BOB DYLAN

ANTHONY SCADUTO

"Pioneers are often written out of history but let it never be forgotten that Scaduto was *the* man. It's scandalous that this book has been out of print for so many years. Its return should be greeted with dancing in the streets". From the foreword by Johnny Rogan, author of numerous rock books including *Neil Young: Here We Are in the Years*, *Van Morrison: A Portrait of the Artist*, and *Timeless Flight: The Definitive Biography of The Byrds*

"Anthony Scaduto's Bob Dylan, although limited by only covering Dylan's first 30 years, is a classic that will forever reward interested readers with tremendous pleasure and rush after rush of fresh insight. Rarely will you find a biography that is such an excellent narrative, such an easy and satisfying read". Paul Williams author of Bob *Dylan: Watching The River Flow* and *Bob Dylan: Performing Artist*

"The author's triumph was that ultimately he persuaded Dylan to talk.... Rereading it close on a quarter-century later, I'm surprised how well it holds up". *Elizabeth Thomson,* editor *of The Dylan Companion and Conclusions on the Wall: New Essays on Bob Dylan*

"I bought it in 1972 and still go back to it now". Patrick Humphries, author *of Oh No Not Another Bob Dylan Book* and *The Complete Guide to the Music of Bob Dylan*

"Still indispensable and in many ways the best biography". Andy Muir editor of Dylan fan magazine *Homer the Slut*

"A wonderful treatment of, and introduction to, Dylan's early life. A quarter century on and Scaduto's biography is still easy to read and hard to put down". Derek Barker editor of Dylan fan magazine *ISIS*

"Dylan's proven to be an elusive biographical subject. Scaduto's attempt ... is about the best and the most comprehensive". *All Music Guide to Rock (1996)*

"Scaduto's book still offers fascinating glimpses into Bob Dylan's formative years". John Bauldie editor of Dylan fan magazine *The Telegraph* and editor of *Bob Dylan: Wanted Man*

Listen, God, look closely after him.
He's more fragile than most people.
Joan Baez, Daybreak

ANTHONY SCADUTO

BOB DYLAN

Helter Skelter Publishing, London
in association with Rogan House

This edition published in 2001 by Helter Skelter Publishing
Helter Skelter Limited, 4 Denmark Street, London.
First published in Great Britain in 1972 by W.H. Allen & Co. Ltd.
Copyright Anthony Scaduto, 1971
Paperback edition published by Abacus, London 1972
Reprinted September 1972
Reprinted, revised edition 0 349 13128 7 April 1973
Reprinted August 1974
First Helter Skelter edition, 1997

Material used in the two chapters, 1971 Father of Night and 1972
Watching the River Flow published by arrangement with the
New York Times Magazine
Copyright 1971 New York Times Company.

Design by Bold.

A CIP record for this book is available
from the British Library

ISBN 1-900924-23-4

Every effort has been made to contact the copyright holders of the pho-
tographs in this book, but one or two were unreachable. The publisher
would be grateful if the photographers concerned would contact Helter
Skelter Publishing.
This edition could not have been printed without the help of
Achim Goebel, Michael Cohen, Hilary Cranny, Michael O'Connell
and Mick Fish.
Main cover photo Michael Ochs archive/Redferns
Inset photo detail UPI/Corbis

Printed and bound in Great Britain by
The Bath Press, Bath

FOREWORD TO THE 1996 REPRINT

It is impossible to overestimate the importance of this book in the history of rock-related literature. Not only was it the first serious study of Dylan's life and work, but also a groundbreaking volume in encouraging publishers that popular music was worthy of respect. These days book shelves are weighed down with treatises on Bob Dylan, with learned sections covering biography, live performances and arcane recordings. Learned broadsheets and pamphlets are available that discuss, in sometimes agonising detail, every aspect of his art. Indeed, Dylan literature has become a sub-genre unto itself, seemingly immune to any fluctuations in its subject's popularity or record sales. It wasn't always so, of course. At the time this book emerged, Dylan was remarkably under-represented in print despite tacit acknowledgements from the quality press that he was a figure of considerable importance.

Timing is crucial in publishing and the arrival of Scaduto's volume at the dawn of a new decade provided the perfect opportunity to reflect on Dylan's contribution to our culture. The book bolstered the confidence of many left uncertain or disillusioned in the wake of *Self Portrait*. For others it provided a reassuring vindication that Dylan always knew which way the wind was blowing. I can still recall a shiver of excitement on first devouring this book and the enormous respect I felt for Scaduto, both as a chronicler and commentator. I wasn't alone. Recently, I was speaking to a friend, now an editor of a music magazine and something of a Dylan authority. He told me that he'd read Scaduto's book before encountering Dylan's music and was so overwhelmed by the prose that he went out and bought album after album over the next few months.

Scaduto's great strength was in covering so many angles. What most impressed was the depth of his research, involving countless interviews with Dylan's lovers, intimate friends and embittered rivals. Before reading this book my view of Dylan was coloured by several screenings of *Don't Look Back* and a handful of anarchic and frequently hilarious press encounters. It says much for Scaduto that he transformed Dylan into a believable flesh and blood figure without sacrificing an iota of the man's mystery. Here was a new Dylan no less intriguing or mercurial than the creature that inhabited my imagination. Carefully sifting myth-making from truth, Scaduto presented a fascinating portrait of Dylan as the chubby-faced schoolboy, the solitary adolescent, the compulsive fantasist, the rock 'n' roller, poet, shaman, media manipulator and inscrutable, protean personality.

The idea of using extended quotes to embellish the narrative brought an even greater sense of authenticity to Scaduto's biography, particularly in the evocation of life in Greenwich Village. While following a strong chronological narrative line, Scaduto was unafraid to break free at times, even devoting an entire chapter to a question and answer interview with Joan Baez. It was a bold move that might have interrupted the normal flow of prose, but nevertheless succeeded. More importantly, Scaduto refused to be limited by the bland confines of biography and wrote enthusiastically about Dylan's art in a concise, engaging and unpretentious manner. Such scholarship would later be superseded by the work of professional academics but few have provided the same sense of exhilaration offered by Scaduto at his best. The review of *John Wesley Harding* and discussion of Dylan's biblical imagery is particularly impressive, especially considering the time when it was written. For some readers, accustomed to requiring mountains of unreleased recordings, the bootleg addendum may look slim but back then it resembled a mouth-watering treasure trove which served as a clarion call to a new generation of tape collectors.

One final consideration about the impact of the book concerns the mystique of the author. This was no high-brow musicologist, chic columnist or *Rolling Stone* radical, but a former crime reporter and self-confessed "Mafia expert". Reading this as an impressionable 18-year-old schoolkid, my mind was full of images of Scaduto calling on a network of police contacts and sniffer dogs to track down the most elusive witnesses to the unmasking of the Jokerman. I know many other people of my age who were equally impressed by the writer's street cred and dogged persistence. When I read in the introduction that he had recorded "hundreds of hours of conversations", it was a degree of research almost beyond my imagination. Such scrupulous interviewing was a lesson to us all. Nearly a decade on, while working on my first book *Timeless Flight*, a biography of the Byrds, it was Scaduto that provided the ideal model of multi-voiced perspectives and contrasting points of view. I'm sure that there are many others who would testify to his influence.

Pioneers are often written out of history but never let it be forgotten that Scaduto was the man. It's scandalous that this book has been out of print for so many years. It's return should be greeted with dancing in the streets.

Johnny Rogan, London 1996

FOR LILLIAN LAGER
who sees the world in a
grain of sand;
who will never live on
Maggie's Farm.

Contents

Thank You, Mr. Tambourine Man

BOB DYLAN, A very private man who seldom gives interviews, finally agreed to sit down and talk to me in January, 1971, after I had been trying to get to him for more than a year. He wanted to know what I had written about him and I agreed to let him see the first rough draft of this book in exchange for an interview—with the understanding that I would not permit him to edit it in any manner. When he finished reading it we talked on the phone.

"I read it," he said. "Some of it is pretty straight, some of it is *very* straight, some of it is *exactly* the way it happened." He went on, still talking in italics as he has always done: "I got nothing against the book, really, but I'll tell you about the book if you like. I just want to clear you up on some of the information you have, which I could do, it's in my power to do.

"Frankly, the book didn't hurt. I mean, years ago I used to pick up these magazines and see articles and stories about me, and sometimes they used to hurt. Your book didn't cause me any pain at all, in fact I rather enjoyed it, because it's not that magazine bullshit."

We met the next afternoon, sitting at his desk shoved against the front window of his studio on a heavily traveled Greenwich Village avenue, and talked for more than three hours. Dylan did most of the talking—he provided personal information that was surprising from so secretive a man: what he thought and felt when he first heard the Beatles; why they helped move him from folk song to rock; even interpretation of his song-poems, discussing those Doomsday poems he had written between 1964 and 1966—almost, but not quite, interpreting himself for me. Again and again, Dylan stressed who and what he is, described what he was thinking and feeling during various crises in his life as a superstar who would rather have been a poet. Hunching his shoulders, speaking with a kind of passionate intensity Dylan explained his interest in this book: "You see, I'm a Gemini. I wouldn't put too much stress on it but, there's a split in the Gemini. He blows hot and cold. I feel that strongly. Right now I'm hot and interested in the book you've done, and I figure I can help you. Six months ago I didn't care what you were doing. Now I care. Six months from now I won't care any more. But now I want to help you."

I thank you, Mr. Tambourine Man, for opening the doors and giving me a peek inside.

This biography of Bob Dylan, man and legend, is the result of hundreds of hours of conversations with those who knew him, loved him, sometimes hated him, often feared him, and usually needed him. This book could not have been written without their help, and I sincerely thank them all. I am especially grateful to: Joan Baez, Suze and Carla Rotolo, Echo Helstrom, and Terri Thal Van Ronk. And so many others: Eric von Schmidt, Dave Van Ronk, Eric Andersen, Jack Elliott, Phil Ochs, Manny Greenhill, David Cohen, John Koerner, Gretel Hoffman Pelto, Ellen Baker, Bob and Sid Gleason, Mikki Isaacson, Eve, Mac, and Peter McKenzie, Mike Porco, Izzy Young, Nat Hentoff, Pete Karman, Carolyn Hester, John Hammond Sr., Sue Zuckerman, and A. J. Weberman.

And special thanks to my editor, Hy Cohen, for much wisdom and understanding.

To all of you, and to those I have neglected here but whose names are sprinkled throughout this book: Love be with you.

1941–1956: *Time Passes Slowly*

"DYLAN USED TO tell us that he came out doing it—out of the womb, singing and playing and writing," folksinger S. David Cohen, formerly known as Dave Blue, likes to recall. That's an exaggeration, certainly, but possibly not by that much; at least, Bob Dylan said it so often (singing like a "demon child ... from inside my mother's womb," he wrote on a Joan Baez album), with so many variations, that he must have come half way to believing it. A man who is cloaking himself in myth must believe in his own magic to make it all work. "After a while," a close friend from the early days recalls, "he didn't seem to know any more what was truth and what was his own creation."

Bob Dylan was born Robert Allen Zimmerman on May 24, 1941, in Duluth, Minnesota. When he was six the family moved to Hibbing, out on the Mesabi Iron Range up near the Canadian border. By the time he was eight or nine, the boy was playing the piano—no formal lessons, just banging away at the family piano and teaching himself. Then a harmonica, and a cheap Sears Roebuck guitar by the time he was ten, and a neck-rack to hold the harmonica. He didn't remember his parents singing too much, he said later; didn't remember swapping any songs with them.

In Hibbing, for a short time the Zimmermans lived in an apartment in a four-family building on Third Avenue, near the Alice School; Abraham Zimmerman, his wife Beatty, Robert and his brother David who was five years younger. Abe Zimmerman was a partner in Micka Electric, as it was known then, a hardware, electric supply and appliance shop on Fifth Avenue, just off Howard, Hibbing's main street. They were small businessmen, the Zimmermans and their relatives. The Stones, Beatty Zimmerman's parents, operated Ben Stone's Clothing Store. The Edelsteins, their cousins, owned a movie house, the Lybba, named after one of the Edelstein women. There was no one named Dylan in the family. The Zimmermans weren't wealthy, but they were respected merchants and they lived comfortably among the mining town's 17,000 Scandinavians, Croats, Slavs, Yugoslavs, Italians—mostly working class Catholics.

Larry Fabbro lived across the street from the Zimmermans. "I can recall playing with Bob," he says. "We must have been about six, a very gentle kid compared to the others. It was a rough neighborhood —kids involved in sports. Bob was quiet, not aggressive at all."

Later, in New York, Bob was to write in a series of poems he calls *11 Outlined Epitaphs* that he had spent the first couple of years as a child in North Hibbing, which was deserted and dead, where the old courthouse stood in ruins with sad-eyed smashed-out windows, and walls crumbling and covered with moss. It resembled the wartime pictures of London or Berlin, a shell-shocked town, bombed into a civic graveyard.

The towns on the Mesabi Range (range means district, not mountains) were once timber towns where lumbermen decimated the Minnesota forests. Then, the mines began to produce. There was so much ore around, so close to the surface, that ordinary mines weren't necessary. Open pits were dug into the earth, great shovels tore greedily into the soil, constantly extending the raw hole. By the end of World War I the mining companies had a problem with Hibbing —the north end of town had been built atop some of the best ores on the Range and the pits had come so close that buildings were sagging and threatening to collapse. Officials of the Oliver Mining Company, which owned the mineral rights under the land, simply moved much of the town and its citizens a mile and a half further south, to its present location on the site of the old mining camp Alice. Huge log-rollers towed buildings down the street, outside of town, and over to the new site, moving houses, churches, saloons, stores, and the Hibbing graveyard.

Today, most of the old part of Hibbing has vanished into what the state touts as "the biggest hole ever made by man," an extraordinary sight, about three miles long, from a half to a mile wide, and almost five hundred feet deep. It covers more than 1,300 acres, and out of it has been wrenched more earth than from the Panama Canal excavation. This huge crater that has destroyed the beauty of the area is probably the state's greatest tourist attraction, "which tells you something about the people out there, who can ravage the earth, create pits and slag heaps and towns where the houses are all red from the ore dust and you could choke to death—and they brag about it," says one of Bob's classmates, who fled the area around the time Bob did. And Linda Fidler, another contemporary, now a television producer in New York: "The thing you have to know about the Iron Range is that it is very suppressed. It's astounding that Bob came out of a non-thinking area, and that's exactly what it is—narrow-minded, everyone conforming to the same point of view, the kids expected to think like their parents and be like their parents. Not much was expected of you, except to make enough to live on and raise a family and be like everyone else."

Echo Star Helstrom, Bob's sweetheart and confidante during their junior year in high school, is a slim blonde who wouldn't conform, who ran around with the tough motorcycle crowd, the "greasers": "The other kids, they wanted to throw stones at anybody different. And Bob was different. He felt he didn't fit in, not in Hibbing. I remember, during the time we were going together, he would drive down to Minneapolis and come back and tell me how great everybody was down there. 'Everybody's with it down there,' he'd say. 'It's so different from Hibbing. They *understand*.' Hibbing was like, well, when I was a little girl it was a happy place to be, but when I grew up it was like having fancy goldfish and plain goldfish in one bowl, and the plain goldfish would just kill the fancy for being fancy. That's what Hibbing wa¹ike. If you were different they would pick you to pieces. Bob rebelled against it. Mostly, he withdrew inside himself, a silent kind of rebellion. And he planned on breaking out, getting away from there."

Echo also recognized back then, what she and everyone else who ever had contact with Bob would call his "paranoia." "He didn't want anybody to know anything at all about him—even before he was famous. He wanted everything to be kept secret."

The beginning of it all was the music, which would open Bob Zimmerman's head as it opened the heads of so many growing up at the end of the repressed fifties, the vapid days of the Eisenhower era, and of the Joe McCarthy national insanity.

He was listening to and toying with standard pop music at first. He would spend hours listening to records in Crippa's, the only music store on Howard Street. Some time in the eighth grade, when he was not quite fourteen, his guitar-picking led him to Hank Williams, "my first idol," he would write on the liner notes to a Joan Baez album. Williams sang about the rattling wheels of the railroad and Bob had spent hours as a child watching the railroad cars filled with ore rumbling away from the pit mines and down toward the Duluth waterfront. Williams, a country blues singer and song writer died in 1953, when he was only twenty-nine. After his death, he became a major influence on all the rock-and-roll groups and singers who turned to the country sound in the mid-sixties. But back then, when Bob began to play his records and try to learn his guitar work and

6

his songs, Hank Williams was strictly for the country music devotees, a young man who shuffled from a tour with Nashville's Grand Ole Opry to country circuit stardom and whose songs broke onto the pop music charts only when other artists recorded them *(Your Cheatin' Heart, Cold, Cold Heart, Jambalaya)*. Bob bought most of the Hank Williams records available and had Crippa's order everything else it could get.

From Williams it was just a short step to the black sounds that would revolutionize popular music, black slave-sharecropper blues, urban blues, rhythm and blues, and spirituals. That kind of music wasn't heard much in Hibbing or in any white communities. Bob would spend hours listening to Gatemouth Page, a disk jockey on a Little Rock, Arkansas, radio station who played Muddy Waters and Howlin' Wolf and B. B. King and Jimmy Reed.

Some time in 1955, when Bob was fourteen, the film *Blackboard Jungle* came to town. Parents, prelates, congressmen and pundits deplored the film because they were certain it would promote mass juvenile delinquency. But the greatest effect of *Blackboard Jungle* came not from the overt teen rebellion shown on the screen, but from the film's theme song, Bill Haley's *Rock Around the Clock,* which kindled another sort of rebellion. Like so many others around the country, Bob's reaction to the song was almost explosive: "Hey, that's our music!" a classmate remembers him shouting. "That's written for us."

If rock-and-roll has a historical beginning, *Rock Around the Clock* is probably it. The first international rock hit, it was a revelation for teenagers who wanted something more exciting than singing along with Mitch Miller. It marked the beginning of the glandular, tension-wracked, raunchy-sensual, black-influenced sound, played by performers who never had a nose bob or capped their teeth. These were performers who never went to the conservatories, but learned to get it together in their basements and garages and slum alleys; blacks, many of them, playing music for kids and by kids.

And it stunned Bob Zimmerman. Elvis Presley and Bill Haley and Buddy Holly really reached him. And especially Little Richard, a young black gospel singer. The Beatles copied his songs and his style, and so did the Rolling Stones. Little Richard, whose first hit, *Tutti Frutti,* opened with a shout and rushed on to a cataclysm. He sang with savage emotion in a shrieking voice, pounding on his piano in an acrobatic style, standing before it, dancing, hopping around. He wore outlandish costumes, drove pink Cadillacs, sported long processed hair piled high in a pompadour. He was the first shaman of rock, the master of what he calls "shakin', hand-clappin', foot stompin', rock-and-roll," and he sold 32 million records in rock's first era. Little Richard became Bob's second idol.

Leroy Hoikkala: "Me and Monte Edwardson were walking downtown back when we were in junior high school. It was probably in late '55, in the ninth grade. We happened to see Bob. I had a set of drums I was fooling with, Monte played the guitar, and Bob was monkeying around with the piano, guitar and a little bit of mouth organ. We got talking about it and Bob said we should get together some time. We should start a group."

They began to work out together, setting up in Bob's garage or in his living room. The Zimmerman home now was at the corner of Seventh Avenue East and Twenty-fifth Street. Bob's parents had bought it a couple of years after coming to Hibbing, a rectangular flat-roofed building with a stucco surface. There, the boys listened to Bob's records, a lot of the new rock-and-roll but mostly rhythm and blues, learning songs from the records. "He was interested mostly in Little Richard, from the first Little Richard record that came out. But he did a little bit of everything, improvising a lot, trying everything. He'd sit down at the piano and play some of the most fantastic chords I'd ever heard."

Bob Zimmerman was a small, chubby, round-faced boy. His light brown hair was cut short in the back but unruly with curls on top. He was very quiet, almost aloof. That's how most classmates and friends remember him: "Quiet, and a loner." The kids he was closest to considered themselves mostly acquaintances. "The common bond was music," one of them says, "but we never got to be close friends." And another: "He didn't travel with any group of people particularly. The kids he got involved with, it was strictly for the music, only the kids who dug music. He'd make music with one bunch of guys and when he felt he took that as far as it could go he'd move on to another group where he could learn more."

Says Hoikkala: "He was like everybody else, but there was the feeling that he had an independent streak and a lot of courage. But he was also a little sheltered. Bob's mother and father were good people. They really watched after him. They wouldn't let him stay up real late at night, things like that."

Bob's first group called itself the Golden Chords. He was the leader because they were playing his music—rhythm and blues and Little Richard. They played a number of gigs during the year they were together: dances, school assemblies, talent contests, anywhere they could get people to listen to them. There were always talent contests around, sponsored by some civic organization. Kids would dance, perform acrobatic feats, juggle, play the accordian, sing like the old Frank Sinatra, or bang out rock-and-roll numbers. Hoikkala recalls one contest they won, but lost:

"I think the Chamber of Commerce sponsored it. We played in the Memorial Building, a big arena where public events are held. Bob did his Little Richard numbers, *Jenny, Jenny* and songs like that, and we backed him. The kids went wild over us. To judge by the applause, we should have won. But we were given second place because of the older people who were there. Bob was very upset he didn't win it."

"You could see something happening to Bob at this time," says another classmate. "He was starting to really dig being a performer. Being up there on the stage and have kids scream over him. Once, after some show, we were sitting in the pizza place, he was way up high with the excitement of it. His legs were bouncing, that jerky knee twitch he had, like he was always keeping a beat. And he was saying, 'Hey we really reached them. We knocked them dead.' Not bragging, so much, not an ego thing. More like a kind of surprise, maybe that he was able to get an audience to react to him. I got a strong feeling that he badly wanted the other kids to dig it, to approve of it. And the more he got the more he damned well was going to get."

Bob was writing songs, back then. Friends remember that he started to write poetry when he was eleven or twelve. Echo Helstrom had a number of his poems, and Dylan has said: "My mother has hundreds of poems I wrote when I was twelve years old." But by his teens, poetry had turned to song lyrics.

Hoikkala: "He was improvising quite a bit, and he was really good at it. He would copy a lot of songs. He'd hear a song and make up his own version of it. He did a lot of copying, but he also did a lot of writing of his own. He would kind of just sit down and make up a song and play it a couple of times and then forget it. I don't know if he ever put any of them down on paper. He didn't do it while we were around him, anyway. He would make something up, maybe change it as he sang it from time to time, and then forget it after a while. We all thought he had a fantastic talent for doing this."

He got his first motorcycle when he was fifteen, while the Golden Chords were together. His friends remember that he desperately wanted a motorcycle, *right now*. "He just kept after his father until they found a good one," Hoikkala remembers. "I went with him and his father to buy it. Somebody over on the west side of town owned it, a Harley-Davidson, about five or six years old. A nice bike. He was all excited, really went wild over it, and his father finally let him buy it. Bob had it painted black.

"A few of us had bikes, and we'd go riding together. One time, my cousin, Bob and myself were riding through a little village. A train was going by. We waited for it to pass and Bob started off across the tracks, to shoot across just as the caboose passed. He got across one rail and suddenly there was a train coming from the opposite direction. Bob threw himself down between the first set of tracks. The train just missed him. Another split second and he would have been killed. He lay there in the track bed and just watched that train go by."

James Dean, the sinister adolescent, became a strong source of identity for Bob: resentful eyes, a mouth filled with scorn, face beat up, bitter, his mother dead, his father gone, friendless, a lone wolf. Resentful toward society, the press agents said, and Dean explained: "My mother died on me when I was nine years old. What does she expect me to *do*? Do it all myself?" He made *Rebel Without a Cause* and *East of Eden* and the teenagers saw themselves in his rebellion and made him their hero. He loved racing cars, but the clause in the contract he signed for *Giant* forbade him to race until the film was completed. And in September, 1955, when *Giant* was in the can, Dean signed on for a race at Salinas. Instead of trucking his white Porsche Spyder to the meet he started driving there, wanting to feel its speed. He got it up to 80—90—a hundred. Near dusk, a Ford driven by a boy named Turnupspeed entered the highway from an intersection near Paso Robles and the two cars collided. The steering wheel went through James Dean, killing 'im instantly. He was twenty-four, and a legend.

"He didn't die," the kids said. "He can't be dead. He'll come back to us." And the peddlers turned out one-shot magazines about his life, sold photographs by the hundreds of thousands, plaster masks, bronze busts, even a bust that felt like real skin when you stroked it. They sold a peek at his death car, fifty cents a head.

Hoikkala: "We use to go to all the James Dean shows those couple of years after he died. And get all the magazines—my cousin, myself, and Bob. We'd go down to the newsstand and get all the magazines that had any articles at all on Dean. He was kind of our idol. This is one thing for sure, that Bob dug James Dean. We idolized him both as a person and an actor. We felt, including Bob, that his acting was actually himself. He wasn't just acting the roles he was in. The roles were him."

The Golden Chords broke up mostly because Bob was interested in black music and Hoikkala and Edwardson wanted to do the more popular rock, where they could get some local jobs and make a few dollars at it. Bob quickly moved on to another group that would play his kind of music; a group that could teach him a little bit more than he knew.

Chuck Nara met Bob at Hibbing Senior High School in the fall of 1955. Nara joined the high-school band, playing drums, and soon a group of boys were getting together for informal jam sessions and to swap records. Nara on drums, Bill Marinak on string bass, Larry Fabbro on an amplified guitar, John Shepard on trumpet, and Tony Connors, on drums.

"We started getting together with him a year later, in the tenth grade," Nara recalls. "There was this group of us with more than just a listening interest in music, and Bob somehow got involved. I think it was probably through his records. I used to have a fantastic amount of jazz records and Fabbro was big on jazz, and Bob had this huge collection of rhythm and blues stuff. So we would exchange records, go from one house to the other to play and swap records. We discovered rhythm and blues mostly through Bob and that brought us together."

Four of the boys—Bob, Nara, Fabbro and Marinak—began playing together. It started with Bob doing Little Richard imitations on the piano in the corner of his living room, and then suggesting they work on an act together. "We kind of did it originally as a lark and then it started getting serious," Nara says. "It got serious because of Bob. He was turned on by Little Richard and doing this singing. No other groups on the Range were doing anything like it."

The informal tenth-grade quartet became more serious about play-ing together after Bob was asked to audition for the College Capers, a dance and talent contest put on by the students at Hibbing Junior College, then located in the high school building. "They were short on talent that year or they would have never considered asking high-school kids," Nara says. "Some of them had heard of Bob's wild singing, so they asked him to audition. That's when we really started working on an act."

They practiced after school for a couple of weeks, Bob standing at the piano pounding out Little Richard-style chords, screaming *True Fine Momma* and a few other of his hits. Bob would direct his side-men, tell them what he wanted to hear, how to accompany him, occasionally playing a Little Richard record to make his point. Fabbro was on his amplified guitar, Marinak on string bass, Nara on a snare drum he'd bring home from school because he didn't have a drum of his own.

Fabbro: "Bob was very much the leader. He had an exact thing he wanted us to do, some little *do dah, do wha* in the background, but otherwise strictly his singing. We were his accompaniment. It wasn't a matter of trying to be a group. It was Bob being pretty much of a personality. He was Little Richard, with rhythm in the background. This was strictly Little Richard."

(Bob Dylan, from an interview a few years later with a Columbia Records press agent trying to get details for a publicity release: "I used to play great piano. *Very* great. Little Richard-style—only I used to play, you know, an octave higher. . . . His records were great records, but they could have been greater records. His mistake was he played down too low. If he played *high,* everything would have compensated. Ah, Little Richard, he was somethin' else.")

By now Bob began to verbalize his dreams of becoming a rock-and-roll star. Nara: "Of all the guys around who were playing, Bob was the only one with a specific goal in mind—that he was going into the entertainment business and was going to make it. He talked about having a group, and going somewhere with records. This was the direction he was going to pursue. We all sat back and, well, I said, 'God, I certainly don't want to be part of any group, that's not for me.' But that was for him, back in the tenth grade."

Anyone who knew him at all well during the high school years, even the girl he was to consider his sweetheart, realized Bob Zimmerman was almost obsessed; he had developed a junkie urgency to express himself in pop music.

But Hibbing was not very receptive; the College Capers audition was something less than a triumph.

"In fact, they literally laughed us right off the stage," Nara says. "Nobody could accept the fact that Bob was screaming and singing like Little Richard. There was some clapping when he got through, but mostly out of courtesy. Not a really positive reaction. Pretty negative, actually."

The audition was conducted by members of the student council, plus a faculty advisor whose task it was to make certain the council members didn't lose their heads. The majority of them all said the group couldn't play: "You just won't fit in." But a couple of student council members objected. They argued: "We can use a wild surprise act. Let them play for us." They were voted down, and the surprise never came off.

Bob did get his Little Richard act on stage a few weeks later, at the high school's Jacket Jamboree Talent Festival. There were two shows, one for the student body during school hours, a sort of dress rehearsal, and later an evening show for parents who wanted to hear what the school was doing with their tax dollars. They were in for a jolt.

Fabbro remembers "some very shocked people" at both performances, even the early one, attended only by the kids. Fabbro remembers the audience reaction this way: "They thought it was a put on. They never heard anything like this before. In fact, even for us playing behind Bob the performance was a lot of noise more than anything else. It was hard for us to even understand the piano playing, it was so loud."

The response didn't distress Bob, however. The boys in his group had the feeling that he knew exactly what he was doing and that if no one else in Hibbing understood, it wasn't all that important to him. Minneapolis, more than two hundred miles south, was the fantasy place for a Hibbing boy who wanted to break away. It had a cool university style. Its Dinkytown, a Greenwich Village-like section near the University of Minnesota had coffee houses where young people could get up and play guitar and try out folk songs. And there were jazz joints that were beginning to get into rock-and-roll. These were places where you could meet black men who really knew black music, and could communicate it with hip immediacy. The kids from the university were living in their own pads and were apparently more sexually free, and more intellectually alive, at least, than Hibbing. Also, the New Left was making its presence felt on campuses across the nation.

Nara remembers going to Minneapolis with Bob in March, 1957. They had taken the bus to attend the state basketball tournament, and they spent much of Saturday afternoon running from one record shop to another, searching out new rhythm-and-blues records: "I was still amazed that he had such a knowledge of music and yet couldn't read music at all." Nara was impressed, also, by something else: "Bob had a few black friends down there, a drummer and a couple of other guys who had organized themselves into a group."

Bob was beginning to spend a lot of time in Minneapolis, going down by bus at first, later on motorcycle or in the family car. He would eventually say, after becoming Dylan the mythmaker and media manipulator, that he had picked up a lot of things from black musicians during the many times he ran away from home. It wouldn't have been in keeping with his later image to talk about the black musicians he visited in Minneapolis, when he had his parents' permission to drive down there on a Saturday.

1957: *The Man In Me*

ECHO HELSTROM IS *The Girl From the North Country,* the girl
Bob Dylan wrote about in one of his more melodic songs (as he was
to write about so many whose lives crossed his). Echo and Bob met
in October, 1957, in the eleventh grade. She hadn't really noticed
him before because, "He was a very clean-cut, goody-goody kid at
the time. Plump and round-faced, not skinny like he became later.
Baby-faced. And quiet. I wouldn't have paid any attention to him
because he was from the right side of the tracks and I was from the
wrong side. It was a question of rich and poor. You either came from
a nice home or, like my place, slightly decrepit. That distinguished
the right side from the wrong." While the Helstroms may have been
somewhat poor, the Zimmermans were by no means rich. Abe Zimmerman's store was not very large, and when miners were laid off
by periodic waves of recession they could not keep up with their
credit payments or make new purchases, and shopkeepers also suffered. Echo's distinction between rich and poor is relative.

Echo: "I was sitting in the L & B with a girl friend. That was the
ice cream parlor and hangout on Howard Street. Bob had been
upstairs in the Moose Lodge, which was above the L & B, playing
guitar and piano with guys in his band. He had a new band then,
different guys than Nara and the others in the talent show. He came
down with his friends and was standing under the lamp post in the
street, playing and hollering, and I thought: 'Who is that nut?' I didn't
know him at all.

"He walked in with another boy, John Buckland, and they came
over and started talking to us. Picking us up, I guess. I think I had
on my motorcycle jacket and a pair of jeans. Very uncouth, for Hibbing.

"We started talking about music. All my life I'd loved music, there
was always music around the house. When I was about thirteen, I
started listening to the rock stuff, and rhythm-and-blues. Nobody else
I knew had ever heard it. You couldn't hear it in Hibbing, you had
to tune in black stations from Little Rock or Chicago, late at night.
I was so hooked by it I used to stay up till four in the morning in the
summer, listening to Chicago after Gatemouth Page went off the air.

"But I couldn't talk to anybody in Hibbing about it. You tell somebody how great it was and they'd think you were out of your head. And when Bob started talking to me about Howlin' Wolf and Jimmy Reed and B. B. King and all the great blues guys, I just couldn't believe what he was saying. It couldn't be true.

"He said: 'You listen to Gatemouth Page!' like he couldn't believe it, either. His eyes got tremendously big. And we just talked about all the great music we'd been listening to that nobody else ever heard of. Everybody else in town was so square, but we could communicate on each other's level, speak the same language."

Bob was excited to discover not only someone with whom he could discuss the blues, but also that she was quite an attractive blond. He said, "Hey, come to my house after school tomorrow. I'll play you my records. Okay?" Echo agreed, and Bob jumped to his feet.

"Let's go back upstairs," he said. "I want you to hear my piano, right now."

"It's locked," Buckland said.

Echo offered a little pocket knife she always carried. She continues: "We went upstairs and Bob opened the lock. Me and John wouldn't dare go in. We were chicken. But Bob went in and played the piano, doing his Little Richard thing."

As Bob was using the knife blade to slip the lock, she asked him: "Bobby, are you Jewish?"

"He got a funny look when I asked him that. I was very surprised. I was always interested in people's backgrounds and it didn't mean anything more to me than asking if he was Slav or Irish or whatever. To me, it was a natural question. But he had this funny look and he didn't say anything. He went inside and started to play and John said to me: 'Don't ever ask him that.'" That was another thing about Hibbing. One of Bob's classmates remembers it this way: "There was a certain prejudice against Jews. I wasn't aware of it until two years ago, when the country club, the only private club in town, admitted Jewish members for the first time. It surprised me, because most of the small business people in town are Jewish. But this club, which had the so-called prominent people in town—the bankers, the officials in the mining company, there was a certain prestige in being a member —didn't admit Jews. It was surprising to me because being Jewish wasn't a big deal in Hibbing. It didn't matter a damn to me or Echo or the other kids, when we were growing up. But there it was. It seemed to matter to the up-tight grownups, and it might have affected Bob."

That was from a Catholic, a member of the eighty per cent or so majority. Linda Fidler, who was raised in Chisholm, seven miles from

Hibbing, knew Bob and his friends and most of the Range well because of the teen habit of *cruisin'*—riding around in cars. They would listen to rock stations, dr⌐p in at kid hangouts along the cruisin' route, see and be seen. Linda's view of prejudice on the Range is a little more carbolic:

"I don't know if there was prejudice against Jews because they were Jews, since there was prejudice against anyone who wasn't Catholic, against anyone who was different. One girl in the eighth grade told me I was going to hell because I wasn't Catholic. That's what it was like. I was upset at not being Catholic, and I imagine it was a lot worse for him being Jewish. It just had to bother Bob."

A couple of years after breaking into Moose Lodge, when Bob was ostensibly going to classes at the University of Minnesota in Minneapolis, a woman who knew him as part of the young folkie set became aware that he was trying to deny his background:

"I had a feeling he was rejecting a lot of things, running from his heritage, sort of traveling in disguise. I was kind of the Jewish mother around and couldn't really get close to him, but I could see this interesting masquerade of his. He was in disguise." And a Jewish coed who dated him for a time: "When I knew him he was in no way being Jewish. That was something he was absolutely not being at all. Even after he knew that I knew he was Bob Zimmerman from up on the Range, he was not being Jewish. He was saying his mother wasn't. ..."

By the time Bob entered high school his father and his uncle were operating an expanded store at the same location, now called Zimmerman's Furniture and Electric. They sold furniture, appliances, and did some electrical contracting. Abraham Zimmerman was in his late forties at the time, small (five-foot-six) and stocky, with black hair and horn-rimmed glasses and usually described as a witty, quiet, gently unassuming cigar-smoker. Like most fathers whose teenage sons developed more than a listening interest in the new rock-and-roll sounds and began to play the music themselves, Mr. Zimmerman didn't approve. Apparently he felt it was all just a phase and Bob was wasting time he should have been devoting to an education and a career.

It seemed to most who knew Bob that he didn't like his father very much. Mr. Zimmerman was a traditional kind of middle class American father; he believed in the American Dream: a man works hard at his studies, works hard at his business or career, becomes financially secure, sires a family, wins his neighbors' respect, and contributes something to the Gross National Product.

"He used to work for me," Mr. Zimmerman has been quoted as saying after Bob had become famous. "He was strong. I mean he could hold up his end of a refrigerator as well as kids twice his size, football players. I used to make him go out to the poor sections, knowing he couldn't collect any money from those people. I just wanted to show him another side of life. He'd come back and say, 'Dad, those people haven't got any money.' And I'd say, 'Some of those people out there make as much money as I do, Bobby. They just don't know how to manage it.'"

Mr. Zimmerman's thinking was much like that of most small businessmen: the eldest son either goes into the family business or he studies for a profession like medicine, or law, or teaching. Bob hated working in the store, and his friends believe some of the tensions between father and son were the result of Mr. Zimmerman's hopes that Bob would enter the business, or become some kind of businessman. Bob, they recall, couldn't imagine that kind of life, aging behind a counter or a desk.

One adult who had contact with the Zimmerman family says: "It was hard to understand what was behind Bob's feeling for his father. And to understand why, at that age, fathers are so disapproving of what their kids are doing. His father misunderstood Bob when he was a kid. Later, when he became famous, he was very proud and hung up pictures all over the store and put his albums in the window and always showed us magazine stories about him. But when Bob was a kid he didn't understand his son at all."

Hoikkala: "Well, I'll tell you. One time Bob wanted a car, this particular convertible, a 1950 Ford with just a gray prime paint on the body and a black top. His father said, 'Well, let's see about it. Let's look it over. No impluse, now.' But Bob wanted the car right then. He had to have it then. His father was a patient man, and somewhat strict, and like a lot of young people Bob disliked this."

Echo: "Mr. Zimmerman was a nice man. I used to wonder why Bob didn't get along with his father. Like, one time we were on the motorcycle and we ran out of gas. As *usual*, Bob sent me after the gas. I was walking down the road and his father came along in the car and asked if I wanted a ride. He said: 'Where are you going?' and I said: 'We ran out of gas and I'm going after some.' He said: 'Well, get in,' and he took me for the gas and drove me back. When Bob saw his father he got so upset and so mad. He mumbled a few things to his father, barely conversation, and when Mr. Zimmerman left Bob started yelling at me. 'What'd you do that for? Why'd you let him give you a lift?' I got so upset. I didn't know I wasn't supposed to. After all, he was his *father*."

Later, in Minneapolis and in Greenwich Village, when he was calling himself Bob Dylan, friends remember his "disguise" as a kind of denial of his father: "When I discovered he was Bob Zimmerman from up on the Range I asked him about it. At that time he was going on about how he couldn't stand his father, and veiled hints that maybe his father wasn't too nice.". And another: "His whole original set of stories was that he was from Oklahoma, an orphan. Then after we learned about the Zimmermans, he would refuse to talk about his folks in Hibbing." And: "He said his father was too hard to get along with so he left home.".

Actually, though, there was no break between Bob and his father. His tales about an unpleasant father, or about being an orphan, were early indications of Bob's recurrent need to create new identities for himself. There was an understandable distance between father and son, certainly. Like most fathers, Mr. Zimmerman was unable to believe his son was up to any good with his guitar-picking, and piano-pounding, and strange, loud singing.

"Mr. Zimmerman didn't agree with Bob's goals," a classmate says, "but he never stood in Bob's way, really. He supported Bob in those first years after high school, gave him money and a kind of moral support. He gave Bob his blessings, in a way. I always thought he was just the right kind of father for Bob: strict about a lot of things, but never so rigid that Bob would really have to run away."

Bob's mother, Beatty Stone Zimmerman, was more understanding. An attractive woman, blonde and fair, she is an older and less hyperactive version of Bob Dylan. While Mrs. Zimmerman may not wholeheartedly have approved of Bob's musical ambitions, she seemed to be closer to her son. "He seemed to like his mother very well," a Hibbing neighbor remembers. "He would talk to me about his mother when I was doing things around the house, tell me how *she* baked a pie I might have been baking, or how she did things. He talked about her as if he liked her. But he didn't talk much about personal things like that. He was very careful about what he said."

Bob Dylan is an outsider, and he was an outsider even as a child. He is one of those outlaws who intuitively reject a standardized society, whose consciousness has not been frozen in the immediate and confining present. But back in those early Hibbing days, he did not fully understand the forces that drove him. He would not begin to understand until some years later. After he had reached a mass audience, he was interviewed by Jules Siegel for a *Saturday Evening Post* article. And he told Siegel, "I see things that other people don't see. I feel things that other people don't feel. It's terrible. They laugh.

I felt like that my whole life. . . . All I did was write and sing, paint little pictures on paper, dissolve myself into situations where I was invisible."

During one of our talks, Dylan conceded that I was "right on target" in discussing the inner Self that he could not repress, that brought him so much pain he had to make himself invisible, and provided him with the strength to reach for higher levels of consciousness.

Eric von Schmidt, folk singer, song writer, illustrator, writer of children's books, was close to Dylan in his early professional years. He recalls: "Dylan's mind seemed to make strange jumps, like electricity. His mind was the most exciting . . . like a calypso mind, making instantaneous sorts of connections, relating seemingly unrelated things and putting them together into something marvelous. He doesn't go from A to B to C and so on—he can jump from A to G while other people are plodding on. He doesn't need to plod. He is able to make connections, not out of something he studies, but viscerally."

Bob Dylan's world was full of danger and his one defense was to make himself invisible in some way. Dylan had to periodically develop fresh masks to deflect the dangers, to preserve his identity, to keep from losing himself in the demands of the outer world.

Ric von Schmidt recalls: "Dylan was continually inventing himself" as a circus hand, carnival boy, road bum, musician, and many other roles in what have come to be called the Dylan myths. One of those myths was that he had started running away when he was ten, got picked up by the police and sent home, and ran away again. But he never actually ran away as a child; he ran from, and within, himself, because of what his parents wanted him to be, what the educators wanted him to be, what Hibbing wanted him to be. After he got to New York and his growing popularity qualified him for a profile in the *New Yorker,* he told Nat Hentoff:

"I was constantly on guard. Somehow, way back then, I already knew that parents do what they do because they're uptight. They're concerned with their kids in relation to *themselves.* I mean, they want their kids to please them, not to embarrass them—so they can be proud of them. They want you to be what *they* want you to be. So I started running."

He was going to be Bob Dylan (whoever Bob Dylan might be), not Robert Allen Zimmerman. As he matured, he built a new identity every step of the way in order to escape identity; he would pursue privacy as some pursue notoriety.

1958: *If Dogs Run Free*

ECHO AND BOB began going steady about a month after they met. He gave her his identification bracelet. "A symbol of our belonging to each other," Echo says. "We were really in love. Everybody laughs at kids when they fall in love, saying how they don't know what it all means or anything, but that's not true. Kids know." They went together for almost a year, breaking up in the fall of 1958, just after their senior year had started. It was a critical period for Bob. He knew he was going to be a singer. He even began searching for a stage name.

Echo: "By the time I met him it was just understood that music was his future. All along we knew there was no other way for him to get out of there, to leave Hibbing. I just knew he had to go on to his career, his singing. I accepted it on those terms, that when school was over, after graduation, he would be off and gone. Get out of Hibbing."

Echo's mother, Martha Helstrom, recalls: "Bob and John Buckland always talked big dreams together about how they were going to make it. They decided whichever got to be famous first would help the other one. They were always planning about being in the limelight, get all the world's attention, stuff like that. Elvis Presley—the idea was to be like him."

By his senior year in high school, Bob no longer impressed his contemporaries as a "goody-goody kid." To most of his friends at that time, Bob was a *greaser*. Greasers roared around on motorcycles, wore black leather jackets, sported greased ducktail haircuts, dangled cigarettes from the sides of their mouths, and usually had one of the *easier* girls hanging on their backs as they sped along Route 169 between Hibbing and Chisholm—cruisin'. There were two basic cliques among teens on the Range: The greasers (the "hoods and hoodesses" as someone called them), and the *right* kids who were rah-rah school, the sports heroes and leaders of school activities. The *rights* ran everything.

Linda Fidler recalls: "Bob was considered part of the tough motorcycle crowd. Always with the black leather jacket, the cigarette in the corner of his mouth, rather hoody. And Echo with her bleached hair and a vacant look; that's mostly how I first noticed him, running around with this freaky girl hanging on the back of his motorcycle, with her frizzy white hair flying and her false eyelashes. It was shocking to me. I tried not to be narrow-minded, but I thought that crowd was a bunch of creeps. We used to laugh at the sight of them on the motorcycles. They used to zip through town and it was funny to see them.

"The thing is, motorcycles were taboo because motorcycle guys were automatically bad. I had to stay away from them. They were terrifying, Bob with his big boots and his tight pants. Another thing, we were all virgins, my girlfriends and I. You just did *not* go to bed with anybody unless you were married to him. These guys on motorcycles, you go out with them and you'd get in trouble, that's what was drummed into us. So we were afraid of them. We would get raped, or something just as awful would happen to us. Every time I would see Bob I would think 'Oh, God,' and practically clutch at my virginity, even though he hardly knew me."

Actually, Bob was no more part of the greaser crowd than he was part of the student establishment cheerleader world. As Echo put it: "He didn't fit in with the bums. I knew the real bums. All my friends were the wrong-side-of-the-tracks people, the dropouts, and Bob didn't fit in with them. He didn't fit in with anyone in town, really.

"We had a lot of great times together. He'd imagine the craziest things, act them out in his head, and then we'd have to go and do them. He'd be quiet most of the time, but when he got one of his crazy ideas his eyes would get so big and he'd carry on so. Everything had to be a big production for Bob, a big adventure. Once we were in his house. We weren't supposed to be up in his room together, but nobody was home and we went up there. He heard Mrs. Stone come in, she was living with them, and he said, 'Oh, my grandmother's home,' and he shoved me in the closet. He said, 'Wait there. I'll tell my grandmother I'm going to the library.' And he went downstairs to talk to her and came back up right away. He put me out on the sundeck outside his bedroom, the deck over the garage. Then he ran downstairs and outside into the street, books under his arms. He started whistling. 'Hang over the railing and I'll catch you,' he yelled. He grabbed my legs and helped me down and we walked away. The house was on the corner, facing two streets, and the whole neighborhood probably saw him trying to keep me a secret from his grandmother.

"He was always playing games. Something between paranoia and games, I guess.

"There was a point there he wanted to be Bobby Freeman, the

singer—you know, *Do You Wanna Dance?* He called me up this one time and said, 'Hey, me and the guys taped this song. Wanna hear it?' So I said 'Sure' and he put it on. It was *Do You Wanna Dance?* But I believed it was him. It wasn't until years later I realized that the kook had been playing the record, it wasn't him at all. He pulled stuff on me like that all the time.

"He hit a little kid with his motorcycle once. I was downtown and I saw him walking on the street and he said, 'I'll walk you home.' Then he pulled me down an alley, big secret, and he told me how horrible he felt hitting this little kid. There was nothing he could do to stop, the kid just ran out between parked cars. 'All I can remember is the orange rolling across the street, the oranɡe the kid carried,' he told me. The kid wasn't hurt much, but Bob was so shook up."

There was something about Dylan, here in Hibbing, that would impress the professional folk singers he would meet in Greenwich Village later on. Bob listened to every conceivable popular music style, from jazz to hillbilly, studying and soaking up those that interested him, learning to imitate, to rework, to transform them into something his own.

At one stage, while he was going with Echo, Bob became absorbed in hillbilly, now called country-western. Echo's mother had a large collection of country music, old seventy-eights from the forties and fifties, and Bob would spend much time playing the records and trying out the songs for himself, on his guitar. Then he, and sometimes John Buckland, would sit on a swing out in the front yard, or on the Helstrom's front steps, and play the songs they'd just heard.

"I still have the records he always played," Mrs. Helstrom said. "Sad, sad songs like *Ohio Prison Fire*, the one about the men trapped in prison and dying because they couldn't get away from the fire. And old cowboy songs. And some on the order of like he wrote in his first album and *Nashville Skyline*. And Hank Snow records. Bob and John played Hank Snow all the time, over and over again. Especially *Prisoner of Love*."

Echo adds: "There was always hillbilly on the radio, and the Grand Ole Opry. Some of them were real sad, miserable songs, people getting killed, or that talk song where this guy runs over a little kid. And Bob and John would also take a lot of straight songs and do them hillbilly style. Like, *Somewhere Over the Rainbow*. These two guys would just start pick-picking on their guitars with that one, and off they'd go like a couple of mountain boys."

But despite the country interest, Bob was still involved in blues and rock-and-roll, at least in his public appearances. And there were a number of such appearances during that winter of 1957 and spring of 1958. Echo recalls these months:

"By this time, Bob had dropped his old group, Chuck and those guys, and picked up others to back him. I can't remember who they were. Maybe Monte Edwardson and another kid. Bob was the leader. He was a nervous, jerky type, always twitching, jumping around, but he was the organizer. I remember one high school show, he was playing the piano again, standing up like Little Richard. The kids would even boo them—talk about prophet in your own home town. Anyway, Bob was playing and I didn't even know what he was singing. I was so nervous, and you couldn't understand what he was singing because all the amplifiers were so loud, and he mumbles anyway. A girl sitting next to me started yelling, 'Hey, he's singing to you,' and I listened close and he was singing 'I got a girl and her name is Echo, I got a girl and her name is Echo.' He just made it up as he went along. Those guys always sat around making up songs.

"Another time they had this show at the Armory, I think a disc jockey from the Hibbing radio station set it up. I remember being nervous again. They turned up the amplifiers so loud you couldn't hear Bob, just guitar noises. I remember standing by the stage and yelling at them: 'Turn down the amplifiers!' But the guys couldn't hear me. It was just a mess. You couldn't hear Bob singing. I wanted it to be perfect. I wanted everybody to know Bob could sing. But the kids in the audience booed and jeered, they wanted to throw stones at anybody who was different.

"Bob was sort of oblivious to the whole fact that people were not turned on by his music. He lived in his own world, and it didn't bother him. There was this cat, playing like they were clapping, when they were really booing. . . ."

Some time in the Spring of 1958, Bob came over to Echo's house with a book in his hand. *Cannery Row,* by John Steinbeck. "This is a great book," he told her, excitedly describing the novel. "Steinbeck is a great writer." And, with that boyish enthusiasm that many would find so infectious, Bob read everything of Steinbeck's. "Hey, hey, do you know Steinbeck wrote *East of Eden,* that James Dean movie?" he once shouted.

"He identified with all the people in the books," Echo says.

Steinbeck was not the only source of Bob Zimmerman's growing disillusionment with the American dream. There were also the stories told by the old miners around town, who had lived through "the troubles" forty and fifty years before. The troubles started in 1907, when the fledgling Western Federation of Miners struck. Oliver Mining and its parent company, the United States Steel Company, rounded up between 7,000 and 8,000 immigrants—Swedes, Finns and Slavs—and shipped them to the Range as scabs. The tactic led to considerable bloodshed, hatred of the "millionaires back East" who controlled the Range, and the forced exodus of most of the beaten strikers.

And then, in 1916, the old strikebreakers went out on strike. It began as an unorganized walkout at the Aurora mine for hi_ her wages and shorter working hours and threatened to spread across the seventy-mile Range. Company agents returned to northeast Minnesota once more. Like company agents everywhere in those days, their assignment was to educate the miners about the glory of Eastern capitalism, and many heads were clubbed, imprinting the message. Eventually, after further beatings and several killings at the hands of company police failed to teach the strikers anything but more militancy, the mine owners gave in and granted a 10 per cent wage increase and an eight-hour day.

But the bitterness engendered by the strikes never completely died. When Bob was growing up, there were still elderly miners around, bitterly reminiscing about the days of company brutality and murder.

Even more personal, more upsetting to Bob, was his direct experience with men and women who were caught up in their own private Dust Bowls.

Echo remembers it this way: "Bob's father used to make him work at the shop sometimes. Bob hated most of all when he had to repossess stuff from people who couldn't pay. He would tell me about it. 'We had to go to this guy's house and take his things away.' I think that's where he started feeling sorry for poor people. Those miners would find a house, buy it, buy furniture on credit because they had jobs in the mine, and then get laid off when times got bad, like they seemed to always be doing. And Bob and this other guy would have to go get all the stuff back because the people couldn't pay anymore. It just destroyed Bob to do that."

Throughout the time Echo was his girl friend, Bob was seriously trying to come up with a name to use professionally; he was trying out a number of stage names and none of them satisfied him. "I can't use my real name," he told a few friends. "I need a good stage name."

Echo remembers: "It was the summer before our senior year. Bob and John Buckland came over in Bob's car. He had that little Ford convertible. He finally had his own car, got his dad to buy him one. They drove over, and Bob was kind of excited.

" 'I found a name,' he said. 'I decided the name I'm going to use when I'm a singer. It's going to be Bob Dylan.' "

Echo says she didn't ask him whether it was inspired by Dylan Thomas because she just assumed that's where the name came from. They had never discussed Dylan Thomas, or poetry—"only music and Steinbeck, even though Bob used to write poems to me." But Echo is certain the story he was to tell later, that he took the name from his mother's brother, a Las Vegas gambler, was just part of Bob's myth-making. And, later, a writer for *US*, a paperback magazine, was to claim that Beatty Zimmerman told him the name had indeed been chosen from Dylan Thomas, that there was no one in the family named Dylan or anything remotely similar to it. (Dylan would not discuss the origin of the name with me. He did say, however, that he first used it on the spur of the moment, without having thought of it before, and that it did not happen in Hibbing but about a year later.)

Echo: "Bob was always running around looking for people who knew something about music. Especially if they were colored. Twice we went up to Virginia, a little further up on the Range, about thirty miles away, because Bob heard they had a Negro disc jockey up there and he just had to go see him. We went to this guy's apartment and he played all kinds of great records for us and talked about all sorts of people who were playing great music. We even had to go visit this guy before our prom night, the eleventh grade prom. Bob had a suit and tie on, I had on my formal, and we drove all the way up to Virginia to talk to this colored disk jockey.

"The prom was miserable. We were so different from all these other gung ho, goody-goody kids and we just didn't fit in. We just wandered around by ourselves. I went home crying, it was so miserable. Probably the crowning touch to the whole miserable thing is that we couldn't dance. He was a lousy leader, and I needed somebody to really push me around. We were stepping all over each other's feet and he was kind of hissing at me between his teeth, 'What's the matter with you? What's the matter with you? Can't you dance?' Finally, he just said, 'Let's get out of here.'

"He was always afraid of being embarrassed. He wanted everything to be kept a secret, he felt that nobody should know anything about him. I remember breaking up with him. It was in school, on a Monday morning, right after one of those lonely weekends I'd been spending because he was running off to Minneapolis. The whole summer I had spent in the house, waiting for the phone to ring, sitting around waiting for him, depressed. He was spending a lot of time in Minneapolis that summer, hanging around and singing and stuff like that. And he probably had girls down there. Anyway, I was tired of it. I saw him in the hallway with a group of his friends and I walked right up to him and gave him his ID bracelet back. He said, 'What's this, what's going on, what are you doing?' Then he pulled me aside, against the lockers, and said, 'Not here. Let's talk about it later. Not here.' He kind of whispered. It just killed him that this was happening in public."

In his senior year, Bob had a group in Duluth. He would run down on weekends, staying over with his cousin who played in the group. And he continued to be close to John Buckland, to dig heavily into all the country music that was around at the time, and the urban black blues. A little bit of folk music began to intrude during this year —urban folk, as distinct from the country sound; Woody Guthrie and Depression folk singers, Aunt Mollie Jackson and her sister, Sarah Ogan Gunning, who wrote and sang about the bitter class feeling and labor violence in their region, the coal fields of Harlan County, Kentucky; protest songs that became accepted and almost taken over by northern urban groups.

School annoyed him, depressed him. A classmate remembers that he was discontent with and bored by the people he had—in his own mind—already left behind. His English teacher grated him especially. She was an elderly woman, and one of her pet ideas was that her students must periodically present speeches in front of the whole class. One day Bob rose and delivered a speech. No one recalls the subject now, but the teacher thought it was not fitting for English students. She ordered Bob to sit down, and failed him. He was furious. He stormed into his next class, a study hall, seething. He quickly dashed off a petition to "impeach" the English teacher, listing her faults, demanding she be fired. And he passed it around. "You gotta sign it," he said. "Gotta get her out of this school." A number of students signed it, but nothing much ever came of it. Since there was no recorded hassle with the school administration, the feeling is he eventually forgot his anger.

He graduated June 5, 1959. The high school year book pictures a young boy, looking grim, and under his name was the legend: "To Join Little Richard." But by this time, Robert Zimmerman had moved into other things.

1959–1960: *Gotta Travel On*

BOB ZIMMERMAN ARRIVED in Minneapolis in September, 1959, entering the arts college of the University of Minnesota on a state scholarship. He was eighteen, a chubby-faced boy from the Iron Range. At first, he lived in the University's Jewish frat house, Sigma Alpha Mu, popularly known as "Sammy." He promised to pledge for it, as so many other freshmen were doing in frat houses all over the campus. Discarding the Hibbing greaser clothes, he now sported the universal uniform of late-fifties collegiates: narrow-lapeled sports jacket, corduroy slacks or neat chinos, striped button-down shirt, white bucks. *Even* white bucks. His hair was short and curly, and he combed it regularly. He was so near-sighted and so vain about wearing glasses that he was constantly squinting, his eyes watery and straining. Some people considered him unfriendly, surly, snobbish, but it was partly that he couldn't see unless he was up close. Like many young myopics he preferred the risk of offending someone to wearing glasses.

Zimmerman attended classes, suffering through freshman English, bored. His counselor saw him as "a talented individual, but kind of lost. He kept strange hours. He was a loner." At first he seemed almost to conform. Echo had come down to Minneapolis to work for a film distribution company, and in the early months there, they would meet occasionally. "He always wanted to spend the night with me but I wouldn't let him. I suppose he wanted to make an impression on the guys in the frat house."

The new freshman was barely settled into his dorm when he made straight for Dinkytown, the small business district on the edge of the campus not far from the Mississippi River, that had become the Minneapolis Bohemia. Dinkytown was the only place in the city where the early freaks could congregate; it was the center for the usual assortment found in all the Greenwich Villages of the country: students, old leftists, New Leftists (just beginning to be called that), ex-everythings, Kerouac-beats, professional intellectuals, bums of all motivations, complexions, and ages, and folkies. "At the time," one Dinkytown escapee reflects, "they all thought they were real great, thought they were going some place. But they weren't going anywhere at all, most of them. Because most of them were people filled with futility."

They all came together in the Dinkytown coffee houses. The Ten O'Clock Scholar, on Fourteenth Avenue between Fourth and Fifth Streets, a block from campus, was the big hangout. About ninety customers could be shoe-horned inside the dingy former restaurant, to sit at unmatched tables and chairs, on bar stools in front of a marble counter in the back near the kitchen, or on a bench that ran the length of one wall. David Lee, who bought the place about ten months before Bob arrived on campus, hired a friend to entertain the customers from a four-inch elevated platform in the front window. That first paid performer was a flamenco guitarist named Gooch whose professional name was "Amigo."

Lee remembers Bob as a "cleancut kid," very intense and determined.

"Do you mind if I play?" Bob asked when he wandered into The Scholar sometime in October. "I want to be a folk singer."

Lee chatted with him briefly, learned that Bob had some experience, and told him it was all right to play. "I'm not going to pay you," Lee said, "but you're welcome to play as long as it's in keeping with the business." Bob nodded. Lee asked, "What's your name?" and Bob replied, "Bob Dylan."

Years later, reminiscing about that conversation, Dylan told me: "I needed a name in a hurry and I picked that one. It just came to me as I was standing there in The Scholar. He asked me how he should bill me and the name just came to me. Wasn't Dylan Thomas at all, it just came to me. I knew about Dylan Thomas, of course, but I didn't deliberately pick his name."

He was Bob Dylan now, wherever he went. Bob Dylan, folk singer. His material was somewhat limited at first. He sang a few traditional folk songs, some country and hillbilly, a couple of Pete Seeger songs, and a lot of material then in vogue because of the popularity of slick, commercial folk interpreters such as Harry Belafonte and the Kingston Trio. He sounded like just another one of the thousands of college kids hooked on the folk revival that started in the mid-fifties.

The Weavers were at the vanguard of the revival, headed by Seeger, with Guthrie as their guru. Much of what they did had a radical overtone, which infuriated McCarthyites and eventually would drag Seeger before Congressional hearings and result in his being blacklisted from national network TV. By 1960, folk music was a conglomeration of styles and influences, from mountain music to Kingston Trio, and Bob was trying it all, still including the black folk and urban blues he had first heard and played back in junior high school.

Bob sang in a traditional folk style. He concentrated more on the melody line than he would later, when his voice became a third instrument accompanied and textured by his guitar and harmonica. His voice was rather nasal, and most people around thought he was an inept singer. Lee's girl friend, a university student who majored in organ and minored in piano and figured she knew her music, would periodically become enraged at this college guitar-picker singing in the front window of The Scholar. She'd come in late some nights and whisper to Lee:

"Make the kid stop singing."

"Why?" Lee asked.

"He's singing in a monotone. He's driving all the customers out of the place."

And Lee would occasionally order Bob to stop singing.

On reflection, ten years later, Lee's girl friend sticks by her guns: "He was a sort of nothing singer. I always used to feel he had adenoid problems and should take them out. He really was driving business away, he sang so badly. He was always off key, way off key and after he'd sing for a while people would leave. He drove me nuts and he drove other customers nuts, too."

But Bob was persistent and sang as often as he could. His friends say he was not a very good guitar player at this point, and his voice and style were an imitation of so much around that they didn't ring true. "He just wanted to get into a situation where he could learn, where his talent and his feel for the music could develop," one friend says. "He learned things quickly and tried everything, and developed at a remarkable speed. But those first few months he was nowhere at all. Just a kid trying damned hard to learn."

He slipped easily into the folk circle. He met David Morton, tall, bearded, "looking like a present-day Christ, an early hippie if ever there was one," a guitar player who lived in a thirty-dollar a month student tenement, without heat or water. At school and at the frat house, Bob was still Zimmerman, but everywhere else he was calling himself Dylan.

During the first few months Bob was telling his newest friends about his rock and roll career: "I had a great rock band up in Hibbing and over in Duluth—so great we made TV a lot and won all kinds of contests." And: "I used to travel with big rock groups all over the Midwest. Played piano and guitar behind some of the hottest rock singers around, like Little Richard." But after he began hanging out in The Scholar, swapping songs and ideas with other Dinkytown folkies, he only talked about his rock background and about Little Richard with college students who would be impressed by that sort of thing. The folkies sneered at rock. This culture was pre-Beatles, pre-drug (although "a few people were blowing grass"), pre-hippie, and rock had not yet become respectable in Dinkytown's intellectual-beat circles.

But the rock myth never died, and there were a number of other myths that Bob gleefully promoted.

From a Dinkytown friend: "He had this whole mythology about being Bobby Vee, the rock singer. He used to go to parties and introduce himself as Bobby Vee, or have friends point him out to strangers as Bobby Vee. And, a lot of times, he would tell us about how he used to work in carnivals, bumming around and playing piano. I was skeptical. But then I heard him play the piano and I never knew really that he could play the piano, so I began to accept his stories at face value. Even part of the Bobby Vee thing. One of the Bobby Vee stories was that Dylan used to play with him, sometimes went on for Vee when he was sick. And we could believe that, at least in the beginning. He also used to disappear from time to time and say he was going to Oklahoma, and it wasn't until a long time later I learned he'd been going back up to Hibbing to see his parents.

"He used to talk about meeting Big Joe Williams and other black blues guys. A whole bunch of stories about great people he knew. Big Joe Williams—I think Bob said he once hopped a freight car down to Mexico with him."

Another friend was later quoted as saying: "He was frightened. So were we all. Going to school is the first time some of us have been away from home. For the first time, you're responsible for yourself. So you defend yourself with a bottle of wine, or by saying you've just been to Oklahoma gathering folk songs, as Bob did. You begin varying your patterns. You get all mixed up. You start to miss classes, you have three drinks in the afternoon. You go to a party. And so it goes."

And John Koerner, who returned to Minneapolis after a few months in the Marines: "The whole bunch of us were kind of emotionally adrift."

Koerner was part of the folk set, along with Tony Glover and Dave Ray, who was still in high school. They played in some of the coffee houses and later became Koerner, Ray, and Glover, a country-oriented group that had a small success for a while and eventually broke up. Koerner met Dylan at The Scholar toward the end of 1959.

"The first time I heard him play, somehow we managed to get together with Len Duriseau, a friend of ours," Koerner says. "We went out back of the Chemical Engineering Building, had some wine, and played. From then on it was just hanging around together, playing at The Scholar and at The Purple Onion."

The Scholar had new owners by now; David Lee sold it at the end of 1959 to Bob Fishman and Clark Batho. For the first couple of weeks The Scholar discontinued the singing, but the customers demanded folk music and Batho and Fishman began looking around for talent as a means of building up their business.

Clark Batho: "When we first saw Bobby he was playing at The Purple Onion, over in St. Paul. I think he was getting two dollars a night. This was the end of January, the beginning of February. We offered him three dollars a night and he came over to sing on Friday and Saturday nights, sometimes Sundays. Bobby and Koerner were there at the same time. Sometimes they'd sing together, sometimes a night for each, sometimes they'd trade it off, playing alternate sets on the same night. When he and Koerner traded it off they'd get two-fifty each in the beginning. Alone, I think I eventually raised Koerner to four dollars a night, big wage.

"Bobby used to play around with the mouth organ on the funny strap around his neck. He thought he was a monkey show. And he was a prima donna, very temperamental. If the crowd wasn't listening to him, wasn't appreciating him, he would get mad and yell at the customers to shut up and if they didn't he would walk off and go down to the basement. That was his so-called dressing room. This was a headache, when you have an entertainer scheduled and people pay thirty-five to fifty cents cover charge to hear him and he doesn't play if they're not listening. You have to keep the crowd happy. If they're happy talking, let them talk."

Hugh Brown, English major, poet, guitar player and Dylan friend: "That was a pretty miserable price for anything, that three dollars for sitting around playing maybe four hours. Nobody liked Clark much. When The Scholar first started it was a very comfortable place. You could go in and sit around all day. But Clark wanted more turnover and he made us all very angry. He took away what we considered to be our place."

Dylan worked The Scholar once or twice a week for about three months. He was still getting three dollars a night and Koerner had been increased to four. One night in late April or early May, Dylan shuffled over to Batho and mumbled: "Hey, I bring a lot of people in, right? I think I ought to get maybe five dollars a night."

"You're not worth five dollars a night," Batho said. "You play only half the time you're supposed to be playing, anyway, so why should I pay you five dollars?"

"Whadda ya mean? Whadda ya mean?"

"Your attitude. It's bad enough at three dollars. It'll be impossible at five dollars."

That was the end of Dylan's apprenticeship at The Scholar. He wasn't fired, exactly; he simply wasn't hired any more.

Hugh Brown: "Bob was very angry. He went right over to the Purple Onion, near Hamline University in St. Paul, and got himself hired for maybe five or even six dollars a night."

John Koerner: "At this time he was just strumming, mostly chords and like that. He was doing standard folk songs. But I do remember him singing some of his own stuff. He was beginning to write his own material."

Koerner doesn't recall any specific Dylan songs from this early period, but some friends have been quoted as recalling part of what Dylan said was his first original folk song, *Blackjack Blues:*

Yeah, yeah, yeah.
How unlucky can one man be?
Every quarter I make
Ole blackjack takes away from me.

"I don't know if he wrote that," says someone who was a very close friend in those days. "I seem to remember him saying, 'This was taught me by Jesse Fuller.' But who knows the truth? At that time it was more important to him that people thought he knew Jesse Fuller than that he was writing his own stuff."

The University's official records show that Robert Allen Zimmerman attended classes for three semesters, from September, 1959 to the Fall of 1960. Actually, however, he stopped going to classes almost completely after the first six-months' torture. As Bob Dylan, he would later give a variety of reasons for dropping out.

He failed English, he said, because he wrote an essay that rather irreverently commented on his teacher's abilities. Or, another time: "Because the teacher said I couldn't talk." He also claimed that he flunked science "for refusin' to see a rabbit die," refusing to participate in the killing and dissecting of a laboratory animal.

"Colleges are like old-age homes," he later told Nat Hentoff for the 1966 *Playboy* interview. "Except for the fact that more people die in colleges than in old-age homes, there's really no difference. ... Colleges are part of the American institution; everybody respects them. They're very rich and influential, but they have nothing to do with survival."

University social life also contributed to the unreality of college. Dylan later explained to a friend: "Carnivals and fraternities—so much crap. A big hoax. You might as well get out and live with some other people."

Again, it was a little more than a distaste for collegiate mindlessness. Part of his attitude toward college was molded by the attitudes of fraternity brothers who began to lean on him. He was calling himself Dylan and working seriously at becoming a professional folk singer, and the other men in Sammy put him down for it. "He changed his name and the other Jewish kids didn't like that," one Scholar habitué put it. "He didn't want to tell anybody he was from up north, and they didn't like that. He was kind of disavowing his heritage and they didn't appreciate that at all. So he just split from that campus scene."

Dylan sought refuge in coffee houses and among the folkies and radicals who congregated in them, and by the time that first semester ended in early 1960, he was changing into what was then still being called beatnik by the straight press. The typical frat uniform vanished, replaced by blue workshirts, jeans, boots, and hair growing toward the shirt collar. He moved into a dreary, partially furnished room above Gray's Drugs, on the corner of Fourth Street and Fourteenth Avenue, a half-block down from The Scholar. He continued to attend classes sporadically, but most of his time was spent with David Morton, Hugh Brown, and their circle of folk beats.

They represented what little hip there was in Minneapolis at the time, ten or fifteen of them, young men and women who sometimes attended the University, sometimes used coffee houses as a more relevant university. If some of them were people "filled with futility" they didn't signal that feeling; they were bright, aware and very radical. A number of older men and women around had been radicals in the thirties, anarchists, even some Communists. Kevin McCosh, who owned the local bookstore that was a radical meeting place recalls Dinkytown's radical scene: "The only way to describe the feeling of people like Dave Morton and Hugh Brown and the other Dylan friends is sort of Marxist-anarchists, sort of predecessors of the New Left. Maybe a fusion of all these things, along with a strong feeling of just *hating* the bastards. A feeling the system doesn't work so throw it out, or maybe a little feeling that it wasn't worth fighting it and you might just drop out."

But it was the music, most of all, for Dylan. Everything else was tangential. "He never read anything," McCosh says. "He never had any part in the radical ideas. It wasn't only that he didn't read any books, but he seemed completely oblivious to everything except music. He didn't know about radicalism. He had contact with all these people, but he didn't know about it at all." A friend: "He was being kind of anti-intellectual. A primitive folk singer who couldn't admit he knew anything intellectual."

The music he was getting into was more authentic; he was dropping the Belafonte-Kingston Trio kind of laundered folk song aimed at the mass market, moving to Jesse Fuller, Big Bill Broonzy, Odetta and Woody Guthrie (although there was still no special emphasis on Guthrie; he was just another folk singer). "Dylan was just learning to sing everything that came into his path, he was into all of the better stuff around. Digging it, learning it, a serious student of all the music around," another friend says.

They were' living a curiously timeless existence, Dylan and his friends. School was a place, not a condition of mind as it is with most students, and it more and more became a place to avoid—except for the common-rooms where they'd occasionally go to get out of the snow, to play and talk. But, mostly, it was nowhere. Dinkytown was where it was at. They spent their time hanging out in bars, the Holland and Triangle mostly, and were drinking a lot of beer and wine. And hardly anyone worked. They didn't need much money. Dylan got a small allowance from home. Hugh Brown recalls: "He went downtown on occasion to get money. I went along once and dropped him off in front of some building and he went in and came out with money. I assumed maybe his parents sent money to this guy they knew in town, and he gave it to Bob. But that was just a guess. He didn't talk about his parents." He made a few dollars singing and didn't have too many expenses besides rent, food, wine and the cigarettes he constantly smoked. He was beginning to consciously adopt the physical trappings of the beats—ignoring personal needs, eating fitfully, seldom changing clothes, seldom washing.

A timeless existence. Much like the characters who lived on Cannery Row. Dinkytown was Bob Dylan's Cannery Row at this point, filled with those saints and sinners and martyrs and wise men extolled by Steinbeck. Dylan summed it up once this way: "There is no tomorrow, it all becomes today." And, at another time: "I don't look past right now."

As he began to meet new Dinkytown people Bob became even more vague, more secretive about his Iron Range merchant's son background. Only his close friends, his classmates, and the men with whom he had roomed at the frat house knew he was actually Bob Zimmerman. Some of them outside the folk circle delighted in spreading the word of Zimmerman's Dylan pose, in *exposing* him. But despite his growing need to change identity Bob didn't seem to care very much that the complex self-portrait he was painting was sometimes filled with holes.

B.D.—3

"When I first met Bobby he claimed he was an Okie, a real Okie," says Gretel Pelto, who was Gretel Hoffman back then. "He never talked about Steinbeck because Bobby was, at least superficially, non-intellectual, a primitive. He sort of *was* one of Steinbeck's characters. He had a whole set of original stories that he was an Okie, that he was an orphan. And that he'd been on the road for years as a piano player. I remember there was a big thing about that. Also that he had lived in California.

"There was this thing about his imagination; sometimes he didn't know what was truth any more. I knew about Zimmerman within a few weeks of the time I met him. He said that Dylan was his mother's name. There were a hundred stories about his background. Then it dawned on us that they were all *stories*. But it didn't matter. He was so vivid, so interesting, so much fun that I came to the conclusion after a while I didn't care about the quote unquote truth about what he was."

Hugh Brown recalls: "He didn't cover his stories very well. It was terribly easy to find him out. Most people didn't let on they discovered it because it didn't make any difference, it was all so terribly unimportant. I for one never minded because I liked Bob. He had a quality, a charm that was hard to avoid."

A Minneapolis girl, her mother a professional photographer, Gretel had been to Bennington for a while, was a dancer, played the guitar, and was part of the scene. She met Dylan in The Scholar around February, 1960, about the time he was giving up on college. He was living above the drugstore by then, a short walk from The Scholar. She would get together with him and play the guitar, and she remembers introducing him to the old New Orleans whorehouse song, *House of the Rising Sun*.

Like so many of those who grew close to him, Gretel found this young kid fascinating. *Charisma* is the overworked word that begins to be used when they talk about Bob at this point in his life; later, others would also be strongly affected by it. Joan Baez for one: "There aren't too many people who have as much charisma as Bobby has. I've never met anybody who has as much."

There were dozens of elements that made up this charisma, both physical and something else: *vibrations* is the modern catchall word that tries to sum up an indefinable charm encompassing more than simple physical attributes. Bob's myopia gave his eyes a sinister look, probably helped along not a little by his continued deep feeling for James Dean and for Marlon Brando. His voice was harsh, filled with accents of unschooled Okies and, in his secretiveness, filled with a quality that Dinkytowners might just associate with men of the soil.

He was manic, too, unable to sit still for long, his leg pumping, constantly moving, always on stage even when appearing to be shy. He had a little boy appeal that made women of all ages want to mother him. There was, also, a Chaplinesque quality about him, humorous, sardonic, sometimes biting. No one knows for certain where the Chaplin images came from; his friends in Hibbing remember his idolization of James Dean, of Buddy Holly and Presley, but no one remembers Chaplin. Yet Chaplin must have played a role because everyone who knew Dylan in Minneapolis comment on it, and when he performed in Greenwich Village later there were obvious Chaplin mannerisms in his performances.

As I talked to Dylan about Chaplin years later, he began to think aloud about Chaplin's influence on him. "If Brando had been into Chaplin I might have got it second hand from Brando because I was diggin' him," Bob told me. I asked him whether it was possible that Bob Dylan was a natural Chaplin figure, that it did not have to come from direct or indirect influences, and he replied: "Yeah, that could be true. Never thought of that. I didn't even see Chaplin's movies. They didn't have any of his movies there in Hibbing."

Gretel: "When he was here in Minneapolis he was still a kid, very much a naive kid. With this great propensity for story telling. And he had a delightful sense of humor."

Someone remembers a party at the apartment of one of the folk-radical crowd, just one of a constant round of parties and drunks. Dylan sat in a corner, playing a few gentle songs for a University coed. *Stunning* her, as some of his friends would put it. After a while he leaned his guitar against the wall, stood up. "Hey, let's go in t' other room," he said. He reached down, took the girl's hands and pulled her to her feet. They walked casually into an adjoining bedroom, dark, private. He closed the door behind him and they remained in the room for a while.

Suddenly the door flew open. A few people at the party stopped talking and watched. Dylan was on his hands and knees, crawling out slowly. His tongue hung out, his eyes glistened, he pantomimed extreme exhaustion. Then he grabbed a drink from someone's hand, tossed it down, and crawled back into the bedroom. He repeated the act several times. Just before it began to wear off ("great sense of timing," a friend says), he picked up his guitar and began to play. No one recalls the girl's reaction.

David Whittaker returned to Minneapolis in February, after some time in Israel. "Resident radical," he describes himself. Others call him one of the first non-students at the university; like Dylan, just hanging around. He lived in Koerner's old place down the street from The Scholar, near Dylan. He played guitar, but not much of it; his was more a social-intellectual influence, an important part of the radical scene.

Gretel and David met shortly after he returned. "I wasn't really Bobby's girl friend, in any sense," Gretel says. "But I was considered to be his girl, I guess. Then I started going with David."

Bob was walking down Fourth Avenue, near The Scholar, one evening in May, just before his nineteenth birthday. He was carrying his guitar, slouching along, when he spotted Gretel.

"Hey, hey, where you been?" he asked her.

"I just got married," Gretel said. "To David."

Dylan's jaw hung loose, his eyes grew wide. He stared at Gretel a moment. Then he stalked past her. Over his shoulder he shouted: "Let me know when you get divorced."

Says Gretel: "I had thought of our relationship as really platonic. If I had thought it was anything more than that I wouldn't have told him about David that way."

Eventually, David Whittaker and Dylan got to know each other and became warm friends. Whittaker is mentioned on the Great White Wonder, one of the many bootlegged albums of unreleased Dylan tapes that were sold under the counter in major metropolitan areas in 1969. On the album, Dylan talks briefly between a couple of songs he recorded in Minneapolis. Just before a talking blues about the murder of a black farmer, Hezekiah Jones, he says: "Hey, man, you oughta see some pictures of me. I'm not kidding." Someone asks "Were they taken at ...? " and Dylan says "Yeah, Whittaker's ... Ummm. I look like Marlon Brando, James Dean or somebody. ..."

Dylan later told me that Dave Whittaker was responsible for an enormous change in him. He said: "I saw Whittaker and it was like that"—motioning with his hand as in a karate chop—"just over and out. I was on this side and suddenly I was on that side. Whittaker, mostly, and also Brown and Morton and the others. You see they were incredible, they were just incredible. The way they were living, the way they thought, nobody was doin' it like them. There just wasn't anyone around like them. Especially David." Bob was hooked on their existential lives, their freewheeling style, the radicalism, the freedom, and they sparked a further transformation in him.

Whittaker says: "I think I had an understanding of where Bob's mind was. We were on the same wave length. There was something about his view of the world—a radical view combined with a sense of humor. And getting more and more, like, humorous. We spent a great deal of time laughing at the world."

Dylan was offered a professional job sometime in the early summer. He was still not very professional although the kids who hung out at The Purple Onion and The Bastille, where he continued to perform, seemed to enjoy him a great deal. But he was basically a kid trying to be a folk singer, a kid still lacking any real direction. As John Koerner recalls it, the job offer came from "some guy who was in town," who asked Dylan whether he'd like to work in a honky tonk joint in Central City, Colorado, a restored frontier town that had become a tourist attraction, complete with saloons, badmen with Western outfits and caps in their six-shooters—and plenty of dancehall girls. Dylan was secretive about the identity of the booking agent, almost guarding the first out-of-town job. One day he simply disappeared.

Kevin Krown, now a music booking agent in New York, remembers meeting Dylan in Denver during the summer of 1960. Krown was eighteen at the time, hitchhiking around the country. He was living at the Salvation Army hostel in Denver, hanging around the Exodus, one of the few folk clubs in the country.

"He was very friendly," Krown says. "Very communicative, very warm and happy to meet people. Said his name was Bob Dylan. He was playing piano in this Central City joint, the Gilded Garter, a burlesque house. Just piano. I didn't know until months later that he played guitar. He was living with this stripper in a hotel down the road. In those days he had money, he was the one doing the buying. He had a job and a few dollars and I was broke. He actually gave me a couple of bucks when I was ready to start hitching again. I gave him an address I was going to stay at in Chicago and told him to look me up if he ever passed through."

But Dylan wasn't quite yet ready to go to Chicago or anywhere else, not ready to leave Minneapolis. He was still basically learning his craft, but lacking that necessary spark that would prod him to move on. He returned to Dinkytown and friends recall his talking about his Gilded Garter experience: "Jesus, what a job. Hey, they had strippers and all kinds of things. Had to play between some real weird people. Hey, it was just—well, Wow."

Rolf Cahn came to town in the Fall of 1960 and all the local guitar players fell under his spell. He was a professional, a noted guitar teacher, with some incredible flamenco work that everyone wanted to learn. Lynn Kastner, now director of the Minneapolis affiliate of the American Civil Liberties Union, back then a young folk concert producer, had set up a concert for Cahn. He had also scheduled a series of guitar lessons by Cahn, trying to pack his week in Minneapolis as full as possible, trying to get Rolf together with Minneapolis folkies. Cahn was staying at Kastner's house for the week, and Koerner and Brown and a number of others took lessons from him —"one huge megalesson," is the way it's remembered; about an hour of intensified guitar work that they taped and that took more than six months to assimilate. Cahn charged a rather nominal fee, about $25 or so, but Dylan didn't want any of his lessons. Some friends believe he didn't want to spend the money, others that he wasn't as interested in technical proficiency as in learning new songs. He was always trying to pick up new material even though he probably had a larger repertoire than anyone else around, and he played more often than any two or three other players in town.

During the week Cahn was in town, Kastner's place became sort of a second Scholar as all the folk crowd hung out there to talk to and play with Cahn. One of them recalls an evening with Cahn, Dylan, Koerner, Brown, Kastner and a few others sitting around picking at their guitars. Someone in the group asked Cahn:

"Hey, Rolf, how 'bout showing us some of that two-finger picking again?"

Cahn was quite pleased to run through it and the guitar players watched, rapt, and imitated him. But Dylan hung back. Cahn asked: "How about you, Dylan?"

"Nah, I gotta learn some more songs," Dylan said. "Show me some of your songs?"

"Sure, but try this first," Cahn replied, and went through a series of riffs and chords.

"Yeah, great," Dylan said. "But I'd rather ya show me some of your songs."

It was, by all accounts, a standoff. The closest Dylan ever came to a formal lesson.

Later, Dylan, Koerner and Cahn jammed together at The Scholar, and the two young folk singers were very excited at the chance to play with a man of Cahn's stature. As Dylan mounted the stage with his guitar Koerner whispered: "Play nothing but blues, Bobby. All blues." And Dylan stuck with the blues that night.

Just before leaving town, Cahn told Kastner and one or two others that Bob was "the most talented guy around." That estimate, from a professional who actually had an album on Folkways, created a number of problems. It fueled hard feelings among some of the folkies because Dylan was a newcomer, still just a kid in appearance and emotions, still rough musically, "and it raised the hackles of jealousy," one of them recalls. But it must have been an enormous boost to Bob Dylan's own estimate of himself, an enormous boost to his link to the outer world.

The spark that fused everything he had learned into a new identity came shortly after Rolf Cahn left town. Koerner says: "I kind of recall a turning point. He'd been listening to just about everything, all kinds of styles, and writing all kinds of styles. Then he heard Jesse Fuller and Woody Guthrie. And then he started going off with the Guthrie thing, and a direction kind of sprang up."

Everyone knew Guthrie's music, of course, but he was more of a legend than anything else, a folksinger-radical who lay dying somewhere, and Dylan knew nothing more about him. David Whittaker seemed to be responsible for turning Dylan to the Guthrie direction. Dylan was sitting at the Whittakers late one afternoon listening to a Guthrie record, when David began talking about Guthrie's autobiography, *Bound for Glory,* describing some of the adventures of a man who was a true-life Okie, a hard traveler, song-writer, folksinger and folk hero.

"You've got to read it," David told him as they listened to Woody's *Dust Bowl Ballads.* "He's from Oklahoma, and the Dust Bowl, and he rode the rails and moved around with the Okies to California."

"Hey, hey, ya got the book around?" Dylan asked.

"No, I haven't read it in years. I don't know anybody who has."

"Let's find it, man, let's find it."

David and Dylan scouted around for a copy of the book. The library didn't have one. It wasn't in any of the stores, not even McCosh's. It took a couple of days until they discovered that Harry Webber, a University faculty member, had a copy. David borrowed it and gave it to Dylan. It was probably the only book he'd read since getting to Minneapolis. "Maybe all year," David says.

"He sat in The Scholar all one day and read it," says Hugh Brown, who helped in the search to locate a copy. "He was just amazed by it. He fell in love with Woody Guthrie right away."

Dylan carried the book around for weeks, talking to everyone who would listen to him. Friends remember Dylan cornering them and reading passages from the book. Especially at the beginning of the book, when Guthrie met a couple of kids on top of a freight heading from out West toward Chicago and, hopefully, New York. Woody played a few tunes for them. And then it looked like rain and one of the kids asked: "Will the rain wreck dat racket box?" And Bob rhapsodized about it.

"Hey, hey, listen to this: 'When the first three or four splats of rain hit me in the face I said to the kids, This water won't exactly do this guitar any good.'

"And," Bob continued, "the kids just pulled their sweaters off and gave them to Woody to wrap around his music box. He put the kids' sweaters on it, and his new khaki shirt, and they all squatted down in the rain in a circle, keeping Woody's meal ticket dry.

"A whole bunch of kids. They all gave Woody their shirts to keep his guitar dry. Hey, hey, damn, that's the kind of people ya meet on the rails. And ya know what, hey? That freight was rolling right through Minnesota at the time. Woody was comin' right through here. Wild!"

David: "He put Guthrie's *Tom Joad* on the phonograph after reading the book and he'd play it all day long, that half-hour song. All day long. Day after day."

1960: *A Song to Woody*

WOODROW WILSON GUTHRIE, a banty rooster sort of a man, with gaunt features and wiry bushy hair and a harsh, nasal voice, has played a unique role in American folk music. Born in Okemah, Oklahoma, in 1912, victim of the Dust Bowl in his mid-teens, Guthrie spent his life writing about people who had been trampled by the system and the men who control it. He wrote over a thousand songs between 1932 and 1952, when his voice and his pen were muted by the onset of Huntington's chorea, the wasting disease that would ravage his body for another fifteen years before killing him. Many of his songs have become a part of the American folk tradition, sung by people who don't even know his name, songs accepted by folk theoreticians and academicians as true folk songs, even though their composer was known. To the folk purists, a song can't be a true folk song until it has been filtered through many voices, like the Bible or the Greek myths, and its original creator has been lost in history.

Not Guthrie, however. He was authentic. He wrote about misfortunes that overtook him and his fellow Okies. And he wrote songs of protest, songs that came out of a rebellious mind inflamed into social consciousness by the Depression and the dust storms. And by the early forties, even the folk purists were forced to hail him as a true folk balladeer and singer.

Guthrie was everything that people claimed he was. Pete Seeger, with notable restraint: "Of his thousands of verses, I think a large number will outlive this century." John Steinbeck called him the essence of the "American spirit." Folklorist John Greenway described him as "the greatest figure in American folksong." And Clifton Fadiman once wrote in *The New Yorker* that Guthrie and his songs "are a national possession like Yellowstone and Yosemite, and part of the best stuff this country has to show the world."

Guthrie was all of that, certainly. Many of his songs will still be important as long as people sing and strum the guitar, songs such as *This Land Is Your Land, Roll On, Columbia, So Long, It's Been Good to Know You,* and some of the other *Dust Bowl Ballads,* as well as many other ballads and talking blues that tumbled out of his head and off his music box strings.

Bound For Glory knocked Dylan out, and he was quickly caught up in the whole romantic hobo life that Guthrie had lived and written about. Dylan had been playing the role of Okie, telling some friends he'd been born in Oklahoma, and others that he had lived there during his many runaway adventures. Guthrie was a ready made identity for a young man in search of a strong image.

Bob Dylan, tracing some of his roots in a conversation a couple of years later: "And then you arrive at Woody Guthrie, who sounds pretty weird and obviously looks like you ... "

He became Woody Guthrie. Paul Nelson, writer and editor, who knew Dylan at the university, would later write: "He was moving so rapidly that one could say his only style was that of transition, both in his artistic and personal life. It took him about a week to become the finest interpreter I have yet heard of the songs of Woody Guthrie."

Dylan's stories began to change to fit his changing identity. "I met Woody once in California," he told friends. A couple of years later, in a Studs Terkel radio interview, he said: "I saw Woody once, a long, long time ago, in Burbank, California. I was just a little boy. I don't even remember seeing him. I heard him play. Must have been about ten. My uncle took me there. It stuck in my mind that he was Woody, and everybody else around me was just everybody else." Some of Bob's friends knew he would have had to be very young to have seen Woody in California, because of Woody's illness, but they never let on that they suspected him of lying. As John Koerner put it: "I never bothered thinking about any of that."

Guthrie brought it all into focus for Dylan. Back in Hibbing his closest friends knew that Dylan's sole direction was music, that little else mattered. Here in Minneapolis the thrust of his ambition was felt even more strongly. He was totally devoted to the music, to his guitar and harmonica, and to Guthrie most of all. Bob was a serious student even though he refused to take lessons from Cahn, and he was learning with remarkable speed. Some of the others were mostly playing around, drifting with no real direction. But not Dylan.

Paul Nelson recalls that Dylan wanted to impress the many Dinkytowners who admired Southern mountain music and the New Lost City Ramblers, and "he developed, in a matter of days, a brilliant and original version of the country staple, *Man of Constant Sorrow.*"

"I ain't interested in no career," friends remember him saying. "Nothing else for me 'cept singing and guitar."

Says Lynn Kastner: "He had quit school because he was going into music. I remember both Dylan and Koerner talking to me about it, and talking to Rolf, because we had some experience. They were asking what it's like, what they'd have to do. I thought Dylan was talented. Rolf and I were both attracted to him and his talent. I enjoyed singing with him, I enjoyed what he did, and he was turned on to what I was doing. And I didn't discourage his ambition. Some of the talk was tied into what he was going to do with his life. And there was no pressure from me to stay in school."

And his friends also sensed a growing professionalism in Dylan during this period. Koerner recalls: "There was a kind of feeling about what he was doing. Like, confidence, or sometimes a touch of *arrogance.* I think he felt it when he was doing it right, he felt he was getting it off. He was confident in that way."

That arrogance flashed through occasionally in other ways. There is little doubt that Dylan knew he had something, and he was impatient sometimes when he felt he was being ignored or put down. He was beginning to demand center stage, even at parties and small gatherings. Everyone played guitar, but only Dylan required that his friends listen to him.

"He went to parties mostly because he wanted to make them into Dylan concerts," one friend recalls. "He would play for hours. He preferred playing *for* audiences rather than playing *with* groups of people. Most of us didn't mind because we were into what he was doing. But there was always discontent with people who didn't like music. There was nothing for them to do but go into another room, but if the party was really big and there wasn't enough space, there would be a conflict between Bobby's concert and the people who wanted to talk."

Bob Dylan, reminiscing about his "training": "I can remember traveling through towns, and if somebody played the guitar that's who you went to see. You didn't necessarily go to meet them, you just went necessarily to watch them, listen to them, and if possible, learn how to do something . . . whatever he was doing. And usually at that time it was quite a selfish type of thing. You could see the people and if you knew you could do what they were doing, with just a little practice, and you were looking for something else, you could just move on. But when it was down at the bottom, when you knew that they knew more than you, well, you just had to listen to everybody. It wasn't necessarily a song; it was technique and style, and tricks and all those combinations which go together—which I certainly spent a lot of hours just trying to do what other people have been doing. That's what I mean by training."

Dylan hadn't bothered renting a new apartment when he returned to Minneapolis from Central City, and through the early fall he was living with a succession of friends and sleeping wherever anyone had room for him, sometimes with Koerner, or the Whittakers, or Gretel Whittaker's parents, occasionally at Ellen Baker's house. Ellen was exactly Dylan's age (one day younger), a student at the university. Her mother was a Minneapolis grade school teacher, her father an industrial chemist who has been a folk music collector for years, with a house full of all the old *People's Songs, Sing Outs!*, and folk lore material up to the rock era, and hundreds of recordings. The Baker house, on Gerard Street, not far from the university, was a second meeting room for the kids in the Folk Song Club at the school, and for other folkies. Once a week or so, for years, the place was filled with kids playing, informal, with coffee and cake and a lot of music.

Ellen met Bob at the Whittakers' place on Fourteenth Avenue, about eight blocks from the University, in mid-September. She stopped off to visit and Bob was there, with his guitar. He was introduced as Bob Dylan.

Ellen remembers: "He seemed quite shy at the time, boyish, but not boyish in that 'Oh, gee, gosh, well' way a lot of kids have. Not cloying. Sort of inarticulate. He didn't say very much but when he did it wasn't the stammering thing. He wasn't taciturn, just shy.

"We talked and he said he was from Hibbing, but I didn't find out his name was Zimmerman until later. We talked about folk and he said he was interested in it, and he mentioned Cisco Houston. I said my father had some old seventy-eights, of Woody, Cisco and others. And like a total collection of bound issues of every issue of *Sing Out!*

that ever was, and a bunch of other kinds of things. And he was really interested in it. He said, 'We should really get together some time and talk about it, about music.' And I said 'Why don't you come over and you can just look through the stuff?' And he said, 'Boy, that would be really great.'

"He came over a couple of days later for dinner. He said something like, 'Boy, I really like Jewish food. It's really nice to come to a real Jewish home for a Jewish dinner.'

"We were sitting at dinner, my parents, my brother and Bob and me, and he was a very polite and just kind of eager and a very nice young man. Mother seemed to feel he was sort of a lost little boy, just kind of eager and impressionable, with no home and no place to stay. He said, 'Gee, can I stay here if I have no place to go?' and mother said it was okay. He ended up staying over that night and on several other occasions, too.

"That first time he was over, Mother said, 'You know you can feel free to stay here and use our shower and I even have an extra toothbrush. And the next time you come over I'm going to insist you do.' And the next time she said, 'Robert, you have green teeth. Go brush them.' She was no Yiddishe Mama, but he *did* have green teeth. His reaction was kind of a boyish, 'Well, Mother knows best' kind of thing. And he brushed. It didn't seem to help much.

"After dinner we looked through my father's books and records. He was tremendously excited over Woody Guthrie. He came across one record in particular, Cisco and Woody singing *Those Brown Eyes* and he played it over and over again. He didn't talk about rock-and-roll at all. He was somewhat disdainful of my own interest in Elvis and the *Blue Suede Shoes* stuff and what was then the hard rock, like the Clovers. When we were together I didn't play that kind of music. I was kind of surprised later when I read on his first album jacket that he had been influenced by Elvis. The only indication I ever had of anything like that was when I heard he had been claiming to be Bobby Vee. But he would only do that when he was with some group that would be impressed by it.

"Some of the people around used to call him 'That itinerant Jewish folk singer.' He wanted so much to be part of what he was singing about. I used to ask him, 'How's the man of the soil today?' And that's what he was. Full of the Jesse Fuller thing, being down to earth, being a man of the soil. When all the time he was the son of a Jewish furniture dealer from up on The Range. The funny thing is, there's a certain mystique about being from The Range, an honorable thing, tough, mine-working, hardy people up there. People from The Range were proud of it. But Bob would rather have been from some place in Arkansas. He wanted to be part of another kind of romantic and glorious tradition, part of some sort of folk Dust Bowl tradition. But he couldn't be a man of the soil with a name like 'Zimmerman,' could he?

"He so absolutely became Woody Guthrie in the months I knew him well, from September to about December. 'We're going to go see Woody in New York,' he used to tell me all the time. He was painfully sincere in his feelings. He had an obsession about Woody Guthrie, and going to see him. And people used to put him on about it, especially when he was drunk. We'd be at a party and a couple of them would say, 'Woody's outside, Bob. Woody's here. Woody wants to see you.' And Bob would go dashing down into the snow in his shirtsleeves, crying, 'Hey, Woody, where are you? Wait, Woody, wait!' It got a big laugh. Very disgusting people."

Ellen's mother sensed some of the conflicts in Dylan. Mrs. Baker recalls: "I had the feeling he was a little lost boy. I felt he was rejecting a lot of things, sort of traveling in disguise. He built a character for himself and it's hard living up to that. I felt it was just a posture, at first. I took it as a kind of *chutzpah* thing, this little kid making a model on a Woody Guthrie. I didn't think of it as genius. I thought it was imitative. Here was Guthrie, who from my youth was a very political figure, and Bob was like singing from the *Little Red Song Book,* doing these songs from the Wobblies song book. He just seemed like a youngster who didn't have much that he felt sure of.

"At the same time, there was this intensity, this singleness of purpose, within the boy. Whatever it was, he got a lot of support from inside himself. He was not compromising. He was going to entertain, that was what he was going to do. He was withdrawn, but I think inside he was on all the time. Once he lighted on Guthrie it all began to come together for him."

Dylan had been in Minneapolis a year by the time Ellen got to know him well, and in that year he had grown a great deal. Professionally, he had come along from a "callow youth" (Hugh Brown's deliberate cliche to describe him) who had been thrown out of The Scholar for annoying the customers, to the Dinkytown folk singer Rolf Cahn picked as the most talented. And Dylan felt the growth, was very much aware that he had something. There was also a toughening of spirit and a deepening cynicism—even about Woody Guthrie. A few who were very close to Bob at this stage felt that in adopting the Guthrie identity Bob was coldly calculating: he knew Guthrie was dying, was no longer able to write or perform, and that a vacuum existed in the folk world. A vacuum that could be filled by a young man named Bob Dylan.

Most of his Minneapolis friends, however, don't believe it was as conscious as all that. More likely, he intuitively seized on Guthrie as the final piece that would fully complete his identity.

"You can't ever get me to buy the idea that he deliberately became Guthrie in order to fill a dead man's shoes," comments one who was very close to Dylan. And John Koerner: "I don't know about conscious designs. What it was, mostly, is that he was going to New York to see Guthrie and to get into a situation where some of the stuff he was doing could develop."

That winter of 1960 Bob was playing at the Bastille where he got five dollars a night, and at the Purple Onion, in nearby St. Paul, for six dollars. In November he moved into a grim, semi-furnished apartment at 711 Fifteenth Street with two friends, Hugh Brown and Max Uhler. It had a living room, dining room and an old decrepit kitchen on the ground floor, on the second floor were two bedrooms and a huge bath. Brown had one of the bedrooms and Max and Bob shared the other. Each contributed a third to the $120 a month rent. There was a constant round of parties and a continual flow of friends living over. One, known as Dirty Dave, reportedly slept for several weeks in the bathtub. After two months of constant hassling by the landlord and neighbors over the noise, the trio decided to get out. One night in December, they dumped most of their belongings in a couple of sheets and sneaked out, owing a month's rent.

Dylan moved into a similarly grim apartment a block away. But he didn't plan to stay very long. "I'm going to New York," he told his closest friends. "I'm going to see Woody. And I'm going to make it big."

But even his closest friends didn't believe he would make it. "We all laughed," Hugh Brown recalls. "It's so easy to say 'I'm going to make it big' and so hard to do it." And Gretel: "I don't think any of us believed he was going to make it. Because it was all so tough. Not that he wasn't good, but there were a lot of good people. And, you see, at this time he was doing very little of his own composing. Mostly singing other people's songs."

No matter how professional a musician and singer Dylan may have become by now, no matter how well he pulled off the Guthrie routine, it was the vision of his folk-poetry that would make the difference, and the people in Dinkytown hadn't seen that vision yet.

One snowy evening in December at the Whittakers' apartment, David recalls: "We had been up all that night, and in the morning we decided to call Woody on the phone. I had learned Woody was in Greystone Hospital in New Jersey, probably from reading something in *Sing Out!*, and Bob just had to call him. So, we called. We got as close as the doctor on the ward, who told us Woody was too sick to come to the phone. 'He can't move,' the doctor told us. And Bob said, 'I'm going to see him. I'm going to New York right now.' And that was the last I saw of him for a while. He just up and went to New York."

Dylan stopped off at Lynn Kastner's house, carrying some clothing, records and books. "Hold onto this stuff for me," he said. "I'm going to New York to see Woody." He left, carrying his guitar and a knapsack.

In leaving Dinkytown behind, Dylan left a large amount of bitterness among some who claim they were once his friends. The basic accusation is that Dylan used people wherever he went, taking from them friendship, love, musical knowledge, street-hipness, and then moving on to someone else from whom he could take a little more. There is a feeling among some of Dylan's old friends that they had been *taken,* that they were manipulated by Dylan for his own uses. Not everyone was entranced by his charisma.

McCosh: "There was something about his personality. Basically, nobody liked him very much. He was arrogant, boorish, aggressive. I think people sort of enjoyed hearing him sing, but he didn't have a very engaging personality. Most of us disliked him as a person."

Lynn Kastner: "A lot of people claimed to have been abused by Bobby."

This dislike for Dylan as a person was based to a large extent on Dylan-as-artist. The only people he drew close to were those who were into the music, who dug what he was digging. Those who were outside the folk scene saw only the posturing of an uneven and very young musician pretending to be something he had not yet become. It was easy to resent him, if you weren't into his music; he played almost constantly, whether he was alone or at the frequent Dinkytown parties. His singing made it impossible for the radical intellectuals who preferred political and philosophic arguments to get into very serious discussions. It's difficult to develop one of those deliciously heated arguments while someone sits on the couch singing *Butcher Boy.*

One afternoon shortly before Christmas, Kevin Krown was sitting in a coffeehouse near the University of Chicago, when a chilled kid wearing a corduroy snap-brimmed cap wandered into the place.

"Kevin?" he asked.

"Yeah?" Krown asked in reply.

"They told me at your place you'd be hanging out here. I'm Bob Dylan."

"Great. Who's Bob Dylan?"

"Remember? The Exodus, in Denver? Ya told me to look you up when I got to Chicago. I got here."

"Oh, yeah," Krown said. "Want to play piano somewhere?"

"I don't play piano any more," Dylan said. "I play guitar."

Krown introduced him to the folkie crowd. "He played guitar in the girls' dorm that night and I listened and it didn't ring. Whatever he was before, he wasn't that now." Krown asked: "What happened? Why you playing the guitar?"

"Well," Dylan said, "I met this guy Woody Guthrie in a hospital in New Jersey and I started playing guitar." He had not yet visited Guthrie, of course.

Dylan remained in Chicago for several weeks. He moved into Krown's place for a couple of days. Then he met a girl—"She grows pot in her place," he said—and moved in with her. He came and went, drifting in and out of Krown's circle, over the next few weeks, playing at parties, coffee houses, dorms.

He was writing a great deal by now, mostly reworking old folk standards into something that he considered his own kind of music, often Guthrie kind of things. The only song from this period that is remembered is his very significant *Song to Woody,* young Dylan's tribute to his idol who was slowly dying in a hospital almost a thousand miles away. Written much in Woody's style, it is a compassionate eulogy by a youth who says he's traveling Woody's road, seeing the world and the people that Woody had once seen, a world that appears to be "a-dyin' " but that's "hardly been born." Gently, with a touching but low-keyed emotion, he makes it clear he's not about to tell Woody what it's all about because Woody knows. There aren't many men around "that done the things that you've done." But most of all he wants Woody to know he loves him.

"Here's one I wrote," he'd say. And he played it again and again, to any who would listen.

"You got that copyrighted?" Kevin asked.

"No. What the hell do I know about copyright?"

"Better do it before somebody steals it."

But no one knew how to get the forms from Washington, what they would cost, the procedures. Krown knew enough to protect him, though. He had Dylan write out a copy in his own hand, date it, and send it to Krown's apartment by registered mail—an effective proof of original authorship.

He thumbed his way out of Chicago in mid-January—heading west, not east. Apparently he had changed his mind and was hitching back to Minneapolis. He got as far as Madison and sent the Whittakers a card from there at the end of January. "I've been broke and cold," he wrote, but he was still elated by his experience. He'd seen Muddy Waters in "dirty smelly Chicago" and had been writing songs "all out of bars and singing 'em to all kinds of people." And, he said, he'd been lucky enough to meet a "bunch of New York people" in Madison.

He headed for the University of Wisconsin the moment he arrived, seeking Madison's own sort of Dinkytown, his guitar always an entree. As at Minneapolis and all college campuses, there was a small folk-leftist set at Wisconsin, living in the radical ghetto just off the campus. There was considerable musical talent around, "not just strumming three chords and singing union songs," as one of them put it. Among the students at Wisconsin was Danny Kalb, then eighteen and already one of the finest folk guitarists around, and probably one of the best white kids playing black blues. With Steve Katz and Al Kooper and some others, Kalb would later form the Blues Project, New York's first rock band, an incredible group that never achieved popular success, but that turned on a lot of Village people to a lot of musical influences.

Jennifer Warren, a sophomore at the time, remembers Dylan's arrival at Madison: "It was very cold, and he was walking along the street, his guitar on his back, and I think he just stopped Paul Brynnis, a friend of ours. He said to Paul, 'I'm passing through on my way to New York. Do you know where I can stay for a while?'

"Paul said, 'We're having a party. Come on up.'

"So Paul brought him to the party at his place. He was a little, wispy kid, sort of skinny. He had a round, little-boy's face. He looked sixteen. When he came in we asked him, 'Who are you?' And he said: 'I'm Bob Dylan, I'm sort of bumming around the country. What would you like me to sing?' and he immediately went into a song. He had a croaky voice. And he couldn't play the guitar worth a shit. A lot of us felt, 'Oh, my God, this poor kid with this thing about Woody Guthrie.' I was tired and the party started to break up—it started to drag, for me, at least, because this kid wouldn't stop playing."

A number of people at the party felt concerned about where Dylan would stay for the night. There was no room at Brynnis's place, so Fred (Fritz) Underhill, another student, offered to put him up. Dylan accompanied Jennifer, Underhill and Fred DeVoer to the apartment they shared on West Johnson Street in another student tenement.

Jennifer Warren recalls: "It was after one A.M. I was tired. We sat

50

in the kitchen and I made coffee. He sat on the stove and started singing again and we couldn't go to bed. All we wanted to do was go to sleep, me especially, and he just went on with song after song. He didn't know anything about the guitar, just picking chord to chord.

"He knew more Guthrie songs than Guthrie knew. He had this Guthrie accent, and it sounded like phony shit. I remember thinking: 'Why the hell would a kid his age want to be somebody else?' Even Fred and Fritz, who were folk devotees, got tired after a while. But he went on until about three A.M. or later.

"Between songs he would talk a lot about himself. He said he'd been bumming around, had met singers, met country people. He said he stopped with this country family somewhere. 'Simple folk,' he said. They took him in. He carried on about them, like 'Wow, they're great.' He was a traveling boy from the road. He came from Minnesota, he said, and left us with the impression he came from the sticks. Said he had left home, and something about his parents. I got this feeling they were crummy people, lower class, unpleasant people. But he gave out very little specifics. It was all very vague.

"He was so single-minded. All he ever did was play his songs and talk about Woody. His whole thing was he was going to New York so he could sit by Woody's bedside because Woody was dying. He said he was planning to see him in the hospital in New Jersey.

"He told us he was going to hit the Village. I remember telling Fred: 'That poor kid. Another incompetent is going to get swallowed by the crowd.' I thought, Jesus, he's going to be eaten up alive."

Jennifer's feeling was based on her awareness of Greenwich Village. She was born and raised there. Her mother is the actress, Paula Bower Smith and her grandfather is Jacob Ben-Ami, actor, director, producer, leading member of New York's Yiddish theater, member of Eva Le Gallienne's Repertory Theater, with a career that spanned more than half a century. Jacob Ben-Ami was on Broadway playing the loving grandfather in Paddy Chayevsky's *The Tenth Man* at the moment Dylan and Jennifer were meeting. A few years later Jennifer would play the role of the wife in Bruce Jay Friedman's *Scuba Duba*. Her knowledge was the first-hand knowledge of that extremely rare breed, a native Villager.

After listening to Dylan for a few hours Jennifer finally pulled out a set of sheets and a blanket, said, "Here's the things," and went off to bed. After a while, Fred and Fritz left him and he curled up under the kitchen table, wrapping himself in the bedclothes, his guitar at his side ready for action.

Others in Madison shared Jennifer's view. Dylan was a tender young kid recreating in himself the whole romantic Guthrie image, playing the lonesome hustler who had been tramping through the wilds of America, playing in carnivals and bars. "Coming on like he was a real professional," Fred DeVoer, who was a graduate student in theater, says, "but when he started playing he wasn't that good, there was very little music coming out of the kid. But he was charming and very interesting to listen to, anyway, because he had a real way with the talking blues thing that Guthrie did—a good way with getting the words over. That was the interesting thing about him."

He stayed around Madison for a couple of days, playing at parties and talking and listening to DeVoer's collection of old blues records. Bob's "Aw, shucks" manner seemed affable enough to those who met him. He played his harmonica at a coffee house, with Danny Kalb, where a basket was passed and they collected a few coins, and he spent some time learning guitar riffs from Kalb. He continued to talk non-stop about himself, his plans, his road experiences. DeVoer remembers that Dylan talked about how he was going to "make it," about his show business ambitions: he was going to make it like Woody Guthrie, and even like Elvis Presley. He talked about them, and others. "Like on a culture hero trip," one remembers.

"Hey," Dylan said once, "I been down South visiting the grave of Blind Lemon Jefferson."

And another time, after doing a bottleneck guitar number rather badly: "I learned that one from Big Joe Williams."

Says DeVoer: "He was doing his season on the road, that Beat Generation thing. He told so many tales I thought he'd been on the road for years. And he was pretty square. He talked like he had smoked a lot of dope and I could tell he hadn't."

1961: *Bob Dylan's Dream*

BOB DYLAN ARRIVED in New York at the end of January, 1961, and later summed up his first impressions: "Everything was so big I couldn't see the sky." The city was shivering with temperatures down near zero, the coldest spell of weather to hit in at least fifteen years. A week before he arrived a foot of snow had been dumped on New York, with drifts ten feet high, and the paralysis that usually grips the snow-bound city lingered for many days. Dylan went directly to Greenwich Village and wandered around, taking in the sights, checking the coffee houses and folk clubs and tourist bars along MacDougal and Bleeker Streets. That evening, lugging his guitar and knapsack, he wandered into the Cafe Wha?, a coffee house on MacDougal. Maddy Bloom, then a waitress there, remembers that Dylan found Manny Roth, who still operates the Wha?, and said: "Just got here from the West. Name's Bob Dylan. I'd like to do a few songs. Can I?"

"Sure," Roth said. "Where you staying?"

"Don't have a place yet. Know anybody's got a place I can crash for the night?"

"I'll see what I can do," Roth said.

Bob climbed up on the stage. Maddy recalls Dylan with his guitar and his harmonica on the wire holder around his neck—"I'd never seen that before. Thought it was unusual and kind of kooky."—and the Huck Finn cap. He sang a couple of Guthrie's songs, and a few others, and between songs he told the audience a little about himself: "I been travelin' around the country," he said. "Followin' in Woody Guthrie's footsteps. Goin' to the places he went to. All I got is my guitar and that little knapsack. That's all I need."

The Wha? was half empty but, Maddy recalls, a number of people in the audience seemed to share her feeling about Dylan: "I remember thinking he was very raw, that he had no professional polish, but that he had a quality of such great innocence, in a way, that you just had to notice him, you had to listen to him. This kid had such a terrific appeal that you couldn't ignore him, you had to listen to him and watch him."

After a few songs Roth took the microphone and told the audience: "This kid has just come into town and he has no place to stay. Can anybody help him out?" There were a half dozen offers, folk buffs from Queens and Brooklyn, straight people, not Village freaks. "I've got room in my place," they said. No one remembers now where Dylan spent that first night, but those who were there remember very clearly that he seemed to drill right into the hearts of the audience.

Within a day or two he was hitchhiking out to Greystone Hospital, a mental institution near Morristown in central New Jersey, with facilities for some non-psychiatric patients like Woody. Dylan was alone, and exactly what took place is known only to him. But Kevin

Krown, recalls another visit to Greystone a short time later: "Guthrie was very shaky, he could barely talk, and he was very difficult to look at. But Dylan would sit beside him and play the guitar for him and somehow they communicated. Guthrie legitimately liked the guy, he even tried to play *This Land is Your Land* for Dylan." By this time Huntington's disease had practically crippled him. He couldn't do much more than strum the guitar with his full hand by now, a chord, and a pause as he struggled for a word, and another chord.

Dylan sent a postcard back to the Whittakers a couple of days after he arrived in the Village, a brief message scrawled on the back of one of those cards printed by the Guthrie Children's Fund, the organization set up to provide for Woody's children. The card carried the classic photo of Woody in a workshirt, holding his guitar in front of him. Dylan's enthusiasm leaps off the card: "I know Woody. I know Woody. . . . I know him and met him and saw him and sang to him. I know Woody—Goddamn." He signed it, "Dylan."

Huntington's disease had forced Guthrie into a hospital for the first time in late 1951 or early 1952. He had begun to have dizzy spells and was wondering aloud whether there was something wrong with him. Jack Elliott, who was living with the Guthries at the time, recalls that Woody used to say it was probably alcoholism which would have been a lot easier to deal with than an incurable and deadly disease. The disease is hereditary, and causes deterioration of certain nerve cells in the brain as the victim comes into middle age. The result is a kind of palsy that progresses gradually until at the end the victim is wracked with tremors that bring physical exhaustion and death, usually by heart failure or pneumonia. At first Guthrie was hospitalized only for brief intermittent periods, but as his illness worsened he required constant hospitalization. He was first signed into Brooklyn State Hospital in 1954. In 1959, he was transferred to Greystone, New Jersey, and by the time Dylan met him, Guthrie had been there for almost three years.

Bob Gleason and his wife Sid (christened Sidsel after a French grandmother) had been fans of Guthrie since the Thirties and when they heard he was in Greystone they went to visit him. Guthrie complained about being confined to the hospital and the Gleasons persuaded hospital officials to let them take Guthrie around Morristown for the day. While wandering around the town, Gleason asked Guthrie if he'd like to spend weekends at their place if the doctors would agree, and Guthrie said he'd love it. The hospital director gave his permission, so long as Guthrie was back at night for special medication. The next Sunday—Mother's Day, 1959—the Gleasons picked up Guthrie at the hospital and drove him to their apartment on North Arlington Avenue in East Orange, New Jersey.

Over the next two years the Gleasons brought Woody to their apartment every weekend, missing only two weekends in all that time. The Gleason apartment in East Orange became a center of folk activity, filled every weekend and frequently during the week with "every stumble bum in creation," as one of them affectionately said of the loose crowd, all come to spend time with the greatest figure in modern folk music. Pete Seeger would come, with his wife, Toshi, and their children. Peter La Farge (son of Oliver La Farge, who won the 1930 Pulitzer Prize in literature for *Laughing Boy*, his novel about the Navajos), part-Indian, cowboy, folksinger, author of *The Ballad of Ira Hayes*, weaver of tall tales. Cisco Houston, Jack Elliott and dozens more. Every weekend at least a couple of Woody's friends would drive out to the Gleasons. They would eat and drink and swap tall tales, and play music. Much of the playing was laid down on Bob Gleason's tapes, some of the most marvelous and priceless tapes around.

When he visited Guthrie, Dylan was told that the Gleasons were bringing him to their home every weekend and the next day Dylan hitchhiked to the Gleason's apartment. Mrs. Gleason remembers that first meeting:

"He came, and he said little except that he loved Woody and wanted to spend time with him. He looked like an archangel almost, like a choir boy, with that little round face and the beautiful eyes. His hair in those days was long and curly and he wore that dark Eton cap. He had a pair of boots that was two sizes too big; everything that child had was either too small or too big. He bought a jacket, for instance, that didn't fit him at all, and I think he paid seventy-five cents for it in one of those Village thrift shops."

Mrs. Gleason apparently (she doesn't recall exactly) told Dylan that Woody would be at her apartment the following Sunday, which was January 29 from the available evidence, and that she expected a few of Woody's friends to show up. And, she added, Bob would be welcome if he cared to make the trip. He certainly did care, for in that card to the Whittakers he's ecstatic about getting together with Woody on Sunday, and with Jack Elliott, Cisco Houston, Will Geer and some others.

Then he made another important stop, not quite the same as visiting the grave of Blind Lemon Jefferson, but possibly part of the same ritual culture hero trip. Bob went out to Guthrie's home in Howard Beach, Queens. It's not clear why he did so, probably just anxious to learn as much as he could about Woody and his family. He rang the bell and a teenage girl opened the door.

"I came to look for Woody," he told her.

"He's in the hospital."

"You his daughter?" he asked.

"No, I'm the babysitter," she replied.

"Hey, can I come in and say hello to the kids?"

The girl hesitated. "I don't know. I'll have to call Mrs. Guthrie first."

Marjorie Guthrie was teaching at her dancing school in Sheepshead Bay, Brooklyn, at the time. The girl called her and said: "There's an awful strange looking kid at the door and he wants to come in."

"Don't let him in," Mrs. Guthrie said. "Tell him to come back when I'll be home."

Mrs. Guthrie had kids knocking at her door all the time, seeking Woody, hoping to learn in Howard Beach some of the secrets of becoming an authentic hobo troubador. "Jack Elliott came and he stayed for two years," Mrs. Guthrie says, laughing at it now.

But by the time the babysitter had put the phone down Dylan was already inside and showing Arlo a new way of playing the harmonica, which Arlo had been playing since he was three years old, some ten years before this. "When I came home from the school," Mrs. Guthrie recalls, "the children told me about the fabulous, wonderful visit they had had with this odd-looking boy. I could tell from the children's response to him that he was probably a warm, kindly and talented kid."

Late Saturday night Bob dropped into the Folklore Center, a combination record and music shop, folk library, folkie booking center and general hangout. "I saw a girl playing with a banjo," he later recalled. "Oh, God! This is it! This is New York! Everyone is playin' banjo faster than I've been playin' guitar. I couldn't really play with them." But he did play, and he left an impression on at least some of the people hanging around at the time. Jack Goddard, writing in the *Village Voice* some time later, described it this way:

"A little over a year ago a short peripatetic young man, his beardless, aquiline face crowned by an old cap, wandered into Izzy Young's Folklore Center on MacDougal Street. Picking up an autoharp, he began mumbling a song about some bloke named Captain Gray. People looked on in amusement as he began hopping around a bit. He was funny to watch, and anybody with half an ear could tell he had a unique style. But few could have guessed on that wintry Sunday morning that a real *enfant terrible* had arrived on the folk music scene, or that within a single year he would emerge as one of the most gifted and unusual entertainers in the whole country."

Dylan showed up at the Gleasons that Sunday, around noon. He spent most of the day sitting on the floor beside the couch on which Woody was sprawled out. "That first time, Bob didn't say a word for a long while," says Camilla Adams Horne, who had worked for years in the folk field. "He was just sitting there most of the time, very quietly, not saying a word. I remember he kept that cap on. And finally he did sing something, and it was impressive. I don't remember what it was because I've heard him sing so many things out at the Gleasons, but it was probably one of Woody's. And I do remember that night Woody saying: 'He's a talented boy. Gonna go far.' "

Bob began visiting Woody at the hospital several times a week, and he showed up at the Gleasons practically every weekend over the next few weeks. By the second weekend Woody was asking for Bobby, and he would ask for him all the time: "Is the boy coming today? When is the boy coming back?" Something grew between them, between the dying originator of modern folk and the boy who was imitating him, idolizing him, and who would soon surpass him. He would talk to Woody when there weren't too many people around, patiently waiting for Woody to form the words that were so hard coming. Woody could not compete with crowds of people talking; he would get excited and stutter and ramble and be unable to put together what he wanted to say. But Dylan would sit at his feet, in a corner, and they would talk. On one of those first Sundays, Bob played *Song to Woody* for him, privately, in the corner, and everyone in the room stopped to listen. And, someone remembers, Woody's face broke into a broad smile of joy, and he said: "That's good, Bob. That's damned good." Dylan seems to have gone to Woody's heart, and after everyone left, Woody told the Gleasons, "That boy's got a voice. Maybe he won't make it by his writing, but he can sing it. He can really sing it."

He also said, "Pete Seeger's a singer of folk songs, not a folk singer. Jack Elliott is a singer of folk songs. But Bobby Dylan is a folk singer. Oh, Christ, he's a folk singer all right."

Another card was sent to the Whittakers, postmarked from New York on February 12. A joyful Dylan wrote Gretel and David that he sees Woody four times a week, has been playing at the Commons (a MacDougal Street coffeehouse) where "people clap for me." And, he says, "Woody likes me—he tells me to sing for him—he's the greatest holiest godliest one in the world."

The Gleasons have a sheet of yellow ruled legal paper and on it, in Dylan's tight but somewhat sloppy handwriting, is *A Song to Woody*. At the bottom of this copy he wrote: "Written by Bob Dylan in Mills Bar on Bleeker Street in New York City on the 14th day of February, for Woody Guthrie."

Kevin Krown clearly remembers that Dylan had written the song while he was in Chicago, a couple of months before this. It's possible Krown is mistaken. It is also possible that this was another minor Dylan deception, trying to leave the impression he had written it only after getting to know Woody. A little later, after he met Joan Baez sometime in March or April, friends remember him saying: "Joannie wants to sing my *Song to Woody*. But I ain't gonna let her. Don't like her. Don't want her to do any song about Woody because she don't *know* Woody."

Bob was holding back at first, at those Saturday and Sunday sessions at the Gleasons, uncertain of his place among a group of some of the most talented folk singers around. But as he won Woody's approval he sometimes sang for the crowd in East Orange, and Pete Seeger, Cisco Houston, Jack Elliott would encourage him, show him some licks, teach him songs, not consciously working on him but jamming with him, accepting him as one of them.

Ramblin' Jack Elliott, as he's long been known, is able to see Dylan from some special vantage points. He had himself become so totally hooked on Guthrie ten years earlier that he imitated his music and his style. The Guthrie magnetism so completely attracted him that he eventually became known as "the son of Woody Guthrie." And, in Dylan's first few months in New York, playing with Elliott at folk clubs and in private parties, Dylan began to absorb some of Elliott's tricks and mannerisms, and folkies would describe Dylan in those earliest months as "the son of Jack Elliott and the grandson of Woody Guthrie" with just a little bit of scorn, at first. There's little doubt that Dylan picked up a great deal from Jack Elliott.

He was born Elliott Adnopoz in Brooklyn, the son of a successful doctor, but at this time very few people around knew him as anything but Ramblin' Jack Elliott, a cowboy from the West. He was ten years older than Dylan, and a decade earlier he had gone through the same shifting identity that Dylan had. Like Dylan, he could not picture himself the son of middle-class Jewish parents and, like Dylan, he created a new identity. He became Guthrie's protege in 1951, knocking around the country with him, playing at radical affairs, in bars, wherever people wanted to hear Woody.

Jack Elliott, on Bob Dylan and Jack Elliott: "Bob was kind of shy, that first day. He had a lot of strong feelings about things. I could tell he liked Woody a lot, and Woody liked him. He was talking a lot like Woody. In fact I told him so one time, 'You sound like Woody,' and he explained he picked it up from an old black street singer he met down in New Mexico, who speaks like that. I used to imitate Woody all the time, and I saw Dylan imitate me direct, doing things that were pure Jack Elliott. He'd already been doing it quite a bit before he got to New York, from my records. A girl friend of his from back in Minneapolis, Bonnie Beecher, the last time I saw her she said 'Bob used to play all your records before he came to New York. He was fond of your voice and he listened to your records and picked up your style,' and I was tickled about that. And then in Gerde's Folk City, he used to get up on stage and sing things like me. I didn't know it was some of me, at first. I thought he was doing it Woody Guthrie style, in the Guthrie-Cisco Houston school. I was tickled to see somebody doing it well 'cause I was really bored with all the other folk singers. There was not another son of a bitch in the country who could sing until Bob Dylan came along. Everybody else was singing like a damned faggot.

"Some of the people around were turned off a little bit because Bob was playing the hobo role. I thought that he was maybe a little too young to pull it off in the style in which he was doing it. He was trying to sound like an old man who bummed around eighty-five years on a freight train, and you could see this kid didn't even have fuzz on his face yet. But I was charmed by it. He was a rough little pixie runt with a guitar. He was headed in the right direction and he had great taste—the words he was singing, the gestures and the mannerisms. Like he was not quite bringing it off, the way he was trying, it wasn't perfected yet. He was very rough. I thought sometimes he had a lot of nerve trying to get away with that bullshit. At the same time I felt unofficially like a coach, teaching him a little bit, in a very loose way. So, secretly, I felt a lot of pride about him every once in a while picking up on something I did.

"I saw him one time, I don't know what it was that I was doing, some kind of gesture I didn't know about and must have just got started on, but he got up on stage right after I did and sang songs and did the same thing I'd just done. He had a great ability to pick things up quickly, but more from hanging out—not a calculated thing.

"Bobby was into a lot of different singers and styles, some of them were people I didn't like and some I never heard of—but that's one of the reasons that Bobby was so colorful, all the different things he was trying on for size. You see, he has a rich way of singing now, but back then it was painful, he was difficult to listen to when I first met Bobby. His voice, he didn't have much control over it. He just aimed for a note—but he aimed for a lot of *good* notes and it was far out, because folk singers weren't doing that kind of thing. He was doing things nobody else was aiming for, so he had the freedom to do whatever he wanted to do.

"There was something else about Bob. He had the same kind of magnetism as James Dean. Dean was the first cat I ever met with that kind of thing, the magnetism and the feeling he was running too fast and was going to get himself killed because he was running too fast. And Bob was the second I ever met."

Dylan was singing before Village audiences every chance he got, hitting the coffee houses primarily. No one would hire him at first, and he was forced to sing for nothing more than the exposure, getting up on the stages of the coffee houses in the afternoons and evenings, before the paid professionals would come on, singing for a sandwich and some coffee, mostly. He seldom shared in the baskets, even. Basket houses were places where baskets were passed around the audience and a collection taken for the entertainers. The audience always believed the performers were unpaid and would starve without contributions, but the truth was the coffee houses were paying at least ten dollars a night, more on weekends, and between eighty and a hundred and twenty-five to an entertainer who had a full week's gig. The basket is said to be the invention of Hugh Romney, later of the Hog Farm collective. Romney, who was working in the Village at the time (and would later meet and marry Bonnie Beecher, one of Dylan's former girl friends from Minneapolis) came up with the brilliant idea to raise extra money for himself and other performers—and it worked. Some performers were making two hundred dollars a week in the coffee houses when audiences thought they were starving.

Dylan sang at the Commons, the Gaslight, and the Wha?, and occasionally when he backed someone who was getting paid he would share in the wages. But usually he got just a dollar or two. Freddy Neil was one of the first to recognize Dylan's talents and had Bob accompany him as often as he could, but the pay wasn't much. Paul Clayton, who came from the old whaling town, New Bedford, Massachusetts, and who sang sea chanties went around singing Dylan's praises to any who would listen. "Bobby worshipped Pablo Clayton artistically," one of the folk singers from those days recalls. "And Pablo became absolutely fixated on Bobby. Bobby could talk about nothing else but Woody Guthrie, and Pablo could talk about nothing else but Bobby Dylan."

There weren't too many paying jobs available, however. The

coffee houses and clubs weren't run by people with especially well-tuned ears, and Dylan was considered a little too off beat even if the professionals were digging him. "Nobody would hire Dylan, he was a freak," blues singer Dave Van Ronk recalls.

He was living a very marginal existence, not quite starving but going hungry often enough. The Gleasons say Dylan took a job for a short time, working as a laborer for the Department of Sanitation removing snow from the city's streets. Huge snowblowers would lift the mounds of soot-streaked snow into trucks which would dump them off at city piers along the Hudson River, where the laborers would shovel it into the waters below. Sid Gleason says she's certain Dylan worked at this whenever he could. David Whittaker remembers Bob talking about the job. But almost everyone else who knew Dylan says it was impossible: "Are you out of your *mind?*" exclaimed one very close Dylan friend, who fed him and gave him a place to stay on many nights. "No man who ever called himself a folk singer would take a straight job, and especially not Dylan. That would have been undignified. It would have been socially unacceptable."

The Mills Tavern, where Bob claimed he wrote the song to Guthrie, was an early hangout for Dylan and Kevin Krown, and their friends. It was a warm place and Rocco, the bartender, was a friendly sort of guy who would give the boys free stew with their beer. Dylan ate a lot of stew. Rocco also permitted Dylan and Krown to sleep in the back when they had nowhere else to go.

But it didn't happen too often. The maternal feeling Dylan aroused in the Midwest served him well in the East, and there were a succession of young women he lived with, and older women who put him up and who very much wanted to play the role of substitute mother to this orphan from the Southwest.

Camilla Horne: "He looked so much like a little boy lost, that we were all concerned for him. He looked sort of undernourished and had a baby face, very sweet, and everyone wanted to take care of him. If he needed a place to stay he never had any trouble finding one."

Mikki Isaacson, combination mother hen and folk collector, who had an apartment on Sheridan Square that was an around-the-clock open house for folk singers and hangers-on: "He had a talent for getting people to take care of him. He would look helpless, bereft. But you never felt he was sponging. He was just somebody in terrible need and you wanted to help—you felt you *must* help him. We didn't even think he was eighteen yet, that's how young he looked. Like a young runaway."

One family, living north of the Village, for personal reasons will be known here as Smith. Mrs. Smith recalls that Camilla Horne dropped by the Smith apartment after learning that Dylan was spending time there, and getting fed occasionally. She recalls: "Camilla wanted to know how Bobby was doing, and wanted to see the lady of the household taking care of him. During her visit she said, 'Bobby, for goodness sakes, you can't go around looking like that. You have to look nice and clean cut. Cut some of the hair off. And take that cap off.' Bobby was very quiet, he looked at me and shrugged, and I said, 'It really doesn't matter how long your hair is or what you wear. You can wear any damn thing you please. Don't dare take the Huck Finn cap off because it looks real on you. You keep it. It's part of theater and a marvelous gimmick.' "

It would appear they were practically fighting for the chance to mother Bobby who had built an orphan myth partly because he had had it with family. And today one woman will charge that the other one had such a bad crush "that she actually wanted to adopt Bobby," while another will say "poor Bobby used to say that if that horrible woman called he wasn't in, because she was mothering him to death." And a man who was around snorts contemptuously that, "They were all out of their Goddamn minds about him."

All of this was taking place during Dylan's first few weeks in New York. He was meeting the older folk artists out at the Gleasons, and the younger ones in the Village, and the women on the fringes, and practically everybody went out of their way to make him feel at home. There was some competition for jobs because they were scarce, and some of the bitchiness that accompanies competition was directed at Bob. On the whole, however, he seems to have been treated kindly by most people he met.

Johnny Herald, of the Greenbriar Boys, brought Dylan to one of the numerous parties at Mikki Isaacson's small one-room apartment —her hotel, she was calling it. After a night in one of the clubs a number of the folk crowd would gather at her place to play for each other "Until the neighbors banged on walls," Miss Isaacson says.

"Bobby sat on the floor that first time, very shabby looking and nondescript. He was slouching, looking so uncomfortable and ill-at-ease I kind of felt he didn't want anybody to know he was there. He didn't say a word. He didn't have a thing to say. One of the boys, maybe Herald or maybe Van Ronk, said to me 'You really oughta hear this kid sing,' and I thought, boy, he's probably a mess. They tried to persuade him to sing, worked on him. I felt he was insecure so I said, 'I'd really like to hear you,' and he came out of his shell. He moved toward the group, sat on the edge of one of the chairs, and began to play. He didn't even have his own guitar with him, he borrowed someone else's. And he sang a song about somebody's death, and I wept. I was just undone by it. He sang it almost as if he was throwing away his lines. He didn't look at anybody, almost as if he was singing for himself, not for the rest of us. And all of these people there, all these professionals, they made it clear they thought Bobby was something special, that he really had it. He knocked everyone out."

The Gleasons gave Bob a bed and fed him whenever he needed it. "He'd come out in the middle of the week, when he was really broke, and have dinner and stay over sometimes for a day or two," Mrs. Gleason says. He had, at the Gleasons, access to records and tapes that were unavailable in Minneapolis, or anywhere else for that matter. The Gleasons had made tapes of old seventy-eights that Woody collected over the years, amounting to possibly ninety per cent of Woody's old record collection, material that Woody himself had collected and listened to. They've swapped material with British folk collectors. And they also have a great many tapes that exist nowhere else, of folk people singing to Woody on those weekend visits. Dylan hitchhiked to the Gleasons during the week to get material he wanted. He would put a tape on, straddle a chair, with his head down on his arms, and listen to the tapes for hours. When he heard something he thought he could use he played that song several times. "He would just listen and copy. He had his own form of shorthand. He'd go maybe twice through a record and he'd have all the words copied, and chord progressions. He'd start in the morning and play tapes all day long, for days on end. He was mostly learning, and working so hard at it."

Dylan seldom played at the Gleasons when Seeger and Cisco Houston and the rest were out there. He was shy, for one thing. And he knew he could take much more from these people than he could give to them. As Jack Elliott put it, "He came from out of town to learn and absorb, and he wasn't the kind of guy who'd be fool enough to try and give a lot of advice and information from the benefit of his long life."

He seemed to be especially drawn to Cisco Houston. Some of it was Cisco being part of the Guthrie legend, which is what also attracted Dylan to Jack Elliott. Cisco was a very gentle man, the kind of man everyone looked up to as an older and wiser brother. "A great cat, no big ego trip, just a nice guy," Elliott calls him. And part of the attraction was that Cisco Houston was dying. Bob Dylan had always been preoccupied with death. Cisco had learned the previous August that he had terminal cancer, but he didn't dwell on this, nor seek sympathy. He was in constant pain and by February he could barely walk, but he continued to perform at Gerde's and other clubs, and at the Gleasons' almost to his death. "There was something courageous about the way Cisco took the fact that he had cancer and it was terminal," Van Ronk says. "Cisco never stopped, never copped out, never showed the white feather." His last performances were during a one week gig at Gerde's at the end of February. He remained in New York for another few weeks and then, knowing his string was running out, he went home to San Bernardino, California, where he died on April 29.

Mrs. Gleason: "We had a little girl living with us, Kathy, she was seven. Bobby loved children. He used to sit and play and sing to her and she adored him. She was scared of men when we first got her, but she loved Woody. When Woody saw a child and he smiled, he just smiled all over, he absolutely glowed, his cheeks and everything just smiled. And Bobby was the same way. He used to go sit on the edge of the bed and sing to Kathy to get her to go to sleep. She would say, 'I'll go to bed if Bobby comes and sings for me,' and he would sing her to sleep. *Jesse James,* she loved him to sing that. And sometimes he would sing the song Woody made up to *Jesse James—Jesus Christ* —and she would get so mad at Bob for singing that."

Dylan did play a great deal at the Gleasons' on week-days, when the established folk musicians weren't around. Because the recording part of the Gleason tape recorder was inoperative during most of the three months Dylan was hitching to East Orange, only one tape was made of his singing.

One afternoon in late February or early March, Dylan was sitting on a large ottoman in the living room, singing to Kathy, when Bob Gleason got the tape recorder going in the next room and got seven songs on tape: *Pastures of Plenty, Jesse James, Gypsy Davey, On the Trail of the Buffalo, Remember Me, Jesus Met the Woman at the Well,* and *San Francisco Bay Blues.* Then some friends showed up and interrupted Bob, who continued to sing for Kathy after she went to bed, but without the tape recorder. That tape was borrowed by a student at nearby Upsala College at the beginning of 1969. She passed them on to her husband, who worked at the college radio station, and he broadcast it. The seven East Orange songs surfaced a short while later on one of the bootlegged albums.

Mrs. Gleason: "He was just living here to there and everywhere in those months. I used to ask: 'Bobby, would you like to take a bath?' He needed a bath. That child needed a bath.

"One thing about that child I loved—if there was snow to be shoveled, he shoveled; if there were dishes to wash, he washed dishes. Bobby didn't bum. I helped Bobby. We gave him money occasionally. But he wasn't lazy. He had to live. He couldn't make it on what he was doing, he was getting just nickels and dimes. They weren't paying him to work in those clubs. He had no place to stay. Sometimes he'd stay with the Van Ronks, sometimes here, sometimes in some of the flop houses in New York. But he wasn't a lazy boy and he didn't expect people to pay his way."

All of the older women around suspected Dylan was smoking marijuana, and part of the mothering included attempts to show him the folly of his ways. "He was hanging around with a pretty blatantly pot-smoking crowd," Mrs. Horne recalls, "and we kept nagging him about it because if he got busted he wouldn't be able to work in a club in New York. I was concerned. I figured this crowd was due for a raid because it was too well known, and I kept nagging at him, and he kept saying he'd given it up."

Mrs. Gleason shared the same suspicions. "So I asked Pete LaFarge to keep an eye on him, and he did. Pete was a tough Indian. He wasn't a big man, but he appeared big and everybody knew he was very powerful. Bob was scared to death of him. Pete would walk into a party where Bob was and stand with his arms crossed, not saying a word, just watching. And Bobby called me one day and said, 'Mom, please get that Indian off my back. I promise I won't do anything like that again.' Every place he was, Pete would come and show up. Bobby knew that his Mom was after him."

One of his closest friends at the time says: "There wasn't that much grass around. None of us were smoking heavy. And Bob wasn't buying back then, he was cheap. I remember once Bob was up at our apartment and we had been blowing grass a bit, and I gave him a little grass for himself that he stuck in his pocket. After a while we left the apartment to go somewhere and I suddenly remembered Bob had this grass and I almost killed him for it. It was never smart to walk around the Village with grass on you, and this fool kid was holding. I made him take it back to the apartment."

Bob Dylan, about his first weeks in New York: "I bummed around. I dug it all—the streets and the snows and the starving and the five-flight walkups and sleeping in rooms with ten people. I dug the trains and the shadows, the way I dug ore mines and coal mines. I just jumped right to the bottom of New York."

His first job that paid anything like substantial money came in April, when he got twenty dollars to sing before the New York University Folk Music Society in the Loeb Student Center on the Village campus. He sent the Whittakers a yellow mimeographed flyer printed by the folk group, announcing he would sing at 6:30 on Wednesday evening, April 5. On the reverse he wrote that he's "gonna sing at the Gaslight" and he asked about Bonnie Beecher. Once more, he signed it "Dylan."

Sue Zuckerman, then a college girl, had met Dylan a short time before this, running into him as he sat in back of the Folklore Center, playing and singing, and she remembers thinking "he looked like he was fourteen years old." She recalls: "A friend of mine belonged to the folk club and told me he was singing at N.Y.U. So I went. There were only about six of us, sitting around this little room, listening to him. And I just immediately fell in love with him, with him and his voice." She and her friends began following him around the Village, "totally entranced by him," catching him in the afternoons at the Cafe Wha? One of her closest friends was a seventeen-year-old girl she had met at camp a few years earlier—Susan Rotolo, who called herself "Suze."

"I told her about this groovy guy I had a crush on, named Bob Dylan. So Suze and I started hanging around with Bob and Mark Spoelstra, hanging around, talking to them, and they hardly knew we were around." A couple of months later Suze would get to know Dylan and she would quickly become one of the important women in his life.

Bob was around the Village only a couple of months when he began to attract a great deal of notice. He had finally found a public stage that, while not paying him a cent, gave him a marvelous opportunity to work, to take the material he had been soaking up and squeeze out something that became Bob Dylan.

The stage was at Gerde's Folk City, then located at 11 West 4th Street. It was owned by Mike Porco, a soft-spoken, old-fashioned man who seemed out of place in the Village folk world. He had bought it in 1959, when it was just Gerde's, brought in bongo players and the like, then turned to jazz. Some time in 1960 Izzy Young and another folk entrepreneur, Tom Prendergast, convinced Porco to turn his place into a folk club. The name was changed to Gerde's Fifth Peg, and the folkies had a club of their own. By the summer of 1960 Porco had renamed his club Gerde's Folk City. It soon became the most important folk club in the nation.

Mondays are traditionally slow nights on the New York club scene. Gerde's was no exception. Porco, trying to figure out how to make Mondays pay off, decided to try an amateur night. He talked the idea around. Robert Shelton, folk music critic for the *New York Times,*

66

and Charles Rothchild, who managed a couple of folk singers, suggested he try a "hootenanny." Woody Guthrie had first heard the word in a union hall in the Pacific Northwest in 1940, describing a union singalong, and he had popularized it in the folk world, using it to mean any group singing or jamming by folk artists. Shelton wrote the word out for Porco, who had never heard it before. Porco figured hootenannies had a little more tone than amateur nights and the idea of getting Village folkies to come in and play for free one night a week, with its potential for attracting large crowds of paying customers, certainly appealed to his businessman's instinct.

So Gerde's Monday night hoots were born. By the time Dylan came to town a few months later, the hoots were stirring much excitement—some of the finest young folk and blues artists around, all on one stage, providing audiences with some of the most advanced musical entertainment available anywhere, and at the same time using Gerde's stage as a showcase, hoping to develop their craft, hoping to build a following, hoping Porco would give them a paying job for a week or two after a stunning Monday night hoot. Many of the hoot-night performances were by younger professionals like Van Ronk, Len Chandler, Judy Collins, Tom Paxton, Jack Elliott and Paul Clayton, and occasionally Cisco Houston would drop in and play, and even young Arlo Guthrie, when he was barely into his teens, did a couple of numbers. Porco was doing an enormous business on Monday nights: his place had a capacity of 175 and it was always filled, with another two or three hundred waiting outside to get in.

Porco: "I remember the first time Dylan came in and asked if he could play at the hoot that night. I told him no because he didn't look old enough, he looked only about 16. I told him to come back with proof of his age and I'd let him play. People were telling me, 'This kid is good, Mike, he plays guitar, harmonica, and he really sings,' so I said he could play if he had proof he was old enough. He came back the next week with proof of his age. It had the name Zimmerman, but I didn't think anything of it because a lot of people were using stage names."

Dylan was telling everyone in New York that he was from New Mexico, an orphan who had been on the road for years. But, as in Minneapolis, he was rather ingenuous and let little things slip out that made friends suspect he was middle class, Jewish, and no orphan. Shortly before Dylan hit the Village for the first time the folkies had discovered that Jack Elliott was actually Elliott Adnopoz, son of a Brooklyn doctor. Then Elliott became seriously ill and relatives from Brooklyn with names like Goldstein had come calling, and his secret was out. One night Dylan was sitting in the Gaslight with Dave Van Ronk and Barry Kornfeld, a musician who is now a Columbia Records producer, and a few others. Van Ronk recalls: "As far as Bobby knew, Jack Elliott was absolutely good coin *goyisha* cowboy. In the course of the conversation it came out somehow that he was Elliott Adnopoz, a Jewish cat from Ocean Parkway, and Bobby fell off his chair. He rolled under the table, laughing like a madman. It was a good thing we were privileged characters in the Gaslight or we would have been thrown out. We had all suspected Bobby was Jewish, and that proved it. He'd be laying under the table and just recovering from his fit and every once in a while Barry or somebody would stick his head under the table and yell 'Adnopoz!' and that would start him off roaring again."

The myth he had begun to create back in Minneapolis became embroidered with finer detail now that he was a thousand miles from home. One of the first stories he told about himself was that he was an orphan and had been raised in an orphanage in New Mexico. There were several foster homes in the new myth, and he had run away from all of them because he had been mistreated or misunderstood. He claimed, also, that he had first heard Woody as a young child, on the radio in the orphanage—"He wouldn't dare say he met Woody in California, to Woody's friends who'd been with him in California," one friend remarks. At the same time, however, he wandered into the Folk Lore Center one day and told Izzy Young, who was not part of the Guthrie circle: "I met Woody once before in California, before I was really playing. I think Jack Elliott was with him. I was in Carmel, doing nothing. During the summer. Woody impressed me. Always made a point to see him again."

Much of the Dylan mythos wasn't direct information, just his letting small *facts* of his earlier days slip out in conversation, then slamming the door shut. The Gleasons, for example, recall Dylan sitting one day, playing with Kathy, and saying: "She reminds me of a girl in one of my foster homes." But they didn't ask too many questions, because he didn't give answers. He would only tell people what he wanted them to know at any particular point: "I used to run away because I couldn't stay tied down," he'd say. "I'd just stay a while and then leave because it was easier leavin' than stayin.'"

Mrs. Smith, who had begun to know Dylan as well as anyone since he was spending much time with her family, recalls: "I once said, 'Bobby, what about your parents? Where are they?' And he said, 'I had so many different foster parents, I don't remember.' I said, 'Oh, you did? What was the name of your last foster mother?' He said, 'I don't rightly remember.' At which time I knew he had parents and wanted them left out of it. I think his mother and father must have had some real problems with him; he was a rough little customer. But he didn't fool us. One night in the middle of nowhere he said, 'You know, I like Robert Graves, the poet. Do you?' I said I'd just finished reading something by Graves and I asked, 'What about Dylan Thomas? Do you like Dylan Thomas?' He just grinned, and he said he loved Dylan Thomas, and I said, 'You don't have to follow in his footsteps and be a drunkard.' And when he didn't say any more about Dylan Thomas I said, 'What's in a name? It doesn't matter.' "

He told most of his friends that he had toured the South, bumming, hanging around with street singers and black artists. Izzy Young made notes of Dylan saying: "Arvella Gray, the blind street singer from Chicago, taught me blues songs about four or five years ago. I also used to know a guy, Mance Lipscomb, from Navasota, Texas. Listened to him a lot. Met him through a grandson, a rock and roller. I started writing my own songs four or five years ago. The first one was to Brigitte Bardot, for piano. Thought if I wrote the song I'd sing it to her one day, but I never met her. I've written hillbilly songs. Carl Perkins, from Nashville, he sings them. Talking blues on topical things. I played the piano with Bobby Vee. Would have been a millionaire if I stayed with him, played piano from Northwest to Montana. Met Jesse Fuller at the Exodus in Denver. Learned the way he does songs, mixed his style in with mine at the time. I heard Big Joe Williams when I was nine or ten in Chicago. I really didn't play so much. I just followed him around. I sung then. I got a cousin living in Chicago, on the South Side."

"The names he dropped were always famous names," Young recalls. "And he always made them just guys he met. Guys who happened to be famous. He never met a Jack Smith from Jersey City. And no one asked a question who this Dylan was, where he came from."

The Gleasons recall him saying he had made a large sum of money as a kid by playing as a backup man for rock-and-roll performers. He went through their albums one day and he would pick one out and say, "I played on that one. Piano on that one. Guitar on that one." Sid Gleason asked: "Are you kidding?" And Bob replied, "Why should I kid you? I even played for Elvis Presley. I played piano on some of his recordings." Mrs. Gleason says: "I believed him. I had no reason not to believe him. Bob was a fantastic performer. He could play piano as well as Jerry Lee Lewis, and I think Jerry Lee Lewis is one of our better hard rock piano players."

Dylan also talked carny slang occasionally, bolstering another favorite tale: that he had traveled around the country with carnivals during a few of his jaunts away from his foster homes. He told one friend (who has it on tape): "I was with a carnival when I was about thirteen, and I used to travel with the carnival. All kinds of shows and things. We went all around the Midwest. Gallup and . . . Lasco, Texas, down there. Was a roustabout. And sang around a lot. I didn't sing very *much,* but I learned a lot of songs in that carnival. A lot of songs people are singin' today, I learned those songs in the carnival. That's why I know all these songs I know today. I didn't learn them now."

Bob Dylan: "Hey, man, there are a lot of things about my life I ain't told ya. Did I ever tell ya I got my nose from the Indian blood in my veins? Well, that's the truth, hey. Got an uncle who's a Sioux."

A few friends had caught a glimpse of the paper he had shown Porco as proof he was over eighteen, and it was whispered around the Village that Bob Dylan was really Robert Zimmerman. But no one knew for certain because Mike Porco wasn't saying anything, and it remained mostly a rumor. Mikki Isaacson: "He was close-mouthed about the Zimmerman thing. It became known in the gang, but he wouldn't talk about it and you couldn't question him. I remember the first time I asked him how to spell Dylan—'Like in Dylan Thomas?' and he said, 'No, like in Bob Dylan.' That's all he'd say. If you went on with the questions he'd walk out."

At the same time, though, he was admitting his Minnesota background to some friends, admitting the existence of a family—possibly because it was clear some of the details were becoming known. But he continued to romanticize it. He told one friend: "I got a great family. Uncles that are just fantastic kind of people. Herman Stone is one uncle, he's a gambler in Las Vegas. I seen him just once, but he's fantastic. And another uncle is a professional thief. I ever tell ya that? Just a fantastic professional thief. Never got caught, that's how fantastically professional he is."

But the folk crowd didn't mind Dylan's poses. Dave Van Ronk's reaction was typical: "We accepted him not because of the things he said he had done but because we respected him as a performer. The attitude of the community was that it was all right, it was cool. He gets on stage and delivers, and that's fine. His pose didn't bother us. Nobody was turned off by it. Whatever he said off stage, on stage he told the truth as best he knew it."

All of the younger folk artists piled down to Gerde's on hoot night, even those who weren't going to perform. They would go to listen to their friends, to encourage and cheer and help each other out. "There wasn't enough work and it was a friendly scene all around, everybody helping the other guy out," one of them recalls.

And, they'll tell you today, everyone thought Dylan was something special. Not that any believed he would make it really big, but there was some quality about him that made it clear he would be a success at least in the folk world.

Terri Van Ronk: "The kid was just great. He was very nervous, with a funny knee twitch. He didn't talk much, just sat for hours listening to people, and then he'd open up and he'd be hilariously funny. Especially with that Chaplinesque thing he had, which was weird. Everybody believed he was a genius. He had that funny pathetic little boy style about him. And a sense of comedy. I remember one hoot night he was on stage for forty minutes, and he kept falling off the stage ... and it was so funny. We had been drinking a little and Bobby couldn't hold his liquor—his beer or wine, really, because we couldn't afford liquor—and we all thought he was drunk. It took us a long time to figure out that when he fell off the stage it was timed, a planned thing, he was falling off within the context of the song, and it was hilarious."

Mikki Isaacson: "He used to do all these kooky things, and they never seemed like a routine. He could even make a comic act out of tuning his guitar, get up on stage and fiddle with the guitar strings and pretend he wasn't able to get it right and cursing under his breath, and we would all be in the aisle with the joy of it. And I'll never forget the thing he did with his harmonica. His eyes were so bad that we didn't know if it was a joke or real, but he'd begin taking harmonicas out of his pockets and laying them down on the table, pulling out one and saying, very *sotto voce,* 'Now where is that E flat harmonica?' then pulling out another one, and not being able to find it. And saying, 'Who's got that damned harmonica?' And it broke us all up. It was so Chaplin-like."

Dave Van Ronk: "He was obviously no virgin on a stage when I first saw him at the Wha?, backing up Freddy Neil. He had been around. And he was something of a natural—a cat who seems to know all the rules and systematically breaks them. He gave the appearance of not knowing anything, but you could just feel he knew what it was all about, and he was deliberately breaking the rules and making it work."

But he was an uneven performer. Mikki Isaacson recalls: "In those days he was afraid of his audience. Suddenly, at the last minute before he was to go on he would say, 'I don't want to do this. Let's go home.' I'd tell him, 'Bob, you've got to go on,' and he'd say, 'No, I'll do it next Monday.' Then he'd get up and do a bad job and get off very quickly. You had to build up his ego a great deal, pamper him, give him a few drinks. He was a creature of moods, like Jack

Elliott was, and if Bobby wasn't in the mood you couldn't get a decent performance no matter what you did. Bobby's friends had to work like hell to keep up his level. We used to sit up front where he could see us. His eyes were so bad we had to sit up as close as we could get, and applaud and look enthusiastic, a whole clique of us. And if we worked hard enough we would get a decent performance out of him. When it was really working there was a tremendous interplay between the performer and us. Not only with Bob, but with Jack and Dave and everyone else. Except that with Dave we would be enthusiastic for him because we really enjoyed it, not because we were trying to encourage him or boost his ego. Dave didn't need that kind of thing, but Bob did.

"Bob was both uptight about it, and casual. Careless. He never prepared for the hoots. I would make a list of songs I wanted to hear and tape it on the back of his guitar, so he wouldn't blank out after finishing one number, and I'd tell him what would be the best material to use back to back. Finally, a while later, he would become very professional about the hoots. He understood the jerks were there before midnight and at midnight there was a big exodus of the high school kids and the straights, and he wouldn't go on until after midnight. If you wanted to see Bob you got there after midnight. You see, he wasn't interested in reaching the crowd at that point. In those days the performers were playing for each other, trying things out on each other and giving critiques and helping each other's professional growth. Most of us felt the straight crowd was a bunch of jerks, and Bob felt that too."

Dylan's enthusiasm reached the professionals. He had a way of letting folk artists know how much he dug them, and they responded warmly because they felt a sincerity in Dylan. Tom Clancy, of the Clancy Brothers, recalls seeing Dylan a great deal at Gerde's, the Limelight, and at the Lion's Head—a noted Village hangout for the folk crowd, *Village Voice* staffers and assorted hip journalists, novelists, poets and freaks. Says Clancy:

"He always wanted to talk about music and songs. He would swap songs with my brother, Liam, after we'd done a set, chatting about songs, chords, music and playing guitar with him. We got to like him very much. He was a strong personality, young, ambitious and strong. You felt he had something to say and, Goddamn it, he was going to say it. He was always saying, like, 'Man, you guys, man, I love this, I love listening to you guys.' He was always kind of bouncy on the balls of his feet when he talked to you, always so enthusiastic about talking to people."

There are others, however, who feel Dylan was calculating, that everything he did was aimed at the big goal: making it. One friend from those days, who got close to Dylan on a personal level, says: "Dylan was the most motivated person you'll ever meet in your life. He talked about being big, playing Carnegie Hall, and going on from there, and he schemed all the time about how to make it. He knew how to use people, knew exactly how far he could use them and he did so. And when he was finished with them, he dropped them."

Izzy Young recalls: "He came into the Folk Center a lot, to play. He was very powerful right away, took over the room right away. Very competitive. He really didn't listen to anybody else. He would sort of wait to sing and then go out. Looking back now, I realize he didn't come in casually like the other kids would come in, Van Ronk and them, just wander in the back of the store and hang around. Bob Dylan was performing all the time, like this was the right time to play his songs and he would play.

"What I'm saying is, he wasn't an innocent kid when he came to New York City. He knew exactly what he wanted, knew how to use people, and when the point came that he didn't have to use them any more he dropped them. In other words, he's sitting with Dave Van Ronk in his apartment for three days, drinking, sleeping and listening, and then he comes to my store and he doesn't say anything about Van Ronk. Or he'd spend a week with Jack Elliott and then go to Van Ronk and not talk about Jack Elliott. He never gave you a feeling he was into anybody else except you."

Dylan lived with the Van Ronks for a while, off and on, in their apartment on West Fifteenth Street. Terri and Dave Van Ronk, just a couple of years older than Bob, befriended him, opened their home to him, brought him into their circle. "My place was a hotel for him," Mikki Isaacson says. "The Van Ronks gave him a home." Dave, one of the more talented blues guitarists and singers of the day, turned him onto a wide variety of new material and musical ideas. Again, not formally teaching, for Dylan would never let on he was taking lessons. But Bob was learning from everyone around. And also, for a musician to publicly say today that he taught Bob Dylan anything would be most uncool and unprofessional. But by all accounts— including Dylan's own acknowledgement later—Van Ronk gave Dylan a good deal of support during his early period of growth.

Dylan was also living in an early crash pad at 629 E. 5th Street, when he started doing hoots at Gerde's, and it upset some of the foster-mothers who wanted to take care of him. "There were a whole mess of kids living in there," one of them reports, "with mattresses spread on the floor just about the only furniture. Bob was living with some little girl from the suburbs who played the lyre. And there was a white kid from the South who was trying to make it as a comedian and who was, of all things, living with one of the most beautiful black girls around. Plus a few other couples. The apartment was clean, that's about the best I can say for it."

A girl who will be known here only as Avril, was in Gerde's one night when she heard Dylan say he had to get out of his place, that he needed somewhere to stay. "She was in love with him, went to Gerde's every night to see him," Mrs. Smith says. "Avril was a beautiful girl, a dancer and a free spirit, and totally magnificent. She offered her place, and he moved in with her on East Fourth Street near Broadway." He lived with Avril for a couple of months before moving on again.

Mike Porco: "That first hoot night Bobby to me was nothing impressive. The audience liked him more than I did, because I frankly didn't realize he had a talent. He was good enough so that I let him come back for other hoot nights, instead of telling him he couldn't go on because there were too many on the list, like I was doing with amateurs. But I didn't know how good he was, really. I wasn't an expert, I didn't know. After a while I saw how much the audience liked him and I talked to Bob Shelton and other people who kept saying the kid is good, and I found out some of the stuff he was doing he wrote himself, and I thought maybe he was good like people said. I made a decision to give him two weeks work there.

"I called him aside and I said 'Bobby, I'm going to put you on in April with John Lee Hooker.' He said, 'Really, Mike?' and he was so excited he was jumping up and down. His first real job, and working with John Lee Hooker who was liked by everybody, and Bobby probably figured, too, that Hooker would bring a lot of people in. I said, 'But Bobby, you have to join the union,' and he said, 'I don't have any money, Mike.' He had to put down forty-six dollars, I think, and I was going to pay him ninety or a hundred, so I told him I'd pay for his union book and take it out of his salary. He said, 'Mike, why don't you manage me? You give me sandwiches when I'm hungry, and you do this and that for me, like a second father, so why don't you manage me?' I told him it wouldn't be fair because I had to take care of my place, and I couldn't spend enough time trying to get him work.

"We went down to the union office, in the back of Roseland, and sat down with the union secretary. He started to ask questions, and he said to Bobby, 'Mike has already spoken to me about you. You're supposed to become famous from what he tells me.' But the man looked at Bob, and I knew he was thinking I must be crazy to think this kid would ever become famous. He gave Bob the contract and asked him to fill it out, and when he filled in the age as nineteen the union secretary said, "I can't okay this because you're under 21. Come in tomorrow with your father.' Bob says, 'I got no father.' The union man says, 'Come in with your mother,' and Bob says, 'I got no mother, either.' Bob was sitting in the center between us and the union man leans back behind him and forms the words with his mouth, asking me, 'Is he a bastard?' and I said 'I don't know.' Then he suggested I sign it as a guardian, and I did. Bob got his union book.

"Then I told him, 'Now you have to get a cabaret card from the Department of Licenses,' and we went downtown to get it. On the way we stopped on West Fourth Street where there was a photo machine, four for a quarter, and he sat down. When the pictures came out his hair was flying all over, it was a mess. I said, 'Bobby, comb your hair, it looks terrible. We'll take the pictures again.' He was ashamed to say he didn't have a comb, and he fumbled around in his pockets and finally he said, 'I got no comb, Mike.' I gave him my comb and he combed his hair. I said, 'If you don't carry a comb you must be superstitious,' and he said, 'How did you know, Mike? I don't believe in combing my hair.' After we got the pictures I gave him two-and-a-half dollars for the license and told him to go down and get fingerprinted and get his cabaret card. He came back with it later, all happy he got it. I said, 'Now you have to do another thing,' and I gave him two dollars and said, 'Go around the corner and get a hair cut.' He said, 'Okay, thanks, Mike,' and he went off. The next day, Tuesday, I saw his hair was cut very little. I looked around him and he saw me and he said, 'You know Mike, I don't believe in going to the barber. I don't trust them.' I think one of the girls cut his hair, just a little trim. And later he told me, 'Mike, I didn't go to the barber. The first time I ever got a haircut I got very sick, and since then I've been very superstitious about barbers. I won't let a barber touch my hair.'

In the week or so before he opened at Gerde's he spent a great deal of time at the Smiths, selecting the songs he would do, practicing, working on arrangements. "Think I'm gonna open with *House of the Rising Sun,*" he told the Smiths one night. "Van Ronk's been helping me on it. Showed me his own arrangement and said I could use it." He sat in a rocking chair and played the song again and again. "Think that's a good opening?" he asked. "Guess I'll use it." The arrangement was the one he used in recording the song for his first album, which would create hard feelings between Dylan and Van Ronk.

Dylan's first major engagement began on April 11, 1961. He was the second act behind John Lee Hooker, an incredible black blues guitarist from Detroit; some of the most widely acclaimed rock guitarists around say that as little kids they were copying Hooker more than any other guitarist in the business. He was little known publicly, because he was black, and the Beatles and Rolling Stones hadn't come along yet to spark an appreciation for the black roots under pop music. But other artists, and a few knowledgeable folk and blues buffs, considered Hooker simply amazing. Hooker had a three-week engagement, starting the week before Dylan was to debut, and Dylan spent every night in Gerde's watching him, talking to him, sponging up his unique urban-country blues guitar.

Woody couldn't make it to Bob's opening, but everyone else was there. As his friends jammed into Gerde's that opening night, Dylan remained out of sight, down in his dressing room, wearing one of Woody's jackets given him by Sid Gleason, and a pair of Mr. Smith's old slacks—from Brooks Brothers. When he came on stage, he seemed very uptight. Some of his friends felt he was standing up there repeating to himself the questions he had been asking aloud during the week before: Will they like me? Anybody gonna be sore that a new kid got this break so fast? Is my luck gonna turn people against me? Apparently still feeling he had been raked by the Minneapolis folkies who were jealous of Rolf Cahn's assessment of him, Dylan seemed to be afraid that Village folkies also would be jealous of his "luck" and turn against him. Then he seemed to shake it off and he began to play *House of the Rising Sun* as an opener. Those standing at the bar stopped drinking and listened to the kid growling and gut-crying the whore's lament. He sang *A Song To Woody,* "like he meant every word," one who was there remembers, and one or two Guthrie songs, and a black blues, and then he was off—five songs in the set, and it seemed to be over before it began.

The Dylan rooting section was cheering loudly from front tables and he bounded off the stage. He ran, he hopped, over to Bob Gleason and shook his hand—the first time anyone remembers Bob Dylan shaking hands. One of the customers yelled, "Hey, why didn't you sing ..." and Bob seemed almost stunned at the request, which sounded like a putdown, but Bob Gleason quickly said: "Do it your way, Bobby. Do it for yourself." And Dylan said: "Thanks, Bob. You helped me. You helped so much." Somebody described him as being stone-cold-sober-high, and he began talking a flood. " ... and Mike loaned me the money for the union. Of course I'll have to pay him back, but he got me the union book and gave me my chance"—"You know, Bob," he said to Gleason, "somebody *does* care. I guess somebody cares, really."—"Do you suppose I'm good enough? I guess maybe I *am* good." He asked Mrs. Gleason: "How did you like Hooker?" and she replied: "I liked him, but I like you better." And he insisted: "No, no, I want to know how you really *like* him." And, Mrs. Gleason says today: "That was Bobby, he was in all his glory but he *did* want to know how I liked Hooker."

By the time his two-week stint was only half over, Dylan was climbing up walls. "I hate that kind of stuff," he was saying toward the end of it. "Hate to play in one place more than a couple of nights. It's such a drag. One week is a drag and two weeks are ridiculous." His friends had to work on him even harder than they had done when he was singing at the hoots, bolstering him, getting liquor into him to loosen him up and, at the same time, trying to keep him from getting drunk and ruining his set.

Still, it was an important engagement for him. It brought no reviews, no public acclaim, no mobs lining up outside waiting to get in. But it cemented the impression of the Village folkies that he was something special, possibly a *genius,* and it resulted in a good deal of talk along the folk underground about this strange little kid who was knocking them dead in the Village. Joan Baez first saw him at this time, and she remembers: "He knocked me out completely. He seemed tiny, just tiny, with that goofy little hat on. And he was just astounding. I was totally absorbed. His style and his eyes and the whole mystical whatever it was—and I just thought about him for days. I was amazed, and I was happy. He really made me happy that there was somebody with that kind of talent."

Bob had to get out of town after that Gerde's gig, and a couple of days after the close he left Avril a note—"Headin' West, be back soon."—and he vanished.

He had been in New York less than three months and he had moved at a remarkable pace in that short time. He had been befriended, fussed over, mothered and smothered and fathered and bothered, was "getting a lot of chicks" (as he put it to a Dinkytown friend around this time), and he had been helped in his craft by some of the most talented folk and blues musicians around. And yet he went away somewhat bitter about his first winter in New York. "He was like paranoid about it," one very close folkie-friend says today. "He felt everyone was out to take him, like it was a plot. So many people went out of their way to make him feel part of the scene and to keep him from freezing and starving, but he sort of accepted that part of it and then got strung-out-paranoid about the few things that were going against him. Like he went up to the *Sing Out!* offices and Irwin Silber [the editor] sort of threw him out. He was there to put out a magazine and he didn't have time to talk to every grubby kid who came in off the street asking questions like they were doing around the clock. Bobby was furious, upset, angry about that. And then there was the first gig, with Freddy Neil at the Wha?, where he got only a dollar or two which is all Freddy could afford to pay him. He became friendly with Silber and with Neil, but he was very offish, because he suspected everyone was out to take him."

Bob Dylan to Izzy Young: "Went up to Folkways Records. I had written some songs. I said, 'Howdy. I've written some songs. Will ya publish some songs?' Wouldn't even look at them. I heard Folkways was good. Irwin Silber didn't even talk to me. Never got to see Moe Asch. They just about said 'GO!' and I heard that *Sing Out!* was supposed to be helpful and friendly, big heart, charitable. I thought it was the wrong place. Must have been in the wrong place, but *Sing Out!* was written on the door. Whoever told me they had a big heart was wrong."

His bitterness flashed through in a Guthrie-style talking blues he wrote at this time, *Talkin' New York,* which he recorded on his first album. It was cold, and he froze to the bone, he wrote, but he made his way down to Green-Witch Village, got up and sang at a coffee house and the owner told him he'd better come back some other time because he sounded like a hillbilly and they were interested only in real folk singers. He played harmonica for a dollar a day at another place and the boss raved about his sound, "dollar a day's worth" of raving. And he'd met people who had no food on the table, but lots of knives and forks to cut up friends. New York was so bad that he headed for "Western skies"—all the way to East Orange, New Jersey, to seek a haven at the Gleasons', apparently.

1961: *Talkin' New York Blues*

EARLY IN MAY, Dylan hitched a ride up to Branford, Connecticut, to the Indian Neck Folk Festival, where he played several Guthrie songs. And he left a deep impression on some—not his music, but his arrogance. "He was being really obnoxious," recalls a young folk singer who would get to know him well later. "He was going through a whole ego thing. Some kid was talking to him, something about music, and Dylan turned on the kid and just creamed him. He was like an animal. He didn't have the cool at the time that he developed later, the hip-meanness. At that early date, it was just being an animal. And he horrified this poor kid, and everybody around. I remember asking, 'Who is that guy?' and someone said, 'His name used to be Bob Zimmerman, but now he's Bob Dylan and he thinks he's tough shit.' "

Dave Van Ronk: "Dylan was always vicious from time to time. This was no lollipop singer, you know. The only trouble about his viciousness, until he became famous he couldn't get away with it."

Dylan returned to Dinkytown at the end of May, picking up the things he had left behind at Lynn Kastner's, and performing in a hootenanny with his old friends. Paul Nelson and Jon Pankake were putting out a quarterly on folk music and artists, *The Little Sandy Review,* and they were overwhelmed by the growth they saw in Dylan. They later recalled it this way:

"The change in Bob was, to say the least, incredible. In a mere half year he had learned to churn up exciting, bluesy, hard-driving harmonica-and-guitar music, and had absorbed during his visits with Guthrie not only the great Okie musician's unpredictable syntax, but his very vocal color, diction and inflection. Dylan's performance that spring evening of a selection of Guthrie and Gary Davis songs was hectic and shaky, but it contained all the elements of the now perfected performing style that has made him the most original newcomer to folk music. Yes, folks, a star was born that night. Bob Dylan was on his way."

On his way back to New York, Dylan stopped off again in Madison and the reaction to him was not as positive as it had been in Dinkytown. He showed up at the Johnson Street tenement apartment where he had spent a couple of days back in January, and he made himself at home for a week or so. Jennifer Warren: "He just appeared again. Fred Underhill asked him to stay with us, and we didn't know how long it was going to be. He dropped his bag and took over my room. People started coming over to see him, chicks and things. He had a sort of cultist thing about him—people gathered about him and he sort of reveled in it. I remember that room, my room ... I was pissed that he took it over. He stayed about a week and he'd bring people up to the room—my room—people interested in his singing or young, slightly weird-looking early hippie chicks, from New York most of them. What I mostly remember is these scruffy girls trying to come on strong to him, and local folk kids who were local pretenders and saw Dylan as king of the folkies. They were all very young, unsophisticated, and the girls especially were young pre-groupie types. Dylan was becoming a little personality, but the people who knew folk music weren't wrapped up in him.

"There were always crowds around him at our place. He would lie on the bed and play, in this dark room, and you could hear this raspy voice. He'd have his eyes closed and the kids would be all around him, and if one of them left or another one came, he wouldn't even open his eyes. I had the feeling he was after doing his own thing, and having people watch him and listen to him. And he was doing the same old stuff from the first time, not any of his own because he apparently hadn't started writing very much yet. I was surprised at his naivete. He was a dumb kid with a big come on.

"Dylan was a taker. We fed him a lot and he took over the apartment, essentially. He never offered money or would buy anything. He just took."

After a couple of weeks Bob returned to New York. Mrs. Smith recalls: "There was a knock on the door and Bobby was standing there with a suitcase in his hand and his old Brown-Martin guitar slung over his shoulder, and he said, 'Hello, I'm back.' There was never any talk about whether he was staying, no wheedling, but he just stayed. How this happened I'll never get straight in my mind. When he came in I said, 'What are you doing here?' And he said, 'I just got in.' I said, 'You're hungry, eat.' This Yiddishe mama said eat. He sat down, didn't say where he was staying, didn't say he was hungry—never would say he was hungry. So he ate and he stayed. That was the end of May and he slept through the month of June in the living room and then my son was going to camp and he told Bobby he could have his bed. And he stayed through July and August."

The Smiths gave him a bed, fed him, and doled out fifty cents a day to him for spending money. He would get up late in the morning or early afternoon, talk a while with Mrs. Smith while he ate, and then head on down to the Village with the fifty cents in his pocket. Sometimes he would vanish for days at a time, usually to stay with the Van Ronks or Mikki Isaacson. He liked mystery and privacy, and not too many people knew exactly where he was going when he left one place, or where he'd been when he returned.

After getting to know Woody Guthrie, Dylan started to write seriously. "He was always working on some song in his mind when he was out in East Orange with us," Mrs. Gleason says. "I can remember him lying on his stomach almost across the dining room table, making notes on scraps of paper, even the edges of newspapers, because he never had anything to write on, and then sticking them in his pocket. Always working on scraps and snatches of songs."

Woody had told him, "Just write. Don't worry where the tune comes from. I just pick up tunes I heard before and change them around and make them mine. Put in a couple of fast notes for one slow one, sing a harmony note 'stead of melody, or a low note for a high one, or juggle the rests and pauses—and you got a melody of your own. I do it all the time."

By June, when Dylan began living with the Smiths, he was writing a couple of hours a night. After spending hours in folk clubs and bars around the Village he'd come in around 4 A.M. and begin to write, lyrics first, scratching them out on ruled legal-sized, yellow paper, later fitting a melody to the words. One of his earliest is something he called *East Colorado Blues,* a rather ordinary reworking based on several cowboy standards, but with Dylan's own road brand on it. The song is about a lonesome man who feels "so bad" stuck in Texas City, which "ain't no friend of mine," and who is pining away for old East Colorado (where Bob Dylan had said he bought the hat with the tag, "Made in Duluth"). The song appears to be one of the many that Dylan wrote but never sang. It appears on none of the tapes now in circulation, and on none of the many hours of tapes the Smiths made of Dylan singing over more than two years. The copy of the song in the Smiths' possession, on the ruled yellow paper, has a note on the other side written to the Smith boy as he was leaving for camp: "Take it easy, but take it, and you'll win."

Another song he wrote at the Smiths' during the first month he lived with them, is one he would use with devastating comic effect at Gerde's, *Talkin' Bear Mountain Picnic Massacre Blues.* The song had its origin in the pages of the New York *Herald Tribune* of June 19. Dylan was sitting in the Gaslight with Noel Stookey who was just about to become Paul, of Peter, Paul and Mary.

"Want to hear something funny?" Stookey asked.

A Harlem social club had chartered the Hudson Belle, an excursion boat, for a Father's Day cruise up the Hudson to Bear Mountain. As the picnickers were crowding the pier waiting for the boat to arrive rumors (later confirmed) spread that about a thousand counterfeit tickets had been sold around town and that those families with fake tickets would not be permitted aboard. The boat docked a couple of hours late and there was a mad scramble to get aboard and a good deal of panic and fighting on all three decks. The cruise was called off and about a dozen people were taken to a hospital for treatment of their injuries. Dylan sat at the Smiths with the story before him and quickly wrote his own version.

"Yippie," there was going to be a picnic and he rushed to buy a ticket, not realizing he would never come close to a bear. He took his family to the pier and didn't think too much of it when he saw about six thousand people there. But when they all started crowding aboard the boat began to sink, and he figured it was a strange way "to start a picnic." The boat sank, all right, amid dogs and cats fighting, and people smashing chairs over each other's heads, and cops rushing aboard, and the last he remembers is all the screaming and shoving and suddenly he regains consciousness somewhere on shore, with a cracked skull and bruised stomach, "bald naked," but lucky to be alive. He finds his picnic basket, and his wife and children, and goes home, to have his picnic in the safety of his kitchen and bathroom. And the last verse recommends taking all the hustlers who stole money from the people and putting them on a boat for Bear Mountain, to have a picnic like the one he suffered through.

The nine verses were spoken, with simple guitar chords as background under the recitation, and the "blues" simply broke up the crowds. "We thought it was hilariously funny at the time," Terri Van Ronk recalls. "Now it's not so funny, but it was then. The thing is, though, that he was beginning to think about and talk about people who were being trod upon. Not in any class way, but just that he hated people who were taking people. He had a full conception of people who were being taken, and he did read the newspapers, and that's what came through in *Talkin' Bear Mountain.*"

Talkin' Bear Mountain and *Talkin' New York,* both Guthrie style talking blues, were among the few original songs Dylan was singing publicly at this point. Although he was doing much original writing he showed his audiences mostly the standard songs that were in every folksinger's tune kit. For example, from a collection of folk songs compiled by John A. and Alan Lomax, Dylan picked up *Dink's Blues.* "Learned it from a lady named Dink," he told friends. Alan Lomax, in writing about the origin of the song, when Dylan was about five years old, says *he* learned it from a black woman named Dink in 1904.

Among other songs in his repertoire was *Poor Lazarus,* about a young black levee worker who was hunted down and killed by a white sheriff, found in the Lomax collection as *Po' Laz'rus; It's Hard to Be Blind,* a reworking of an ancient folk song, *It's Hard to Be Poor;* and a rewriting of the old spiritual, *Gospel Plow,* and of *He Was a Friend of Mine.*

His talent and the presence can already be felt on these old tapes, but his style wasn't altogether successful. This was 1961, and the people around Dylan were warning him that he was an anachronism, singing the songs of the Thirties and earlier. Woody Guthrie was already almost outdated, but Dylan continued to sing and write songs with a Guthrie appeal to them.

Mrs. Smith: "I said to him once, 'Woody is a man of his own times. Why do you try to live in his times?' And he asked, 'Why don't you think I should sing the songs of the Thirties?' So I told him, 'Because it's not your era. Sing of your era. Don't do what all the other folk singers are doing. What the hell does the boxcar mean to them? What does it mean to you?' I said, 'What's so nice about riding a boxcar? When Woody rode a boxcar it was real, he came out of the Dust Bowl, he didn't have anything to eat. That was the truth of the Thirties. You never knew that kind of life. Don't lose yourself in Woody's shadow.'

"Around this time, Bobby was saying he wanted to go to San Francisco, and I asked him, 'How are you going—by boxcar? Or are you taking the train?' And he started to giggle and said, 'I'm gonna take a train, they're so nice to ride.' Giggling. He was no fool. He knew what was going on. He knew the old folk songs weren't him. He was just searching for whatever *was* him."

The search was made relatively easy by the intellectually turbulent atmosphere in which Dylan found himself. He seldom discusses the influences on him, except for his great debt to Woody Guthrie; "Open your ears and you're influenced, it's all around you," he would say. But friends deliberately tried to get him out of the Thirties. Van Ronk, for example. A voracious reader, with an appetite for politics, social problems, and poetry, as well as for blues and folk music, Van Ronk argued with and sometimes lectured Dylan for hours on his own special brand of New Left radical-humanist thinking.

Jack Elliott: "Dylan never talked much, but Dave could actually get him to start arguing. I'd sit in and listen to Bobby argue for many long hours, mostly with Dave, about politics and the world and everything. Him and Dave, both like bulls, locking horns for hours." And, while he had not appeared to be paying much attention to radical thought in Minneapolis, it touched him here in New York.

Van Ronk, by most accounts, also got Dylan into the French symbolist poets, particularly Rimbaud, and into Villiers and Bertolt Brecht. Dave talked about them, quoted them, during the long sessions of arguing, but Dylan continued to carry off the American primitive role, the Woody Guthrie kid who never read a book in his life. Van Ronk: "Being a hayseed, that was part of his image or what he considered his image at the time. Like, once I asked him, 'Do you know the French symbolists?' And he said, 'Huh?'—the stupidest

'Huh' you can imagine—and later, when he had a place of his own, I went up there and on the bookshelf was a volume of French poets from Nerval almost to the present. I think it ended at Apollinaire, and it included Rimbaud, and it was all well-thumbed with passages underlined and notes in the margins. The man wanted to be a primitive, a natural kind of genius. He never talked about somebody like Rimbaud. But he *knew* Rimbaud, all right. You see that in his later songs."

` The Van Ronks had a wide circle of active radical friends. Some even defied the State Department ban on travel to Cuba and went down to see what Castro was building. Dylan was thrown into the center of this group. But it was not only the Van Ronks who shaped his thinking about the deficiencies in the nation. Pete Seeger was still singing his songs of gentle protest, spreading his imperturbable humanism, despite a Congressional contempt indictment and a blacklist that kept him off television and some college campuses. Seeger, one of the more innocent menaces to American Society, had been called before the House un-American Activities Committee in the summer of 1955 where he was indicted and convicted on contempt charges for refusing to answer questions about his personal and political beliefs. Eventually the courts dismissed it all as absurd, but in March, 1961, during Dylan's first New York winter, the Seeger trial appeared more tragic than absurd. "They're framin' him," Bob said. "They want to shut him up."

And there was always the example of Woody Guthrie. Even as he was dying, Guthrie continued to lash out against injustices of all kinds, just as he had all of his life.

One man who helped fuel Dylan's imagination was Richard M. Buckley, known as Lord Buckley, "a most immaculately hip aristocrat," someone has called him. Lord Buckley was a monologist, but that's as lame as calling Dylan a singer. Lord Buckley was truly extraordinary. Born in California in 1905, he began working nightclubs in Chicago during Prohibition when Al Capone ruled, and gangsters, hookers, pimps, chorus girls and sporting men were pop culture heroes. He swung into it all and he learned the language and mores of the streets, and of the black jazz musicians with whom he shared the stage and life, and he incorporated them in the visions and allegories he wove. A white man speaking the slang of black jazz musicians, he used the language of the hip to bring fresh insight into the meaning of, for example, the Nazz—namely, Jesus, or appraising good and evil in his monologue "The Bad-Rapping of the Marquis De Sade, the King of Bad Cats."

Buckley was important in Dylan's development, although Dylan never met him. In November, 1960, as Dylan was leaving Minneapolis, Buckley collapsed and died in his New York hotel room. But he was still being talked about when Dylan first hit town..

A number of people introduced Dylan to the Buckley magic, including Bill Cosby, who was doing some Buckley monologues at the Gaslight, and Hugh Romney. Dylan crashed at Romney's place occasionally during that summer, and Romney got him an album of Lord Buckley's material. Dylan borrowed it, took it to Mikki Isaacson's, and studied it the way he had studied Guthrie.

Miss Isaacson: "He had collected a lot of material over the years, songs and things, and he asked me to take all these scraps of paper laying in his guitar case and type them out for him. One of the things he had me do was a routine off the Lord Buckley record, the one about the hanging of a black man. Bobby was so very anxious to learn it, and for me to type it for him. He was so excited about it, kept playing it on the phonograph over and over again 'til I was going out of my mind."

Buckley's monologue was called "Black Cross," which Dylan turned into a talking blues, *Hezekiah Jones,* about an "ignorant nigger" farmer who bought books and read a lot and annoyed white illiterates. The white reverend they sent around to cross-examine him found Hezekiah "don't believe in nothin'." And Hezekiah said he certainly did, he believed man should be "beholden" to his neighbors, not worship God out of fear of His wrath. "There's a lot of good ways for a man to be wicked," the white minister shouted, and Hezekiah was lynched. He deserved it, his neighbors said, for he "never had no religion."

Dylan was beginning to write about people who were trod upon. They were like the people Woody Guthrie had written about, poor and abused, but Dylan brought them up to date; the children of Guthrie's Dust Bowl subjects, perhaps. But as Jack Elliott puts it, Dylan had a lot more "information" available, and his imagination and language could soar and dive, and he could get away with things that would have made Guthrie look foolish had he tried them. And Lord Buckley was one of the burrs under Dylan's saddle.

But all these artistic and political forces working on him would take a little time to percolate.

Ric von Schmidt: "The first time I heard about Dylan was through Robert L. Jones, who was my brother-in-law. Robert was a good singer and he was invited down to the Indian Neck Festival that year and when it was over he came back and he said: 'Hey, there's this guy down there you really gotta hear. Bob Dylan, he sounds like Woody Guthrie and he sings these funny songs.' So, some time in June, Dylan showed up in Cambridge with Jones. Dylan was young and puppy-like and sweet and just real live, open and warm. I felt that very much. We got together at my apartment on Boyleston Street and I played some stuff like *He Was A Friend of Mine*. I got that one from the Library of Congress, and he was very impressed by that concept of being able to take the black expression in that kind of song and being able to sing it. He wasn't at that time quite able to handle material that related to the blues, and he was still feeling around for a way to do that. And *Baby, Let Me Follow You Down,* I played it for Bob that day. I had learned it from Geno Foreman, who was the son of Clark Foreman, the civil rights leader.

"I can also remember Bob and me driving around East Cambridge that day, looking for this street where somebody lived who we decided to see, just moving around in a kind of haphazard way. And we were playing harmonicas. Both of us were pleased that we could play harmonicas together in a duet and have it sound pretty good. I can't remember whether I was playing the crossed harp and he was playing straight, or vice versa, but I remember we played some very nice easy things for the harp, and then we switched. He played the crossed and I played straight.

"We drove out to Roxbury where Jones was. He had a croquet set and Bob was gung ho on everything, he'd try everything, and I still have visual flashes of the croquet game. Bob was so close to spastic, he was one of the most uncoordinated guys at that stage. He couldn't hit the ball, and he couldn't finish the game, he was wiped out. It was kind of a delightful game, he could never make the mallet come in contact with the ball."

As the summer began melting the city asphalt, Dylan was spending much time at the Van Ronk's apartment on West 15th Street, often sleeping over, practically living with them when he wasn't staying uptown at the Smith's.

Terri Van Ronk had started managing her husband that spring, after they both decided his manager wasn't doing anything to promote him. By summer she decided to "become a grown up manager" and was beginning to handle some of the singers in their circle who needed managers: Van Ronk, Tom Paxton, Mark Spoelstra, and Dylan. Terri got Dylan his first out-of-town gig (and an out-of-town engagement was a mind-blower, because there were very few clubs around outside the Village that would book folk singers, "there was literally no place to get a singer up on a stage outside town," Terri recalls). She called Lena Spencer, an actress who runs a place up in Saratoga Springs called Caffé' Lena, and asked her to book Dylan. "She didn't want Bobby. For a whole year I had been finding her someone at the last minute to fill out an act, she'd call me and I'd go around to Spring Street where a lot of people were hanging out and get her a performer. So I told her that for a whole year every time she needed a favor I'd come through and now I needed a favor, and she booked Bobby for the weekend. After it, she called me and said not to bring him back again."

Dylan wasn't too well received at Caffé' Lena. The audience wasn't composed of the folk enthusiasts who flocked to the Village, and they didn't pay much attention to the young kid singing about Woody Guthrie and hoboes. At one point it was so noisy in the place that Bill Spencer, Lena's husband, had to get on the stage and tell the audience to quiet down. Dylan didn't talk about it when he got back to the Village, but Spencer, who thought Dylan had enormous talent and was furious at the indifference of the audience, told Terri and others what had happened at Lena's. He got up on the stage and told the audience: "You may not know what this kid is singing about and you may not care, but if you don't stop and listen you will be stupid all the rest of your lives. Listen to him, dammit." His little speech didn't help very much; Dylan's two-night stand was not an overwhelming success.

But Terri couldn't get him too many other gigs. The Club 47 in Cambridge refused to hire him because he was too much of a freak for the folk crowd. The owner of the Second Fret in Philadelphia heard a tape of some of Dylan's early Guthrie interpretations and snapped: "Why should I hire a Jack Elliott imitation when I can get Jack Elliott for nothing?" (Elliott had filled in at the Second Fret for the dying Cisco Houston a couple of months earlier, without pay, a benefit for Houston, and apparently they figured down in Philadelphia that Elliott felt a desperate need for work and would perform just for the exposure, "for nothing"). Terri spoke to an executive at Vanguard Records and he said he wasn't interested in Dylan, he wouldn't go over at all. Years later, after Dylan became the most important singer in the folk bag, this executive found in the bottom of his desk a note of his conversation with Terri which said, "Bob Dylan—nothing doing" and he went out and got himself drunk.

One job he got that summer excited him a great deal. Harry Belafonte and his producer, Hugo Montenegro, were trying to come up with a slightly different sound for the popular singer, one that would

lend a more gutsy blues sound to his rather commercial interpretation of folk and blues. They decided on a hard-driving harmonica,
and Dylan was asked to back up Belafonte. He would get fifty dollars
a session, a princely sum since he hadn't made more than a few
hundred dollars as a Village professional. But more important, was
the chance to get into a recording studio for the first time.

He was ecstatic about the session, Mrs. Smith recalls, going off with
his harmonicas, soaring as high as an eagle. But he returned dejected,
annoyed, angry. Belafonte is a total professional, a musical perfec-
tionist. He will work on a song, do it again and again and listen to the
replays and then do it again, until he has it exactly the way he thinks
his record should sound. To Dylan, coming up in the loose and casual
coffee houses and folk clubs, where you make a mistake and laugh at
it and maybe repeat it the next time for the chance to laugh at it
again, the perfection Belafonte sought was too much. He stamped
back to the Smiths' place afterward and announced that he had quit
after only one song.

"Over and over again," he told the Smiths, pacing angrily around
their living room. "Who needs that? The same thing again and again.
That ain't singin'."

"But it's a chance to work with a big star," Mrs. Smith said.

"Yeah, but I can't stand that kind of thing," Dylan replied. "I ain't
goin' back. Can't work like that. How many times can I play the same
song over and over? The whole thing was overdone. A drag."

As a result, Dylan appears on only one cut of Belafonte's album,
The Midnight Special, playing harmonica on the title song.

Kevin Krown was spending much of his time trying to promote
Dylan. He made the rounds of record companies with Dylan tapes.
No one was interested. He called Robert Shelton, folk music critic of
the *New York Times,* trying to get him to listen to Dylan and write
an article about him. At first, Shelton didn't respond, but after seeing
Dylan at Gerde's one night he decided to do an interview with Dylan
and try to persuade his editors to run it. Dylan began to duck him.
"Did you call Shelton yet?" Mrs. Horne asked Bob day after day, and
he'd reply: "No, not yet. Tomorrow." Mrs. Horne says: "I don't know
why he kept stalling. Bob was most diffident, in some respects. It may
have been insecurity. But then again he was a lot brighter than most
people gave him credit for. He may have had his own plots going—
that once he would get another booking at Gerde's an article would
be more valuable to him. Maybe that's why Bobby kept stalling
Shelton."

The young Bob Dylan, as remembered by Ric von Schmidt and Barry Kornfeld, sitting around a midtown Manhattan apartment reminiscing for an interviewer:

Ric: I think Bob's whole career reflects his fear of being out of control. Of losing control over his audiences. I think everybody who gets out there fears that to some degree.

Barry: Then this would explain his *pretending* to be out of control. Like at one of his early gigs, where he's wearing the Huck Finn cap. He got up and started running some rap. It was cute, but he backed himself into a corner and you sat there and wondered, "How's he gonna get out of that one?" And he'd come up with a mind-blower and get out of it all right. But the thing is he had it up his sleeve all the time, and he'd run the same riff the next night.

Ric: That goes back to his being a primitive musician. There is a thing you can pull out of yourself by that sort of tight-rope walk he does. He looks like he's going to fall off it, but he gets out of it. If you can get out of these things it sweeps an audience along with you like nothing else. I think this is a key thing with a primitive performer working with a sophisticated audience, which is what the folk audience was. The only way to create performance tension is to go way beyond what the audience thinks your capabilities are, and somehow pull it out.

Barry: You have to remember something about Dylan and his ability. He always professed an inability, he always said he didn't know anything, but somehow miraculously incredible moves appeared at the last minute, and it becomes clear he knows a hell of a lot.

Ric: A lot of it has something to do with the fact he's able to make those mind connections, viscerally, not something that was learned.

Dylan demonstrated that tight rope walk at one concert that has been preserved on tape. On the last Saturday in July, the Riverside Church, which operates a non-commercial FM radio station in upper Manhattan, put on a folk hootenanny—a day-long showcase for established and newer artists working in every form of folk song. Bob Dylan joined Jack Elliott, Dave Van Ronk, Cynthia Gooding, Tom Paxton, Victoria Spivey and dozens more at the concert which ran for about a dozen hours.

Bob, one of the earlier performers, was introduced as "a newcomer, a boy from Gallup, New Mexico," the MC said. He played a few riffs on his guitar and then broke it off and said: "Came up here in a hurry, don't know what to do," immediately establishing himself as a kid who needs a lot of tea and sympathy. He began to sing: "Oh,

I wish I was in London . . ." and it was strange, this kid was putting stresses on syllables that were seldom stressed before, bending notes and lyric lines, mumbling some words to get past them so he could come down hard on the ones he wanted to stress. It wasn't a black sound, not a polished folk sound, something a bit different, and possibly a bit incompetent . . . on first hearing.

He got a little more than a polite hand and he started strumming to get into the second song. Suddenly, he stopped. He said: "This harmonica holder isn't holding too good, together.." (Pause.) "Seems like it's gonna strangle me here, it's just a hanger, a coat hanger." The audience remained still, feeling for this kid who was handicapped musically because all he had to hang his harmonica on was a coat hanger and it wasn't working too well. He started to sing: "She promised to meet him . . ." and ran through *John Lewis,* a nice kid singing a standard folk song, and getting a hand that was a little more enthusiastic now.

He blew into his harmonica. "Uhhh . . . sing ya one a Woody Guthrie's songs . . ." He began to play the guitar, then stopped. He turned to other artists on the stage behind him and asked: "Anybody got a knife?" There was no response. He turned to the audience: "Any one a you people got a knife?" Chuckling. Somebody passes a small knife up to him. "Well, this ain't surely a big knife." (Pause.) "Show you a little trick." He fooled with the coat hanger, unsuccessfully: "Got a bigger knife?" The audience laughs. "That wasn't the trick," he said, throwing the line away as well as any experienced comedian might. "I really ain't no comedian," he insisted, but he kept at it for a while, blowing a couple of notes into the harmonica, trying to get the thing working. Then he gave it up and played *Poor Lazarus* and got an even bigger hand than before.

Then: "This is a friend of mine, Danny Kalb. He plays the guitar, sings, and all that." (Pause.) "I'm gonna play harmonica." Applause. And Dylan and Kalb got off a superb railroad song, Dylan's harmonica chugging out the sounds of the engine behind and in and out of Kalb's singing, and the audience was up and whistling.

Many, many hours later Dylan was called out to do a final song, to close out the show, because he had found a real harmonica holder somewhere. And he came out with Jack Elliott, the two of them making a grand entrance, hopping towards the mike and strumming as they came. They broke right into a schlock-rock duet, a takeoff on the Coasters and other rock (ugh!) groups of the day. "Doo-wah, doo-wah . . ." Jack chanted several times to a modified rock beat while Dylan played the harmonica. And then Dylan sang, improvising teen-rock lyrics:

"You said you'd ask me/you said you'd ask me/to the senior prom/
Found out I had acne/now you won't ask me/to the senior prom/
woooo—ooo." And a second chorus, with more Elliott doo-wahs in
the background: "Got me a shotgun/22 rifle/I got it my birthday/I
killed my parents/'cause they don't underrrstand/They don't think
you need her at all ..." And strutting off, playing, a grand exit.
"More!" the audience demanded, "More!" It was a Dylan audience
all the way; he'd won a houseful of fans after a long walk on that
tightrope.

Pete Karman, a young writer for the *New York Daily Mirror,* went
up to the Riverside show to do an article. He brought with him two
of his friends, Carla Rotolo, who worked for folk collector Alan
Lomax, and her younger sister, Suze.
Both sisters were very attractive, and presented a startling con-
trast. Carla was dark, with glossy black hair, and Suze was fair, with
long-flowing hair the color of wheat. Suze was seventeen. She has
been described as "kind of like a Botticelli woman," by one who
knew her at that time. She also struck almost everyone she met as
a highly intelligent woman, one of the brightest young women in the
Village folk crowd. Carla and Suze knew most of the artists from the
Village, and they were permitted free movement backstage. A couple of days later Suze described it in a letter to Sue Zuckerman:
"When Cynthia Gooding was MC-ing for the foreign music section,
I left and went into the studio room. Dylan was fooling around with
some cameraman and he made me sit on his lap while the guy was
taking pictures. It was fun. I wore Dylan's hat for a few hours. Suddenly I was in a sound-proofed room with John Wynn, Jack Elliott
and Bob Dylan. We were hopping around while poor Bob was trying
to rehearse. Jack kept telling me what an upsetting thing it is to
realize the view that sidewalks are getting every time a female walks
on them. He said all his life he's been trying to think of ways of lying
prone on the sidewalks and become invisible. He pointed out that his
jealousy of the sidewalks of the world was so overwhelming it almost
kills him. The funniest Goddamn five minutes of talk I've heard in
a long time.
  "Jack Elliott was cutting up on stage every time the Greenbriar
Boys or Bob was trying to perform. Jack himself gave an excellent
performance. At night Anna Bird had a party which was great, small
but damn good. Carla, Pete and I spent the whole night with Dylan
and Bruce. Dylan gave us a private concert, a repeat of the private
one I'd gotten that afternoon in the soundproofed room. He's a good
composer, too. He and John sang a song that lasted a half hour,

completely impromptu. John lead-singing and Bob trying to play his guitar like Johnny does. Dylan giggling his adorable giggle all through it. The song was called *Beautiful People:* I'm going to that beautiful land/with those beautiful people/wearing beautiful underwear/and those beautiful people/are waiting for me.

"Got home at four in the morning. Pete drove me, Carla and Dylan home. More crazy things happened but I couldn't type anything else."

Suddenly, their friends say, Dylan and Suze began going together. It was summer and there was no school for Suze and no work for Dylan, and they were together a great deal. Suze was living with Carla in the Village and their widowed mother, Mrs. Mary Rotolo was living with friends. Mrs. Rotolo had given up her apartment the previous March because she and Suze were going to live in Italy where Suze planned to study art. But several days before they were scheduled to leave, their car was involved in an accident, and Mrs. Rotolo and Suze were seriously injured. They had no apartment, and when they were released from the hospital each went to live with a different set of friends during their recuperation. After a month or so Suze moved in with Carla, and Mrs. Rotolo continued to live with friends while she looked for an apartment. Suze was always around the Village and so was Dylan, and they quickly became very close.

"They were two kids bouncing around together, two innocent children falling in love," one girl in the crowd remembers. "It was very pretty, at the beginning. It was like the picture of them walking along West Fourth Street that's used as the cover for the second Dylan album."

Others were reminded of Hansel and Gretel. Wherever they were, they were alone; a crowd of ten or fifteen might be at Mikki Isaacson's place and all decide to run down to Gerde's, and Bob and Suze would have to be dragged out of a corner where they had been sitting, apart from the others, in their own little world. And when they walked over to Gerde's, Bob and Suze would be arm in arm, as on the album cover, but always apart from the others in the crowd.

Dylan stirred the maternal instinct in older women, and he stirred another basic impulse in younger women. Sue Zuckerman says: "He roused a sexual instinct. It's difficult to describe him. I always dug the way he moved. It was pleasing to watch him move, and he had that sort of rough kind of appeal, not all pretty and fancy, but definitely an individual who was very different from most people hanging around in those days. He just had a very special sort of identity. Even before he was known, he just stood out personally. Also, he was into the James Dean-Marlon Brando quiet rebel sort of thing, that was definitely part of it. And at one time he was kind of earthy, and the kind of twang when he talked, so refreshing from the New York accent. One of the things appealing about him, although it was more of a nervous habit kind of thing, was that he'd sort of giggle. And whenever he sat still, he wouldn't be able to sit still—just moving, always moving, it was fascinating, all that nervous energy."

There were two distinct groups of folk singers and patrons in the Village at the time. One consisted of the younger interpreters like Van Ronk and Elliott, who were more concerned with music than with intellectual arguments about the purity of folk song. The other group believed folk was an antique art, that the songs which came out of the hills of Tennessee and the plains of Montana should be sung the way they've always been sung, that if John Lomax found and recorded a song as sung by slaves, the song should be sung the way the slaves rendered it, even a hundred years later. "Low folk" and "high folk" they called it, and the highs considered Dylan the lowest of the low. He had a startling approach to folk songs. His interpretations were a total departure from intellectually acceptable musical forms. And the folk purists detested his work and spoke about him contemptuously. Dylan, whenever he heard about it, simply shrugged and continued doing it his way.

But up in Cambridge, the folk scene was "loose and goosey, while in New York they were ready to shoot down the younger guys," von Schmidt says. For a while, Dylan was almost commuting between the Village and Cambridge. Besides the comfortable scene it offered, Bob was drawn by von Schmidt's marvelous ability to handle the black sound that Dylan wanted so badly to learn.

Von Schmidt: "I think his attitude towards me and Van Ronk and anybody who knew a little bit more in terms of chords was that he wanted to pick up on it. He wasn't really looking for ideas, but looking for instrumental chops. Van Ronk and I represented a coming together of black expression and that's what Bob wanted at this time. I felt this later, from time to time, about Bob, it was Van Ronk's and my connection with the black funky thing that was at first appealing to him. It was the amalgamation of the black sound that made Van Ronk and me momentarily important to him."

Some time in early August, a couple of weeks after meeting Suze, Bob returned to Cambridge with a couple of other folk singers. They dropped into the Club 47, which was the center of the young folk sound in New England, the place where Joan Baez had begun to sing. Dylan was called to the stage and he did a couple of songs, including *Talkin' Bear Mountain,* and then he was introduced to some of the folk crowd. Among them were Carolyn Hester, who was appearing regularly there through the summer, and her husband, Richard Fariña.

Carolyn was a warm, fresh-faced young folk singer from Texas, with long blond hair and looking so delightfully wholesome that when the *Saturday Evening Post* was later doing a story on the folk boom, her picture was used on the cover. She had sung at festivals and folk clubs around the country, had made two records for small labels, and was signed to Columbia by John Hammond, director of talent acquisition, a few months earlier, in 1961. Fariña was a darkly impetuous and bubbling young man of prodigious talent as a folk singer, song writer, novelist and short story writer. Dick and Carolyn had seen Dylan work at Gerde's, had heard his name talked about all over the Village, but had never met him. Dylan struck it off well with them and the next day, Carolyn, Dick, von Schmidt and his wife and infant daughter, all went off to Revere Beach.

Carolyn Hester: "This was the first time I ever got a good look at Dylan, got to talk to him. His hair was pretty long then and I loved the way he looked. But he seemed to be in bad health, he seemed to be living out in the street. His hands were very rough, very tough, but almost feminine in a strange way. He was in a shirt and jeans, and when he took his shirt off his skin was transparent. He had his harmonica with him and played it, and had music very much on his mind. He got talking, and he and Richard and Ric would joke a little about things, and talk about *San Francisco Bay Blues* and other songs, and Ric was very interested in Dylan and wanted to get together and trade songs. When we went back to the Club 47 that night I had to sing, and I think Richard did an Irish song. And then we made a point to have Dylan come up and sing maybe four or five songs, because we felt very fond of Dylan by then. He hadn't talked about ambitions or what he wanted to do, particularly, and we didn't know he was writing songs. As a matter of fact I don't think he was that much, although he did do *Talkin' Bear,* but talking blues was Guthrie and a lot of kids do them and that was nothing unusual. He was just around listening to songs Ric had, traditional songs, and that was it. I don't think at that time he had sufficiently in mind what he was going to do, to be able to talk about it. Maybe he was working on it and we didn't know it, but he didn't talk about it. He was around for a week up in Cambridge and we were very friendly.

"I don't remember exactly how Dylan came to work with me on my first Columbia album. It may have been Richard saying to Dylan, 'Gee, if we get into some gigs or something we'll bring you in, too.' And the record was the first thing to come along. Richard and I were talking about what could be acceptable to the folk crowd and still be a little advanced commercially—to reach out, to be a little different from Joan Baez, say. Odetta had put a bass on her record, so we thought a bass with my guitar and also a harmonica—my father had played a harmonica on my first record—so we thought that's what we'd do. And when we got down to New York around the first of September we asked Dylan to play the harmonica for my record.

"He was happy about it. I went to the apartment where he was staying with Suze and Carla, off Sheridan Square, to see him and talk about my record. He taught me *Come Back Baby* there. Dylan impressed me as being, again, totally absorbed by the music. It seemed to me he didn't put his guitar down hardly ever, I think at that time, by September, I was beginning to get the idea he was writing, he may have sung me part of a song but he didn't emphasize what he was doing. He was very happy he was going to play the harmonica, going to get a record date. He was concentrating on me and our meeting and our music and he opened right up and gave me this song. He may have played a couple of things for me that I could use on the record, one was a Guthrie song and this other one, *Come Back Baby*, was very bluesy, which was very, very different from anything I had on the record.

"The second meeting was a week or so later. Richard and I were staying at the apartment of Ned O'Gorman, the poet, on West Tenth Street. John Hammond came by, to listen to what I had worked up, and Dylan was there, and Richard. Just the four of us. I remember one wall was all a window and there was a garden in the back and the sun was streaming in. Dylan was sitting next to Hammond on the couch and I was sitting in front of them singing and Dylan was playing his harmonica and they talked to me about *Come Back,* the song Dylan gave me, and Hammond liked that song very much. He said, 'Okay, our first session will be ...' and he set a date for the end of September. And he liked Dylan, I could see he liked Dylan, which made us happy."

John Hammond: "I saw this kid in the peaked hat playing not terribly good harmonica but I was taken with him. I asked him, 'Can you sing? Do you write? Why don't you come up to the studio? I'd like to do a demo session with you just to see how it is.' I was sitting there thinking, 'What a wonderful character, playing guitar and blowing mouth harp, he's gotta be an original.' It was just one of those flashes. I thought, 'I gotta talk contract right away.'

"You see, I had come back to Columbia about a year before and I was distressed at the fact we weren't into too many kids while Mitch [Miller] had been running the show. The first thing I did was to sign

Pete Seeger, he was still under indictment for contempt of Congress, still being blacklisted by CBS, our parent, but I felt he would give Columbia a better image with the kids. And we were willing to take a chance on a controversial artist because he was obviously a great artist. I was just waiting for somebody with a message for kids when I met Bob. And I just had some good success. I had brought in Aretha Franklin, and I was in fairly good shape at Columbia. I told Bob, 'I don't have too many artists to produce, and I'd love to record you.' So we made a date for him to come to the studio."

But Dylan would first go into the studio to record for someone else. Victoria Spivey and Lonnie Johnson opened a two-week engagement at Gerde's on September 12. Miss Spivey, born in Houston in 1910, began recording the blues when she was a teenager, and began writing the first of what is probably as many blues numbers as Guthrie had written white folk songs; *Black Snake Blues,* her earliest song and recording, was one of the best-known and most-recorded blues songs of the Twenties, selling 150,000 copies in one year. That was a phenomenal performance, for Victoria is black and the records of black artists were released as "race records" and never came near the sales and popularity of white musicians. But *Black Snake Blues* and the recordings of a couple of other black artists of the time made it obvious to the major record labels that race records were big business, and they leaped into the market. Miss Spivey became so popular that, while still under twenty, she was given the starring role in King Vidor's "experimental" all-black film, *Hallelujah.* By 1961, she had her own small record company, she and her manager, producer and historian, Len Kunstadt, trying to develop a larger interest in some of the neglected black blues artists such as Lonnie Johnson and Big Joe Williams who are owed such a large debt by blues-influenced rock groups that have gone on to fame and fortune.

Victoria Spivey: "Dylan was hanging around Gerde's every night we were there. We took him for granted, I think. He was so meek and so humble, like a pet, just like a little baby boy. A poor little baby, a tiny little thing. He was the kind of boy you wanted to pull the sleeve on his sweater down so it looked right, or straighten his tie, except he didn't wear a tie. But he was a no-talking man. He didn't talk about nothing, or, when he did talk, he talked in riddles. Jive talk, always jiving. That was Bobby Dylan.

"The first night I was aware of him, really, he came up and put his arms around me and said, 'You're the most gorgeous creature,' and I asked, 'What can I do for you?' And he said, 'Nothing, I just like you.' And we just used to hang around and talk. And Big Joe Williams was there a lot. I know Bob Dylan loved Big Joe Williams and Big Joe

Williams loved Bob Dylan, and they used to get on the stage at
Gerde's and play together. Big Joe and Little Joe or Joe Junior we
used to call them. Joe and Bobby told us Bobby used to follow Joe up
and down the streets of Chicago, that Big Joe was his inspiration.

"I told Bobby that Big Joe was gonna record for me and he said,
'Moms, you want a little white boy on one of your records?' Bobby,
you know, had no color denomination to him at all, everybody was
people, not color, so I said, 'What do you mean? You're just one of
my sons,' and he said, 'You should have a white boy on some of your
records,' and I said, 'You got some around?' And he said, 'Yeah, me.'
So I told him we'd get together."

Big Joe was scheduled to go into the studio to record for Spivey
Records, and Dylan kept pressing for a chance to record with him.
Len Kunstadt was against using Dylan for a couple of reasons; for one
thing, he felt that if anybody should get a recording chance it should
be a black artist who could use the work; for another, using a white
musician might destroy the ethnic authenticity of the recording. But
Miss Spivey insisted, and Dylan went into a West Forty-sixth Street
recording studio with them on a warm afternoon in late fall and laid
down at least four tracks with Big Joe, playing the harmonica behind
and around Williams' strong guitar and sandpaper-rough Delta blues
voice. Two of them have been issued, on an album featuring tracks
by Miss Spivey, Williams. Lonnie Johnson and Roosevelt Sykes, called
Three Kings and the Queen. Dylan plays harmonica and harmonizes
with Williams on *Sitting on Top of the World* (and makes it sound as
if Big Joe was accompanying Dylan's harmonica) and plays a driving
bluesy harmonica on the second cut, *Wichita* ("This is Big Joe, and
Little Junior's blowin' his harp," Williams calls out, and Bob gets off
a harmonica riff and after another chorus Williams calls out, "Play for
me, Junior," and Dylan drives it on). The other material in the Spivey
files, not yet released, include Bob and Big Joe playing *It's Dangerous,* and at least one other song.

Len Kunstadt: "They got it down in one take. Perfection. They
sounded like they had been playing together for fifty years or so. In
my opinion, Dylan was fantastic. Big Joe is a difficult artist to play
with, that's why he's a solo artist. He's a genius, with an extraordinary
ear, and he plays very fast, never the same way twice, and you
couldn't keep up with him. He's erratic, irregular, unpredictable,
and I've never seen anybody follow Big Joe that well. Simply amazing."

Miss Spivey: "Dylan's a born genius of a musician."

Mike Porco booked Dylan into Gerde's again for a two-week engagement, beginning September 26, with the Greenbriar Boys on the same bill as the lead act. Dylan was ready for the *Times* now, and Shelton was there for the opening night. A couple of days later Shelton's enthusiastic, almost rhapsodic review ran under a four column headline that said: "Bob Dylan: A Distinctive Folk-Song Stylist."

"A bright new face in folk music is appearing at Gerde's Folk City. Although only twenty years old, Bob Dylan is one of the most distinctive stylists to play in a Manhattan cabaret in months. . . . When he works his guitar, harmonica or piano, and composes new songs faster than he can remember them, there is no doubt that he is bursting at the seams with talent.

"Dylan's voice is anything but pretty. He is consciously trying to recapture the rude beauty of a Southern field hand musing in melody on his porch. All the "husk and bark" are left on his notes and a searing intensity pervades his songs. : . . Dylan's highly personalized approach toward folk song is still evolving. He has been sopping up influences like a sponge. . . . His music-making has the mark of originality and inspiration, all the more noteworthy for his youth. Mr. Dylan is vague about his antecedent and birthplace, but it matters less where he has been than where he is going, and that would seem to be straight up."

The review simply amazed everyone, and it created some jealousy in folk circles. None of the singers who'd been knocking themselves out had ever been treated to such an effusive bit of puffery by Shelton. The critic was friendly with all of the folkies in the Village, yet had never given any of their careers the boost he gave to Dylan.

Jack Elliott: "I remember that review. I was really turned on by it because it was beautiful and true, but I was a little burned because Shelton gave me a review a little before that, but not like Bobby's. It was nice, no putdown, but he flipped out over Bobby so heavily. I remember feeling, 'Gee, whiz, Shelton, you gave him a jet-propelled push there.'"

There was a good deal of backbiting about the review, but Dylan didn't let on that it bothered him. He was totally ecstatic about it, and carried it around in his pocket until it was falling to pieces. And his joy showed through from the stage at Gerde's. Manny Greenhill, Joan Baez's manager, was in Gerde's the night the review was printed and recalls: "He did a talking blues on the review. He read it to the audience and then did a talking blues about how he stayed up all night, reading it, missed a meal, read it again. It was delightful. Boy, that kid could write."

Carolyn Hester: "The day of my recording session was the day the review was printed, and Dylan brought it with him. He was absolutely delighted with it. He would laugh and sort of shyly say something like he didn't expect it and he was so new in town and wasn't that a bitch and wasn't he lucky. And Dick and I had the article, and Bruce Langhorne who was playing guitar with me on that session, he had it, too. And Hammond saw it. We were in the studio working every day and I could see Hammond was getting more and more interested in him."

Dylan played harmonica on three of the songs on her album, *Come Back Baby, Swing and Turn Jubilee,* and *I'll Fly Away.* And the more Hammond saw of him the more impressed he became.

Hammond: "So he came in and made some demos, he did *Talking New York* as the first one, and when I heard him I flipped. I told him. I wanted him to record for Columbia, and I had the contract drawn up. We sat in my office and I said, 'How old are you?' and he said he was twenty and I said, 'I have to get your contract signed by your parents' and he said, 'I don't have any parents.' I asked, 'Do you have any relatives?' and he said, 'Yes, I have an uncle who's a dealer in Las Vegas' and he added, 'John, don't worry, you can trust me.' He had a romantic point of view at this time. As Bob Dylan he had no parents. He said he had no manager and I told him, 'I'll get you the best deal possible from the company. We usually start an artist at two per cent of royalties but I'll start you at four.' It was unprecedented to start him at four. Seeger was getting five, and he was established."

David Kapralik was director of pop A & R at Columbia at the time, and had veto power over new artists. He recalls: "John brought him to my office. Dylan seemed retiring, introverted, a little insecure, but quite sincere. He didn't say much, he just kind of checked me out. Maybe a day later John was saying to me, 'Dylan's an extraordinary young man. I don't know if he is going to sell, but he has something profound to say. Not in a commercial way, but in a personal way.' John was so enthusiastic about him, and I respected John so much that when he was so enthusiastic I wouldn't dream of saying no to him. I authorized the contract before even hearing Dylan."

Bob ran down to Mikki Isaacson's place and burst into the apartment. "I've got it!" he cried. "I got the contract." He waved a couple of sheets of paper around, hopping all over the place. But he wouldn't let anyone see it and he wasn't believed, at first. When the folk crowd learned he had actually been signed by Columbia, the jubilation outweighed any jealousy anyone may have felt because it was a break-through: the first of the younger male folk singers to be signed by a major record label. "It was a good sign," Suze Rotolo recalls.

Israel Young, who ran the Folklore Center and produced folk concerts, and is a member of the board of *Sing Out!* decided to produce Dylan in his first concert. The reason is noted in an October 23 entry in the folk world journals that Young has kept for years. "I'm very excited by Bob Dylan. I'm producing a concert so I can hear him entire. Purely from the way he talks he seems to have greatness in him, an ability to stand on his own."

Young's journals for this period contain an interview with Dylan, conducted mostly because Young wanted material for concert program notes, but also because he feels he is a part of the history of folk music and should record it all. The interview took place on the afternoon of October 20, Dylan responding to Young's questions, or just rambling, while Young patiently wrote. These are some of Dylan's ramblings:

"I didn't know the term 'folk music' until I came to New York. 'Folk music' is just a name. I sing a lot of old jazz songs, sentimental cowboy songs, top forty hit parade stuff. People have to name it something so they call it folk music. Now there are very few people singing that way. There's been no one around to cut records like the old Leadbelly, Houston and Guthrie. There are young people singing like that, but they're being held back by commercial singers. People who run radio programs don't play the ones singing like that. Folk music is being taken over by people who don't sing that way. It's all right, but to call it folk music ...

"I don't want to make a lot of money, I want to get along. The more people I reach, and have the chance to sing the kind of music I sing. ... But people have to be ready, they have to see me once already. People often say the first time they hear me, this isn't folk music. My songs aren't easy to listen to.

"The concert isn't going to be a planned concert. I can offer songs that tell something of this America. No foreign songs. The songs of the land that aren't offered over TV or radio and very few records. Offering a chance to hear them.

"I won't join a group. Groups are easy to be in. I've always learned the hard way. I will, now, too. When you fail in a group you can blame each other. When you fail alone, you yourself fail.

"I play a lot of cards. Believe in 'dead man's hand,'—the aces and eights. It's time to cash in when you get aces and eights, dead man's hand. Sounds illogical? The other things I believe in are logical. Like the length of my hair. The less hair on the head, the more hair inside. Wear a crewcut and you have all that hair cluttering around your brain. I let my hair grow long to be wise and free to think ... Or religion. Got no religion. Tried a bunch of different religions. The churches are divided. Can't make up their minds, and neither can I. Never saw a god; can't say until I see one.

"I've been with Jack Elliott ... Jack hasn't taught me any songs. Jack doesn't know that many songs. He's had a lot of chances."

That last item on Jack Elliott was rather unfair; Young calls it "an early example of the Dylan killer instinct." The fact is that Dylan leaned very heavily on Jack Elliott's material and style when he performed at the concert Young produced a couple of weeks later, on the night of November 4. Young rented out Carnegie Chapter Hall, a small room on the fifth floor of the Carnegie Hall building with seats for two hundred. He put tickets on sale at two dollars each. The hall cost him $75, printing costs of the tickets and programs another $35, he gave Dylan $20 even though the agreement had been that Dylan's fee would be a half share of the profits—and he lost money because only about fifty people showed up. Young recalls: "Al Grossman had spurred me on to produce the concert in the first place, telling me how much he felt Dylan was going to make it. I didn't know it, but Grossman already had his manager's fingers on Dylan by then, when everybody thought Dylan was a free agent. But Grossman wasn't telling anyone. Grossman was supposed to help get people to the concert, but he never even showed up himself. He didn't come to the concert. Suze came, and Bob's friends, but no Grossman."

The concert was a flop. "He did so many Jack Elliott things," Young recalls, "even raising his leg the way Jack does, using those Elliott mannerisms, and using practically all Elliott material. Bobby thought it was a failure, he called it a flop."

A friend of Dylan recalls: "He really messed it up. He sounded too much like Elliott, and he also performed indifferently, like he just didn't care because he didn't have a good audience. He didn't even bother doing his own songs, except maybe for *Song to Woody*. His ego seemed to be bruised because only his friends were there, he wasn't reaching anyone new."

A tape of that concert exists. Listening to it now, years later, you can feel the force of Dylan's raw talent. He starts off quite strong, singing *Pretty Peggy-O* (which would be used on his first album) and then into one of his sympathy-inducing little boy talks:

"Kind of got lost comin' up here tonight. Took a subway, ended up at 166th Street ... Almost got run over by a bus. Took another subway down to 34th Street and walked up here." He strummed a few chords. "Uh, come pretty prepared tonight. I got a list on my guitar. This is a new list. I used to have one on my guitar about a month ago that was no good. Figured I'd get a good list, so I went around—I put the list on first—then I went around to other guitar players and sort of looked at their list and copied down songs on mine." (Pause.) "Some of these I don't *know* so good."

He got off a couple of good ones, especially *Gospel Plow* and *Song To Woody*. And then it began to fall apart: an old Leadbelly song, done without much feeling; an Irish ballad he said he learned from Liam Clancy which failed badly; and *Fixin' To Die,* in which his guitar work is sloppy and the singing sounds forced. And Dylan never quite got back into it. After all, fifty people at your first uptown concert can be rather disheartening, especially since he frequently had more than that number listening attentively at parties and in the folk clubs.

1961–1962: *It Hurts Me Too*

BY THIS TIME Suze's mother had found an apartment, the penthouse at One Sheridan Square, the same building in which Mikki Isaacson lived. Suze moved in with her mother. Bob had been living on Avenue B, on the East Side; now he moved for a while into the Hotel Earle, on Waverly Place, where Jack Elliott and Peter La Farge were staying. He then moved in with Mikki, to be near Suze.

Mikki: "It looked as if Suze was his first big love. It was a beautiful thing to see. Whenever Suze was around Bobby was so sweet. Sweetness wasn't a part of his personality, and neither was compassion. He was a bit of a terror. But when Suze was around he was gentle, sweet and loving. A complete change. She could make him jump through hoops. One thing, he wouldn't go to sleep at night unless Suze was there to stroke him and put him to sleep. He looked like he was terrified to be alone. He wasn't lover-ish about it, more like a four-year-old child. Suze couldn't go upstairs to her mother's apartment until Bob went to sleep. Maybe he was acting, and putting us all on. He was always good for an act, always performing his kid stuff about Suze, but even in acting it showed how desperately he wanted Suze."

Suze also took over much of the mothering Bob seemed to require. She got him to change and wash his clothes a little more often, and she broke down his fears and persuaded him to have his eyes checked; he had lost his glasses a year earlier. Miss Isaacson recalls: "He would have terrible head pains because of his eyes. Every now and then he would throw his whole body backward on the bed, his hands covering his eyes, and almost screaming in pain. It would last for an hour or more and he used to say, 'I got to get to an eye doctor. Ain't had my eyes checked in six years.' And every time he had one of these attacks, I'd say, 'Bobby, won't you *please* go to an eye doctor and see what can be done about it?' But he would always treat me like a mother who was nagging him, and I deduced from it all that he was afraid to get his eyes examined. Suze eventually got him to go, and it turned out all he needed was a new pair of glasses." Suze also took upon herself the job of getting Dylan primed for the stage. He was still uneven, as a performer, still required pampering, and Suze would make certain he had the extra drink to loosen him up. "He was often drunk on hoot nights but Mike Porco never knew," one friend says. Suze played up to him and "loved him up," as Miss Isaacson puts it, while others taped to the topside of his guitar a list of songs they thought he should sing, so that he wouldn't have an excuse for coming off stage early. On many nights, though, he was a phenomenal performer. One night at Gerde's, for example, he broke a string on one guitar, picked up a banjo and broke its strings, ran over to the piano and began to pound out some wild blues and hard rock Little Richard things. Jack Elliott jumped up on the stage and started playing his guitar, and he and Dylan bounced long riffs off each other, and the audience wouldn't let them stop.

Suze's sister, Carla, and their mother, were far from happy about Dylan. "In comes this scruffy, dirty, slightly strange and totally poverty-stricken little boy of nineteen, and your daughter falls in love with him. You can't be too ecstatic about that," Terri Van Ronk recalls. And Miss Isaacson: "I remember Carla coming around, talking about how worried she was about Suze and Bobby, their relationship was so intense, and Carla kept saying, 'I know Bobby's going to make it.' Suze, Carla and I, we were so sure Bob was going to make it, we knew it. I met Mrs. Rotolo and talked to her and tried to convey that Suze was safe. Everybody felt so protective about Suze. We wanted to protect her against her mother finding out she was staying out too late, and protect Suze from finding out Bobby was off on a toot with some other girl."

Bob spent much time in the Rotolo apartment. Mrs. Rotolo was a charming, gracious woman, articulate, sensitive, thoughtful. "She's one of those rare Italian women who kept their face and figure into middle-age," a woman in the folk crowd recalls. "She didn't like Bobby too much. I can remember being up there once when she wasn't being too nice to him. She used to call him 'Twerp,' but she had a certain amount of style, and she put it in a way so that he couldn't get upset about it. After all, he was a twerp."

Within days after signing the Columbia contract, Dylan rented an apartment on West Fourth Street, just off Sixth Avenue. He was forced to pay the previous tenant $350 for some broken furniture. The rent was $80 a month for a place described by friends as absolutely raunchy, a tiny bedroom and living room, and a "kitchen" in which a bachelor and a box of corn flakes could barely fit. Bob asked Suze to move in with him, but she resisted at first. One of the women around remembers Dylan worrying that Suze was only seventeen, and the age of consent in New York State is eighteen, and asking: "How do you live with a girl when she's under eighteen?" The response: "You wait six months." But Dylan wasn't about to wait, and he continued to press Suze to share his place. He had grown totally dependent upon her.

He was a kid who was searching for approval and love, and needing them desperately. For all his denial of roots—or because of it—for all his drifting, he desperately needed an anchor. He felt rejected several times in the previous two years. Echo had returned his identification bracelet. Gretel married David. When he went to live with Avril, Mrs. Smith recalls, he told Jack Elliott, "I finally have a girl," but Avril returned to California in May, while Bob was traveling back to Dinkytown. And Suze was the kind of girl a young man falls in love with. Dylan was totally obsessed with her, totally caught up in her warmth and openness, the gentleness and the beauty and the intelligence that everyone else saw in her, and caught up in his own special needs for a woman to love him. Suze, he would later say, is "the true fortune teller of my soul." His love for her was real, it was intense, and it was touching at times. One of the Smiths' tapes, made after Thanksgiving dinner that year, when everyone was sitting around while Bob played, gives an indication of his need for her. Dylan was playing for the small and very appreciative audience of his closest friends, the Smiths, Kevin Krown, a half dozen other kids his age— his biggest boosters. It was the kind of party he thrived on. And, in the middle of a song, he suddenly stops and asks: "Where's Suze?" She went to the bathroom, someone tells him, she'll be right back, and Dylan says, "Oh, okay," and he fools around with his guitar, tuning it, then with a mandolin, carelessly fingering it, not resuming his private concert until Suze returns to the living room.

It was very pretty Hansel-and-Gretel in the beginning, but there were also very destructive elements in their relationship. Bob Dylan was totally possessive about his women, a trait that seems common to many artists and entertainers. One noted super-groupie has put it this way: "A woman who loves a musician has to reconcile herself to the·fact, right up front, that she must come second to his music, that his music is the most important thing in his life. It takes a special kind of chick to be able to do this, to want to become almost a slave." Suze was not about to become that sort of vegetable. She didn't simply want to hang around being Bob Dylan's woman, completely swallowed by him and his career, even as she loved him. She painted and sketched constantly, had some artistic talent. She had been encouraged by her artist father, and she wanted a chance to develop.

Suze was close to a group of actors in the Village who were involved in putting on some Bertolt Brecht plays. She helped paint the scenery, got involved in staging, and wanted to act. She also wrote a great deal, was much better read than Bob, heavily into the poetry of Rimbaud, Villon, Robert Graves, Brecht. "The creative one," Dylan called her. She doesn't appear to have been the kind of teenager with dreams and no ability, flightily skipping from one glamour-ambition to another; she had been thrown into the Village artistic cauldron quite young, it all broiled within her, she had a large intelligence, and those who knew her believed she could work out an artistic destiny. She believed it, too. She had to be her own self; at the same time, Bob needed a woman who would be a mere reflection of himself. That is not an oversimplification nor is it exaggeration; it was felt by everyone who was close to Suze and Bob during the couple of years they bounced from one emotional crisis to another. Each had special needs: Dylan was unable to recognize Suze's needs or to take them seriously; Suze knew she could not suppress her own desires and continue to exist as a human being.

At the end of November, 1961, Suze went into the studio with Bob for one of his recording sessions and even at this early date in their relationship she recognized her fears and confided them in a letter to Sue Zuckerman:

"The funny thing is that I don't want to get sucked under by Bob Dylan and his fame. I really don't. It sort of scares me. I'm glad and all but I just have a funny feeling about it. I can't put my finger on it but it's there. It really changes a person when they become well known by all and sundry."

Pete Karman recalls: "The relationship was extremely intense, and neither of them knew how to handle it. They would go from idyllic love to intense hatred and back again in a few minutes. Both were green behind the ears and didn't know how to handle what was happening to them."

Bob Dylan cut the album in only three or four sessions, working alone and working quickly, and it cost Columbia precisely $402 to get it down. They remember him standing out on the studio floor, with all the equipment and folding chairs around him, the harmonica around his neck and the guitar cradled in his arm. At one point, when Bob couldn't find something with which to fret his guitar for *In My Time of Dyin',* he borrowed a lipstick holder. Suze's feeling that Bob would be going through some fast changes began here, in the studio, as she saw the way Hammond and others were handling Bob. She told a friend: "Dylan's got them treating him like he's the new God." Hammond recalls: "He was just a doll in the studio. He was completely inexperienced, popping every P, and he didn't play the greatest guitar, but he was so enthusiastic."

Bob Dylan, after completing the record: "There was a violent, angry emotion running through me then. I just played guitar and harmonica and sang those songs, and that was it. Mr. Hammond asked me if I wanted to sing any of them over again and I said no. I can't see myself singing the same song twice in a row. That's terrible."

   Dave Van Ronk: "We had a terrible falling out about *House of the Rising Sun.* He was always a sponge, picking up whatever was around him, and he copped my arrangement of the song. Before going into the studio he asked, 'Hey, Dave, mind if I record your version of *Rising Sun?*' I said, 'Well, Bobby, I'm going into the studio soon and I'd like to record it.' And later he asked me again and I told him I wanted to record it myself, and he said, 'Oops, I already recorded it and can't do anything about it because Columbia wants it.' For a period of maybe two months we didn't speak to each other. He never apologized, and I give him credit for it."

Albert Grossman is probably the best-known, most successful, and aggressive artist's manager in the music business. There are some who will defend him. Kapralik, who later left Columbia to manage Barbra Streisand, and is now managing the highly successful rock group, Sly and the Family Stone, says of him: "He was bright and astute. I had nothing but good contacts with him. He fought hard for his artist. Now that I'm a manager I have the deepest respect for any manager attuned to what an artist has to say and who fights his artist's battles. And this is what Albert does."

The basic charge against Grossman is commercialism: "Anybody who goes with Grossman has to accept his premise that financial .success is the absolute goal," says one who has worked with Grossman and with Dylan. Grossman was from Chicago originally. He ran the Gate of Horn there, creating audiences for singers such as Big Bill Broonzy and Odetta. A folk singer with a massive voice, and a range that encompasses every coloring of sound, Odetta was beginning to .achieve some acclaim in 1956 as something very special in folk music. She had been managed by her husband but, when he became ill, Grossman became her manager and moved to New York. In 1959, the Kingston Trio amazed everyone in the folk field by getting their version of the old folk standard, *Tom Dooley,* on the top of the popular charts. They continued to have hit after hit, and made a lot of money putting folk music into the juke boxes. Others began trying to figure out how to cash in. Grossman came up with the perfect formula in Peter, Paul and Mary, a Kingston Trio with sex appeal. This established his reputation as a star-maker, as some kind of genius manager, even as he was being criticized for commercializing folk and for being an excessively sharp operator. A chubby man who moved in light, graceful steps, he was called "the floating Buddha."

Grossman was already operating behind the scenes by the time Dylan cut his first album. He seems to have been managing Dylan very early, without a contract, but he never let anyone know he was Dylan's manager. The accepted story has always been that Shelton, the *Times* critic, brought Grossman to Gerde's to see Dylan a couple of nights after his opening, after the Shelton rave review. Terri Van Ronk still believes she booked Dylan into Gerde's for that second gig,. but Mike Porco says it was Grossman who persuaded him to hire Dylan again. And, from Izzy Young's scrapbook, dated October 13:

"After listening to (another folk singer) for two nights last week I'm beginning to feel he won't make it. Grossman thinks that Bob Dylan has a much better chance of making it. I just made an arrangement with Bob Dylan to do a concert early in November. Al Grossman spurred me to do it."

Adds Young, nine years later: "We didn't know at the time that Grossman was managing him. Everybody thought Dylan was a free agent, but Grossman had his fingers on him much earlier than that. He would come in here and promote Dylan with me, friend to friend, and he would promote him with ten other guys, and all of us would be promoting Dylan—for Al Grossman. He was using us. Nobody knew he was managing Dylan until long after the record came out. I once asked Dylan if I could manage him and he said, 'Well, I'll see. But I think I want to be alone.' And actually he was being managed by Grossman. That's how Grossman always did things."

Grossman's secrecy is understandable. Bob had not yet signed, and Grossman was not about to let anyone know he was anxious to get Bob as a client. It was smart business, but what grates people today is that he was working as a manager and pretending to be something else again.

Apparently Dylan didn't sign with Grossman immediately because of his own suspicious nature, that "paranoia" again. He researched Grossman as thoroughly as possible. He asked John Hammond's advice and Hammond remembers: "I said I knew Albert, we had worked together on the board of the Newport Folk Festival, and I told Bob I could work with Albert. 'He's not the grooviest guy around but if you want to sign with him, go ahead.' " Bob asked the manager of another very big folk act what he thought of Grossman and was told, "He's the most effective guy you can find. But you'd better sign a two-year contract, if possible, instead of the standard seven-year contract, just in case it doesn't work out."

He went up to Grossman's office a couple of weeks after Shelton's review and signed a contract—for seven years. Terri Van Ronk: "I was up in New England trying to get work for Bobby and Dave at the folk clubs, and there wasn't anything doing. When I got back I was told Bobby had signed with Grossman. I was angry, and I didn't see Bobby for a while. But it was a very intelligent thing for Bobby to do. My managing Bobby was kind of a joke; there wasn't that much managing for anybody to do in those days, and Grossman was one of the few real managers around."

Suze continued to turn aside Dylan's pleas to live with him. At the Thanksgiving dinner at the Smiths, Bob mentioned that he was going to take a trip out West, to Cleveland and Minneapolis, possibly get a couple of club dates.

"Suze, are you going with him?" Mrs. Smith asked.

"I'd like to," Suze replied. "But my mother says I may as well marry him if I'm going to do that."

"I agree," Mrs. Smith said. "What are you waiting for? If you love someone . . . he wants to marry you . . . he's asked you . . . if you love him, then you marry him."

"I'm too young, I think. I want to grow up a bit." Suze paused for a moment, thinking, and then it poured out of her: "I want to paint, I want to try it, seriously. I don't know if Bob and I would be good for each other. It's so hard to talk to him, in many ways. Sometimes he doesn't talk. He has to be drinking to open up. I think he may need too much from a woman, someone to take care of him and all of that. I don't know if I can do it."

Dylan returned to Minneapolis in mid-December, and Suze remained in New York. His Dinkytown friends were surprised at the further changes in him since his last visit the previous May. One of those who had always been closest to him recalls: "When he came back that December, right after the first album was cut, we sat and talked and we had a conversation about this character he was creating. He was very explicit about creating a character. He talked about how he was styling the language into a certain image that he was acting back there in New York, building a character that would sell. Those are the words he used, 'building a character that will sell.' This was something so far from the Bobby of a year before that I was truly surprised by it. He had always been an actor but had never been aware of himself as an actor." (About that "character that will sell," Dylan on reading it commented: "Absolute trash. I was never into that thing about building a saleable character. It was never my trip, whatsoever. All the changes I was going through, that was never one of them.")

John Koerner: "It was obvious he had grown. He was friendly and all that, but it was obvious he was into something stronger than we got into. You could see it, something forceful, something coming off."

Dylan played a great deal around Dinkytown. One night at the Whittakers he sat and played for hours and Tony Glover, who had taught him some harmonica work when both were playing The Scholar and other coffee houses, taped a good many of his songs. Dylan gave copies to several friends, and the tapes are now in circulation, underground, prized by serious Dylan collectors. There are twenty-six songs on the tape, his basic Gerde's repertoire, among them *Baby Please Don't Go, Hard Times in New York Town* (how mean and dirty the big city is), *Dink's Blues,* several of the Woody Guthrie VD songs written for the government, *Hezekiah Jones,* and *East Orange, New Jersey.* There is a long shaggy dog story about a folk club where everyone plays chess. Dylan is paid off in chess pieces, takes his king and queen to a bar, orders a beer and gets a couple of pawns in change; the routine was borrowed from Lee Hayes of the Weavers, and Dylan proves he would have been a flop as a standup comedian.

Bob Dylan, to a Dinkytown friend: "Wait'll you hear my album. Everybody at Columbia is just flipped about it. John Hammond, he's the big producer, you know. Well hey, he says I'm gonna be bigger than Presley. Bigger than *Presley!*"

When he returned from Dinkytown he finally convinced Suze to move into the West Fourth Street apartment with him. He was way up high with happiness; about Suze and about his career. The album was going to be released soon. And people were knocking on his door. He was asked to sing at the Blue Angel, a plush uptown room, but turned it down because he felt it was too posh and unreal for him and his material. And the big businessmen were becoming interested in him, particularly the Music Corporation of America, then a talent agency. One of the executives at MCA heard an advance copy of Dylan's first album and called John Hammond to set up an appointment with Dylan. "I've got two possible things for him," the executive said. "I want him to audition for the Ed Sullivan Show, and I want to see if he can play Holden Caulfield. We own the rights to *Catcher in the Rye* and we think maybe we finally found Holden Caufield in your boy."

Dylan went up to the CBS TV studios, protesting all the way. "I don't like to push my music on anyone." He was shown to a studio, got up on a stage in a huge room and, while a half-dozen men in dark Madison Avenue suits sat and listened, he went through several of the numbers on his first album, *Pretty Peggy-O, Man of Constant Sorrow,* and *Song to Woody* among them. The executive types didn't know what to make of him.

"Sure different," one of them said. The others agreed, completely noncommittal in front of Dylan. As he left with the MCA agent, he asked what had been going on in there. "They said they never heard anyone like you before," the agent replied. "They need time to decide what you are."

"They heard me, didn't they? They either like me or they don't."

"It's not that easy," the MCA man said. "You're far out, but they have to decide whether you're far out enough to sell."

"I guess they think I'm cute and funny," Dylan snapped, and he went back to the Village and described his experience to everyone he met. Later, over a glass of wine, Dylan told a friend, "I'm not going up there again."

"They'll call you," the friend said. "Just wait."

"Maybe so," Dylan replied. "But they ain't telling me what to sing."

The Holden Caulfield idea fell through, and the men from the Sullivan show wouldn't call Dylan for another year, and when they did, they would indeed try to tell him what to sing.

Bob Johnson, one of Dylan's friends from the University of Minnesota, came to town during Christmas recess. Months before, Johnson had spent a week drinking with Dylan in Village bars, bouncing around, living wherever Dylan happened to be living at the time— mostly in the crash pad on East Fifth Street. Then Dylan had been

warm, open, happy to see him, even taking him to Greystone to visit
Guthrie. But now, at Christmas, he had changed a great deal and
Johnson felt he wasn't welcome at all. "About the only thing I can
remember," Johnson says, "is that Dylan wasn't around much, and
Kevin was saying, 'Now that he's cut a record he's too big for us.'"
Krown recalls: "He started to grow very aloof after Grossman got
him."

The album was released at the end of February, which was considered an extraordinarily short time for recording and releasing an
album, especially by an unknown artist. It's clear that while some of
the music men at Columbia felt they had something special in Bob
Dylan, the businessmen were less than enthusiastic. *Bob Dylan*
didn't fully mirror what Dylan himself was up to because he was still
moving so fast. The material on the album was already something out
of his past even as he was laying it down. The only originals were
Song to Woody and *Talkin' New York;* the rest was an uneven assortment of songs that he had been doing for a long time. Much of it has
that special Dylan charm, distinctively Dylan interpretations, but the
unique stage charisma that added so much to Dylan's singing doesn't
come through on a record. *Bob Dylan* didn't light up the skies; it sold
only five thousand copies the first year, just enough to break even for
Columbia. (It has sold more than 200,000 copies through the end of
1970.) The enthusiasm at Columbia was so soggy, in fact, that some
didn't want to release it at first. It is said in the industry that Columbia didn't know what it had in Bob Dylan. One executive thought
Bob was a far-out comic and should try some laundered Lenny Bruce
routines. Another thought he was a harmonica player who should be
stuck on some country or bluegrass records. A third executive, according to industry scuttlebutt, was spending many of his working
hours trying to undercut Hammond's power in the organization, and
he tagged Bob Dylan with a label: "Hammond's Folly." Some time
before Dylan was scheduled to cut his second album, one of the
executives called Hammond and said: "John, I think we're going to
have to drop Bob Dylan." Hammond replied: "Over my dead body."
Hammond didn't have to offer up his body, however, because he was
relatively unassailable: he had the reputation of knowing his music
—Columbia's strength in its jazz catalogue is attributable to Hammond—and he was the man who had originally brought Goddard
Lieberson to Columbia, and Leiberson was now the firm's president.
There was another card in Hammond's full-house hand. "Johnny
Cash was one of Dylan's big boosters at Columbia," Hammond says.
"Way back there in '62, whenever Dylan was in the studio or playing

in town, Cash would come around. They hung around together back then. Johnny dug me because I brought Seeger to the company, and I brought Dylan to the company, and he was behind me all the way. Cash was behind Dylan every which way, everybody in the company knew it. Cash made it known he thought Dylan was a giant. There's no higher recommendation possible." Dylan's contract was not dropped..

1962: *Blowin' In the Wind*

EVERYTHING THAT HAD been fermenting in Bob Dylan suddenly bubbled over into a series of "protest" or "topical" songs that he wrote at this time. The songs were remarkable not because they pointed the finger at the ills of our society; minstrels had been doing that since the first dragon ate the first knight. Dylan's songs reached beyond political sloganeering; many of them were touched with poetry. "He wrote songs that hadn't been written yet," Joan Baez said recently in discussing Dylan's early work. "There aren't very many good protest songs. They're usually overdone. The beauty of Bobby's stuff is its understatement. Anything that's brilliant is an understatement like that . . ."

Suze Rotolo is considered one of the most important influences on Dylan during this period. She had moved into the West Fourth Street apartment with him soon after his return from Minneapolis in mid-December, and she brought him the love and the anchor he needed. She brought him other things besides, heightening his growing awareness of the poetry of Rimbaud, Villiers, Villon, Robert Graves, Yevtushenko and Brecht, especially Brecht. Suze also seems to have splashed something very flammable on the sparks of social consciousness that had always been in him. This was 1962, eight years after the Supreme Court ordered desegregation of schools, and schools were still black or white, and Negroes were growing increasingly more militant. The Congress of Racial Equality had sponsored the first of

112

the "freedom rides" the previous May, and by the end of that summer of 1961 hundreds of Negro and white college students, ministers and professors were in Mississippi jails for demanding equality on buses and in terminals. In dozens of communities, also, whites and blacks conducted sit-ins at lunch counters. In Albany, Georgia, the Reverend Martin Luther King, Jr., was arrested at the end of December, along with about seven hundred demonstrators from the Student Non-Violent Coordinating Committee and other civil rights groups.

Suze was working for CORE as a secretary and envelope stuffer. She spent many hours telling Bob about the realities of the black man's life as she saw it from her desk at CORE, where the phones rang day and night as field men called in to describe the latest segregationist brutalities. And so one of Dylan's first protest songs, *The Ballad of Emmett Till,* was written for CORE.

From the journals of Izzy Young: "February 1, 1962. Bob Dylan came in and said: 'Wrote a song the other night. *Ballad of Emmett Till.* After I wrote it someone said another song was written about him, but not like it. I think it's the best thing I've ever written. Only song I play with a capo. Stole the melody from Len Chandler, a song he wrote about a Colorado bus driver.' "

The song, written in the traditional ballad style, recounts the story of the fourteen-year-old Chicago black youth who was visiting his uncle in the Mississippi Delta during the summer of 1955 and made the mistake of whistling at a young white woman. Till was beaten, shot to death, and thrown into a river. The murderers went unpunished.

Dylan's concern was not with the civil rights movement alone, however. Some friends believe Suze's radical bent was broader than that, and that she passed it on to Dylan. Mrs. Smith: "I talked him out of singing for a socialist club before he met Suze, even though he would have made twenty dollars and could have used the money, because I was afraid he might be tarred with guilt by association. He was too young and too early in his career for that. And then Suze came along and she wanted him to go Pete Seeger's way. She wanted Bobby to be involved in civil rights and all the radical causes Seeger was involved in. Suze was very much with the cause, something developed from her own background and the memory of her father. She used to talk about him, he had been active politically, and this was a part of her being. She influenced Bobby considerably, that way. I was disturbed by it at the time, because I was afraid Bobby would be hurt taking a radical stance."

Suze denies being a major influence on Bob's political thinking. It was in the air, she says, all around, and everyone influenced him; everyone was involved, it was there, that's what those days were all about. She was, of course, only one of many who were caught up in the civil rights movement, in all radical movements. A number of folk singers, such as Len Chandler, Gil Turner and Peter LaFarge, were following Pete Seeger's lead and turning out topical songs. Even those who were not writing at the time—especially Dave Van Ronk—were urging Bob to forget the Guthrie-Thirties and get on with the business of the Sixties. "Guthrie's dying, and his generation is dead," someone remembers Van Ronk shouting at Dylan during one of their endless wine-soaked, back-biting sessions. "You can't keep rewriting the songs they wrote. Do your own songs. Their songs are for the history books. You're just going to be a history book writer if you do those things. An anachronism."

Dylan already knew that, for in his eleven months in New York he had learned something about Woody Guthrie, and about himself. He told Nat Hentoff, for the *New Yorker* profile: "After I'd gotten to know him, I was going through some very bad changes, and I went to see Woody, like I'd go to somebody to confess to. But I couldn't confess to him. It was silly. I did go and talk with him—as much as he could talk—and the talking helped. But basically he wasn't able to help me at all. I finally realized that. So Woody was my last idol."

Dylan had romanticized Woody, as so many did and still do. But after he met Woody, and met people who knew him and had done some hard traveling with him, he realized that Woody for all his enormous talent, was no more than human. He was a man of enormous ego, who didn't much care to hear any but his own songs or his own conversation. He was somewhat irresponsible: he'd start drinking heavily before a concert or a hoot, even though he knew he'd get so dead drunk that he couldn't get up on a stage, and when he was singing with the Almanacs, someone was assigned to keep him out of bars and away from his drinking companions. His irresponsibility extended to his women, and children—practically every woman who has ever had contact with Woody has been deeply hurt by him, his closest friends will tell you, and he left progeny all across the country, some bearing his name and some not, pretty much ignoring them all except for the last, Marjorie Guthrie's children by him. Dylan learned all of this from Woody and those who loved Woody most deeply but had no romantic illusions about him.

Another interpretation is that Woody deliberately tried to destroy the romantic image Dylan had of him, "shattering even himself" as idol, as Dylan put it in "11 Outlined Epitaphs," the poems accompanying his third album. Years before, when Woody decided it was time to wean Jack Elliott from the same hero worship, he left Elliott somewhere in California and vanished. Eventually, he sent a card back to Elliott, saying simply: "Dear Jack: Fuck you. Woody." Elliott went off on his own, devastated, and not until years later did he realize that Woody had done it *for* him. Perhaps Woody was also weaning Bob Dylan.

Woody taught him, Bob has written, that even men who are idols have reasons for what they've done. There was a paradox about Guthrie. Despite the authenticity of Woody Guthrie, despite the very real social consciousness of the man that flowed into his thousand songs, Guthrie to some extent became, like so many others who were lionized, a part of his own myth. Not commercial, not like the slick Hit Parade music men he held in contempt. But the *simpleness,* that was part myth. Guthrie was a very complex man, a man with "a devouring curiosity," Pete Seeger had called him. He read everything he could, the Bible, Rabelais, Walt Whitman, Will Rogers, left wing tracts. He was totally political, as deeply involved in radical thought as any man around. He had a huge intellect: Albert Einstein is said to have delighted in talking to him down at Princeton, Franklin Delano Roosevelt sat with him in bull sessions in the White House and, later, Eleanor Roosevelt often had him up to Hyde Park. Guthrie's simpleness was, in part, a pose; he was a simple, noncommercial, authentic folk primitive because it was expected of him, and because he was most comfortable in that role. Dylan grasped the reality of Guthrie. About a year after meeting Woody for the first time, the following was taped in an interview between Dylan and a Columbia Records public relations man:

Dylan: "Woody was a *glorified* folk singer. Woody was a man that went back—don't print this on the record. . . . But, but, but, Woody was a man who dwelled on simpleness because he was getting attention for it . . ."

Dylan used his *Song to Woody* on his first album, but later he would get almost defensive about the song. The Smiths have several tapes of Dylan sitting around playing and talking, and at one point Mrs. Smith asks: "Bobby, would you do the Woody Guthrie one for us?" Dylan can be heard handling another copy of the song he wrote out for them, crinkling it, and then he says: "I left out a whole verse here I never sing. There's a verse here I never sing." He reads it, obviously stalling, and after a while he begins to pick out a traditional tune, then fools around tuning up his guitar, and finally begins playing a topical song he had just written, *Ballad of Donald White.*

Later, in the Studs Terkel interview in Chicago in May, 1963,

Dylan refuses to sing the song. He said: "I never sing it. I only sing it to Woody . . ."

Terkel asks: "You couldn't sing that now?" and Dylan replies "No," and goes on to another song, one of seven on the Terkel tape. Dylan would continue to pay homage to Guthrie as an influence, but he would no longer make it sound like idolization. (At the same time, his public statements about Woody as his "last idol" only contributed that much more to the mystique-veil he always wrapped himself in.) In any case, Dylan broke out of Guthrie's very powerful grip, something that Jack Elliott admittedly was unable to do.

Elliott: "Here I imitated Woody and learned from him and picked like him and I got hooked on the Ramblin' Jack Elliott image, and just never imagined that somebody like Dylan could come along and learn from Woody and then turn around and write stuff for *today*. But Bobby was always very aggressive. He knew what he wanted, he had a goal and he shot for it. He was a well-disciplined person, as crazy as he seems. He was a fighter and he didn't forget what he was going for, even though he was like every other screwed up guy who usually ends up on the Bowery, a screwed up weirdo like we all were, drinking all that wine and stuff. He had a very strong drive, and he just went into those songs because his drive made him build it all up."

Another element in Dylan's development as protest writer was the creation of a forum. Pete Seeger had toured England in the fall of 1961 with his wife and youngest daughter, and everywhere he went he was struck by the fact that young folk-poets were writing songs about the things that troubled them, atomic annihilation or computer emasculation, or the nuclear submarines that the U.S. Navy had stationed in Scotland. Seeger was even presented with a new album filled with songs dealing with the housing problem in the British Isles, *Songs to Swing Landlords By*. When Pete returned he began talking aloud about the dearth of folk protest in the United States. He revived the idea of putting out a folk magazine that would be an outlet for topical songs that Pete felt certain were probably being written but were unable to break through Tin Pan Alley barriers. The idea had been presented about a year earlier by Pete and by Malvina Reynolds in the columns of *Sing Out!*, but it was dropped because it was felt there wouldn't be enough interest. But now, at the end of 1961, Sis Cunningham, who had been involved in folk since the early forites, when she worked with Pete and the Almanac Singers, decided the times were ripe for a topical song publication. She founded *Broadside*, a mimeographed four-pager scheduled to come out twice a month (more or less), with the help of Seeger and Gil Turner, a singer and writer and occasional MC at Gerde's. Turner

116

rounded up Village people, urging them to write those songs that were eating at them and get them printed in *Broadside*. He dragged young folk singers up to the *Broadside* offices, where a dozen or so would sit around and each would play his latest song. Phil Ochs was there fresh from the University of Ohio, where he had been studying journalism and found folk song; Turner, Paxton, Spoelstra, Chandler, La Farge, and Dylan, were also hard at work. Songs were literally pouring out of Dylan by the time the first *Broadside* was published, in February, 1962. He would read an item in the newspaper or see something on television, or hear a political argument, and dash off a song about it. Sue Zuckerman, who occasionally slept over in the apartment on Fourth Street with Suze and Bob, recalls watching television with them one night (February 12, 1962). The program was about crime and capital punishment—a film called "A Volcano Named White:" A 24-year-old black man was sitting in his prison cell in Texas talking about his life, its oppression, his cries for help that were ignored, until he finally killed someone and was now waiting to be executed. "Bobby just got up at one point," Miss Zuckerman says, "and he went off in the corner and started to write. He just started to write, while the show was still on, and the next thing I knew he had this song written, *Donald White.*"

Suze Rotolo: *"Donald White* was only partly a journalistic approach. Dylan was perceptive. He felt. He didn't read or clip the papers and refer to it later, as you would write a story, or as other songwriters might do it. With Dylan it was not that conscious journalistic approach. It was more poetical. It was all intuitive, on an emotional level. Not as a newspaper rewriteman, although it may have on occasion seemed that way. It was more than just writing, it was more like something flowing out of him."

Another close friend says: "He would get a conversation going with other people, then lean back and absorb, learn, and from that would evolve a song. He had this way of interviewing people, getting them to talk with him. He would say something and then remove himself from the conversation and listen, sponge it up. He would never really get involved in a conversation. Sponging, that's how he learned."

Around the time he wrote *Donald White* the newspapers were filled with debate over the wisdom of building fallout shelters, with the Governor of New York signing a bill encouraging such shelters (and some politicians were rushing to worm their way into shelter-building firms for a piece of the action). There were stories about people who had built such shelters and stocked them with food, and outfitted them with guns to shoot down their less far-sighted neighbors who were certain to come pounding to be let in when the bombs began to fall. Some clergymen even said they could condone killing under those circumstances. The folk crowd sat in the Gaslight and The Kettle of Fish next door, and laughed about the stupidity of it all. One night Dylan went back to Fourth Street and wrote an acerbic song to a gentle melody, *I Will Not Go Down Under the Ground,* in which a man answers Death's pitchmen who are preaching that the world will soon end in a hydrogen explosion. "I'm going out to enjoy the flowers and the mountains and the streams, to live, and if death comes I'll face it with my head held high and will not go slinking into some tomb." (Dylan never released his recorded version of the song but he can be heard harmonizing with Happy Traum on an album of *Broadside Ballads,* put out in 1963, and still available. The album also contains other songs Dylan wrote at this time, including *Blowin' In the Wind,* sung by the New World Singers. "Blind Boy Grunt" sings *John Brown,* about a boy who goes off to war with his mother cheering him, who discovers that the enemy's face looks just like his, and who returns with his own face shot away, handless, a brace helping him walk. He drops his medals in Mother's hand and staggers away. "Blind Boy" also sings *Only a Hobo* and *Talkin' Devil* on the album. "Blind Boy" is Dylan hiding his identity because he was under contract to Columbia.

1962: *Don't Think Twice, It's All Right*

IN APRIL, DYLAN wrote *Blowin' in the Wind,* which became an anthem of the civil rights activists and made Dylan the spiritual leader and troubador of the Movement. *Blowin' in the Wind* came to him during a long discussion in the Commons, a Village coffee house, about civil rights, and the failure of America to fulfill its promises. The conversation finally petered out and everyone was quietly staring into his beer. An idea flashed—"your silence betrays you." Dylan made some notes on a scrap of paper and, after finishing his drink, went home and began to write.

Later, Dylan would refuse to talk about his songs ("They speak for themselves.") even to his friends, but at this early stage, he was still open and very excited at the songs coming off his pen. He told some friends, "The idea came to me that you were betrayed by your silence. That all of us in America who didn't speak out were betrayed by our silence. Betrayed by the silence of the people in power. They refuse to look at what is happening. And the others, they ride the subways and read the *Times,* but they don't understand. They don't know. They don't even care, that's the worst of it."

Dylan later told me, "That's true, about *Blowin' in the Wind.* I say that to you because it means a lot to me, that song. It means a whole lot to me."

Dave Cohen remembers that the first thing he had ever heard Dylan play was *Blowin' in the Wind.* "He was writing it and I was strumming chords for him while he was getting it down," Cohen says, "and then we ran over to Gerde's to play it for Gil Turner." Terri Van Ronk recalls: "A day or so after he wrote it, he asked me to stop by and get the words, and either he or Suze wrote them out for me. He went around singing it for everybody, and everybody was knocked out by it."

Blowin' in the Wind was published in *Broadside #6,* at the end of May, and it slowly began to gain favor among folk singers, both professionals and the kids on the campus. It has a simple melody that doesn't intrude upon the metaphysical poetry of the lyrics. How many roads must a man walk down ... ? How many miles must a dove fly ... ? And, if Dylan's answer is vague, his questions are clear and sharp, and the song admirably fulfills Yeats' definition of *sincere* poetry: "It must have the perfections that escape analysis, the subtleties that have a new meaning every day, and it must have all this whether it be but a little song made out of a moment of dreamy indolence, or some great epic made out of the dreams of one poet and of a hundred generations whose hands were never weary of the sword." With *Blowin' in the Wind,* Dylan proved his ability to write folk poetry as meaningful and effective as Woody Guthrie's.

One of the folk singers around then says: "That was high drama, it really was. Here's this kid who was practically a freak, scruffy-looking and a twerp, and in less than one year on the professional folk scene he turns out something every bit as good as Guthrie's *This Land Is Your Land* or Seeger's *If I Had a Hammer.* I mean, it just boggled the mind. Pete Seeger was running around saying, 'I've never seen anything like it. The kid has to be a genius.' But the kid was more than a genius. He was a reincarnation of *all* the folk geniuses there ever were. It's spooky, really it is."

Dylan tried to explain *Blowin' in the Wind* a couple of months later, in remarks for *Sing Out!* in which he said:

"There ain't too much I can say about this song except that the answer is blowing in the wind. It ain't in no book or movie or T. V. show or discussion group. Man, hip people are telling me where the answer is but oh I won't believe that. I still say it's in the wind and just like a restless piece of paper it's got to come down some time ... But the only trouble is that no one picks up the answer when it comes down so not too many people get to see and know it ... and then it flies away again."

Dave Van Ronk to Bob Dylan: "Hey man, you're really getting into something with those songs. Welcome to the twentieth century."

The songs tumbled out of him, and practically every issue of *Broadside* had a new Dylan. Some of them came with strong line drawings by Suze. *Masters of War,* for example, in *Broadside #20,* has a drawing by Suze, a man with a Picasso sort of face, a knife in his right hand and a fork in his left, beginning to carve up the globe while a family looks on. A second drawing depicts a baby carriage on tank tracks, a rifle fastened to its side. *Masters of War* is about the men who profit from war, who build guns, and planes and bombs, who hide in their mansions while young men go off to die.

Although it would be another year before Dylan's name and his music would become widely known, the people around him were thunderstruck at what Bob was doing. He seemed able to turn out a dozen songs a day, on any topic, and most of them displayed more flashes of brilliance than any other songs being written by anyone else at the time.

Phil Ochs: "The first time I heard him sing his first few songs, at some party or at the *Broadside* offices, I thought, 'This guy is it. He's the best writer, the best singer, that anyone has ever heard.' And I wondered what the future had in store for him. He was just so extraordinary."

Joan Baez: "I remember vaguely being at a party and he had just written *God On Our Side,* and I was in that state of disbelief that anybody was turning out something like that."

Bob Dylan to Pete Seeger, during an interview for a local radio show:

"I don't sit around and write songs with the newspapers, like a lot of people do, spread newspapers all around and pick something out to write a song about. It's usually right there in my head before I start.

That's the way I write. But I don't even consider it writing songs. When I've written it I don't even consider that I wrote it when I got done. .... I just figure that I made it up or I got it some place. The song was there before I came along. I just sort of came and just sort of took it down with a pencil, but it was all there before I came around. That's the way I feel about it."

Meanwhile, Dylan plunged ahead wholeheartedly. He told Gil Turner: "I don't have to bullshit anybody like those guys up on Broadway that're always writing about 'I'm hot for you and you're hot for me—ooka dooka dicka dee.' There's other things in this world besides love and sex that're important too. People shouldn't turn their backs on them just because they ain't pretty to look at. How is the world ever going to get any better if we're afraid to look at these things?"

Later, when he moved away from protest and folk song, Dylan insisted he had used that sort of music mostly as a way to become more widely known. He told Nat Hentoff, for the *New Yorker* profile: "Some of that was jumping into the scene to be heard and a lot of it was because I didn't see anybody else doing that kind of thing." He put it even more strongly to close friends. Joan Baez remembers asking him what he was thinking when he wrote the protest songs, and Dylan said: "Hey, hey, news can sell, right? You know me. I knew people would buy that kind of shit, right? I never was into that stuff."

Dylan returned to Dinkytown again in March, 1962, carrying copies of his first album. He called Echo who recalls: "He brought me his first album and we started talking about his music. He told me he was in folk and I said, 'Folk? You mean that hillbilly garbage? What the hell are you doing that stuff for?' And he said, 'That's the coming thing. That's how I'm going to make it.'"

Bob Dylan, opportunist, doesn't ring true with those who were closest to him when he was writing and performing protest songs. John Hammond: "When he first came here he was thinking and talking about injustice, and about social problems. Bobby really wanted to change things. He was uptight about the whole setup in America, the alienation of kids from their parents, the false values. From my leftist point of view he was just superb, and it was real." Phil Ochs insists: "He definitely meant the protest. At one point he was definitely a left-winger, a radical, and he meant every word he wrote. He was just going on to bigger things when he started denying it, that's all." And Dave Van Ronk: "He was no opportunist. He really believed it all. I was there. He absorbed what was around him, believed it, but he didn't really understand it. He only absorbed the superficialities. It's entirely possible he fell into the *Broadside* bag knowing what those songs could do, but he believed. He meant it. Basically he still believes it, but he's in another bag now. He does happen to be a genius who is entitled to a certain amount of nonsense."

Van Ronk's assessment of Dylan's motives is probably closest to the truth. Dylan's main drive was to make it as an entertainer, but rock-and-roll was dead in this pre-Beatles era, and the only way to do it was alone, through folk. As Bob told one friend:

"I had just made up my mind very early that if there was anything you wanted, you really had to make an attempt to sacrifice everything, a lot of things. There was nothing I really wanted, you see, like money and things. I didn't want anything like that. I knew whatever I did had to be something creative, something that was *me* that did it, something I could do just for *me*. And I made up my mind not to have anything. I was about seventeen, eighteen, and I knew there was nothing I ever wanted, materially, and I just made it from there, from that feeling. But then I realized I couldn't make it with a group, there just wasn't anything doing for groups. I had to do it alone. So I decided to do it alone through the folk thing."

And he later told an interviewer: "I tried to make it in rock-and-roll when rock-and-roll was a piece of cream. Elvis had struck. Buddy Holly was dead. Little Richard was becoming a preacher. And Gene Vincent was leaving the country. I wrote the kind of stuff you write when you have no place to live and you're very wrapped up in the fire pump. I nearly killed myself with pity and agony. I saw the way doors close; the way doors that do not like you close. A door that does not like you needs no one to close it. I had to retreat."

Retreat, of course, was folk—and protest. And yet, simply because he never lost sight of his goal—to make it as Presley had done— doesn't mean he didn't have a social conscience. One of those friends who meant the most to Dylan in the early Village days says:

"I don't know if he was really believing the protest, or if he just knew it was the right thing to do at the time. Right in terms of his career. And in terms of what he thought about the world, about how things had to be changed. Probably both: he believed it very strongly, and at the same time he knew it could give his career a shot."

When Bob went to Dinkytown for a few days that March, he didn't completely endear himself to his old friends. They were thrilled at his mounting success, but made slightly uncomfortable by futher evidence of his arrogance. At one party someone asked him to play and Dylan snapped: "I get paid for playing, and I ain't about to play for free. You know what I'd get paid if I was doing this in New York?" (Actually, he wasn't making very much—Columbia did not give him an advance, and he made only $180 for the two weeks at Gerde's.) Eventually he did play, but the thing was rather sticky. He also hurt Echo, who describes how he played with her emotions:

"After he gave me the album and we talked a while out on the street in front of where I was working, he asked me to go to a party with him. I told him I didn't know if I could make it—he had always been talking about his wild parties, where girls didn't wear blouses, and free love and all of that, and I didn't dig that scene. But later I decided I'd go. I called him and told him I was coming and he seemed all shook up. Maybe he was afraid of getting involved with me. I didn't have any bad intentions. He was now a friend, not a sweetheart, and I just wanted to go and see him. I knew he was going to play and everybody was happy for him, and I wanted to see him. The party was at David Whittaker's place. I was standing in the kitchen talking to some guy and Bob came in. 'I want you to come and live in New York,' he said. I said, 'What will I do in New York? And besides, you're supposed to be in love with Joan Baez, that's what we all hear back here.' I was so upset and so mad because he was being cruel, and I just ran down the stairs and he yelled from the top of the stairs, 'Wait, where ya going?' and I walked all the way home."

A Dinkytown friend who was at the party recalls: "Bob told her to come to New York, but he was just teasing. I remember him asking later, 'What am I going to do? I think she really wants to go with me.' "

The rumors about Dylan and Baez were nothing more than rumors at that point. They were seen together occasionally, but they were simply a couple of professionals with music in common. Dylan, in fact, was still telling people he couldn't stand Baez—and some felt he was jealous of the heights she had attained. He later wrote on her album, *In Concert/Part 2*, that when he got to New York he believed that "the only beauty's ugly" and that people who told him about Joan's special beauty didn't reach him, Joan's voice and charm didn't get through his "fence of deafness." It wasn't until much later, he writes, that the fences fell and he could love her. Bob never used that word, "love," but it sings from every line.

But at this time, in 1962, he was pretty much avoiding contact with Joan Baez. Still the rumors were strong, and once in a while Joan would get annoyed and do something outrageous to provoke the gossip-mongers. One night she walked into Gerde's with Bob. All heads turned and everyone buzzed. Joan went into the lady's room, shoved a T-shirt under her dress, and wandered around the club, looking pregnant.

But Bob was totally caught up in Suze. "They lived a kind of wasted life," a friend recalls, "like everybody else, sitting around and rapping with people, very poor." They would play poker a lot, with the Van Ronks and others, penny ante. Bob would give Suze five cents, for he had very little money, and if she lost it she was out of the game. And if he lost the twenty cents he allowed himself, he dropped out. But whenever he had a solid hand he would turn to Suze and say, "Give me three cents, I've got a winner."

The conflict between Suze and Bob grew deeper in their first months of living together. She was making illustrations for some of his *Broadside* songs, and painting, and had gotten Bob to begin to paint. But she was feeling more submerged every day. "He won't let me do anything," she told one friend. "He just wants me to hang around with him all the time. I had to stop working now that he's making some money, and he doesn't want me to do anything for myself. I have to be myself, too, but he can't understand that."

Suze's mother had been married, to a professor from a college in New Jersey, and they were again making plans to spend the summer in Italy. Suze wanted very much to go, but she also did not want to leave Bob. Dylan kept telling her that it was all a plot on her mother's part to break them up. Most of their friends felt her mother was trying "the classic breaking up of a kid romance," as one of them put it. That's what Dylan went around telling everyone. However, Carla and Sue Zuckerman and a couple of others, who were Suze's confidantes insist that Suze made her own decision, based primarily on the fear she had expressed while Bob was cutting his first album. Dylan, she felt, loved her only in relation to his own ego and that he would keep her down until she became nothing more than a lovely, ego-less musician's chick.

Terri Van Ronk: "Suze didn't know what to do. She ran around for a month asking whether she should go. I gave her some advice that just about ended my friendship with Bob. I told her that if she went she shouldn't expect Bob to wait the summer for her, and if she didn't go she might completely regret it. I told her to make up her own mind, instead of telling her to stay with Bob the way Bob would have wanted me, and we had a falling out."

They sailed on June 8—Suze, her mother and her stepfather. The trip took eight days and as soon as Suze settled in Perugia, she got a transatlantic call from Bob, urging her to turn around and come home. She cried for hours, she told a friend, and she was tempted to tell her mother she was going home. But she stayed. Bob wrote her many letters, most of them repeating what he said, in effect, in one of the first: "We wasted a lot of time playing cards at the Van Ronks, sitting around bullshitting with a lot of people. Come on home and let's get to know each other, dig each other." But Suze stayed, and she fell in love with Italy. "She got a taste of freedom," one friend says. "When she was with Bob she found she 'was withdrawing into herself, that all the openness was turning sour and inward. He sapped all the life out of her. She was unable to work or paint. And they wouldn't talk or communicate when they were together, just watch TV a lot, or Suze would sit there and listen to Dylan play. The whole thing was pretty bad. Both of them had better things to do with their lives than be heavies in a melodrama. But that's what it was."

There was another viewpoint about Suze leaving Bob. Mrs. Smith expressed it this way: "Suze took herself off to Italy knowing he would never be cruel enough to pay her back for leaving him, for walking out on him just when he was beginning to find his own way. Grossman had him, it was happening, it was just a question of time, and she hit him with the kind of ego destruction that no one can take."

Dylan spent the following months grieving over Suze. Some friends felt he was acting, and overdoing the melodrama. Others believed it was sincere. All are agreed that Dylan seemed to be falling apart as the summer wore on. Mikki Isaacson's recollections are typical of all Dylan's friends:

"He was totally down after Suze left. Kind of lost. He wouldn't come near the rest of us in the beginning. You'd meet him on the street and he wouldn't respond. Physically, things began to happen to him. He didn't eat and he was neglecting himself. He got scruffier looking—back in the beginning, when he looked scruffy, he was at least clean. He showered a couple of times a day. But after Suze left he began to really look dirty. He started drinking, too, after she left. And there were all kinds of rumors about drugs, but he wouldn't talk to us about it. We were all trying our best to keep Bobby together. I know he was falling apart at the seams. His performances began to fall below his usual stuff. He'd get up on hoot nights at Gerde's and he would be bad. He was so depressed we were afraid he was going to do something to himself. People would stop each other and say, 'Have you seen Bobby? What's happening to Bobby?' "

Suze wrote Bob often at first, but then began to taper off. She had been scheduled to return around Labor Day, but she stayed on through October and November. And, Miss Isaacson recalls: "Bobby would be running around the Village looking lost and skinnier, a real mess. When he talked about Suze, he'd always say: 'I don't think she's ever coming back. How can I get her to come home?' And there was a great deal of effort on everybody's part to encourage Bob to hope for the best. We kept telling him that Suze hadn't left for good, that she'd come back and love him as she always had."

Mrs. Smith recalls: "One time he came for dinner when Suze was still in Italy. We had been hearing rumors of drugs and when he didn't take a drink I suspected maybe the rumors were more than rumors. He talked about Suze and I said, 'Well, Bobby, you have to let her find her way a little bit,' and he just grunted. And when he left, I stopped him at the head of the stairs and said, 'I've been hearing rumors, and I don't like the rumors. If you're sick in any way, on drugs of any kind, I don't care what they are . . .' and he interrupted and said, 'I'm not on drugs, believe me I'm not.'"

Bob Dylan, to a friend: "I gotta get away. People are recognizing me, they're stopping me on the street and asking me what I meant in *Blowin' in the Wind,* and what's the true meaning in my other songs. They're driving me flaky. Gotta get out of here."

Bob Dylan, to an interviewer: "I wander around the city a lot, I take the ferry to Staten Island or I walk down by the river. Or maybe I'll sit around all day with a painter I know."

On August 9, Bob wandered over to the Supreme Court building in downtown Manhattan, where he legally changed his name to Bob Dylan. He wasn't about to permit his anguish over Suze to make him lose sight of his main goal: making it as a folk singer. The Columbia public relations factory had been going to work on Dylan. Billy James, a young PR man who struck it off well with Bob, got Seventeen Magazine to send a writer around to interview Bob that Spring. Result: a big spread in the September issue. Several other magazines showed an interest in Dylan. John Hammond sent him up to see Lou Levy, head of Leeds Music publishing, and Dylan was given a five hundred-dollar advance to sign with a Leeds' subsidiary, Duchess Music. Duchess published most of his early songs, including *Song to Woody* and *Talkin' New York.* And then, industry scuttlebutt has it, Artie Mogull heard *Blowin' in the Wind* and wanted to get him for Warner Brothers, which was then buying the Witmark Music publishing firm. He talked to Dylan and convinced him he'd be better off with a large firm that had its own recording company. Dylan agreed and, the story goes, Mogull gave him a thousand dollars to buy back his Leeds contract. The head of Leeds was out of town. Dylan talked to someone else in authority, and the deal was consummated.

While Suze was gone the songs continued to flow from him. His finest early work was written in those months in 1962 after Suze left. Mikki Isaacson recalls: "We were driving up to my parents' house that summer—Dylan, John Herald, and Jean Redpath. On the way up I saw through the rear-view mirror what Dylan was doing in the back seat. He had a spiral notebook, a small steno book, and he must have had four different songs going at once. He would write a line in one and flip a couple of pages back and write a line in another one. A word here and a line there, just writing away."

At least a dozen songs were written for Suze in this period. "This was a strange time," Dylan told me. There are references to Suze, to the girl he thinks he has lost, in *Down the Highway*, a travelin' blues song, and in *Don't Think Twice, It's All Right*, where he tells his woman—she's "a child I'm told"—he gave her his heart and she wanted his soul, and that she wasted his "precious time." Dylan describes it: "It's not a love song, it's a statement to make me feel better." *Farewell* (never recorded by Dylan), and *Restless Farewell, Bob Dylan's Dream* about lost friendships; *Honey Just Allow Me One More Chance,* an exuberant adaptation of an old song Dylan said he had heard played by a Texas bluesman; *Tomorrow is a Long Time* ("He used to play that in his room all the time, the one about him wishing he could lie next to her again, nothing in the world is like her beauty, I remember him writing it and singing it," one friend says). There were more, and they seemed almost to be endless, the special brand of Dylan love song, written for Suze.

As has already been noted, Dylan did not sit around and grieve and write pretty ballads about love or raunchy blues about nasty women, but continued to work hard building a reputation in *Broadside* circles. He was too disciplined, too self-controlled, to permit grief to get in his way. During the seven months Suze was gone, and while he was turning out boy-girl songs in remarkable quantity, he was also writing the finest protest songs around. None of them would equal *Blowin' in the Wind,* but some would come close, and all would enlarge his image among the professionals and on the campuses. Two of his most effective songs were written within days of each other, at the beginning of October. James Meredith tried to break down the color barriers at the University of Mississippi. He was turned back several times, with Governor Ross Barnett personally barring him from the campus, and President John Kennedy called out the troops who got Meredith inside. Rioting broke out, and two men were killed, and Dylan wrote a bitter song, *Oxford Town*, about the man who couldn't get in the front door because of the "color of his skin."

At almost precisely the same time the nation was enmeshed in the Cuban missile crisis and marching along the edge of nuclear war. Dylan sat around one night at the end of September talking with friends about the very real possibility that it was all unwinding to a violent end, and he went to a friend's apartment and wrote *A Hard Rain's A-Gonna Fall.* "I wrote that at the bottom of the Village Gate, in Chip Monck's place," Dylan told me. "It was his apartment, a real cruddy basement apartment but it had wall-to-wall carpeting and the carpeting even ran up the walls. It was a great place. That's where I wrote *Hard Rain.*"

It is a song that is important on a number of levels. *Hard Rain* is stunning evidence of the maturation of a young artist, a divining rod that points the direction in which his writing would begin to move. And it is poetry. *Hard Rain* is filled with spare, sparkling images that evoke the terrors of national injustice and of international-insanity-diplomacy. Never mentioning nuclear war or fallout, the evils of segregation or man's inhumanity to his own kind, but forcing the listener to conjure with such terrors out of his own emotions.

Hard Rain impressed the professionals, much as *Blowin' in the Wind* had. Pete Seeger began singing it at his concerts, and less well-known singers had to include it in their song bags.

"Boy, you're really like the Woody of today," Jack Elliott told him one night in the Gaslight. Dylan took exception to that: "I've gone 'way far beyond Woody," he said. "Woody was good in his time, he served his purpose. But I've gone far beyond that."

Bob Dylan, on *Hard Rain:* "I wrote that when I didn't figure I'd have enough time left in life, didn't know how many other songs I could write, during the Cuban thing. I wanted to get the most down that I knew about into one song, the most that I possibly could, and I wrote it like that. Every line in that actually is a complete song, could be used as a whole song. It's worth a song, every single line. Because I was a little worried. . . . It's not atomic rain, though. Some people think that. It's just a hard rain, not the fallout rain, it isn't that at all. The hard rain that's gonna fall is in the last verse, where I say the 'pellets of poison are flooding us all,' I mean all the lies that people are told on their radios and in the newspapers, trying to take people's brains away, all the lies I consider poison."

From Izzy Young's notebooks: "December 3, 1962. Bob Dylan just ambled in to ask for mail and to tell me he just finished a group of new songs. He looks as he usually does. He said he just made a single for Columbia of *Mixed Up Confusion* and was disgusted after the third session and left. Doesn't know which of the three versions they'll use. Said he wrote the song on the way to the recording session."

John Hammond recalls: "Albert Grossman and John Court"—Grossman's associate—"insisted on coming up to all the sessions and

Court was trying to tell Bobby what to do and trying to tell me what to do and all the rest, and I ordered them out of the studio. They were saying, 'This isn't good, I don't want him to do this,' and I said, 'John if you don't like it you can leave.' And he did. Albert stayed around and Albert had the brilliant idea that Bobby ought to be recorded with a Dixieland band on *Mixed Up Confusion*. It was a disaster."

The single, Dylan's first, was released at the end of December but was quickly withdrawn from the market. It was a bluesy song, but rather a shocker for the times: Bob was accompanied by Dick Wellstood playing a bopping, Jerry Lee Lewis-style piano, Herb Lovell on a hard-driving drum, plus two guitars and a bass—a full rock and roll band. Not Dixieland, on the version released, but hard rock, brought up to date and fused with Bob's country-folk singing. "Bright country rock," is the way Dylan described it. The record, with *Corinna, Corinna* on the reverse side, was felt to be a mistake, not in keeping with Dylan's growing image as a protest writer and singer. Rock, after all, was a dirty word by this time, for much of the hard brilliance of early rock had turned to mush, had degenerated into mindlessness (The Beatles and Stones wouldn't transfuse the sickly pop scene for some time yet) and, with few exceptions, rock music was pre-teen pap.

Dylan was also taping some of his newest songs for his second album. During one of the sessions Hammond talked to Dylan about using backup musicians to flesh out his low-keyed readings of his songs. "Bobby, you should be recording in Nashville," Hammond said. That was before everyone in the industry was rushing to Nashville to take advantage of the superb studio musicians working there. One night, during a recording session, Don Law, head of Columbia's Nashville operation, was in the New York building. "Don, you have to come up and hear this Dylan kid," Hammond told him. "He's got to work with Nashville musicians. We don't have the kind of guys around here who can play for him. This isn't the right scene for Bob." Law went into the studio as Dylan was recording *Oxford Town*, listened to the lyrics for a while, then turned to Hammond and said, "My God, John, you can never do this kind of thing in Nashville. You're crazy." And he walked out of the studio.

One night at the end of December Dylan rushed into the Kettle of Fish, where a group of his friends were sitting at a back table. "Hey, I'm going to London," he shouted. "The BBC wants me to do a TV show. Gonna pay a thousand bucks." After they all congratuated him someone asked, "When are you leaving?" Dylan replied: "Right away. The show's middle of January, but I'm going over to find Suze in Italy."

He dropped by the Folklore Center and told Young: "The only reason I want to go to England is to look for Charles Dickens."

Bob went to Italy after the first of the year. He rushed to Perugia, but Suze had left for New York just a couple of days before. Dylan later told me: "I was in Italy with Odetta. Suze had gone back to the States and that's when I worked up the melodies of *Boots of Spanish Leather* and *Girl From the North Country.*"

Of *Spanish Leather*, Dylan said "This is girl leaves boy." The song is written in a dialogue, the girl who is sailing away asking whether she can send him anything when she gets across the sea, and the boy insisting he wants only her return, "unspoiled," asking that she comes back with her "sweet kiss." And then he gets a letter from her, written on the ship, in which she says she doesn't know when she's returning and her words make him feel that her "mind is roamin.*" And, he says, you can send me boots of Spanish leather.

Dylan had told friends that he had been carrying *Girl From the North Country* around in his head for a year or so and it suddenly came bursting out after he failed to locate Suze. This song about an earlier romance motivated by the loss of his present woman, is one of his loveliest songs of that period.

Dylan headed for London, to look up Dick Fariña. He and Carolyn Hester had separated and Fariña had run into Ric von Schmidt a few days before Dylan arrived, and when the three of them got together they settled into a couple of rooms in a hotel in the South Kensington district. They worked in a couple of clubs together and played a lot of music everywhere they went.

Von Schmidt hadn't seen Dylan for at least a year, and he now sensed a remarkable sort of change in him: "At this time Bob had the most incredible way of changing shape, changing size, changing looks. The whole time he was there he wore the same thing, his brown jacket, blue jeans and cap. And sometimes he would look big and muscular and the next day he'd look like a little gnome, and one day he'd be kind of handsome and virile and the following day he'd look like a 13-year-old child. It was really strange. I've seen people do this physical thing but I've never seen it so markedly apparent as on Bob during that period. You'd never know what he was going to look like.

"I think he was searching for an identity at that time. But I don't think it was conscious; if it was conscious it had nothing to do with attitudes. As I think back, it was physical. He physically looked different. He just seemed like Bob Dylan, but in a whole different version each time, wearing the same clothes but making incredible changes, like Plastic Man."

Dylan appeared in a TV drama on January 12 that was, by all critical standards, a bomb. Critics dismissed the drama outright, but at least one of them was kind to Dylan—"Bob Dylan as a hobo guitar player was interesting," the *Daily Mirror* man wrote, "although his type of singing could not be judged against this sorry-go-round."

For some reason Bob didn't tell von Schmidt and Fariña about the TV show; "I'll be damned, I didn't know that," Ric said when told about it years later. Dylan also neglected to tell them about another incident during his London trip, an encounter with poet Robert Graves. Says Jack Elliott, who heard the story from friends in London: "Rory McEwen took Bobby to see Graves. Bobby was very rude to Graves, from what I hear. He wanted to read his poetry to Graves, wanted to get his approval or something, possibly, and he came on a little too strong." Bob later told some of the Gerde's crowd: "Son of a bitch Graves was on a big ego trip. Couldn't dig anybody but himself. Old bastard won't listen to anybody younger than him." And he told Suze that Graves was an old guy, a little old man instead of the giant he had expected, and that Graves was more interested in his own head and didn't give a damn about Dylan.

Two days after his TV show Dylan, Fariña, von Schmidt and Ethan Signer, a member of the Original Charles River Valley Boys, went into a recording studio at Dobell's Jazz Record Shop in London and laid down fourteen songs. The album includes "Blind Boy Grunt" harmonizing with Fariña and von Schmidt on a couple of cuts.

After the recording session they went to a folk club and von Schmidt was treated to a rare insight into Dylan's ability to focus so completely upon himself that the outer world didn't exist. Von Schmidt tells the story this way:

"We went down to this club and everyone was juiced to begin with, and we thought the recording session was so great that we just carried that session to the club. Dick made us think we could just walk in like at the 47 and alternate with whoever was on stage, but when we got there this Israeli chick, with her boots and tambourine, said, 'Well, I've been hired for the night and you boys are not going to get on stage because this is my show.' But we kept at her and we went backstage and we said, 'Look, can we get on stage between your sets?' Somehow or other we were going to steal that stage. She looked at her watch and she said, 'You can have seven minutes.'

"Another guy whose name I can't remember had some very fine grass, and we had taken a bottle of gin from the recording session, and we were all drinking and smoking and getting outrageously high.

This poor Israeli chick, as soon as she got off the stage it was all over because there were so many of us and so little of her. In fact, there were more of us than there was an audience.

"We each went out and did a thing, and the chick realized there was no way to regain the stage and she gave up, and the final thing was Dylan. He had been smoking very heavily. I saw him several times do this: seem so wasted you had the feeling he would fall off the stage and wouldn't be able to regain it. This strange coordination of his, this playing back and forth between coordination and uncoordination. He had everyone amazed, those English people who are used to sitting and hearing someone sing *McPherson's Lament* and knowing all the words. And here was Dylan up on the stage and he wasn't even playing at first, he was just weaving around the apron of the stage making dope-remarks, saying, 'Hey, we're underwater,' and people saying, 'What? What? Doesn't look like underwater to me, mate.' And I thought, 'Oh my God something is going to happen to Bobby,' he was so out of control. I started sobering up, started to worry, thinking he should just shut up and play.

"There was a little stool almost on the very apron of the stage, and Bob would be playing with his guitar and talking dope remarks, and then he'd collapse right on the stool. Just like Chaplin. And somehow I started getting a connection between the ballet and Dylan. First it horrified me and then I realized this is one of the greatest things I've ever seen in my life. He was doing it. He had all these people buffaloed, doing this great thing, and if they hadn't been so confused they would have seen this was Chaplin reincarnated. He would get up and play a little bit—he did start to play and sing some standards and some of his own things—and then he'd fall and land right on the stool. He never missed that stool.

"And while this was going on the English audience got into a deeper state of shock, near total shock, because in came this guy in kilts, like he should have a dirk in his argyle socks. This was a guy who had started out at this very small club and had graduated from this club and was playing in a big bar in Trafalgar Square or something. It was his first night at Trafalgar Square and he had come back here to celebrate his triumph and sing with the Israeli chick, and the place had been taken over by these outrageous Americans. When he walked in everybody sucked in their breath; he was back from his triumph and here's this guy weaving around on *his* stage, singing, and nobody had the slightest idea what he was doing—this Chaplin ballet.

"Bobby was drunk, and stoned, and he was as close to out of control I've ever seen anyone, and always at the last minute he would pull it back. This is a difficult thing for any performer to do, especially when the audience is as hostile as this was, and not only hostile but no more than three feet away.

"The guy with the dirk was sitting there wanting to get on stage and fuming. He lit a cigarette with this big match that lit up the whole place, and he sat there smoking and looking at Dylan and he couldn't take it any more. He started talking to Dylan, putting him down, only about a foot away from him. And Dylan at first was pretending to ignore him, and after awhile Dylan really did ignore him totally. Dylan just went on talking and playing and weaving around and on and off the stool, doing this Chaplin dance, and this guy was smoking cigarettes that just disappeared in a single puff. And finally this guy realized that even though he had all the people there on his side, Dylan was refusing to say anything to him and the audience was growing impressed by this. And little by little the guy was disappearing, just shrinking down to nothing and finally he just ceased to exist. Dylan wouldn't admit he existed, so he no longer existed. And the last thing was he threw his cigarette on the floor in a shower of sparks and stalked out of the club, and Dylan went right on staggering around the stage.

"It was one of the most total wipeouts I have ever seen. I learned a little bit of what can happen to you if no one will let you exist. Here this guy was the love of the crowd and Dylan wouldn't let him exist, so he had no existence. It was stunning, one of the strangest and most beautiful evenings of music, performance and control I've ever seen."

1963: *Masters of War*

SUE ZUCKERMAN RAN into Bob in front of Gerde's in the first week in January, 1963. "She's back," Dylan cried, giggling with obvious pleasure. "Suze just got back."

"He was really strange," Miss Zuckerman recalls. "I hadn't seen him in a long time and he looked dilapidated, like he was falling apart. He'd lost that boyish glow. He changed a lot over those seven months, because of Suze. And he was out of his mind that she returned."

Suze also seemed to have changed, physically and emotionally. Her long hair had been cut, she dressed with a touch more sophistication. She seemed to be quieter, "like she was just observing the scene and trying to make decisions about what she was going to do, with her life and maybe a career," Carolyn Hester recalls.

Within days of her return Suze was back with Bob, in the West Fourth Street apartment, and almost immediately the old stresses returned to shatter their relationship. Suze complained to friends that Bob wouldn't permit her to lead any life of her own. She had taken a part-time job in a luncheonette, working a couple of hours a day simply to have something to do, and Bob said to her: "You don't need that. I got money now. I don't want you to work." She stopped working. She told other friends he objected when she signed up for a three night a week course at the School of Visual Arts.

Their friends could see Dylan "overpowering" Suze. He had the sort of personality that dominated everyone, no matter who else was around. Those who knew them well say that Bob ran Suze ragged with emotional binges. To everyone else, on the surface, he was the ultimate cool. But with Suze he would break down as a youngster might, shouting and screaming and crying—"crying constantly"—overwhelming her. He'd sit in a corner with her and whisper: "Hey, it's me and you against the world," and, one friend says: "He made her a vegetable. Her head was blown by all that, she couldn't help but get swallowed up in it." She was unable to work or paint, when Dylan was around. They barely talked—she told friends she couldn't understand why he was unable to communicate with her when his songs communicated with millions—and they'd spend much of their time watching an old TV set someone had given them. Only occasionally, when Dylan would leave for a few days to do a brief campus tour, would she be the old Suze, gay and busy and chatting with delight about everything around her. When he returned, "she became a zombie again."

He had been working on the second album, *The Freewheelin' Bob Dylan,* and he had a Columbia photographer take a picture of him and Suze, walking arm and arm along West Fourth Street. "The cover's the most important part of the album," he told friends as he passed around advance printings of the album jacket. It shook up everyone. "She was the envy of every folk singer's chick in the Village," Terri Van Ronk says. "It was a big ego trip, being on a record jacket." Some friends believe Dylan was deliberately trying to affect Suze's ego, "to give her some of the taste of what he was getting, and to make his hold on her a little tighter," one of them says. But the ploy wasn't enough to keep Suze from sensing the unreality of it all.

Sue Zuckerman: "At that point Suze got more into the scene, more and more people were sniffing around and Bob was more in demand. The whole scene, running around and going places and being recognized and being followed, was so strange. I got a taste of it one time. We went some place with Dylan and some guy was coming on strong to me, and I was wondering what was going on. It didn't occur to me. And then he said, 'Why don't we *all* go'—and I realized he was trying to get close to Dylan through me. I felt it was weird, so you can imagine how Suze must have felt, being in that kind of position all the time, in that whole scene.

"It tormented her that there was no peace, no privacy, and above all the paranoia—that she couldn't trust anyone, that every one except her old friends were trying to get to Dylan through her. A large part of it was justifiable paranoia, because it was really happening that way, and a large part was that Bob's paranoia was probably rubbing off on her."

The relationship was not as totally painful as friends picture it now. Bob and Suze were in love and there were moments of true tenderness and compassion between them. If Bob's obsession with music and the growing ego that came with an awareness of his strength often intruded, if Suze's fear of ego loss, of "getting sucked under," of being loved by Bob not for herself but for gratification of his own psyche-needs, cast a gloomy shadow over them both, their lives were not yet fully enveloped by it. Bob could demonstrate in touching ways how he felt for her. Mikki Isaacson recalls having dinner with them one night in their apartment. Suze baked a cake that Bob loved, but on this night it turned out badly. Bob dug into it with great enthusiasm anyway, and exclaimed: "Sue, that's great. Can I have another piece?"

But close friends did feel that Suze was, as one of them expressed it, "just a young chick wondering how to break off with a guy, or whether she actually wanted to break off with him at all."

Further, Suze's early fear that their relationship would suffer because Bob was certain to be famous was fast becoming reality; he was by now the most talked-about citybilly around. The Columbia publicity machine had laid the groundwork and Grossman was building upon it, shrewdly using other artists under his control to promote Dylan. Grossman also managed Odetta and Peter, Paul and Mary, and a number of other artists, and all of them began singing Dylan songs on campus tours and concert dates. Especially *Blowin' in the Wind;* Peter, Paul and Mary, smooth and commercial and enormously popular, sang it everywhere they went, and they went everywhere. They always introduced it with the line: "Now we'd like to sing a song written by the most important folk artist in America today, Bob Dylan." By late spring Bob Dylan was almost as well known on campuses and almost as idolized as Joan Baez. And on every campus, young and radical guitar players were struck by the power of his songs and, also, by the fragility of his person. He seemed almost a reincarnation of James Dean, a crushed young man whose pain seemed honest and deeply felt, was written all over his face and body. He projected hurt and fear, in his wounded eyes and anguished voice.

It was Dylan's work as a composer rather than performer, the startling imagery of his writing, that brought him his first wide audiences. For Dylan by now had transcended all his earlier influences and had taken the topical folk song beyond journalism—the topical song, at first, because that was the idiom in which he felt he had to work. Very deliberately, he was trying to bring poetry to what was usually only rhyme in the hands of most writers. He was conscious of himself as a poet. "The words to the songs aren't written out just for the paper," he would later tell an interviewer. "They're written so you can read it, you dig? If you take away whatever there is to the song—the beat, the melody—I could still recite it."

Dylan's method of composing is further evidence he considered himself a poet more than a songwriter: he sat and wrote a poem, and later found a tune, stole it, rewrote it, or composed one. And, he deliberately smoothed the transition from standard folk to his own songs by pinning his lyrics to a traditional framework. "I'm using the old melodies because they're there," Farina quoted Dylan in a magazine article. "I like the melodies. Besides, if they can hear the old melodies in my new songs, they'll accept the songs more. It ain't the melodies that're important, man, it's the words. I don't give a damn 'bout melodies."

The words, poetry—Dylan believed he could pull it off, writing poetry for a wide audience, for the people of the streets. Rimbaud had done it, and there was much of Rimbaud in Dylan and his contemporaries: Rimbaud was an arrogant, rebellious young man, questioning the authority of government, church, educators, a man very much like a cat on the Village streets or a Kerouac road bum, leading a scruffy life, existential before the word was coined, a heavy drinker and a heavy user of hashish and opium.

Dylan's idiomatic pungencies, his skill at narrating a dramatic story rather than revising a headline, his ability to mimic the rhythms of natural speech in his verse, took him beyond all his contemporaries, made him a poet of the people—especially the young, the disoriented, the idealists, the activists believing they could build a new world. "He was like a dramatic poet," says folk singer and composer Eric Andersen. "Like Shakespeare, he wrote about things that all sorts of people could relate to, without having to be superintelligent. He spoke in a common language, and he opened up the language of song quite a bit." Dylan used his guitar and harmonica—and, later, a rock band—to lend nuance to the poems, to end the divorce of music and poetry brought about by the printed page. In his liner notes, long letters, program notes, even a piece written for a folk magazine, *Hootenanny,* Dylan's writing was in the form of poetry.

His consciousness of the uses of language is clear in the way he handled the topical song. He seemed to recognize the vapidity of topical songs built on headlines, and he came up with something much more effective, dramatically and poetically; he took the specific and made it universal by finding its underlying meaning.

A comparison of the way Dylan and Phil Ochs each handled the murder of civil rights leader, Medgar Evers, points it up. Ochs, and everyone else writing the *Broadside* song, saw the killing as simply a story to be set to music. The tradition is old and honorable. Ochs, in *The Ballad of Medgar Evers,* tells how Evers, as a boy of fourteen in Mississippi, saw a friend hung because of his color. The lynching was branded on his brain. And then, quite simply, without melodrama, Ochs writes about the killer who waited in ambush and shot Evers down. And when they buried him, the nation gained a killer but lost a man. Dylan, however, handled it differently in *Only a Pawn in Their Game.* He immediately establishes that a bullet fired from ambush takes Evers' life, but from there he takes it several large steps forward. The man who fired that bullet is not to blame. He is only a pawn in the game, a game in which the politician preaches to the poor whites that they're better than blacks, and the politician rises to power on his demagoguery while the poor whites remain "on the caboose," at the bottom of the heap. Governors, sheriffs, soldiers, all the law enforcement crowd—and the preachers and educators— teach him that his white skin is a protection, teach him to walk in a mob and to lynch blacks. And they buried Evers "as a king" but when the man who fired the gun eventually dies, his epitaph will be that he was only a pawn in their game.

Bob Dylan, to a friend: "My songs speak for me. I write them in the confinement of my own mind. If I didn't write I think I'd go insane."

The Dylan mystique had already outgrown the Village scene by the time of his first major concert, at New York's prestigious Town Hall, on the night of April 12, 1963. Eric Andersen recalls: "I was up in college at the time and I had a friend who hitchhiked down to that concert. When he came back he said it was like the most incredible thing ever, to see somebody get up and do what you're feeling. It blew their minds.

"You see," Andersen adds, "this was the most together period in recent American history. Like the first Woodstock, happening way back then. The old left, the new left, college singers, everyone started sensing the vibes. People were sort of aware of what started to happen, students especially. The word began to spread and college kids from the Midwest realized something incredible was happening, like the age was filled with tremendous spirits. Dylan and those cats were singing about the Vietnam War when everybody else thought it was still a 'conflict.' That whole scene was generating a lot of vibes, and Dylan had the heaviest vibes of them all. Dylan was sowing the seeds of the decade."

Carl Oglesby, radical theoretician, writer, folk singer, song writer, is a former president of Students for a Democratic Society. SDS had come into being in 1962, born in response to the failures of the old left, the liberals, the unions, and other one-time radical groups at exactly the moment Dylan's songs were becoming known. By the time of the Town Hall concert a year later, SDS was in the vanguard of the Movement (a role it held until it was later splintered and destroyed by the Weatherman madness). Dylan played an inestimable part in the early years of the Movement. More than simply political activism, the Movement was a reflection of the new youth culture; a culture that embraced folksong, dancing, rock, drugs, a search for human values, a belief in the paramount importance of the individual and of human relationships, mysticism—cliched as "The Aquarian Age" or the "Woodstock Generation," but real beyond all cliches. All of these were part of politics, for the Movement defined politics as a kind of personal life force. "Within that context," Oglesby says, "Dylan's early songs appeared so promptly as to seem absolutely contemporary with the civil rights movement. There was no time lag. He wasn't a song writer who came into an established political mood, he seemed to be a part of it and his songs seemed informative to the Movement as the Movement seemed informative to the song writer. This cross-fertilization was absolutely critical in Dylan's relationship to the Movement and the Movement's relation-

ship to Dylan. He gave character to the sensibilities of the Movement."

The Town Hall concert was an enormous success. Shelton, in the
Times, once again extolled his virtues ("a folk musician who breaks
all the rules of song writing except those of having something to say
and saying it stunningly"), and Dylan was reviewed in *Billboard* and
other industry publications. He unveiled *Hollis Brown,* a song about
the oppression and death of a South Dakota farmer; *Who Killed
Davey Moore?,* which once again goes beyond the usual story-telling
song by asking who was responsible for the death of the fighter in the
ring, three weeks earlier: "Not me," says the referee, who could have
stopped the fight but was afraid of being booed by the crowd; "Not
us," answers the crowd that only wanted to see a fight; "Not me," say
the manager, the gambler, the sports writer, and the boxer who
knocked him out and killed him. And their denials condemn them
all as killers.

Dylan sang *Hard Rain, John Brown,* a dozen more. And then, to
a standing ovation, he recited a poem, "Last Thoughts on Woody
Guthrie," a long evocation of old memories, a youth searching for
himself by the railroad tracks, down the road, in fields and meadows,
on the banks of streams, in the "trash can alleys." And, he says,
somehow during that search so many years ago, Woody was his companion. However, he seemed to imply, that was years ago, behind
him now. And it was.

Bob had almost completed the second album, *The Freewheelin'
Bob Dylan,* when Grossman descended from his Park Avenue office
and pounced on Columbia executives with a series of demands that
added up to an attempt to get Dylan away from the record company.
Grossman had discovered, a few months earlier, that Dylan had
signed the Columbia contract when he was under age. Lawyers said
the contract was illegal. Grossman got Dylan to send a letter to
Columbia repudiating the contract, demanding the return of all
tapes and masters. But Columbia's attorneys, pointed out that Dylan
had been in the studio several times since turning twenty-one in
May, 1962, and the contract could not be broken. Now, as Dylan was
finishing up the album, Grossman and his associate, John Court,
charged into the studio.

John Hammond: "Relations with Grossman were not the most
pleasant because I got Bobby to repudiate that letter and to sign a
new contract, which made Grossman very uptight. I don't think
Grossman has ears and I don't think he has taste, even though I
respect him a lot for what he did with the Gate of Horn, giving Big

Bill Broonzy and people like that a shot. But Grossman came in the studio and got in the way."

Grossman couldn't break the contract but he began demanding that Dylan be taken away from Hammond. Grossman went to David Kapralik and said: "We don't want John Hammond to record us. We don't want anything to do with any producer at Columbia because you don't have a producer who understands Bob Dylan." At around the same time, Hammond says, he asked to be released as Dylan's producer and, he recalls, he suggested that Tom Wilson, a young black producer, be given a chance to see if he and Bob could work together. Grossman and Dylan went into Kapralik's office one afternoon, Dylan remaining silent, and Grossman softly demanding: "Take Hammond off Dylan." Kapralik replied: "Okay. I don't know why you're taking that position, but there's a young man just signed to the label I'd like Bob to meet and see if he can get together with him." Wilson was called into the office and, because he was black, neither Grossman nor Dylan could turn him down out of hand. Dylan and Wilson talked for a while, and the next day Grossman called Kapralik and said: "Wilson's okay."

Dylan returned to the studio immediately to tape several more songs. "I got enough for a full album, plus some," he said, "but I can't be sure what I want to use. A couple sound too folksy for me." He finished working in the third week in April and the album was scheduled to be rushed out at the end of May. Dylan was happening. Nat Hentoff had interviewed him for a *Playboy* article on the new phenomenon of the citybilly. *Time* wanted an interview. Other national publications expressed interest.

And there was the Ed Sullivan Show. Finally, after a year, they did call and they wanted Bob to appear—an enormous break, for Sullivan's show had one of the largest audiences in the country and, most important, no one was trying to dictate what he would sing. Bob chose *Talkin' John Birch Society Blues,* and when he sang it for Sullivan and Bob Precht, producer of the show, they were delighted with the song. It is a spoof about a man who joins the John Birch Society because he's learned there are Communists everywhere. He searches high and low, under his bed, in the stove, in his glove compartment, down the toilet bowl, but they always seem to get away. He figures maybe they're inside his TV set so he opens the back and gets a shock; the Reds caused it, he's sure, the hard-core kind. He changes his name to Sherlock Holmes and the first bit of detective work turns up the fact that there are *red* stripes in the American flag —"Oh, Betsy Ross." His investigations make him certain that Eisenhower, Roosevelt, Jefferson and Lincoln were all Russian spies, and

140

the only true American is George Lincoln Rockwell. He is certain Rockwell hates Commies because he picketed *Exodus*. After all his investigations have been completed, the Bircher is at home, investigating himself and hoping he doesn't discover anything he hadn't known.

During rehearsals on a Sunday afternoon in May, hours before the show, Dylan was told by Stowe Phelps, editor of program practices for the CBS network, that he could not sing the song because there was a possibility it libeled members of the Birch organization. "Are ya out of your fuckin' mind?" Dylan shouted, according to one who was there. "What the hell can they sue about?" Phelps said: "I'm sorry, Bob, but that's the order from the lawyers. They won't let us use it." Precht and Sullivan both apologized, asked Dylan to sing something else. "Bullshit," Dylan almost screamed. "I sing that or I sing nothing." And he stalked off. Sullivan later told TV columnist Bob Williams:

"We fought for the song. We pointed out that President Kennedy and his family are kidded constantly by TV comedians. Governor Rockefeller is also kidded, among others. But the John Birch Society —I said I couldn't understand why they were being given such protection. But the network turned us down. They told us they understood and sympathized with our viewpoint, but insisted they had previously handled the Birch Society and their lunatic behavior on network news programs and couldn't take the subject into entertainment. We told CBS, 'It's your network, but we want to state that the decision is wrong and the policy behind it is wrong.' "

The controversy spilled over to Columbia Records, a wholly-owned subsidiary of CBS. CBS's lawyers and officials discovered the song was scheduled to be included in Dylan's second album, and they ordered it taken off. Hammond, who was no longer producing Dylan but had been producer on *Talkin' John Birch,* Kapralik, and others in the company argued against the suppression on the grounds that the lawyers were being too conservative-pig headed and also that other Birch songs had been recorded, including a fairly recent one by the Kingston Trio. Their arguments were fruitless, and the song was deleted.

Dylan has been attacked in some quarters for permitting CBS to dictate what he could record. During the height of the controversy over the record he had been running around the Village telling everyone: "They'll kill that song over my dead body. That song's going in the album." But it was ripped out of the album, and that is pointed to now as the first Dylan *sellout.* A revolutionary hero simply doesn't permit the mass merchandisers to censor him; Dylan let himself be censored; hence, he sold out. Actually, Dylan could not have done much else, short of becoming an accountant and forgetting music. The Columbia contract gave the company the right to censor questionable or libelous material. Dylan was still relatively powerless, a kid with a lot of promise but no real influence. If the fuss over the Birch song had occurred in 1965, when Bob Dylan was a power, when his albums each grossed over a million dollars and his songs were being recorded by everyone, it is likely he could have won the argument. But not in 1963. His first album had been a flop. He had no track record as a moneymaker. If he was going to record for anyone he had to record for Columbia, on Columbia's terms. He had no choice but to accept the decision.

Dylan was almost totally crushed by it. Dave Cohen recalls: "He was very upset. He disappeared for three days or so. I remember Suze, Van Ronk and Terri asking if I'd seen him." In a short time, however, he was shrugging it off: "Who needs all the hassling? Just gonna keep writin' and all those cats can screw." And he smiled when someone pointed out: "Man, you got a lot of free publicity. A real underdog."

He made some last minute changes himself in the *Freewheelin'* album. He explained to a friend: "There's too many old-fashioned songs in there, stuff I tried to write like Woody. I'm goin' through changes. Need some more finger-pointin' songs in it, 'cause that's where my head's at right now."

At least two different *Freewheelin'* albums, possibly three, were released in small quantities by mistake before the final approved version was circulated. One of the albums, a few copies of which got out in the East, contained the forbidden *Birch Society Blues*, and *Let Me Die In My Footsteps* (a new title for *I Will Not Go Down Under the Ground*). There was also *Ramblin' Gamblin' Willie*, a delightful Dylan tale of a Southwest gambler and card shark who sires at least twenty-seven illegitimate children and supports every one of them with his gambling winnings. He finally gets a bullet in the head from an angry loser and, when he falls, reveals the dead man's hand—aces backed with eights—that Dylan told Izzy Young he believed in. The album also contained a song called *Solid Ground*. Another copy of the album, about three hundred of which were released in California, did not contain *Solid Ground*, but had in its place *Rocks and Gravel*, a Southern railroad work gang blues.

The album as eventually released did not contain those five songs. The Birch Society song was forced out and Dylan ruled out the other four. It's not clear why he deleted *I Will Not Go Down Under the Ground*, for it was one of his better topical songs and Terri Van Ronk recalls everyone asking him to record it because they thought it was so good. The other three were clearly Guthriesque and Dylan had gone beyond that stage. These songs were replaced by four others that Dylan cut in late April, with Tom Wilson as his producer: *Girl From the North Country*, *Bob Dylan's Dream*—songs about Suze, mostly, and Echo—and *Masters of War* and *Talking World War III Blues*. The last was nothing more than a partially worked out idea in Dylan's mind when he went into the studio, and which he improvised while he was being recorded.

One of the songs on the album, *Don't Think Twice, It's All Right* (written while Suze was gone, putting her down because she wasted his "precious time"), created some controversy in folk circles. The melody is based on a song called *Who'll Buy Your Chickens When I'm Gone* discovered by Paul Clayton during a folkloring expedition in Appalachia. Dylan made use of it. Legally, he had as much right to the tune as Clayton did, since it was in the public domain. But, most of their friends believed, Dylan had a moral obligation to give Clayton credit for it and make him a co-author, which would mean giving Clayton half the royalties. As one very close friend expressed it: "Everybody who knew about it felt that Bob was making enough money by the time the album started selling big that he could have given Clayton the tune royalties. We felt that if a guy is making the kind of money that Bob was making and he cops something from a friend—and one who is starving—the least he can do is quietly take care of him. Some of us told Bob how we felt, but we could never get a response out of him. He wouldn't talk about it. Clayton complained, but not to Bobby. He excused Bob, really excused him because he was obsessed by this little kid, Bob Dylan. Everybody else's attitude was that he should have sued the little bastard."

Of course, it is possible that Dylan was quietly taking care of him, for some months later Clayton accompanied Dylan on a cross-country tour, all expenses paid. It is not clear, however, whether he was given a salary. Clayton eventually did get "a substantial sum" from the music publisher, Dylan told me.

In late April, Dylan went to Chicago where he appeared at The Bear, a jazz, folk and gospel club at Ontario and Wabash. He did not get paid for the two nights at the club which had just opened and had no liquor license. Howard Alk, the owner, said he couldn't afford to pay Dylan, but Al Grossman booked him in anyway because he wanted Dylan to get exposure. The booking also gave Grossman a news peg on which to earn some promotion. A short time before, Grossman had gone up to WFMT, Chicago's class FM radio station, and talked about Dylan to Studs Terkel, the Chicago interviewer, writer and institution, and to Terkel's producer, Ray Nordstrand. Grossman had always been low key in pushing his artists, Nordstrand remembers, but he was excited the day he came in to talk about Dylan. "I've got some test pressings of a new kid," he told Nordstrand. "You've got to listen, you've got to hear him." Says Nordstrand: "That time it stood out because he came on strong. He knew he had something good." Dylan was booked for a Terkel interview.

It was broadcast live on May 1. Dylan repeated a number of the myths—that he met Woody in California when he was ten, that his life was spent "just out around the country, through the southlands, and in Mexico for a while." But through much of the interview Dylan appears to have been speaking frankly, trying to explain himself and his work. Later, as the fame and the paranoid reaction to fame, and the myth, began to grow, Dylan's interviews would become tortuously convoluted as he used the interview situation as part of a larger drama in which Bob Dylan was dramatist, director and leading man. But at this point he needed Terkel and Terkel's audience much more than they needed him, and except for an occasional runaway tale, he appears to have been quite open.

(For the record, Dylan sings seven songs on the Terkel tape, *Farewell, Hard Rain, Bob Dylan's Dream, Spanish Leather, John Brown, Davey Moore, Blowin' In the Wind.)*

From the Terkel interview:

Terkel: "Back in the Thirties there were young people feeling passionately, under one label or another, more or less pigeonholed. But what you stand for, you belong to nobody but yourself . . ."

Dylan: "I think maybe it's just the times, now's the time maybe you have to belong to yourself. I think maybe in 1930, from talking to Woody and Pete and other people I know, seems everything then was good and bad, and black and white and easy to see and . . . you only had one side or two. You stand on one side you know people are either for you or against you, with you or behind you, or whatever you had. Nowadays, don't know how it got that way, but now there's more than two sides, not black and white any more. . . .

"I seen so many people before I got to New York that are good people, that maybe are poor, maybe a little poorer, and there are other people telling them why they are poor and who made it so that they are poor, and to take their minds off that they are poor they have to pick out a scapegoat. . . .

"It seems like we're talking about pounding a nail in a board—there's a board there and all the nails are pounding in all over the place and every new person comes around to pound in a nail finds that there's less space. And I hope we haven't got to the end of the space yet."

Terkel: "You're looking for a fresh piece of wood?"

Dylan: "No, I'm content with the same old piece of wood. I'm just looking for a place to pound in the nail. Some of the people are the nails—being pounded."

Terkel: "What led you to the idea of writing these songs? Was it always with you?"

Dylan: "Yes, it's always been with me, but can't really say what led me to. . . . I can only say I look to do a lot of things. You know, I'm one of these people that thinks everybody has certain gifts when they're born. I got enough trouble trying to figure out just what it is. I figured first it was . . . I used to play the guitar when I was ten, you know, so I figured maybe my thing was playing the guitar, figured that was my little gift. Like somebody can make a cake, somebody else can saw a tree down, other people write. Nobody's really got the right to say that any one of these gifts are any better than any other body's, you know, 'cause you get them, that's the way they're distributed out and everybody gets the same thing. And I ain't saying that this is exactly what my gift is, maybe I got a better gift, but as of right now I ain't found it yet. I ain't even callin' it a gift, that's only my way of tryin' to explain something that's very hard to explain." (Suppressing a laugh.) ". . . Like music, my writing and that, is nothing. Like this guitar, I don't consider sacred. This guitar could bust and break, it's pretty old now, I could still get another one. It's a tool, for me, that's all it is, it's just my tool. It's like anybody else has a tool, some people saw the tree down or some people go spit tacks. I go to saw the tree down, I cut myself on the saw. I spit tacks and I swallow the tacks. Sort of got this here tool, and that's all. I use it as a tool. My life is the street where I walk, that's my life. Music, guitar, that's my tool."

Freewheelin' was released a couple of weeks after the Terkel interview and was an immediate success, selling at a steady ten thousand copies a month, bringing Dylan an income from the record of about $2,500 a month. Hentoff's *Playboy* article on folk was printed in the June issue, and gave Dylan a good deal of space. Hentoff called him "a penetratingly individual singer, as well as an expert harmonica whooper and guitarist the most vital of the younger citybillies." Hentoff was also working on the editors of the *New Yorker* for a profile on Dylan. *Time's* last issue in May gave him two columns and a photo. While the story—titled "Let Us Now Praise Little Men"—ridiculed him somewhat, it was as much praise as putdown, and any kid who was not yet fully aware of Dylan and what he was all about could probably figure out from the tone of the article that many adults found something disturbing about Dylan. For every adult who snickered at the *Time* putdown, it's possible at least one kid decided to listen for himself.

"It ain't nothin' just to walk around and sing, you have to step out a little, right?" Dylan had said to Fariña one morning when they were together in London the previous January. He added: "Take Joanie, man, she's still singing about Mary Hamilton. I mean, where's that at? She's walked around on picket lines, she's got all kinds of feeling, so why ain't she stepping out?"

Joan Baez was a young lady with the most stunningly pure voice in folk, a Renaissance smile and an Elizabethan-oriented repertoire. The only protest song she was doing at this time was *What Have They Done to the Rain?*, Malvina Reynolds' touching portrait of a boy standing alone in a nuclear-infected rainfall. Joan had only a little contact with Dylan up to this point and, although she continued to be "amazed" whenever she heard one of his songs, she didn't hear too many of them. Not the least reason was that for a time she wasn't listening to anything at all. "I'm really lazy," she explained in an interview. "I must have a block about it." She agrees that Dylan's criticism was valid; she was not singing protest songs because: "There weren't any. He wrote them. He wrote songs that hadn't been written yet." But she was not very aware of Dylan for more than a year after his reputation started mushrooming. And then Emanuel Greenhill, her manager, forced her to listen. He had been given an acetate of Dylan performing a dozen or so of his songs and had been asking Miss Baez to listen, but she kept putting him off. Finally, during a tour of the South just before *Freewheelin'* was released, he borrowed a phonograph, took it to her hotel room, and made her listen.

"Again, I was stricken by the genius of it all," she recalls.

Joan and Bob met again, a short time after this, at the Monterey Folk Festival, in May. His understated approach to his biting lyrics roused the audiences, and Miss Baez suddenly became aware that his songs provided depth and substance to the "desperate sort of thing" that had driven so many of the young to folk music. These songs could fill the gap between the traditional folk song she had been singing and the malaise that their generation felt.

Dylan affected Miss Baez in another way, as he had affected so many other women: "I wanted people to hear him," she recalls. "I think we liked each other, and I really loved him. It was a funny thing. I wanted to take care of him and have him sing. . . . I mean, brush his hair and brush his teeth and get him on stage. . . I wanted to have as many people hear him as possible."

After the Monterey Festival, Dylan went with Miss Baez to her home in Carmel and he lived there for several weeks. He wrote, he played dozens of his songs for her, and she began rehearsing them for use at her next scheduled concert dates. She asked Dylan to be her unannounced guest during her next concert tour later that summer, and Dylan agreed. Joan was providing him with a ready-made audience, the kind of young audience that could most appreciate Dylan and spread the word about him. Of all those promoting him, Joan was probably the most important and the most effective.

By his return to New York and to Suze in June, Peter, Paul and Mary had released a single of *Blowin' In the Wind* that immediately became an enormous hit. In the first two weeks it sold well over 300,000 copies, the fastest-selling single in Warner Brothers history, and it swept the country. Even black rhythm and blues stations in the South, which had ignored the trio in the past, were playing the record. The racial crisis in the South was deepening and folk song had become a vital morale booster for the Southern blacks and northern whites who joined them in the civil rights struggle. *Blowin' In the Wind* became the most sung "freedom song," north and south, black or white, and its author the most widely known protest singer. One weekend in July, Dylan went down to Greenwood, Mississippi, to perform at a concert with Pete Seeger, Josh White and Theo Bikel to assist the voter-registration drive there. And the appearance of this pained, almost-crushed, near-tragic figure gave his music authenticity. He remained in Greenwood and Jackson for several days, hanging around with black activists and students.

One thing must be stressed here: Dylan may have been an opportunist on occasion, but he did not lend his voice to the civil rights movement as part of a design to increase his popularity "He had no color denomination," Victoria Spivey has said. That was not quite accurate. If anything Dylan was probably highly aware of color, for the black music had touched him deeply back in Hibbing, and the black experience had touched his very strong feelings for the oppressed. Maybe he was simply romanticizing it all, as he had romanticized the hobo, but he was totally sincere about it. In Hibbing and in Minneapolis he went out of his way to meet any black man connected with music; in New York he developed close friendships with a number of black men and women. *Friends,* not symbols. The few I have been able to reach have demonstrated a lasting loyalty: "I won't give you an interview unless Bobby says it's okay," they said, years after any real contact with him.

1963: *The Times They Are A-Changin'*

THE NEWPORT FOLK Festival at the end of July, was literally Dylan's crowning moment. When the three days of traditional and protest music and folk workshops in the seaside Rhode Island resort were over, Dylan was being hailed as "the crown prince of folk music" by the mass media. It was a Dylan triumph, almost a Cecil B. DeMille ending to the tale of a poor orphan boy who makes it, complete with 46,000 extras playing the role of fans. But it was real, and it was all Dylan's.

Newport was also the scene of the transformation of Bob Dylan—hobo minstrel, into Bob Dylan—the eclectic poet-visionary-hero who was orchestrating a "youth revolution." He looked thinner and more undernourished, more ascetic and pained than ever before; his bones stuck out, and his skin—the color of sour milk—appeared to be stretched to the ripping point. He generated visions of a young man on a death trip: rebellious, living fast and dangerously; we'd better love him now and pay attention to him now because tomorrow he may be dead.

And they loved him. Most of the crowd at Newport were young high school and college students, a large percentage of them lugging their own guitars and banjos. Even before Dylan himself appeared, every time one of the performers mentioned his name, or sang one of his songs, the crowd cheered. "This song was written by the most important folk artist in America today," Peter Yarrow began, as he usually did, and the audience roared as Peter joined Paul and Mary to sing *Blowin' In the Wind*. This audience seemed to know the song and the artist, before the first note was struck.

When Dylan was finally introduced it was to a stunning ovation, second only to that given Joan Baez, and there were even some teenage squeals for him. Dylan sang *Playboys and Playgirls*, an acidic

148

poke at some American institutions, ranging from Hugh Hefner and his bunnies to fallout-shelter builders, lynch mobs, red-baiters and race-haters, and war mongers, who "ain't gonna run" his world any more. Pete Seeger joined him in the song, and called on the crowd to sing along with them. And when Dylan started to sing *Blowin' In the Wind,* Joan Baez was so moved by it that she joined him, her clear soprano flowing behind and above and around his harsh nasal voice, and all of those on stage rose from their chairs and celebrated his triumph with him: Seeger, Bikel, Peter, Paul and Mary, and the Freedom Singers, harmonizing Dylan's song. And the crowd roared and shouted for more and the performers were all so affected by the ovation that they improvised a striking finale to the performance, all of them locking hands, swaying from side to side, singing *We Shall Overcome.*

Near the very end of the weekend's last concert Joan Baez took the stage again. "Tonight is one of the most beautiful nights I've seen," she told the crowd. "I'm all up here with it. I feel sort of like exploding." She sang, and her voice never seemed so powerful, so moving, she gave what many felt was the finest performance of her career. And, for her third encore, she called out Bob Dylan and together they sang *With God on Our Side,* and Bob was indeed the reigning prince at the side of the folk queen.

For those in the crowd who had never heard Dylan or his songs before, the effect was electric. They had come to take part in a movement, and they discovered a prophet.

"The crowd was fantastic," was all Dylan would say of the biggest weekend of his career. "Just fantastic."

But there was another kind of Dylan performance. Behind the scenes in Newport's giant Freebody Park, and at the motel where most of the performers were housed, Dylan strutted with a giant twenty-foot bullwhip, lashing with it, over and over again. What do you do with that? someone asked, and Dylan replied: "I flip people's cigarettes out of their mouths. That's what I do with it, man." He rattled a people with his arrogance, with the walls he erected aroun   lf. He was the center of attention wherever he went, his mus.   s the music being sung from the stage, his songs were the ones being discussed and analyzed at the afternoon music workshops. Some of the traditionalists made it clear they despised Dylan for his style, his youth, and most of all because it was his magic that had attracted the largest and youngest crowd in the history of the festival.

And the fans went after him, asking what he meant by certain songs and images, trying to get close to him. It frightened him. "You could begin to sense the fear," says one young folk·singer who was there. "Bobby was touched by a fear of it all, starting back there at Newport when it all began to get together for him."

Eric Andersen: "He was very paranoid about this attention, he didn't dig people prying. He was pretty cool about the fame and all. There wasn't much flashing of ego, but he did become nervous and furtive. He was secretive, and he'd invent things. He couldn't really be straight about anything so he sort of closed the book on himself."

Dave Van Ronk: "I remember at the Festival, some of the crowd came and charged after him. They were running after Bobby and we were running away from them. We got in a damn station wagon and got away from them. I was sitting on the tailgate and Bobby was inside and he said: 'Get used to it, Dave, next year it'll be you.' It terrified him. He was paranoid to start. All of a sudden five million people were pulling at his coat and picking his brain, and he couldn't take it when just five people were doing that. His feeling, basically, was that the audience is a lynch mob. What he said was: 'Look out, they'll kill you.' He never trusted anything or anybody in his life. At the same time, the man has some notion of the basic dignity of a human being. If you are a brilliant person, the wages of your brilliance are not to have your clothes torn off or your mind invaded. And that's what they started doing to Bobby."

Bob Dylan, to a group of friends at Newport: "Wish I could do it all and stay in the places I'm comfortable. Where they don't know me and don't stare at me. The attention is too much commotion for my body and head. The world's scary, sometimes."

Dylan, to another friend: "I once thought the biggest I could ever hope to get was like Van Ronk. But it's bigger than that, now, ain't it? Yeah, man, it's bigger than that. Scary as all shit."

And he talked a little about his songs, and some of the influences on him. He told an interviewer: "Man, I don't write protest songs, I just react. I got all these thoughts inside me and I gotta say 'em. Most people can't say 'em. They keep it all inside. It's for these people I write my songs. . . . I was influenced by Brecht. Used to be Woody, but not any more."

There was much of Brecht around the Village, in off-Broadway productions. As mentioned earlier, Suze herself was working on *Brecht on Brecht*, an anthology of Brecht material that opened later that spring at the Sheridan Square·Playhouse. She was doing scenery and props and Bob would come to rehearsals, listening to the cast of six recite Brecht's poetry and sing the songs he had written with Kurt Weill. Suze remembers it was Dylan's first contact with Brecht and he was impressed by the poetry and the songs, especially *The Black Freighter*.

Dylan later talked about influences from that period. "Brecht was important to me," he told me. "But there were a lot of other things. Like, *The Hostage*. I don't know if it was the play itself, the action on stage, or what, but it really got to me." Behan's play about the IRA is set in a societal prison of the mind. All the players stomp and shout and sing and the young British soldier who is being held hostage can't make much sense of any of it. And after all the farce and folly, there is a sudden wrench as the soldier is executed. Dylan saw the absurdity of political posturing. In the end, only the victim is pure.

Suze was at Newport and some who were there sensed that she and Dylan were still having their problems. One of the folk singers remembers seeing Suze sitting around, "wistful, sad, like Ophelia," looking through a lattice-work fence with the sun streaming on her face and burnishing her hair, watching Paxton, Seeger, and then Dylan, singing to thousands. And watching him with Baez, especially Baez.

"Well, what kind of rumors do you hear about Bobby and Joanie?" she asked one friend as talk about their intense affair grew even more persistent. The friend answered: "The same kind of rumors you hear." Suze considered that for a moment, and then said: "Bobby couldn't love Joan Baez. He couldn't love *anybody* that big."

Baez's first opportunity to bring Dylan up as an unannounced guest artist came immediately after the Newport Festival. She held several concerts scheduled in the East: the Camden Music Fair in New Jersey on August 3, Asbury Park a week later, a date in Connecticut and one in Massachusetts, and the Forest Hills Tennis Stadium on August 17. At each performance Joan would sing alone for the first half, doing several of Dylan's songs, and then after intermission call him out, sing with him, let him sing several songs alone. While there was some grumbling from a few purists who objected to Dylan, most of the crowd was demolished by the appearance of the skinny little kid who was becoming a greater idol than Woody had ever been.

The Forest Hills appearance was an especially important one for him. There were 14,000 people there, very young and very hip, and reporters and critics from the New York papers and all the trade publications. When she came out after the intermission Joan began: "There's a boy wandering around New York City and his name's Bob Dylan. You all know about him. Bobby Dylan says what a lot of people my age feel, but cannot say. It just so happens that Bob Dylan is here with me tonight." When the ovation finally died, he sang *Blowin' In the Wind, Pawn In Their Game, With God on Our Side,* and a song he had composed a couple of days before. *Troubled And I Don't Know Why,* which tickled the crowd by castigating the establishment's boob tube: the TV squalled, roared and boomed and bounced around the room, but it didn't say anything at all.

Bob, Joan, Odetta, Peter, Paul and Mary, Mahalia Jackson, Harry Belafonte and dozens of other performers who had been raising their voices to benefit the civil rights movement took part in the March on Washington on August 28. Two hundred thousand demonstrators, black and white, filled the nation's capitol to jog the national conscience. The Rev. Martin Luther King Jr. gave the most eloquent speech of his career ("I have a dream . . . I have a dream . . . 'Free at last! Free at last! Thank God Almighty, we are free at last!' "). Ossie Davis introduced the entertainers, Dylan sang *Pawn in Their Game,* Baez sang *We Shall Overcome,* and Peter, Paul and Mary did *Wind.* What was blowing in the wind was an optimism, Dr. King's dream, "a dream deeply rooted in the American system," but even then, as the speeches and the songs filled the seat of national government, even before assassinations would lead so many to abandon the dream, Dylan was questioning the reality of it all.

"Think they're listening?" he asked, glancing towards the Capitol. "No, they ain't listening at all."

David Whittaker: "I came from Minneapolis for the March. Dylan, in Washington, could still go to an open party—he was at a party with Baez and they were very close—but he was beginning to feel the pressures. I remember him saying, 'I can't go on the streets,' and I said, 'Why? Do they think you're Bobby Darin?' Then I went up to New York, to West Fourth Street. Suze had just split. And even though he was quite wealthy by now there was nothing in the place but two mattresses, a card table, four chairs, and a refrigerator he didn't dare open. I went to see if there was any beer and Bob screamed, 'Don't open it! There's stuff growin' in it!' It was a funny time. You realized something was really happening with him, Peter, Paul and Mary sang *Blowin' in the Wind* in front of 200,000 people. He sang. And yet when he got back to New York he was still the same guy, not taking care of himself, sleeping in his clothes, doing strange things. A funny time."

Suze had left just before the March on Washington, had gone to live with her mother and stepfather in New Jersey. She left because the recurring arguments over their relationship wore her down; because, she told friends, when she and Bob were getting along it was good, but when they weren't it was bad and she just wanted out. One argument on a sweltering night in mid-August was especially bad.

Dylan left the apartment and went to Gerde's, and a while later Suze called him there and said she was leaving. He rushed back, tried to talk her out of going, but he couldn't budge her. They talked all night, into the dawn. As the streets of the Village began coming to life, she called Carla and some friends and they helped her move her things out.

Dylan got out of town after Suze left. Albert Grossman had bought a large house up in Bearsville, adjacent to the art community of Woodstock, a hundred miles upstate from the city, and Bob spent a great amount of time there. "I'm going through bad times," Dylan told a few close friends. "It's blowin' my head." Some who were close to him at the time believe he "was near a breakdown"—and Grossman helped pull him over the bad times. Dylan wandered through the woods during the day, clearing his head. He wrote in the mornings and at night in a room which had a bed, table, typewriter, and little else.

"If it wasn't for Albert," Dylan later told Bob Shelton, "I could be on the Bowery now Albert's the greatest manager that ever lived in the whole century of the world."

Grossman appeared to be more than a manager at this point. He had become almost a substitute father, running Bob's life in most respects. A number of men and women who were in the Dylan circle at this time say that Grossman was telling Bob what to eat, where to sleep, that Dylan was confused, uncertain of what was happening to him, where he was going, and he accepted Grossman's guidance.

To those who were around them at the time it also appeared that Grossman was feeding Bob's distrust of people, his paranoia. Grossman's attitude—and Dylan's—was that outsiders were trying to use them, to take advantage of them, to con them in some way. (Dylan still feels that people were trying to use *him* in those days. "This thing you wrote about my manipulating others," he told me, "why can't you say I've been used as much as I used other people." To a great extent, Bob was used by others, and this is a part of the enormous stresses that would soon begin to afflict him and change the course of his life.) Because the attempts to manipulate Dylan were so obvious much of the time, the Grossman-Dylan attitude was that only close friends were to be trusted; any newcomer was likely to be an enemy, *was* an enemy, until he passed some great test of loyalty and proved he was true and was not likely to break a trust. Also, if a man did not suit the Grossman-Dylan values, he should be excluded from their company. This was especially true of writers; they were less reliable than anyone else. One of Grossman's stock demands was to see an article before it was printed and, although he didn't press

Victoria Spivey and Bob Dylan at one of his first recording sessions, 1961.

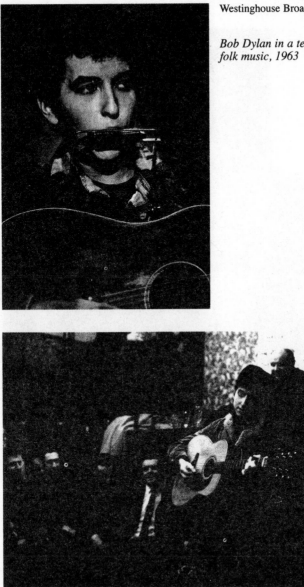

Westinghouse Broadcasting Co.,

Bob Dylan in a televised tour of folk music, 1963

Brian Shuel / Redferns

Bob Dylan at the Singers Club Christmas party in London, 22 December 1962.

rtrait of the artist in 1965.

Joan Baez performing at an anti-Vietnam War rally in London,
29 May 1965

ylan contemplates Hamlet's Elsinore castle at the start of a world tour, 1966.

Bob and Sara Dylan with their children in Woodstock, 1968.

Bob Dylan with Woodstock neighbours, 1969.

David Redfer

Bob Dylan performing with The Band at the Isle of Wight festival in front of 200,000 people, August 1969.

it, enough writers did agree to be edited by the Grossman office. Much of the material printed about Dylan in those days, amounted either to press releases or Dylan word games.

Bob's feelings about Grossman were ambivalent. On the one hand he appreciated Grossman's enormous talents as a manager, but he also deeply resented Grossman for changing what had been the simplicity of his early days in the Village and making his life a huge hassling operation. And when the money started to pour in, Dylan began worrying if he was getting a fair shake from the Grossman office, whether the investments and tax setups were to his best advantage, whether somebody was possibly frittering away some of his wealth. Grossman's maneuvers to get Dylan away from Columbia, his treatment of John Hammond, made Dylan feel guilty. "He shouldn't of done that to John," Dylan once told a friend, and although he never said more than that, it was clear he resented Grossman for it.

"Bobby was confused, really mixed up by it all," one friend says. "Grossman was telling him how things should be handled, people at Columbia were telling him something else again, and friends had a lot of advice. He didn't know who was giving him straight poop."

His need to work, and his obligations to Columbia, also helped him get over the rough times after Suze left. He went into the studio in late September and early October 1963, and laid down his third album, *The Times They Are A-Changin'*. The second album had already sold about 100,000 copies with reorders amounting to another 100,000 or so, and Dylan's income had risen to about $5,000 a month. "I'm makin' money," he told writer Chris Welles. "But it's botherin' me. The money's wrong. It don't make sense. It's all so weird." He was, he said, going through "head changes" on the third album.

The Times They Are A-Changin' stamped Dylan even further as a spokesman for the restless and rebellious young, particularly the title song which warned the dinosaurs—writers, critics, politicians—not to stand in the way of the flood waters of change that were engulfing the world.

The album also contained *With God On Our Side* and several new protest songs including *The Lonesome Death Of Hattie Carroll* which generated a lot of excitement. Phil Ochs recalls: "We sat down and listened to the final version of the album and Bob softened up when *Hattie Carroll* came on. He said: 'That's the one, that's the song I really like.'" Also on the album were *The Ballad of Hollis Brown,* and *North Country Blues,* both moving accounts of people who were beaten down by the system.

The head changes were apparent in the songs about personal relationships that would point the way to Dylan's future work. Although folk purists began to criticize Dylan for letting his personal vision intrude on his social message, those songs—among them *One Too Many Mornings* and *Boots of Spanish Leather*—were a vital element in Dylan's hold over his youthful audiences. The sentiments meshed perfectly with the search for spontaneous human expression.

The album closes with Dylan's testament, *Restless Farewell*. In that final song he tries to step back from personal involvement, telling his audience that he is not really a prophet; he is just a man who loves his freedom and doesn't want to be locked in to any stance; that his songs were written because he had to get down every thought that came into his head to keep from going insane; that they were written for himself and his friends and had no deeper design; and that he was bidding them farewell and not giving a damn.

A number of forces were working on Dylan during this period that contributed to profound personality changes.

There was, first of all, what some old friends have called the "mindguard"—a special kind of bodyguard whose duty was not only to protect him from the groupies (the less desirable ones, anyway) and other fans, but to protect him also from those whom he felt were making demands on his head, on his time. These included old friends, mostly, and some fellow folksingers with whom he no longer felt comfortable "because, in his paranoia, he thought we all hated him for his great talent," as one of them put it. Dylan's reaction to the fame seemed strange to his friends. Most who have made it, who have become big stars in the pop culture, go through enormous ego changes. For years scruffy kids bounce around for a buck, and then suddenly they're rich and have all the women they can ever hope to use, and hundreds of thousands reaching out to touch them, and the ego simply goes wild. But there seems to have been little of that with Dylan. "Basically," says Phil Ochs, "he was a very human person and wanted to keep human relationships from souring. And I think he felt that slipping away because of his fame, in the way people reacted to him." His friends didn't understand why, and were confused and hurt by his withdrawal.

The mindguards traveled with Dylan wherever he went, spent much time with him up in Woodstock, protecting him and changing his head in other ways. Among the Dylan entourage was Geno Foreman, son of Clark Foreman of the Emergency Civil Liberties Committee. Geno was a young folksinger, part of the crowd that hung around the Club 47 in Cambridge; he had a wild raucous way of singing that pre-dated Joe Cocker's spastic style by ten years. And Victor Maimudes, a dark, strange young man who had once played Lincoln in a high school production and is described by friends as "a frustrated actor and frustrated guitar player." Victor got into the folk scene by hanging around with Jack Elliott in Topanga Canyon in California in the mid-Fifties. He showed up one day in Woodstock with a friend's wife, and he was hired as Dylan's road manager and companion. Also part of the group were Albert and John Maher, sons of a wealthy Texas industrialist, and Paul Clayton, who remained loyal to Dylan despite the hassle over the melody for *Don't Look Twice*. Many of them were heavily into drugs, popping all kinds of pills and experimenting with acid and mushrooms. Smoking and snorting, they were stoned much of the time.

Recalls one woman who was intimate with Dylan: "Bob was one of those rare people who get their strength from some inner self. But when I first knew him, in the protest period, he was putting it down and denying it. The inner self was just part of the things you didn't talk about, it was understood. He was aware of Zen, some of us were getting into that, but he was into reality at the time and he was putting the inner self down. He was writing protest and he had to push everything else aside and jump into that all the way. He was always that kind of mystical person, but during the protest period he was playing some other role. Later, when it was all evolving for him, he was into things like Byron and began to get into his head more. Later, I'm certain Bob got into acid or one of the mind-expanders. We used to have arguments about drugs. He was always saying he was in favor of chemistry. 'I'm pro-chemistry,' he would say. He would try anything to open his head. And after he got into the drugs he stopped denying that thing inside himself. He began looking for it, believing in it, working with it and letting it flow over him. The drugs got him back to that mystic inner self."

In a 1969 interview with Jann Wenner of *Rolling Stone* Dylan acknowledges, "I was on drugs, a lot of things," and while he says the drug experience heightened his "awareness of the *minute*" and of the mind, he insists drugs did not influence the writing of his songs. Still, the songs he was beginning to write at this time—*Chimes of Freedom* and *Tambourine Man* among them—were directly related to the drug experience. Just as the work of the San Francisco and New York poets, some of them once called Beat—Ginsberg, Corso, Sanders and Kupferberg of the East Side rock group, the Fugs, Duncan, Ferlinghetti, McClure, Whalen and others—reflected their drug culture. These poets were also directly influencing Dylan. Ginsberg met Dylan around this time, and he expanded Dylan's perceptions as much as drugs did.

There was a growing awareness that folk was dead, both for Bob Dylan and as a public fad. In the beginning he was a folk singer, and for a couple of years that was a deeply satisfying role. But by the release of *The Times They Are A-Changin'*, he had been into drugs, had gone through the head changes, and had begun to weave tapestries that could not be confined to the standard ballad. He knew that he could get away with it now, could carry his audience along with him, could possibly reach that goal—"Bigger than Presley!"—because he and Joan had gone beyond folk. They had a wider constituency; all those disaffected kids were digging something deeper than folk music. Folk fans don't buy a quarter million record albums. Folk, in fact, had been taken over by the moneymen from a new Tin Pan Alley and destroyed, as rock had been destroyed earlier, everyone getting rich turning the music into the plastic house plants of folk-pop. Dylan later told a friend, who has it on tape:

"I had to hold a lot of things back before. That's why I was doing other kinds of writing, because I could of never got away with it in song. People would never understand, they would have killed me. I would have been dead, they would have chased me off the stage, I would have been a total failure. I held it back because I had to survive, I had to make it back then, I couldn't go too far out. If somebody was going to give me three hundred dollars for doing a certain thing, it wouldn't be too hard to do that thing. I'd just do it. My ideals aren't that important to me, what you might call ideals. I didn't really care. I didn't have what people call ideals. So it didn't matter a damn. I needed bread, and I had to scuffle. That's all. But I don't have to scuffle any more. I can do it my way now."

The conflict with Suze was also a catalyst for change. Dylan had things to say about women, and love, and the quality of human relationships, and they could not be said in the standard folk ballad. That's one reason he was writing poems he never intended to set to music, as in "11 Outlined Epitaphs" on the back of *The Times They Are A-Changin'*. Suze had returned to the Village in mid-September after a few weeks with her mother in New Jersey, and went to live with her sister, Carla, in an apartment on Avenue B, in the East Village. One day Dylan came around to the apartment. He persuaded Suze to let him stay, and he moved in with them. Carla soon asked him to leave, mostly because there were no doors on any of the rooms, no chance for privacy, she explains. But Dylan ignored her. Carla asked him to swap apartments—let her use his West Fourth Street place—but he refused. "Need it for practicing and stuff," he said. And he stayed, unable to give Suze up. Friends who visited them say they spent much time arguing, or watching TV. Seldom talking.

And there were other tensions. Pete Karman recalls one night in late September when he was sitting around in the apartment with Bob, Suze, Albert and John Maher, when someone rapped on the door. Dylan got up and opened it and Geno Foreman swept in and shouted: "Hey, Bobby, I hear you're makin' it with Joan Baez." Suze's face went through several color changes in the next room, and Dylan was urgently whispering: "Shut up, will ya? Shut the hell up." And the evening was a wipe out.

Karman: "The relationship between Dylan and Baez seemed to be very close by then. The King and Queen—that's how Bobby was talking about it. He had that image of himself, that he was the King and Baez was the Queen. And still he was worried about Suze because he knew she was very uptight about that."

Suze's feelings didn't keep Bob from flying to Hollywood in October, to appear as Joan's guest at the Hollywood Bowl. His reception was not quite triumphant, however. A very vocal minority of the audience booed and otherwise expressed their displeasure when he took over the second half of her program. A few of them later sent angry letters of protest to the Bowl management complaining that they had paid to see Baez and weren't much interested in Dylan— "that screeching fool," as one of the letters described him.

A week later Dylan filled Carnegie Hall with a couple of thousand young rooters, most of them adoring teenagers who had bought out the house. These were fans, not folk music *afficianados.* It was as enthusiastic a crowd as any Dylan had ever experienced and they cheered every one of the twenty songs he performed, the protest songs, the bitter anti-hero love songs, a couple of early Guthriesque ballads. And what came through from his songs was a feeling of hopelessness—and helplessness, a feeling that the world was screwed up and that we should hate the people responsible for it. As an introduction to the song, Dylan put it right to his audience: "Met a teacher who said he didn't understand what *Blowin' In The Wind* means," he said. Laughter through the house; the kids knew all about those stupid teachers. "Told him there was nothin' to understand, it was just blowin' in the wind. If he didn't feel it in the wind, he'd never know. And he ain't never gonna know, I guess. *Teachers.*"

But there was something else, here at Carnegie Hall, a public hint of the head changes Dylan said he was going through at this time— a feeling that instead of searching for answers to the old problems one must turn one's back on the problems, rejecting easy formulas and easy solutions, search deep inside oneself instead. *Lay Down Your Weary Tune,* sung near the end of the concert program, is an early indication that Dylan had moved from folk-protest to a kind of radical-anarchy, a mysticism akin to William Blake or the Eastern philosophers.

The Carnegie Hall audience's style was further proof that something had happened to lift Bob Dylan out of the folk trap. "It was very strange," Terri Van Ronk remembers. "Like the precursor to Beatlemania. Bobby's first big skyrocketing was right there in that Carnegie Hall gig. When it was over and we were all backstage, they began to plot the getaway from all these little girls who were screaming outside. Suze and I were delegated to go out and act as decoys. We went out the stage door and started walking up the street in the opposite direction from where the car was parked, and a whole bunch of kids began to follow us. Suze got a little panicky and she began to tell them to go back, that Bobby was still inside, and after a while they finally believed her and they all ran back. And Bobby came out, flanked by Geno on one side and Maimudes on the other, and we all pushed our way to the car. Bobby was terrified over mobs, and that was a mob. Like something I literally had never seen before, little girls hanging on top of the car and policemen pulling them away so Bobby could get out of there safely. I can understand the panic that performers go through, after seeing that."

Suze's reaction was that Carnegie Hall was "a horror show, all these people chasing you up the block, that really sent it home that anybody around Dylan was as much in danger as he was."

Abe and Beatty Zimmerman were at the concert, flown in from Hibbing by Bob and ensconced in a west side motel, all expenses paid by the wastrel son who had become famous. Dylan no longer tried to hide his origins from his friends, for the *Little Sandy Review* had written about Dylan-Zimmerman for its very small audience of folk professionals and enthusiasts. While Bob continued his little games on his friends and on Suze about his hard travelin' with carnivals and circuses, and his Indian blood and gambler uncle, he did want his parents in New York to share it all. The Zimmermans were out front, in the best seats in the house, and then backstage (where Mrs. Zimmerman asked Suze: "Can't you get him to cut his hair?" and told her that she just couldn't believe the audience had been screaming for her son). But Bob's parents were ignored by the teenyboppers; for them Bob was publicly still the James Dean orphan rebelling against a world he never made.

But the secret was out the next day, when *Newsweek* hit the stands with an exposé of Bob's middle class roots. It quoted Dylan as insisting that he had never been Robert Zimmerman—"Dig my draft card, man. Bob Dylan"—and, when asked about his parents, Dylan is said to have responded: "I don't know my parents. They don't know me. I've lost contact with them for years." The article went on:

"A few blocks away, in one of New York's motor inns, Mr. and Mrs. Abe Zimmerman of Hibbing, Minn., were looking forward to seeing their son sing at Carnegie Hall."

The story also called him a fraud, a kid who faked his atrocious grammar, who claimed he hated the commercialism of music "but he has two agents who hover about him, guarding his words and fattening his contracts." It said he scorns reporters who try to interview him, "but he wants to know how long a story about him will run and if there will be a photograph."

The article was true enough, of course; Dylan was an image maker who wanted to be a pop star. But the writer made it clear he was interested only in a hatchet job on Dylan when he repeated a rumor that had been kicking around for some time—one that was clearly untrue—that *Blowin' In the Wind* had been written by a New Jersey high school student who had sold it to Dylan. The student, who was named, denied it, but the rumor was published anyway.

In a sense, however, Dylan and Grossman had it coming to them. As had happened to so many others before him, the writer for *Newsweek* had been promised Dylan's cooperation in an interview, but then at the last moment either Dylan or Grossman (there are several versions but most credit Grossman) told the writer there would be no interview. The writer then went out to Minneapolis and Hibbing and dug up Dylan's background. On his return he threatened to publish all the gossip, and Grossman backed down and set up an interview. It was brief; Dylan became nasty and broke it off, and the hatchet job was printed.

Dylan was deeply hurt by the *Newsweek* article. "Why did they do that?" he asked Chris Welles who, after trying for eight months, had finally got Dylan to sit still for a *Life* feature interview. "Man, they're out to kill me. What've they got against me?"

1963–1964: *Chimes of Freedom*

DYLAN WAS ON his way uptown to Grossman's office on the afternoon of Friday, November 22, 1963, when John F. Kennedy was shot
in Dallas. "I watched it at my manager's office," Dylan later told me.
"The next night, Saturday, I had a concert upstate, in Ithaca or
Buffalo. There was a really down feeling in the air. I had to go on
stage, I couldn't cancel. I went to the hall and to my amazement the
hall was filled. Everybody turned out for the concert. The song I was
opening with was *The Times They Are A-Changin'* and I thought,
'Wow, how can I open with that song? I'll get rocks thrown at me.'
That song was just too much for the day after the assassination. But
I had to sing it, my whole concert takes off from there.

"I know I had no understanding of anything. Something had just
gone haywire in the country and they were applauding that song.
And I couldn't understand why they were clapping or why I wrote
that song, even. I couldn't understand anything. For me, it was just
insane."

When he returned to the Village he, Suze and Carla sat and
watched the national tragedy through the rest of the weekend and
into the Monday morning funeral. Like so many across the nation,
they were engrossed in the events unfolding before them: the murder of Oswald, the funeral, the continual replays of the death of
Kennedy, the confirmation of a new president, the widow refusing
to change her blood-soaked dress because she wanted the world to
see her husband's blood, to see what it had done. Through it all Dylan
sat and watched and said little, just feeling the emotion of it. He
drank a little wine, and played Berlioz's *Requiem* over and over.

Eric Andersen: "You can't separate Dylan from history in the sense
of what was going down, the way he reacted to a chain of events. The
first being Kennedy's death; I think that got him out of politics. He
might even have had fears of assassination himself, being the center
of attention and saying the kind of things he was saying. Kennedy's
death brought home that there were a lot of maniacs out there in this
country. He realized the divisions were there, and he sort of wanted
to remove himself from politics, because he was probably scared of
getting knocked off himself.

"Right after Kennedy, things started to get strange. The immunity that had been. . . . Well, folk music looked like it was going to be pretty heavy. Folk music had a medieval flair to it, and pageantry, it had a feeling of truth and of, yes, we can do it, just freedom, and everybody's going to get it together and it is just going to be won. And Kennedy, he was sort of like the shadow of flight, he sort of protected this kind of thing. And then that bird got shot out of the sky and everybody was exposed, naked to all the frightening elements, the truth of the country. It had flown, that force had lost out. And people were depressed. The streets were very cold, man, when I got to the Village right after that, and I could feel the vibes change immediately. And Dylan got scared. . . ."

Phil Ochs also felt it in Bob: "Oh, yeah, I was overcome with it. Yeah, that feeling was everywhere. I was almost destroyed with that very same thing. You're sticking your neck out, a public figure, and there's an obvious fear. You're political and obviously the bad guys are on the loose and maybe gonna kill anybody who's out front, and you get scared. Bob never talked about it, but it was there."

Although many felt it in Dylan at the time, he denies it today. "I didn't feel it any more than anybody else," he told me. "We were all sensitive to it. The assassination took more of the shape of a happening. I read about those things happening to Lincoln, to Garfield, and that it could happen in this day and age was not too far-fetched. It didn't knock the wind out of me. Of course, I felt as rotten as everyone else. But if I was more sensitive about it than anyone else, I would have written a song about it, wouldn't I? The whole thing about my reactions to the assassination is overplayed."

Yet, despite Bob's denial, the murder did have an enormous effect on him. He signaled that feeling to very close friends, and a couple of weeks after Kennedy's death, Dylan gave a disastrous speech that indicated how much the assassination had troubled him. He went to the grand ballroom of the Hotel Americana in New York to accept the Tom Paine Award of the Emergency Civil Liberties Committee for his work in the civil rights campaigns. "As soon as I got there I felt uptight," he later told Nat Hentoff. "I began to drink. I looked down from the platform and saw a bunch of people who had nothing to do with my kind of politics. I looked down and I got scared. They were supposed to be on my side, but I didn't feel any connection with them. Here were these people who had been all involved with the left in the Thirties, and now they were supporting civil rights drives. That's groovy, but they also had minks and jewels, and it was like they were giving money out of guilt. I got up to leave and they followed me and caught me. They told me I had to accept the award. When

I got up to make my speech I couldn't say anything by that time but what was passing through my mind."

What was passing through his mind and what he said was this: "It took me a long time to get young and now I consider myself young. And I'm proud of it. I'm proud that I'm young." The people sitting at the tables in furs and jewels were far from young, most of them, and Dylan told them they should retire, they "should be out at the beach . . . relaxing in the time you have to relax. It's not an old people's world. . . Old people, when their hair grows out, they should go out." The audience was still able to laugh. And Dylan went on:

"They talk about Negroes, and they talk about black and white. And they talk about colors of red and blue and yellow. Man, I just don't see any colors at all when I look out. . . . There's no black and white, left and right, to me any more. There's only up and down, and down is very close to the ground. And I'm trying to go up without thinking of anything trivial, such as politics. That has got nothing to do with it. I'm thinking about the general people, and when they get hurt."

Members of the audience began to lean over, asking what he was talking about, why he appeared to be denying the value of what they were doing. But Dylan didn't seem to notice and he plunged on:

"I was on the March on Washington, up on the platform, and I looked around at all the Negroes there, and I didn't see any Negroes that looked like none of my friends. My friends don't wear *suits*. My friends don't have to wear *suits*. My friends don't have to wear any kind of thing to prove they're respectable people. My friends are my friends and they're kind, gentle people if they're my friends. And I'm not trying to push nothing over."

There was a smattering of applause, and Dylan began to think of Kennedy's murder, which had been deplored by speaker after speaker that night, and he said:

"I'll stand up and be uncompromisable about it, which I have to be to be honest. I just got to be, as I got to admit that the man who shot President Kennedy—Lee Oswald—I don't know exactly what he thought he was doing, but I got to admit honestly that I, too—I saw some of myself in him. I don't think it could have gone that far. —I don't think it could go that far. But I got to stand up and say that I saw things that he felt, in me—not to go that far and shoot. . . ."

Some members of the audience began to boo and hiss, and Dylan went forward: "You can boo, but booing's got nothin' to do with it —it's uh—I just uh—I've got to tell you, man, it's Bill of Rights, it's free speech and . . ." Someone broke in and said his time was up and

Dylan later claimed the chairman began kicking him under the table, and he finished up by quickly saying he accepted the award in behalf of James Foreman and the Student Non-Violent Coordinating Committee, and he went off amid boos and some applause, beat it out of there.

Dylan's putdown of his hosts and his inability to verbalize what he was feeling, created a minor furor in the older elements of the civil rights movement. Dylan felt ashamed and guilty at first, and he dashed off a long letter-poem to Clark Foreman and other members of the ECLC, which started out as explanation and apology. He was not making fun of bald heads, he wrote; what he meant to condemn was bald minds, and in any case he didn't know why he had talked disparagingly about old people and had suggested they retire to the shore. He cannot make speeches, he wrote, he is just a writer and singer, and perhaps he should have let it go with a couple of songs. When he talked about Oswald he didn't mean the deed, which spoke for itself. He meant that he was sick of hearing that we all share the blame for every killing, every lynching, every church bombing in the South, every "President-killing." It is too easy, Dylan wrote, to say "we" and spread the guilt around equally. "I must say 'I' alone for it is I alone who is livin' my life." Long and rambling, the letter explained every word Dylan had spoken and asked, "Do you understand?" It was clear he didn't think they could ever understand because some of them were the kind of people who would not give him a chance to be understood and who could say Bob Dylan was the one who really shot the President. God, he wrote, it is so hard to hate, and so tiresome.

Within a few days Dylan was beginning to feel even more estranged from the older leaders of the civil rights movement, from the organizations. One friend recalls him saying:

"They didn't understand me because they got mind-blinders on. They couldn't understand that Oswald was like me, and like you. He was uptight about the times we're livin' in, about all the lies they feed ya, about the history books that tell ya facts not worth a damn, but never once tell you how somebody *feels*. That's what Oswald was about. That's what I'm about. But those people can't understand. They don't know what's happening. All they can see is a cause, and using people for their cause. They're tryin' to use me for something, want me to carry a picket sign and have my picture taken and be a good little nigger and not mess up their little game. They're all hung up on games. But the games don't work any more."

By the middle of January he seemed to be more nervous than he'd ever been, restless, complaining that something was wrong, that he didn't know what to do with his life. "I gotta get away," he told a friend. "Need time to think, to dope things out." The Grossman office had set up a couple of concerts across the country—Atlanta, Denver, San Francisco and Los Angeles. Ordinarily Dylan would have flown to keep the dates, but this time he had other ideas.

"Hey," he said to Pete Karman, the *Daily Mirror* writer, "wanna ride cross-country with us? Gonna do some concerts. Ramble 'round the country. Show ya some of the places I been, like Central City, Atlanta, Greenwood. Hit New Orleans for the Mardi Gras, even."

"You have concerts in all those places?" Karman asked.

"No, just a couple. But wanna get out and ramble around. Meet people. Stop in bars and poolhalls and talk to real people. That's where it's at, people. Talk to farmers. Talk to miners. That's where it's at. That's real."

Friends say he wanted to do the Woody Guthrie thing, even though he was beyond the Guthrie stage. "You gonna ride a boxcar?" someone asked him. He only smiled; what he was going to ride was a brand new Ford station wagon, bought by a company called Ashes & Sand, a holding company that Grossman and the lawyers had set up because Bob was becoming a rich man, worth at least a hundred thousand dollars and with prospects of at least three and four times that much from song royalties alone in the next year or so. Dylan insisted money didn't mean anything to him. "If I need money, I just go to my manager and get it," he said, "and if I spend that and need more, I just go back and get more." He had always done as he pleased, but money gave him the freedom to do it in a new style. Ford station wagon style, which wasn't quite Rolls Royce style, but getting there. Plus a very thick sheaf of Traveler's checks.

But most friends felt he was sincere when he confided, "I want to go out and feel what the people are feeling, find out what's goin' on."

Suze was happy to see him go. She wasn't satisfied at the way their relationship was going, and she was bored much of the time because they just sat around when they were together.

The Dylan entourage drove through the Holland Tunnel and onto the New Jersey Turnpike on the morning of February 2—Dylan, Karman, Paul Clayton and Victor Maimudes, who was behind the wheel. Dylan had put his three companions on the books of Ashes & Sand. All expenses were to be paid but only Maimudes, who was officially the road manager, was on salary.

The car was filled with used clothing that Dylan had collected for the striking miners in Kentucky. And Dylan's typewriter. "Gonna write all along the way," he said.

That first night they stopped in Charlottesville, Virginia, where

Clayton had a house. The drive down had been uneventful, which is surprising considering that they were all stoned, Clayton high on pills, Dylan and others on grass. As soon as they arrived Dylan called Suze back in New York, then he and his companions spent the night playing Monopoly, drinking wine, smoking to maintain the high edge of psychic excitement.

They went into town the next day, wandering the streets in the downtown area, dropping into a bar for a couple of drinks and moving on again. "Hey, man," Dylan shouted as they passed a record shop. "Gotta see if the new album's out yet. Wanna pass 'em around to people." They shuffled into the shop. "Got the new Dylan album?" Dylan asked. The girl behind the counter looked up. Lord help her, that's Bob Dylan, that man there with the funny cap, surrounded by a couple of freaks. She stumbled out into the aisle, to a bin labeled "Dylan" and pulled out a copy of *The Times They Are A-Changin'*. "How many you got?" Dylan asked. The girl counted them out, ten of them. "I'll take them all," Dylan said.

He leaned against the counter, under a large poster with his picture on it, signing Traveler's checks, and the word flashed through the store. "That's Bob Dylan." "Where?" "Over there." Four or five kids moved closer, suppressing moans and squeals. Dylan looked around at them, and his guard moved in around him. "Man," Dylan said, "there's a lot of *people* in here. Let's split." He hustled out to the street, followed by several of the customers. "They're closin' in on us," Dylan said. "Let's move." They began to trot, the kids catching up, then to gallop, into the car, roll up the windows, race away. "Man, that was close," Dylan said. "They almost got me."

Later that morning they were on the road again, Clayton driving, Dylan studying the map: "Hendersonville, North Carolina," he said. "You gotta take this highway"—shoving the map in front of Clayton —"and right outside Hendersonville is where he has his place, Flat Rock. That's where he lives."

They entered Flat Rock late that afternoon, pulled up to a gas station. Dylan jumped out of the car. "Where's Carl Sandburg's place?" he asked the tall gangling mountain man in coveralls. "You know, the poet." The mountain man considered that for a while. "You mean Sandburg the goat farmer?" he asked.

"No, I mean Sandburg the poet."

"Don't know about no poet. There's a Sandburg has a goat farm. Wrote a book on Lincoln. Little guy. Littler than you, even. If that's the one, take this road two miles up there, turn left after the little bridge, can't miss it if you're sober."

Stoned, they didn't miss it. They pulled up to the farm house and knocked on the door. A small, bearded, wizened man came out.

"You're Carl Sandburg," Dylan said, not asking. "I'm Bob Dylan. I'm a poet, too."

"How nice," Sandburg said, his smile saying *another kid who wants to be a poet.* But he tried to be gracious and said, "Come, sit a while." Mrs. Sandburg joined them, smiling but not saying anything.

"I've written some songs, Mr. Sandburg," Dylan said. "I know Woody Guthrie, he's very sick in a hospital, he talked about you a lot. Got some songs here I'd appreciate you listening to." He handed Sandburg one of the albums and the poet took it and said, "That's wonderful," but it was clear he was simply being polite. They chatted awhile, Dylan rambling on about folk music, and his own songs and poems, subtly telling Sandburg he was a young poet and Sandburg should recognize him because he recognized Sandburg as an older poet. And Sandburg smiled at this scruffy kid promoting his album, hyping himself as a poet, Sandburg polite but not particularly interested.

After about ten minutes Dylan said, "Well, gotta go. Nice meeting you," and he turned and skipped down the steps and into the car. His entourage piled in after him and they drove off, quickly, Dylan slouching down in the front seat, very quiet, staring straight ahead. Someone handed him a joint and he puffed deeply and said nothing. He was obviously annoyed at his encounter with Sandburg, hurt that the poet had never heard of him.

They entered Hazard, Kentucky, in Harlan County, coal-mining country, the next day. The first stop was the Post Office, to look for a thick envelope sent them from New York in care of Dylan, general delivery. The envelope was there. It contained a quantity of marijuana, sent by friends; all along their route similar envelopes filled with grass would be waiting for them in similar Post Office buildings.

The second stop was a place to eat. Dylan was paying the bill when he spotted a crock on the shelf, with flowers and the word "Marijuana" imprinted across the front, designed to hold teabags or sugar in the kitchen of a suburban split level and to provide some chuckles for the neighbors. Dylan giggled. "Gimme one of those," he said. He double-timed it to the car and spilled all the dope into the marijuana crock and put it up on the dash board. "What a gas," he said, giggling, and they all broke up. "If a cop stops us we'll tell him we're English and carry our own tea." They all broke up again. "Insane!" Clayton shouted.

Dylan drove. He was a bad driver, erratic, and his companions tried to keep him away from the wheel. He found the mine union headquarters and Hamish Sinclair, an organizer Bob had met on his earlier trip South, greeted him, but half-heartedly, clearly distracted. "Got a whole bunch of clothes in the car for your people that need 'em," Dylan said, and Sinclair was pleased. But he was very busy. There was trouble in the coal fields and several miners had been arrested. Sinclair was on the phone for an hour, then had to run out to the mines, and Dylan was getting depressed. "I know he's got problems, but shit . . ."

Dylan stalked out, and the four of them piled into the car again. As they drove into the countryside beyond Hazard, past mine towers and slag heaps, they came across a man trudging along the side of the road. "Pick him up," Dylan said. "He's a miner. Look how black he is." The man was a white man but his pasty face and rough hands were streaked with coal dust and sweat.

"Can we buy ya a drink?" Dylan asked. The miner agreed and directed them to a bar up the road, where they ordered drinks. "This guy's groovy," Dylan said. "Real miner." He turned to the man. "Been a miner long?" he asked. The man nodded. They threw questions at him—Ever been in a cave-in? Gotta shop at a company store? Company cops ever beat you?—stereotyping him as The Miner, grooving on being with a real miner, not seeing him as a man with a wife and kids, struggling to get along. And after a while they left him, drinking alone at the bar, and climbed back into the station wagon.

A feeling began to come over Karman that none of it was quite real. Dylan was looking for sensations, without involving his intellect, and Karman couldn't understand that this is the way his mind works. Dylan had seldom been articulate, but now he barely verbalized his impressions at all. His whole *trip* was more feeling than logical thinking—this is where it's at, it's what's happening, oh, wow!

And when he did talk, it was to work out some poetic images, testing their reactions: "Time don't exist, it's an illusion, the other side of Dali's clocks." And: "Know where God is? The river, that's God. The river's right where you're standing, and it's up in the mountains, and it's down the bend, and into the sea. All at the same instant. Very same instant. If there's a God, the river's Him."

As Victor drove away from Hazard, Dylan climbed into the back of his station wagon, put the portable typewriter on his lap, and began to write. Later, Karman got a look at the page: *Chimes of Freedom* was the title, a poem that would later become a song, perhaps Dylan's description of an actual mystical experience.

They drove through the night, completely stoned. At the Atlanta

Post Office in the morning they picked up another batch of dope and replenished the dwindling supply in the jar, and Dylan gave a concert that night at Emory University, a black college. A number of Dylan's friends from SNCC were there, and afterward a select group of people returned with him to his motel room—kids in the civil rights movement, enough groupies to make everyone feel welcome, to take the edge off the hard travelin', and plenty to drink and smoke. Dylan called Suze, to tell her the concert went off well, and they hung around for a couple of days, filling up on the pleasures.

They moved on to Mississippi, to Jackson and on to Tougaloo College, the black school that was a center of the black freedom movement. A police cruiser followed them briefly, as police followed every out-of-state car obviously filled with nigger-loving outside agitators. They made it safely to the school and Dylan gave an impromptu concert of his protest songs in a small room.

Through Mississippi later, and Louisiana, driving at top speed, the dope jar on the dash board and not caring about Southern cops. Clayton leaned out the window in one town, as they flew past three or four young rednecks sitting in front of a store, and shouted: "Muthfuckers!" Putting down everything they saw, deliberately courting danger. And they all laughed from up high.

New Orleans was alive with tourists, in town for Mardi Gras week. Dylan found their motel where there was only one room available for the four of them, and they quickly headed for the Latin Quarter. "Gotta find the black bars," Dylan said. "That's where it's happening." He led them into one place and they got thrown out by the bartender who didn't want trouble with white cops. In a second place they had a couple of drinks, talked with black patrons, and were thrown out when a cop came by and wanted to know if they were part of a desegregation movement. And into another place, Dylan enchanted by the owner, a huge man in woman's clothes, a transvestite who called himself Wanda. And then off to the streets again.

There were a dozen people trailing them by this time, who had to see what this Pied Piper was up to. A white street singer and poet, Joe B. Stuart, became part of the entourage for a while. Everybody flying high, floating through the town, Dylan at the head of a freak carnival procession.

Out in front of one bar they came across a young white street singer who was busking—playing for the coins of passersby—his guitar work and singing style a fusion of Leadbelly and Guthrie. "Hey," Dylan said, "can I borrow your guitar?" The singer handed it over and Dylan began to sing a couple of things off his first album. "Man," the kid exclaimed, "you sound just like Bob Dylan." Bob's face was impassive. "Saw Dylan once," he said. "A place in the Village. He's all right, I guess."

They returned to their motel room and Dylan was talking in elliptic, flashing images: "No one's free, even the birds are chained to the sky." And saying: "Rimbaud's where it's at. That's the kind of stuff means something. That's the kind of writing I'm gonna do."

The guy's freaky, Karman thought. He asked: "You moving away from social protest stuff?" His voice sounded disapproving, and disappointed.

"You becoming a critic?" Dylan snapped.

"Hell, I only know your protest songs mean something to a lot of people. . . ."

"Hell with 'em," Dylan said. He 'went to the typewriter and banged out a few lines, then turned to Karman. "Even the birds are chained to the sky," he repeated.

"You're only saying that 'cause you're stoned," Karman said, and walked out.

They had to race out of town after a couple of days, racing through Louisiana toward Denver, where Dylan had a concert that he would miss if they didn't hurry. "Drive, Pablo, drive," he shouted at Clayton from the back of the wagon where he sat with his typewriter, working on *Chimes of Freedom* again, and on other songs. Clayton drove, high on pills, disdaining the marijuana on the dash board; a child's head, marijuana.

But on entering Dallas, Dylan had an urge: "Let's go see where Kennedy was killed." They drove around, looking for the Texas Book Depository and Dealey Plaza, four months after the murder, lost in downtown Dallas. "Where's Dealey Plaza?" Dylan asked, leaning out the window, and no one knew, four people, and five, and six, and none of them knew the place. At least, that's what they said. The seventh man they asked, answered: "You mean where they shot that bastard Kennedy?" Dylan didn't answer, and the Texan gave them directions. For about a half hour they wandered around the murder scene, Dylan grim and silent, and then back in the car and on their way, and all of them shouting out the windows, condemning all Texans as assassins.

They made it to the Denver Folk Lore Center, the local freak haven, with several hours to spare. Harry Tuft, the young operator of the place, apologetically told Dylan the concert had not sold too well, only about half the tickets gone. Dylan didn't react at first. He hung around, enjoying the hang-loose feel of the place and the kids. Then: "Hey, tell you what. Let's cancel the concert in the big hall and do it right here. I'd rather a small place, anyway." Empty seats: the performer's nightmare.

But the concert was a success, Dylan getting it on and living up to the audience's expectations. For weeks there had been rumors that he would not come, that he had been killed, or gone insane, destroyed by a System-conspiracy. On stage his appearance seemed to justify these fears, his fragile body, his wounded voice. James Dean's death, now Kennedy's, had done that to this generation: they were certain their leaders, their heroes, would be taken from them. Dylan —because he was like a broken-winged sparrow—appeared the most defenseless, the most vulnerable.

Karman had some straight friends in Denver and he went to visit them for a couple of hours and they blew his mind, he says. They were so warmly normal and average and stable, while Dylan and his group seemed on the edge of some dark cataclysm, totally unreal, always stoned, speaking in unintelligible parables. Karman felt as if Dylan was backing him into a padded cell.

They all were, in fact, almost thrown in jail. Karman was behind the wheel as they drove through the mountains in western Colorado and, as they were climbing one very steep hill along a narrow two-lane road, they were caught behind a funeral procession.

"Pass the Goddamn thing," Victor shouted, from the seat directly behind the driver.

"That's illegal," Karman said. "You're not supposed to pass a funeral."

They argued a bit, Victor growing more insistent, Pete standing his ground. Suddenly, Victor threw a leg between Pete's shoulder and the door, shoved Pete to the passenger side, and jumped behind the wheel. He gunned the accelerator and the car shot out of lane, on a blind curve, swinging around the last car in the procession, past one big limousine after another.

The station wagon finally pulled abreast of the hearse. "Okay, we made it . . ." Victor started to say and Dylan shouted: "Cops!" At the front of the procession a state police cruiser paced the way, its dome light gently revolving, and before Victor could slip back behind the hearse the trooper spotted him and waved him to pull over. The funeral procession ground to a halt.

"The stash!" Dylan shouted. "Hide the dope!" Karman grabbed the marijuana jar from the dash board, bobbled it like a nervous first-year quarterback, and passed it back. Dylan shoved it under a rear seat.

The cop walked over to the driver's side and if they were all high a moment ago, they were now as sober as they'd ever be. "The registration," the trooper said, in a soft Western drawl. Dylan pulled it out of his pocket and handed it over. Ashes & Sand was listed as the owner. The cop glared at the four freaky-looking guys in a brand new car and not one of them could safely be identified as Ashes & Sand.

"What are you people doing?" the cop asked.

"We're a group," Dylan said, holding up his guitar. "Like the Kingston Trio, but there's four of us. We sing." He couldn't say he was Bob Dylan because the cop probably had never heard of Bob Dylan, but a group like the Kingston Trio might work. Dylan strummed a few chords and sang. Clayton joined him. The other two remained silent, for fear of giving it away. And the cop finally said: "Okay, get on out of here. And be careful." Victor drove off, slowly. Dylan leaned his head back. "Stop at the next gas station, Victor boy. I got something to do."

They raced through Central City, which was closed up because it was off-season, and Dylan told them about the summer he spent there; "Played rinky tink piano for the strippers in an old timey western ginmill. Right out of Gunsmoke." They stayed over in Reno for a couple of days, gambling, Karman losing all his money, and then they pushed on towards San Francisco. Dylan had a concert in the Berkeley Community Theater and it had been sold out for weeks in advance. The undergraduates at the University and kids from as far north as Oregon and as far south as San Diego had joined the pilgrimage.

"By this time I was disillusioned, my mind was being blown," Karman recalls. "Dylan was a very strange character. His notion of reality was like nothing else I'd ever experienced. I sort of was getting the idea *I* was crazy. I was beginning to feel crazy when *they* were crazy, Victor a freaky nut and Dylan very weird and Clayton always high on pills, and I just had to break away from them."

Karman had friends in San Francisco and he went to see them the night before the concert. They reinforced his feeling that some kind of insanity had struck the wandering minstrel and his entourage. But Karman was completely out of money, having dropped his last cent at the gambling tables, and he decided to stick it out to the end. A few hours before the concert he asked Victor for a pair of tickets, for his friends. "What are you talking about?" Victor demanded. "We got no tickets to spare for friends."

"For Christ sakes, they're my *friends,*" Karman said. "Of course you've got tickets. There's always plenty of tickets for the performer to pass around to friends."

"Sure," Victor said. "But *his* friends. Not your friends."

Dylan came in at that point and listened to the argument for a moment. Then he broke in: "What do ya want out of me, Peter?" "I don't want anything out of you," Karman said. "I just asked for a couple of tickets for friends and I'm getting hassled."

"You want tickets, right?" Dylan asked. "Then ya want something out of me."

"I've never asked you for any . . ."

"I brought ya to a party for Peter, Paul and Mary," Dylan shot back. Karman remembered it, of course. A birthday party for Peter Yarrow, a couple of months earlier, and Karman had been in a down mood and had stayed out of everyone's way and Dylan was bringing it up now for the first time: "I take ya to a party and ya act cool and ya sulk all night, in front of my friends. Ya ignored all my friends."

"What are you talking about?" Karman asked. "If it bothered you back then, why didn't you say so? Funny time to be bringing it up."

"Ya ignored my friends," Dylan insisted, "and now ya want tickets for your friends. Very strange. You trying to use me, Peter?"

Karman's brain felt like it was being wrenched around inside his skull. "I'm beginning to think I'm crazy," he shouted, "when it's really you guys who are crazy. You're all out of your minds. I'm going back to New York before I get as crazy as you guys are."

The concert is one of those memorable events that is still talked about in the San Francisco area. Dylan was never so attuned to an audience, his kind of audience, the hippest, most radical and aware college students in the country, and he held them the way few entertainers ever hold an audience, few Holy Roller gospel preachers either, for that matter. And when he came back after intermission and introduced Joan Baez—a stunning surprise—it electrified the audience. Dick Fariña, who had been divorced by Carolyn Hester and had since married Joan's sister, Mimi, has written:

"Had a literary audience been confronted by Dylan Thomas and Edna St. Vincent Millay the mood of aesthetic anxiety might have been the same."

When the concert was ended, Dylan, Clayton, Maimudes, and a new member of the group, Bob Neuwirth—a folk singer who replaced Karman—drove down to Baez's home in Carmel. Fariña, who was there with Mimi, later recalled in a magazine article that Dylan brought French fried almonds, glazed walnuts, bleached cashews, dried figs, oranges and prunes. Joan's mother, visiting from Paris, cooked a beef stew. They all sat around later talking about old friends back east, in Harvard Square and the Village, a gathering that wasn't much out of the ordinary, except that it was the King and Queen— and by now that's what the fan magazines were calling them. They played some old Everly Brothers records, Clayton sang some of the whaling and sea songs in which he specialized and a few Appalachian folk songs, and only once did anyone mention Dylan's music. "You know, Bobby," Joan said, "I'm thinking about recording a whole album of your songs." Dylan replied: "Sure thing." That's all.

Suze was very upset by the time Bob returned to New York after his six-week absence. Toward the end of his trip he hadn't bothered calling her at all. He had tried to keep her from seeing people and holding down a job, as has been pointed out, and yet he was gone for more than a month and had stopped calling her. When he returned it was as if he had slipped downstairs for a pack of cigarettes. And he seemed a lot meaner now.

Jack Elliott: "When he got famous around then, he got kinda mean. He was very quick, very sarcastic, dealt with people like a boxer, parrying blows and remarks and skipping out in a hurry. Which was good. Dylan's way was the only way not to hurt yourself. These people just hang on and bore you to smithereens. It's an energy drain. You have to shut the door on fans and groupies, even it if means running little numbers on them."

But Dylan began to run some of his numbers on friends, using them as targets.

Carla Rotolo: "As things got worse and worse for him, in terms of demands on him, he got tighter and nastier. He'd tell people he's got the truth, he was going to show everybody everything, tell them he had the truth about it all. That's where he started using bayonets on people. He could look at you and pick out a weakness and suddenly grab it and use it on you. Which is what he did with everybody. He'd find their vulnerable spots, and just demolish them. At that time he was very vicious to everybody."

Sue Zuckerman: "Once we all went down to a little Chinese restaurant near Carla's place on Avenue B, Bob, Pete, Suze and myself and a friend from college. We were talking about politics and history and Bob wouldn't let anyone get a word in edgewise. But what he was doing was just fabricating what he called facts. It was about history, and the forces of history, and he was trying to talk about the things he felt emotionally, but he insisted they were facts. He couldn't back anything up, but he insisted they were facts and everybody should know them. He wasn't letting anybody else speak, his whole attitude was that nobody else had anything to say on anything, and after a while Suze got up and left the restaurant kind of upset. His attitude wasn't pretty. He used to say, 'Dave Van Ronk always kids me that I never read any books but I know more than ...' and that kind of thing."

Carla: "I used to stay in the Limelight 'til four in the morning because I didn't want to go home. I'd come in and see them sitting in the room with the TV set, or a lot of people around, and there was no privacy, absolutely none. I felt I was some kind of freak. I began to think I was crazy because he had a way of telling you, 'You're full of shit, you're this and that,' and even my head was blown. I thought I was flipping out. Once I said to him, 'Hey, man, again, let me take your place on Fourth Street and we can swap apartments and everybody'll be happy,' and he started coming on like the song he wrote about it all, *Ballad in Plain D,* about my being lousy for this reason, and rotten for that reason. And a parasite. How could he call me a parasite when for a long time I was the only one with a job? But it was just devastating, the way he could twist somebody's words back on themselves and make them feel he was right and they were wrong.

"You must remember something about Bobby at this point in his career: he couldn't sort things out for himself because of where his career was going, he just couldn't get himself together, he was going through a weird time. And one reaction was using the bayonet on everybody around him."

Suze's sister and her closest friend may not be the most objective witnesses available (especially since Dylan used his sharpest hooks on Carla in *Plain D,* getting revenge on her as he was to get revenge on so many others in his songs) but their recollections of Dylan's "viciousness," are corroborated by practically everyone who had contact with him at the time: Baez, Elliott, Ochs, Van Ronk, Dave Cohen, among them. It was not constant, Bob was frequently warm and funny and almost open with his nearest friends, but on many occasions when his mood swung to a dark, savage side, he ran his numbers on everyone.

For Suze and Bob, it all came to a head in March, during an argument that was more heated than any before. Dylan's version is in *Ballad in Plain D.* Suze, he writes, was caught in the middle of an argument he had with Carla, the "parasite" sister. But what actually happened was between Bob and Suze who broke down completely. Bob left the apartment and Suze once more went to live with her mother in New Jersey. It was the final break between them, although Bob attempted to get Suze to return to marry him for almost another year.

"He took it badly, very badly," one friend recalls. "He used to come around the apartment and pound on the door and shout, 'Let me in,' but Carla wouldn't open the door. Suze came back to live with Carla in a couple of weeks and Dylan kept coming around, but

she didn't want to have anything to·do with him. In a couple of
months, she'd see him occasionally and spend time with him and
their friends, but she refused to go back to him. It was too late. It was
over. He'd lost her by then, although he couldn't realize that for a
long time. He kept asking her to come back, but for Suze it was all
over."

1964: *Mr. Tambourine Man*

"I HAD HEARD the Beatles in New York when they first hit," Dylan
told me in 1971 as we sat in his studio. "Then, when we were driving
through·Colorado we had the radio on and eight of the ten top songs
were Beatles songs. In Colorado! *I Wanna Hold Your Hand,* all those
early ones.

"They were doing things nobody was doing. Their chords were
outrageous, just outrageous, and their harmonies made it all valid.
You could only do that with other musicians. Even if you're playing
your own chords you had to have other people playing with you. That
was obvious. And it started me thinking about other people.

"But I just kept it to myself that I really dug them. Everybody else
thought they were for the teenyboppers, that they were gonna pass
right away. But it was obvious to me that they had staying power. I
knew they were pointing the direction of where music had to go. I
was not about to put up with other musicians, but in my head the
Beatles were *it.*·In Colorado, I started thinking it was so far out that
I couldn't deal with it—eight in the top ten. It seemed to me a
definite line was being drawn. This was something that never happened before. It was outrageous, and I kept it in my mind. You see,
there was a lot of hypocrisy all around, people saying it had to be
either folk or rock. But I knew it didn't have to be like that. I dug
what the Beatles were doing, and I always kept it in mind from back
then."

Dylan went to England in May for a concert tour. In London the

Beatles, the Rolling Stones, Eric Burdon of the Animals and members of some of the other rock groups that were changing the structure of pop music came out to see him. After his concert in London, Dylan spent some time with the Beatles—striking it off especially well with Paul McCartney and John Lennon—and they got stoned together; Dylan turned on the Beatles to marijuana. Bob later told one interviewer, "We just laughed all night, that's all, just laughed all night," not mentioning dope because back in 1964, you didn't publicly admit using the stuff.

The English tour made a large impression on him, for the Beatles and the Stones demonstrated with great force that rock-and-roll was viable once more. During the years Dylan had turned to country and folk, rock-and-roll had degenerated to commercialized pap. But the British groups returned to the original black roots and transformed what they heard into something that once more had a breath of life to it.

Bob Dylan, to a friend on his return to New York: "My God, ya oughtta hear what's going down over there. Eric Burdon, the Animals, ya know? Well, he's doing *House of the Rising Sun* in rock. *Rock!* It's fuckin' *wild!* Blew my mind." Burdon's rock interpretation of that old folk song was the first folk-rock, although it wouldn't be called that until Dylan returned to rock.

For Bob Dylan, protest was completely dead at this time. He would never again write a song of explicit protest. Although he would continue publicly to perform the best of his protest songs for another year he was deliberately moving away from the *Broadside* niche. The shift was gradual, for Dylan knew one thing about his audience: "You gotta keep control over them. You can't jump from one mountain to another. You gotta bring them along with you through the vallies so's they can see what's behind them and where they're goin' next. Nice and easy."

To Phil Ochs: "The stuff you're writing is bullshit, because politics is bullshit. It's all unreal. The only thing that's real is inside you. Your feelings. Just look at the world you're writing about and you'll see you're wasting your time. The world is, well . . . it's just absurd."

To a friend, who has it on tape: "I stopped thinking in terms of society. I'm not really part of any society, like *their* society. You see, nobody in power has to worry about anybody from the outside, any cat that's very evidently on the outside, criticizing their society. Because he *is* on the outside, he's not in it anyway, and he's not gonna make a dent. You can't go around criticizing something you're not a part of and hope to make it better. It ain't gonna work. I'm not gonna go along with things the Johnsons and McNamaras do, I'm just not gonna be a part of it. I'm not gonna make a dent or anything, so why be a part of it by even trying to criticize it? That's a waste of time. The kids know that.

"The kids today, by the time they're twenty-one they realize it's all bullshit. I know it's all bullshit. Kids realize it's really a drag to plan for tomorrow their whole life, realizing in really hard terms that tomorrow never comes. You always wake up and it's today. There is no yesterday, tomorrow never seems to come, so what's left is today. Or nothing. There's no reason for anybody not knowing what's real, if they'd only open their heads."

And he began to express aloud the fears that friends sensed after Kennedy's assassination:

"All I can say is politics is not my thing at all. I can't see myself on a platform talking about how to help people. Because I would get myself killed if I *really* tried to help anybody. I mean, if somebody *really* had something to say to help somebody out, just bluntly say the truth, well obviously they're gonna be done away with. They're gonna be *killed.*"

What Dylan was saying struck a chord on the campuses, among SDS members and those within other radical groups in which political naivete was giving way to a deeper radicalization based partially on Marcusian realities about industrial society and the one-dimensional man it has spawned. Says Carl Oglesby, about Dylan and SDS:

"Even after abandoning the anthem writing period, when he turned to a new kind of literary epic, Dylan became more political in mood than before. At a certain period in a young man's life he will say, 'How many more years?' and a little bit later on, having been around and seen what happens, casing the joint and getting a better sense of the immensity of the forces in play, he knows it takes a damn long time. The change involves understanding that laws are not written out of scruples of human instincts; that's not how they're made. If anything they are dim reflections of the realities of power. By the Sixties, Dylan and the Movement and everybody just knew the world is run by these criminals in power, knew how powerful these criminals are. The lamentable deaths, the betrayals, the losing of hope—it comes as no surprise. That's where Dylan moved to, where the Movement moved to at precisely the same time."

There is also another factor in what many have called Dylan's loss of commitment. He had become more certain of himself as an artist, as a poet; not simply a folk-poet, in the Guthrie tradition, but an artist from whose grave-dark mind began to spring epic images. Bombarded by visionaries such as Rimbaud, Brecht, Byron, Ginsberg, and the anonymous authors of the Bible, among others, the songs that were beginning to flow from him were growing more transcendent, less concretely objective, increasingly filled with the shapes of vivid fantasy, with the motifs out of the collective unconscious.

"I have to write for myself now," he told one friend. "There's stuff in me bustin' to get out and I'm not gonna hold it back."

He told another friend: "You have to vomit up everything you know. I did that, I vomited it all up and then went out and saw it all again."

A part of what Dylan was into had been summarized by Rimbaud, almost a hundred years before:

"The poet makes himself a seer by a long, prodigious and rational disordering of the senses. Every form of love, of suffering, of madness; he searches himself, he consumes all the poisons in him, and keeps only their quintessences. This is an unspeakable torture during which he needs all his faith and superhuman strength and during which he becomes the great patient, the criminal, the great accursed —and the great learned one!—among men. For he arrives at the *unknown!* Because he has cultivated his own soul—which was rich to begin with—more than any other man! He reaches the unknown and even if, crazed, he ends up by losing the understanding of his visions, at least he has seen them!"

Dylan saw them, and flashed through unspeakable tortures over them during the next two years, until his motorcycle accident in 1966. In our conversations later, Bob made it clear he had experienced precisely the mystic damnations Rimbaud had written about.

Dylan's shift also reflected the latest alteration of his self-image. Dylan put it this way, in a discussion taped by a friend:

"I'm not really a social critic. I knew where to put the song back then, I knew where the slot was, that's all. When I wrote those songs they were written within a small circle of people. I took the time out to write those things, in little rooms and all. I can remember that. Stopped to write them consciously. The other stuff I was doing, resembling more what I'm writing today, they came from inside of me and I didn't have to stop to write them. They don't resemble the protest songs at all. I was me back then, and now I'm *me.* You dig? I can't ever be the me from back then, I can only be *me,* from today. And the me from today is involved in a bigger circle of people."

Typical of a man who changes identity from time to time, Dylan had to deny past accomplishments. Only what he is doing now mattered: "There is no yesterday, so what's left is today." This was not a pose, for Dylan, not conscious additions to his myth. Bob Dylan was continually seeking a new identity because his psyche could no longer comfortably live with the old. He had to move on.

Bob Dylan did not sit down one warm spring day in 1964 and consciously work out his future, did not analyze, calculate the options available, and suddenly leave protest and move on to something else. Dylan was not a coldly scheming general conducting a campaign of media conquest, although he and Grossman sometimes made it seem that way. He was, actually, beset by fears, uncertain, confused. He had been forced to mature in a goldfish bowl during the previous two years. Dylan's intimates say that people were reaching for him, demanding to know what was in his head, that Grossman and others were working on his ego by, among other things, telling him he couldn't do much wrong because he was the great Bob Dylan, that sycophants were sucking up to him and hustlers were trying to manipulate him for their own gain, and everyone was giving him conflicting advice about his career. "He was getting hit from so many sides," says one writer who spent time with him, "that he just didn't know what he was up to any more."

"I'm hungry, and restless, and pretty damn wretched," Dylan said at this time. "I used to think I was smart, but I don't know any more. Don't even know if I'm normal."

He was a personality before he could become a person, a fate that has destroyed many talents. His fans made him a symbol, a hip existential hero, and it weighed heavily on him. He was feeling more threatened by it all, and he began to spend a lot of time in Bearsville and Woodstock, and grew even more elusive than before.

Dave Van Ronk: "He finally had to face the reality of the fame, and it scared him. He never trusted anybody in his life. Now there were a lot *more* people grabbing at him, to mistrust."

And yet, although he was beset by fears, he believed his audiences were ready for a "new" Dylan, that he could bring them along with him. To those around him it seemed Dylan had an intuitive sense of his power, of his ability to make it all work for him. "He never made a mistake, in terms of theater," Eric Andersen says. "That comes out in his songs—theater, and the theater never went wrong."

The first public awareness of what was swirling in him came at the Newport Folk Festival in July, 1964. Dylan had, of course, written and performed non-protest, personal songs before; *Bob Dylan's Blues,* on the second album, actually started with a spoken introduction that was a put down of the commercial folk song: "Unlike most of the songs nowadays, that're bein' written uptown in Tin Pan Alley, most of the *folk* songs, that is ... this song was written somewhere

down in the United States." And many of his other songs were outside the protest idiom. But in Newport, 1964, Dylan provoked a
storm by singing love songs—negative bitter songs of love gone
wrong. The audiences were captivated by this Dylan; the kids responding to a young man who was suffering as they were. But the
professional upholders of the folk tradition were aghast. *Sing Out!*
published a long impassioned letter to Dylan, begging him not to
change, demanding he not give up protest. "I wouldn't mind so
much if he. sang just one song about the war," Irwin Silber, the
magazine's editor, was quoted as saying at the time. Others accused
Dylan of selling out to Grossman, to Columbia, to the fast buck.

The shouting grew more shrill a month later, with the release of
Dylan's fourth album, which contained many of the songs he performed at Newport. The album title, *Another Side of Bob Dylan,* told
it all.

Dylan talked about this with Nat Hentoff. He had gone into the
studio one evening only a month before the album was released and
Hentoff was there to watch and to interview him for a *New Yorker*
profile. Hentoff, who has been around music and musicians for a long
time, believes Dylan has been honest with him most of the time, has
expressed what he was actually feeling and thinking at the time, not
running his little games on Hentoff as he did with most interviewers.
(The one exception, with Hentoff, is the *Playboy* interview published
in 1966, a put on that will be discussed later.) Dylan and his producer,
Tom Wilson, planned to do the album in one session, trying to get
it down on tape as quickly as possible because Columbia wanted it
ready for the fall sales convention. When he came into the studio he
brought with him a group of friends, including Jack Elliott and Victor
Maimudes, several bottles of Beaujolais from which he drank as he
worked, seven new songs in various stages of completion, including
some he had sung at Newport, plus a half-dozen others that were
incomplete ideas still locked inside his head.

"There aren't any finger-pointing songs in here," Dylan told Hentoff before beginning to work. "Me, I don't want to write *for* people
any more. You know—be a spokesman. From now on I want to write
from inside me, and to do that I'm going to have to get back to
writing like I used to when I was ten—having everything come out
naturally. The way I like to write is for it to come out the way I walk
or talk."

Later, in a restaurant in the Village, a friend stopped by as Hentoff
was finishing up his interview. The friend asked Bob whether he had
stopped doing the old folk songs to concentrate on his own material
and Bob replied: "Have to. When I'm uptight and it's rainin' outside

and nobody's around and somebody I want is a long way from me—
and with someone else besides—I can't sing *Ain't Got No Use For
Your Red Apple Juice.* I don't care how great an old song it is or what
its tradition is. I have to make a new song out of what *I* know and
out of what *I'm* feeling."

The album was a stunning reversal and made it clear beyond doubt
that Bob had abandoned folk in his search for, depending on your
point of view, greater meaning, or greater fame. Bob Dylan was no
longer the anthem-writing revolutionary. Much of it was clearly autobiographical, songs about the imperfections of man, forcing his
audience to face themselves. A song is an *experience,* Dylan has said;
you don't have to understand the words to understand the experience, and trying to understand the full meaning of the words may
destroy the feeling of the experience. Or, as Picasso said it: "Everybody wants to understand painting. Why is there no attempt to
understand the song of the birds? Why does one love a night, a
flower, everything that surrounds a man, without trying to understand it all?" More and more, as his songs defied analysis, as experience overwhelmed definition and verbal communication collapsed,
Dylan would resist those who tried to understand every word of what
he was saying. Everyone is free to find their own meaning in Dylan's
songs.

The central theme of *Another Side of Bob Dylan* is love and personal freedom. Most of the songs are caustic comments on human
relationships. Love is more than facades and games and knots; it is
mysticism and fantasy, honesty. It is part of that inner world that
society has forced us to repress; it is Eros, not *Vogue.*

Many of the songs seem to be written to Suze, but are also directed
to all women. *Ballad in Plain D* is most obviously a song of Carla,
Suze, and Bob, and the destruction of a love affair. *It Ain't Me Babe*
tells Suze and all women that the search for an illusory Hollywood-
romantic love, for someone who will die for her, who will pick her
up each time she falls, a lover "for your life," has turned him to stone
because he cannot fulfill such terms. *All I Really Want To Do* tells
his woman that he is not attempting to destroy her mind, to bring
her down or make her spin, to crucify her or classify her, that all he
wants is to "be friends with you." *I Don't Believe You,* telling Suze
he doesn't understand why she turned her back on him, why she acts
as if they've never met. And telling all women that he can play that
kind of game, can pretend they have never touched. And *To
Ramona,* a lovely song that rings farewell to a woman over whom he
grieves because she is trying to be part of "a world that just don't

exist," a fake dream-world, a vacuum, filled with worthless words that have "twisted and fed" her mind and made her believe that the "finishin' end" is upon us; a world filled with worthless people who made her believe she must be like them. And, he says, it makes him sad that he can't help her, can't show her the truth.

There is a second theme to the album, Bob Dylan explaining his view on another level: that involvement in causes is lifelessness. Dylan has discarded what he now considers the barren political moonscape, denouncing the old myths in a song that sums it up for him, *My Back Pages*. He laughs at himself as an impotent musketeer waging false battles (as Phil Ochs has put it). By extension, he sneers at all the other impotents who continue to believe they can change the world by protesting against the criminals and their crimes. In six verses and four minutes and 20 seconds, Dylan plumbs deeply into the futility of his times, illuminating with "flashing images" (Dylan said it) what so many of the nation's young were feeling about the American-Hollywood-TV-textbook-Dream. *My Back Pages*, taken together with the rest of the songs and with the liner notes, meshed perfectly with the mood of the disaffected generation.

In *My Back Pages* Dylan says the old slogans and the old symbols don't work. In the "love" songs he argues that the old consciousness doesn't work; that we must get beyond consciousness and into ourselves and others. The poems that take the place of album liner notes are part of the collage that Dylan was building, part of the experience of Bob Dylan. Go fight your own battles, he says to Joshua, for Dylan has to go to the woods for a while to live and to dream, because he has learned that nothing makes sense, anywhere. That he has no answers, no truth. Except, maybe, don't play *their* game; discover in your own head what it's all about.

Once more, Bob Dylan was completely in step with his times. At the very moment flower-power and turn-on-tune-in-drop-out and other anti-authoritarian ideas of the youth-drug culture were taking shape—before becoming media cliches, at the instant Jerry Rubin and Allen Ginsberg and Timothy Leary started proselytizing a generation, Bob Dylan was there. Starting right here, with *Another Side of Bob Dylan*, and on through the next several albums, he would have an incalculable effect on the growing radicalization of the young. He helped create a cultural climate that made it possible for the Beatles and most other rock groups around to break out of the three-minute vise of popular song and to pass along their own visions (or pseudo-visions) and add their voices to the attack on a valueless and corrupt society. Dylan became an unofficial leader of the Movement and of all those causes that add up to a truly new generation,

possibly even a "children's crusade," as someone has called it. "The
movement is a school," Jerry Rubin says, "and its teachers are the
Fugs/Dylan/Beatles/Ginsberg/mass media/hippies/students/fight-
ing cops in Berkeley/blood on draft records/sit-ins/jail."

Dylan denied he was a leader of anything. "I agree with everything that's happening, but I'm not part of no Movement," he told
Nat Hentoff. "If I was I wouldn't be able to do anything else but be
in 'the Movement.' I just can't have people sit around and make rules
for me." The denial was in keeping with the radical-anarchistic spirit
of the Movement. Anyone perverse enough to say he wants to be a
leader is going to lose any following he may have had, for the Movement abhors formal leadership. Dylan clearly was on the same wave-
length.

Dylan's role as hip hero was, in a sense, stage-managed by Bob
Neuwirth who encouraged it and almost directed it. As Fariña described him, Neuwirth was one of the original hipster nomads who
shuttled back and forth between Cambridge and Berkeley. He
became a Dylan companion after Pete Karman dropped out of that
strange cross-country trip the night of the Berkeley concert. Neuwirth had worked the Club 47 in Cambridge when it was *the* folk
center of the East, playing an easy country-folk at the time Baez, von
Schmidt, Hester and other young singers were making it there. It is
said he was every bit as talented as Dylan, but never had Dylan's
obsessive drive. Neuwirth seemed to dissipate himself in a hundred
directions. He is Dylan's age, and at that time resembled him in a
striking way: skinny, small, nervous, wasted, jumping around all the
time, manic, with a very quick mind and a fast, caustic wit, elusive,
almost as secretive as Dylan.

Eric Andersen recalls: "Dylan was coming around to play the hoots
again in 1964. He wasn't always up in Woodstock, he'd come down
to Gerde's and the Village to see what was happening. He had made
it, he sort of came to check it out. Ochs was running around sort of
maniacal, telling everybody how great it was when actually everything was all uptight. The bandwagon had broken down, the political
topical thing was gone, everybody was on his own trip. And Neuwirth was around on his own trip."

Another singer, part of the Dylan set: "Neuwirth was a scene-
maker, a very strong cat. When he got to New York in 1964, he
started hanging around Dylan. And Dylan started to change at that
time. Part of it was Neuwirth, he was a real strong influence on
Dylan. Neuwirth had a negative attitude, stressing pride and ego,
sort of saying, 'Hold your head high, man, don't take shit, just take
over the scene.' He was the kind of cat who could influence others,

work on their egos and support those egos. His whole negative attitude fell in perfectly with what Dylan was feeling, because of Suze and the fame and all the rest of it.

"Neuwirth gave everybody a devil-may-care attitude. His thing was very nebulous, sort of Prince of the Scene, always on the scene and always around, a big personality, and he got Dylan to be a personality. Neuwirth was sort of a famous people collector, the kind of guy who would say, 'Hey, let's go see Marlon Brando,' then call him up and get together with him. He got Dylan into that trip."

Eric Andersen: "Dylan understood that he was kind of a hip hero and he practiced it, but he didn't really dig it because it wasn't real. Only it took him a while to discover it wasn't real."

As Dylan underwent the transformation into a "personality" he began to turn his back on old friends, many of whom grew angry because they felt he had used them. The Smiths, for example, hadn't seen much of Bob in the past year and were somewhat bitter about it, that he had lived with them when he was unknown and in need of food, shelter and companionship, and slowly moved away from them as he grew famous. He had almost completely cut himself off from them by this time, and Mrs. Smith wanted to know why. She recalls:

"We saw him backstage at a concert, before he went on. Bobby was racing back and forth, getting ready, and we talked to Joan Baez for a while. We helped him with something on his trousers. And then I said to him: 'Why haven't we seen you? Shall it be my backyard or your backyard?' And this boy, as fast as lightning, said, 'There are no backyards.' "

One of the pressures on Bob was his obligation to fulfill a book contract. A number of publishers learned that Dylan was writing his autobiography. An editor at MacMillan moved quickly and signed him to a contract. The book was to be called *Tarantula,* and Dylan devoted a great deal of time to it. He had talked about his original conception of the book to Studs Terkel, in May, 1963: "It's about my first week in New York . . . Not about the big city, really. The big city's got nothing to do with it. It's about somebody who has come to the end of one road, knows there's another road there but doesn't exactly know where it is, and knows he can't go back on this one road. . . . It's got all kinds of stuff in it which doesn't add up, thoughts in my head, all about teachers in school, all about hitchhikers around the country. These are friends of mine, too, you know. College kids, going to college. And these are people that I knew, and everyone's sort of a symbol, I guess . . . for all kinds of people like that. And like

New York is a different world, especially I'd never been to New York before, and I'm still carrying their memories with me so I decided to write it all down. . . ."

The concept changed, somewhere along the line, and the book became what Dylan calls "collages . . . no rhyme, all cut up, no nothing, except something happening which is words. The book doesn't begin or end."

But *Tarantula* didn't work. Dylan was doing songs and albums, going on the road a lot and taking his typewriter with him to write the book, and very upset that he had a deadline. It became a drag for him. It grew less lucid as he went along, more stream of consciousness that both defied meaning and lacked the emotion of poetry. Much of it was absurdist word-play. Dylan was unhappy with it, but still he plunged ahead, forcing himself to write. There was a feeling among some friends that he was seeking some sort of approval from the literary establishment which had ignored him.

Dylan was performing publicly as often as he could, doing many concerts across the country. One of the more important was a program at Philharmonic Hall in New York, Saturday, October 31, Halloween night. Columbia Records taped the show, hoping to get a live album out of it. Dylan did about eighteen songs, and the tape indicates he had reached a high level of musicianship by now—his guitar and harmonica work had grown enormously, and he demonstrated a great deal of control over his material. He also showed he was able to take his songs less seriously than most of his audience. Introducing *The Gates of Eden* Dylan smirked: "This is a sacrilegious lullaby in G minor." At one point he told the packed house that overflowed on seats on the stage: "Well, hope you're all havin' a good time. . . . It's Halloween and, uh, I've got my Bob Dylan mask on." He performed some protest songs, among them *Hard Rain, Hattie Carroll,* and *Davey Moore.* And he stunned the audience by bringing out Joan Baez after intermission. They did four songs together, including *With God On Our Side.*

But this was mostly the new Dylan: *Gates of Eden, It's All Right, Ma, (I'm Only Bleeding),* and *Mr. Tambourine Man;* each of them personal visions from the mind of a popular poet, some of them difficult for an audience to understand at first hearing. "An introspective, symbolist piece that moved in and out of this listener's comprehension, but still conveyed a strong mood," Shelton wrote of *Tambourine Man* in his *Times* review. The new songs, differing in quality, in texture, in color, were still all of a piece in stressing personal freedom as man's basic reason for being. And personal freedom meant liberation from all the cultural hangups imposed by the authoritarians, all the societal structures that deny truth and create walls between us all.

Tambourine Man would become the most important of his songs in this period. Artists rushed to record it, and it rose to the top of the record charts. Some old Dylan friends claim the song is based on a story told Dylan by Ivars Perlsbach, a friend from back in Dinkytown. Ivars had been born in Latvia in 1944, when the Russians were pushing back the Germans. Ivars and his mother were placed in a Russian internment camp. His mother eventually escaped with her two-year-old son in her arms, and made her way through the winter snow to the American lines, traveling with a group of other refugees. All across northern Europe they trudged, and the only joy they had was at night, when they made camp, for then the local folk musicians would come and play for them. The children enjoyed the tambourines most of all, and they would ask: "Play a song, mister tambourine man."

Dylan denies the story. "That's just not true," he told me. *"Tambourine Man* had nothing to do with Ivars. The song just came to me. I never heard any story like that from Ivars."

Many Dylan fans believe *Tambourine Man* was about a dope trip. For Dylan, though, it represents an awareness of his life that goes beyond the temporary insights that drugs may sometimes bring. Dylan was beginning to feel that his success had trapped him in the same artificial value system that had enslaved most of society. He was, he told me years later, beginning to recognize that something false and evil was happening to him, but he was not yet able to understand what it was. *Tambourine Man* represents Dylan's first attempt in song to reach out for something beyond the immediate present, for something to help him climb out of this miserable cage in which we live, away from the "twisted reach of crazy sorrow."

1965: *It's All Over Now, Baby Blue*

ROCK WAS BEING transformed into something vital again by some of the finest musicians in the country, many of them conservatory drop-outs who refused to accept the conventional wisdom in music any more than they would accept it in their life styles. The so-called British invasion had helped churn it up, and Dylan never forgot how much the Beatles had stunned him. And in the Village many of the most talented musicians were moving into electric instruments and the rock beat. Dylan caught those tremors of the new musical direction. Bruce Langhorne was into it. Danny Kalb, Al Kooper and Steve Katz were members of the Blues Project, playing gigs at the Cafe Au Go Go on Bleeker Street. They had come together in 1964 as the Danny Kalb Quartet (Tommy Flanders rounded it out). After playing some background on an album of blues numbers recorded by Dave Van Ronk, John Koerner, Eric von Schmidt, Geoff Muldaur, Kalb and a couple of others—an album called *The Blues Project*—they adopted the name for their group. (Among the supporting musicians on that original Blues Project album is a "Bob Landy," who is Bob Dylan. On one cut, he is playing the bottom part of the piano while von Schmidt plays the higher register.) The Fugs had come together in a small theater on St. Mark's Place in the East Village and their members included poets Allen Ginsberg, Gregory Corso, Ed Sanders and a half dozen fine rock musicians and chorus members. They were wild in appearance, outrageous in lyrical content, heavy on the music, and when they moved to spots along MacDougal Street they generated enormous excitement. In Chicago, Paul Butterfield had put together his Butterfield Blues Band, with Mike Bloomfield as lead guitar, fusing electric instruments with the black blues he had grown up with in Chicago's black bars. Dylan knew them all, and they helped move him into rock.

The clincher came in the first months of 1965, when the Byrds, a California folk group, demonstrated what could be done with Dylan's songs by performing them to a modified rock beat. The previous summer, when Dylan was cutting the album, *Another Side,* he had asked Jack Elliott to sing *Mr. Tambourine Man* with him. Elliott didn't know all the words and the song didn't work out. A tape of that out-take was sent to David Crosby, one of the more intelligent musicians around, then leader of the Byrds. The group had been experimenting with electric instruments and they cut a single, *Tambourine Man* backed with Dylan's *All I Really Want To Do.* Bob was sent an advance copy and, a member of his set recalls: "He was stunned. He ran around saying, 'Fuckin' wild!' For Bob, it was like the Animals rocking *House of the Rising Sun* all over again. Rock worked."

He went into the studio at this time to work on his fifth album, *Bringing It All Back Home*—the title indicating a return to his rock roots. He brought with him Bruce Langhorne to play lead guitar, and eighteen songs, some of which he had written in Woodstock over the last couple of weeks. Tom Wilson had several other studio musicians waiting, and Dylan worked with them, tirelessly, drawing on his own musical knowledge to create the canvas of sound he was trying to paint. It was Dylan's concept, all the way, but he was able to draw out of the other musicians their ideas, their musical feel, using them as he had used his friends back in Hibbing, to give his music a substance.

Bringing It All Back Home was released in March, 1965, and eventually became his first million dollar seller. The album erupted on the scene like an earthquake. Seven songs on the first side backed by electric instruments and the lyrics—in such symbolist poems as *Subterranean Homesick Blues, Maggie's Farm, Bob Dylan's 115th Dream,* and some of those written for the Philharmonic Hall concert: *Gates of Eden, It's All Right, Ma, and Baby Blue*—were again denounced as a complete "sellout" by the folk purists. *Sing Out!* attacked him: "It's a pity and a frustration, for if ever the world was in need of the clear and uncompromising anger and love of the poet, it is now." The writer called the new Dylan "a freak and a parody," not realizing that by opening up the language, using more complex images than ordinarily found in song, reaching a larger audience with rock, his new attitude was more critical of the social order than before. The previous album had been bad enough, but at least those songs of personal pain were performed with an acoustic guitar and sounded folksy. This new one, however, was rock. Presley stuff. Bob was becoming a teenage idol, and that was completely unacceptable.

Joan Baez also felt Bob was betraying those committed to reform. Just before *Bringing It All Back Home* was released, Dylan and Baez began doing a series of formal concerts together; Dylan was no longer an unannounced guest but shared the bill with her. Ric von Schmidt had drawn a poster, a simple water color with a Toulouse-Lautrec feel to it: Baez and Dylan playing their guitars, above them the announcement: "In Concert: Joan Baez & Bob Dylan." It was used only once and then discarded. The reasons depend on who's telling the story. Joan's manager, Manny Greenhill, recalls that Dylan rejected the poster because it pictured him in his poor-boy cap and by now his image had changed. Von Schmidt recalls that Greenhill didn't like it because Bob was too prominent, and Grossman didn't like it because Joan seemed to be the focal point.

"It was a great concert tour," Dylan told me. "I have nothing but fond memories of it because it really worked so well."

Joan and Bob had been lovers for at least a year, spending as much time together as they could manage, considering she lived in California and he in New York. Joan's attitude continued to be one of helping Bob with his career, helping him get exposure, wherever possible, even though he had reached and possibly surpassed her level of popularity. Normally, Joan never worked two nights in a row, but she did for Bob. She performed at a solo concert in Convention Hall, Philadelphia, packing 11,000 fans in on March 5, and the next night she played the New Haven Arena with Bob. She played a couple of other successive gigs with him later in the month, and on stage they seemed to be as close as any King and Queen could be.

But Bob was ready to move on. His attitude toward Joan was beginning to change. He and Neuwirth began criticizing Joan for her "naivete" about the value of commitment. Joan was in the process of founding the Institute for the Study of Nonviolence, her school in the Carmel Valley. She was one of the "outside agitators" the police denounced after she appeared at Sproul Hall during the 1964 Berkeley demonstrations. She was totally committed to moving people to become forces for good in the nation. Dylan and Neuwirth told her she didn't know what she was doing, didn't know the meaning of the words she sang and spoke, that movements were a waste of time in the face of the realities of power, and they hurt her. Further, while Bob was criticizing her for her commitment he made it clear that he was more interested in being the "rock and roll king," as Joan puts it, than in any kind of social involvement. "I'm not responsible for those kids," he told her after one concert, and she felt that he meant what he said.

A member of that last tour recalls: "There was serious conflict. When we were finishing up the tour there were real blowups and everybody was walking gingerly. Dylan was very upset much of the time, towards the end of it, and even Neuwirth was walking gingerly."

The word around Village folk circles has always been that Bob proposed marriage and Joan turned him down. However, as we'll see later, Joan says they joked about getting married, that it wasn't a formal proposal. But she concedes that Bob must have come away pained.

Immediately after the concert tour Joan and Bob and their aides —Grossman, Greenhill, Neuwirth and others, plus a film crew from Leacock Pennebaker, Inc.—went over to England to do a tour that has come to be known as the *Don't Look Back* tour from the film that was released two years later. It became pretty obvious by the time they got to London that Bob had dismissed Joan as no longer having any meaning in his life. They never sang together again.

There is some question among some of those who were close to Bob and Joan as to which came first, Bob's break with Joan, or his meeting Sarah Lowndes. Dark-haired, attractive, a former model who has been described as "a mystical kind of chick when Bob met her, into all sorts of Eastern religions just at the time Bob was into the I Ching and Ginsberg's Buddhist stuff." They met some time in late 1964 and she seems to have captivated him. "She accepted him for what he was, without trying to groove on knowing the great Bob Dylan," one friend says, "and without asking what he meant by his songs, like most chicks did." She was a friend of Grossman's wife, Sally (the young woman posing with Dylan on the cover of *Bringing It All Back Home),* and was a frequent guest at Grossman's place in Bearsville, where Dylan continued to spend much of his time. Sarah was living in the Chelsea Hotel with her young daughter. Bob, who had given up his West Fourth Street apartment, usually stayed with friends or in a hotel when he came to town. Now he took an apartment at the Chelsea to be with Sarah.

It is possible, some friends say, that Dylan deliberately hurt Baez to break off the relationship, because of Sarah. Others believed he grew closer to Sarah only after months of turmoil with Joan, and after their relationship had dissolved.

1961–1965: *Visions of Johanna*

JOAN BAEZ LAUGHS with genuine pleasure as she remembers incidents from back then, during the years she and Bob were so very close. She sat in a counterfeit Scandinavian-modern chair in a New York City hotel room, her arms hugging her knees to her chin, in blue denims, blue-striped polo shirt, her hair cut a lot shorter than it's ever been, and you're caught once again thinking she's so much more enchanting than her photographs. Her black eyes sparkle, she laughs often, her smile is lightning quick. She turns serious as she recalls something painful from those days. Then the smile comes again as she remembers something funny, or as Gabriel, Joan and David Harris's son, age six months, gurgles in his playpen.

She had seldom talked about Bob in the past, she explains, because "there are so many people who live vicariously off people like Bobby, and I hate it when it happens." And, also, "out of a loyalty to Bobby." But once she began to reminisce about what it was like, being with Dylan, "I realized that everybody who talks about him must really like it because in all our lives there's so few things that ring real."

We talked for about three hours, in that hotel room.

Let's start with how you first met Bobby.

JOAN. I guess it was in the Village, I heard his name whispered around, it was in Gerde's Folk City and he was singing his song to Woody. And he knocked me out completely. As I remember him, it seems he was about five feet tall, he seemed tiny, just tiny, with that goofy little hat on. I think I went back a couple of times to hear him. And he was just astounding. I was knocked out, totally absorbed. I thought, "God." His style, and his eyes and the whole mystical, whatever it was, and I just thought about him for days. I was amazed, and I was happy. He really made me happy that there was somebody with that kind of talent. I'm really hooked on geniuses and any time it happens along I really get excited.

Did you meet him that first night?

JOAN. He came over that night. Somebody said "Oh, you gotta meet Joan," and he came over and there wasn't anything I could say. I said "far out" or "beautiful" and Bobby mumbled, "Hey, hey, too much." I don't know what he said, something equally as dumb, and that was all.

Tell me about the early days with Dylan, the first period. Did you get together?

JOAN. Bobby was always just out of reach the way he probably is for most people. And, I can't remember the order of how, I remember vaguely being at a party and he had just written *God on Our Side* and I was in that state of disbelief that anybody was turning out something like that. There was a lot of mystique about him, and also hiding. But sweet and funny you know, the really wonderful thing about him is that sense of humor, it's really terribly funny, and cynical. And forming, you know, he was forming.

You brought Bob up as a guest on a number of your concerts. Had you drawn close?

JOAN. Not really, I wanted people to hear him. I think we liked each other and I really loved him. I wanted to take care of him and have him sing. I mean, brush his hair and brush his teeth and get him on stage. ...

I get that from most girls and women who knew him in those days, this great maternal. ...

JOAN. Yeah, it was very maternal. And then I wanted to have as many people hear him as possible. I asked him to appear with me because he was brilliant. I loved him, I loved his music, I wanted people to hear him. That was it. I mean, I wanted to share him. And he dug it. He'd get drunk and scared but he dug it. I guess the concert I remember most was Forest Hills. I was always afraid for Bobby. He didn't seem to have the stage fright kind of fear. He seemed to submerge that and it came out in paranoia about people afterwards, like coming at him for autographs. He was so terrified. I remember times later when we sang together officially, you know, at those concerts where nobody could decide how to arrange the names so his wouldn't be higher than mine, and mine higher than his—all that crap. Afterward, he'd have these big getaways all planned, it was just bullshit. I think that in a way he needed people pounding on the car and breaking the car antenna and climbing under the hood and everything.

He'd say "Wow, fucking my mind, I can't stand this whole shit." Obviously there were other ways to get out of a building. One time we got out of a limousine somewhere, when we were doing concerts together, and two girls came screaming, "There's Bobby." They came screaming at him, and he said "Oh, wow, let's run," and I said "You dumb ass, just stand here," and I took his hand, and he was like a little kid and they came up all hysterical and teary and I said "Now stop acting so stupid and he'll give you his autograph." And then he calmed all down. They looked a little embarrassed. It was beautiful. I said "Just talk to them a minute, Bobby," so he did. He gets control the minute he sees he can have it, but I think he genuinely was terrified of people like that.

But Bobby had no conception that he could calm down the kids who were ready to tear his clothes off?

JOAN. I think he probably learned some of that, but certainly at the beginning, when we did concerts together, he didn't understand this. Because it's a conflict. You want the people to scream and holler and love you and climb up on the stage and pull at your hair. I mean you want that because it's irresistible to an ego because ego doesn't understand it. It has nothing to do with love, nothing to do with anything genuine. It's just hysteria. And so you feed on it in a way, and the other half of you recognizes that it's baseless. But then Bobby also had the genuine fear of being hurt, I think, and being trampled. Because you can see yourself get trampled.

Did he have a fear at all of the audience? I'm told by people who knew him back in '61 at Gerde's that they had to put drinks into him, a lot of wine into him, bolster his ego to get him to get up and perform.

JOAN. I saw it come out in very different ways. He never had the traditional stage fright the way I did, sit down and have diarrhea and feel nauseated for forty-five minutes before a concert. He was always bopping around writing songs. But it would come out in another way, a sudden furious tantrum because his coat was stolen one time. That scene you probably heard about—it was unbelievable. This horrible little coat. I'm sure to this day he thinks I must have stolen it. Because I used to try to get him to—it had throw-up all over the front of it. I guess he got drunk and threw up on it. It was his favorite. It was this shitty-looking horrible brown thing, there are hundreds of pictures of him in it. It smelled horrible . . . was too short, it was short in the sleeves, made him look like a poverty-stricken little Welsh schoolboy.

Which is exactly the effect he was trying to attain.

JOAN. Yeah, and I was really working on him, trying to get him to get rid of that jacket. And one night we showed up backstage—I guess we must have left for a while and gone back to the dressing room—and his jacket was gone. And he had a tantrum, I mean like a five-year-old, and he screamed at the policeman and the policeman scurried out, and he screamed at who else was there and they all scurried out. I think Neuwirth was there. And there was that kind of tension that I would always think would have something to do with

194

having to perform. That night was amazing, though, because I wouldn't scurry out. He was really wildeyed with fury. "My fucking jacket . . . somebody took my fucking jacket, and all you fuckin' cops get out of here, and you fuckin'—and fuck fuck fuck. . . ."

I said "Oh Bobby, take it easy" or something, and he started to blow up because nobody was supposed to talk to him like that. And I asked "You want to practice or do you want to have a tantrum?" Or some equally dumb maternal thing like that, and then he calmed down. He said "I'm not mad," I mean I've seen that in other people before and I don't know what you'd call it, but he refused to admit he was mad. He switched roles, we practiced, he gave a brilliant performance in the first half. At intermission I said, "Gee, you ought to get pissed off more often," and he had another tantrum. I mean it was terrible. He said, "I was not mad," and I said "No, you were furious, but I won't talk about it here."

This thing was his form of stage fright?

JOAN. I have no idea. It happened at other times, too, but it seemed to me that was all built up around—I mean it happened at times when he wasn't performing. Things like that. To me it would seem like tension of having to perform or having to be who he was.

A number of reviews of concerts where you performed together said Bob detracted from the program, and there were also complaints from people at the Hollywood Bowl in '63.

JOAN. I think he was drunk or high on something, and he went on much too long. He could never resist singing what he had just written and he had just written *Lay Down Your Weary Tune*, it was forty-five minutes long.

The one that somebody called 'War and Peace'?

JOAN. Right, it was just endless. Of course, I was perfectly happy, except I was concerned. I've always had an audience conscience. I've always worried about making them tired or whatever, and he wasn't.

He was drunk when he sang his War and Peace song?

JOAN. I don't know if he was drunk.. Yeah, I guess he got drunk a lot. Audiences got sore at him, and I should have known better because it wasn't good for him—people getting mad at this little punk who came out of nowhere, singing these forty-mile-long songs.

What was his reaction? Was he aware that the crowd was hostile?

JOAN. He just seemed very young when this happened. He seemed young and smaller than usual, and I just wanted to protect him all the more. He'd say something like. . . . Oh, he'd never talk about it. But if you brought it up, then he'd admit, "Hey, wow, ooh . . ."

Hollywood Bowl is a weird place. You see, in different places he was received differently. In Boston, as I recall, he was received well.

He was drunk there, though, and that's another thing I think is stage fright, too—getting loaded so he wouldn't feel anything. He did beautifully, no matter how he was. He would stand up and sing whether he was smashed or straight. The concerts were fun. I mean I just looked forward to him as the funn*est* part of the concert for me, and I'd ask him up on the stage, and we'd sing mostly his stuff—a couple of other things we did. I guess we did *Butcher Boy*. But he'd just come up and sing, and in the hipper places people just went wild. They just loved him. He'd sing some stuff alone, and then we'd sing some stuff together.

When we used to sing concerts together and he'd start getting keyed up like that coat thing, oh, he'd start screaming about who was taking charge of the getaway car, who was this and who was that. I'd slip a Librium into his coffee. I don't think he ever knew that. Sometimes I'd slip two of them and a couple of times it helped. I could see him sag a little bit and, whew—he was this bundle of nerves.

And he was never aware of it?

JOAN. The Librium? I don't think so. I think he would have been pretty pissed off if he had known.

And did the Librium improve his performances?

JOAN. He didn't need improving. It just improved my nerves a little bit.

Did it improve his stage presence?

JOAN. He did relax a little bit.

I think Dick Fariña in his piece in Mademoiselle *quotes Bob as saying something along the lines of "Joannie's still singing* Mary Hamilton. *That's not where it's at." The impression has been left that Bob turned you on to the protest in music, in song.*

JOAN. No. Not at all. Not in my spirit. In songs, yes. There weren't any I could sing until he wrote them. He wrote songs that hadn't been written yet. There aren't many good protest songs. They're usually overdone. The beauty of Bobby's stuff is its understatement. Anything that's brilliant is an understatement like that. You don't have to hit anybody over the head with it. Even his most blatant stuff, when he was really young, it's still clever enough so that it's not dull or heavy.

Yes, there's a stamp of genius even on the . . .

JOAN. On absolutely everything he ever wrote. Even the crummy stuff. I mean, some of it's crummy, kind of crummy.

Getting back to those hostile audiences. His basic feeling about audiences, as I get it, is not quite yours. You're concerned with your audience, he's concerned with his material and himself more than the audience.

JOAN. I could never figure out what he was concerned with. I mean the most real conversation I ever had with him—which was the beginning of Bobby and my splitting—was after the last concert we did together. I can't remember when or where, it was somewhere on the East Coast. . . . But, ah, we were having fun. There were a lot of people up in the hotel. That's when Dan Kramer took those goofy pictures of him ironing my hair and stuff. We felt good together, it had been fun and everything. And then he said—you know, you'd get these private-private talks, you'd have to go and hide under a couch somewhere and talk—and he hauled me off to the bathroom and said, "Hey, hey, let's do Madison Square Garden." And I suddenly had a really funny feeling, and I said "What are we gonna do with Madison Square Garden?" And he said "I don't know, man, it'll just be a gas to do Madison Square Garden." I thought about it a minute. "I'm scared," I said. "I think what it means is that you'll be the rock-and-roll king, and I'll be the peace queen," and he always put me down when I talked like that. He'd say, "Bullshit, bullshit," but the fact was that night the kids in the audience had been pleading for *Masters of War, God on Our Side,* any song that he'd ever written that meant something to them. And he knew immediately what I meant when I said I'd be peace queen and he'd be rock-and-roll king, and he said, "Hey, man, I heard those kids, I heard them, right? I can't be responsible for those kids' lives." I said, "Bobby, you rat, you mean you're gonna leave them all with me?" He said "Hey, hey, take them if you want them, but man, I can't be responsible." It didn't mean he didn't love them, you know. I think he was just afraid. But it was real, he meant it. And that was the last time we ever sang together.

Why was it the last time?

JOAN. Because of that. I think so. That was the end of that tour. We didn't continue it. I think after that he came with me a couple of places where I was singing.

What about Don't Look Back. *My impression was that was the last time you sang together.*

JOAN. I never sang with him. He wouldn't let me sing, to put it bluntly. I should never have gone on that tour. It was sick. You see, originally I was going to go to England and have a concert tour, and in the middle of that Bobby's rise to fame came so fast that a few months later, we thought we'd go together and do split concerts. By the time it got around to England, Bobby was much more famous there than I was, and so Bobby just took England. I mean I didn't even bother with a tour. But, you see, I thought he would do what I had done with him, would introduce me, and it would be very nice for me because I'd never sung in England before. That's what I had in my mind. And by the time we got to England, whatever had happened in Bobby's mind—I'd never seen him less healthy than he was in England—he was a wreck and he wouldn't ask me on the stage to sing. And I was really surprised. I was very, very hurt. I was miserable. I was a complete ass; I should have left. I mean, I should have left after the first concert. But there's something about situations like that—you hang around. I stayed for two weeks, and then when I walked out the door in the film, I never came back after that. I went to France and stayed with my parents. They lived in France then. But it was one of the really most painful weeks in my life because I couldn't understand really what the hell was going on.

Understand there was a proposal of marriage on Bobby's part at one point which was around the time that you last . . .

JOAN. Well, I wouldn't put it that formally. We joked about it, you know. You see, Bobby and my coming together was inevitable: crown prince and Newport and all that stuff. It was inevitable. I was involved with other people, and he was involved with other people and when we finally shed all the other people and met—then we were together. But it was something that just had to happen in the course of our lives.

The whole king and queen thing, as the pop journalists were putting it, was inevitable?

JOAN. I think that we both would halfway kid about it and get scared and back off. I wouldn't say Bobby proposed to me. No, we talked about it. We talked about getting married. And we kidded about it because we knew, in a sense, we almost felt it was inevitable, too. But luckily we both had enough sense to realize that it would have been a complete disaster. But I think what happened was that I expressed it before he did. He would have, probably, eventually. But he was still in the joking stage and I said, oh, you know, it'd never work out or something. . . . And after that was the switch, after that he never was. . . . I mean, after that it was as though he was trying to get back at me. . . .

Well, he's got a highly developed sense, a need for approval.

JOAN. And *prrride.*

And Pride. And obviously this was a rejection of him.

JOAN. Yeah, I think that's what happened. He was on the East Coast and I was on the West when that came about in a phone conversation. And ever after, it was as though he was playing around with my soul. But you see we were still going to go to Europe, which was really dumb on my part because I should have understood his kind of psyche and how he was going to feel. "Hey sure, sure come to Europe, you can help me out," is what he said, and I thought that meant I would sing with him, and I think probably, originally, he planned on it and then decided against it.

Were you aware at the time, before you got to Europe that he was bigger than you, so to speak.

JOAN. Yeah, I knew that perfectly well, which is why I cancelled my tour. I was just perfectly happy in that position, that I'd go to Europe and then. ... When the plane landed in England, I think Bobby was torn because he was scared and he wanted me by his side. I couldn't tell that then, and I stayed back because I felt very much that I didn't want to impose on his scene. It was Bobby's tour, and I stayed about ten feet in back of him, literally not noticed by anybody. That was fine. But a couple of times, as I think back, he gave a look. It was like 'Help,' and I couldn't decide whether it was more important to go and help him.

What was the situation?

JOAN. It was just coming out of a building, out of the airport after a press conference, and he went like this (signaling), like 'Come here,' but I didn't want to jump into his scene. Maybe it was stupid modesty, maybe I should have, 'cause maybe he needed me then. But I didn't jump in. And that happened a couple of times. Then after that he never asked again, so then I never saw him. I mean I was like never allowed. ... Oh, I went into the room and stuff, but it was that stupid revolting scene. Bobby would get the record player and put on his record, sit with his back to everybody and type, and everybody'd sit around and eat. It was really revolting. The most human he got was that night in the film where he'd been typing and we sang some stuff, or I sang a song he'd written and forgotten, and then I kissed him on the head and left.

And that was the last real contact you had with him?

JOAN. No, I saw him once years later, in a concert in San José. I went to see him in San Francisco and then San José, I think. Or two nights in a row, I think, in San Francisco, and then I spent late into the night with him in San José. But he was not being real. He was getting into these arguments with people about. ... I remember him saying, "Hey man, if ya gonna bomb Hanoi, whyn't the fuck, man, they bomb Hanoi? I mean, I don't give a fuck if they bomb Hanoi." It was all sort of saying, "Hello, Joanie," I felt, when he couldn't say anything more real than that. And that was when he was married and he didn't tell me he was married.

Yeah. That was very confusing, too, And he. ... I don't think. ... I think he didn't want to be around me, or I was too much to bother with, or he was genuinely not interested at that point. I feel now as though I really imposed myself. I should have gone home, but people don't. I mean, when you're around somebody like Bobby, you do impose. I mean, you stay around until everybody is kicked out.

Why is that? What is there about him?

JOAN. Charisma, probably.

Yeah, but what's the charisma all about?

JOAN. I've never understood charisma. There aren't many people who have as much as Bobby has. I've never met anybody who has as much. My husband has a different style of it, when he speaks. But it would never be as glamorous as Bobby's because it's telling people to do something.

I get a feeling that David is not manic the way Bobby is.

JOAN. Yeah, there's also the charm about Bobby's being maniacal. I mean you can't resist watching it, see which way it's going to go next, even if you stand there and get hit over the head with it.

Did you feel this in the very beginning?

JOAN. Oh, yeah, the charisma, and it was obvious he was on the edge of something. You see, I think Bobby comes closer to being psychotic than neurotic. I just say that because of the couple times that he got drunk and turned against friends, just turned on them, and I couldn't believe it. I would never buy it. It wasn't real. I would stand there and fight him.

I guess the most I did take was in England, and I'm amazed when I look back that I took that much. But I loved him and I couldn't believe that he was, you know, just being so hurtful. And even when he was sick, at the end of that tour when he got so sick, and God I was just in agony. I didn't know how sick he was, and I wasn't allowed in his room.

What was he sick from?

JOAN. Oh, hell I don't know, I think he over-ate in Sweden or something. They all went off. . . . I mean you live with Albert Grossman, you're gonna eat. Everybody said "I'm tired of being in England, let's go someplace where there's a good restaurant." I don't know if they went to India or someplace, but everybody took off and came back sick. And I didn't know whether Bobby had tonsillitis, syphilis or just a stomach-ache or what, but he was pretty sick and that's when he called in Sarah. But he would see my mother, he'd see everybody, but he wouldn't see me.

I went out and bought him a shirt, something. I mean I wanted to tell him that I loved him, that I cared for him, that it didn't matter what was going on and everything, and I was glad Sarah was there because she seemed to care for him, you know, somebody to take care of him. And I bought him a shirt and went to the door and, I'd never met her but I guess that's who came to the door. And she took it and I never heard anything after that. That was the closest I got to seeing him. And then I left England.

My basic feeling about Bob, as a revolutionary, is that in the beginning he was writing understated yet still the basic protest, topical song. Somewhere along the line he moved from the anthems to the more personal stuff, introspective, and yet truly more radical. Did Bob ever talk about where he was going, talk about the writing, talk about the Movement?

JOAN. No, he just denied everything he'd ever done as he moved along.

Even personally? I know he denied it to newspapermen.

JOAN. Yeah, he said to me something once. . . . Of course, I have to distinguish between before and after that one phone call. Before, he was more honest with me, but it would take me sometimes four hours to get something out of him that I knew was the truth. And then he'd say, "Hey, don't you never tell nobody, man. You're the only fuckin' chick who's ever made me do that." I mean, 'cause nobody had the patience.. . . .

Like what? Remember any of it?

JOAN. Yeah, one night he shouted at Victor. Bobby was in one of his psychotic frenzies about. . . . I don't know what it was about, but it was at my house in Carmel, and he said, "Victor, Victor, you're nothing but a road manager." I said "Bobby, what a way to talk. Is that . . . ?" And he said, "Hey, why don't you keep out of this?" And I said I didn't want to hear him talk like that in my house. Then it all simmered down and later on I said, "Bobby, why did you talk that way, why are you rude to me?" He said, "Hey, the only reason I said what I said to you is that you looked hurt, right?" I thought, "Did I look hurt? I *did not* look hurt." I said "I *did not* look hurt, I wasn't hurt, I was mad." He said, "Hey, you were hurt," and I said "Bobby, I *wasn't* hurt and you know it," and he said, "Hey, hey I know it, hey, but don't ever tell nobody." He said, "Hey, you're the only chick who pins me down on that kind of shit, hey. I don't want to hear about it, I don't want to think about it." And then he was in a good mood again and we laughed. But I can't *believe* it. He does that to people all the time, and they really think, "Oh, I must have looked hurt."

You were able to pin him down. Did you ever pin him down on his writing, or his feelings?

JOAN. No, it came to a draw. I said something about *God on Our Side*. "What were you thinking when you wrote that stuff?" He said, "Hey, hey, news can sell, right?" and I said, "Oh, Bobby, speaking of selling, you don't think I'm gonna buy *that*, do you?" He said, "You know me, I knew people would buy that kind of shit, right? Hey, I never was into that stuff," and he denied it all. I said, "Well, you can deny it till you're blue, but you know I'm never gonna believe it." I never carried it farther than that.

He never talked about the radicals he knew or the radicalization of his own head?

JOAN. No, he'd never admit to anything like that.

Even with you?

JOAN. He teased about songs, I got him in some songs, but not the radical ones. It was like *Four Letter Word*. I remember he'd just written it all out on paper, and he said, "Hey, can ya dig this?" I read it off, he hadn't finished the last verse yet. He said, "Bet ya can't guess what's gonna happen," and I said, "Sure I can, you're gonna go back to the girl's house and fuck her." And he said, "You bitch, how'd you figure that out?" And I said, "Cause that's what you always do." It didn't take any genius on my part. Teasing, things like that. But I don't remember ... because I don't know if it was clear to Bobby what he was doing when he was writing those songs. But you can't take *God on Our Side* and pretend you wrote it because you thought it was gonna sell.

In your book, Daybreak, *you call him the "Dada King."*

JOAN. Oh, he was so busy saying, he was busy being dada, everything's crazy, sort of comical, cynical or however you want to put it. And he was avoiding being real with anybody by doing that. I mean he had *weird* stuff going on. He'd just written *Visions of Johanna* which sounded very suspicious to me, as though it had images of me in it. I mean, I can't ever say that publicly. But he'd been talking to Ginsberg about it. First of all he had never performed it before, and Neuwirth told him I was there that night and he performed it. And that was very odd. I was listening to the song and sort of inwardly wanting to feel flattered, but wondering whether—you know, I mean, everybody in the world think Bobby's written songs about them, and I consider myself in the same bag. But I would never claim a song. But certain images in there did sound very strange. Then Ginsberg came up at one point and said, "What do you think *Visions of Johanna* is about?" And I said, "I don't know, Ginsberg, your guess is as good as mine." He said, "No, no, what do you think it's about? Bobby says ..." and then he reeled off this pile of crap that had nothing to do with anything. And I said, "Did Bobby say that or did you make that up, Allen?" I had the feeling the two of them were in sort of cahoots to make sure I never thought the song had anything to do with me. I had that feeling a lot. And I wouldn't give any. ... I mean Ginsberg was trying to get me to say I thought the song was written about me, and I would never say that about any of Bobby's songs.

You had the feeling Ginsberg was acting as Bobby's front man?

JOAN. Yeah, I did. You see, he had been hanging around Ginsberg. That's another great story, funny story, of how I meet Ginsberg for the first time. And by the way, I dig Allen. He's crazy, but I dig him. It was at a party. I guess Bobby and I must have given a concert. I was feeling very off Bobby that night, so Bobby was trying to make it with some redhead. He got very drunk at this party, and he was flirty-flirty-flirty-flirty, talk-talk-talk with this redhead. And so I started talking with Neuwirth and hanging out with Neuwirth. I think Neuwirth had on a blue velvet jacket. Anyway, Ginsberg came up, introduced himself and announced he wanted to fuck Bobby. And I said, "Well hello, what's holding you back?" And he said "I'm shy." I said, "Isn't that sad?" I can't remember much more about that meeting except that's all Ginsberg wanted to talk about. I was a little insulted myself. I hadn't realized he wouldn't have any interest in me at all and was just using me to get to Bobby. Then Bobby was completely and totally drunk. We got him out in the car and he was, oh, maudlin. I don't remember what he was saying, but I said "Ginsberg wants to go to bed with you," and he said "Oh, oh, far out," and then he passed out. Probably threw up on that horrible little jacket again. You see when people fall in love with Bobby they do it all the way. Just 'Bobby, Bobby, Bobby.'

In Daybreak *you said you've "seen him fake a regular heartbeat . . . He put us all on but mostly he put himself on . . . a bizarre liar . . . a huge transparent bubble of ego." You almost drowned in it. You heard "the pleadings, the words, the denials," and almost drowned in it.*

JOAN. He just did seem like a huge ego bubble, I mean, frantic, and lost, and so wrapped up in ego that he couldn't have seen more than four feet in front of him. . . . Well he can't anyway without his glasses. And also, see, I'd written him a note on Ralph Gleason's typewriter saying could I come back and see him because it would make it easier for me. I still felt terrible from London. Obviously, in a way something in me was still in love with Bobby. I mean that's hard to get over because, I mean it's not real. It's just that when somebody ignores you, you always wonder where you've missed and want to get back to be okayed—"Do you still like me, do you still like me, am I still okay in your book?" And that's what the note was really saying and apparently Gleason handed him the note and Bobby didn't even look inside. He said, "Oh yeah," or something, and was very vague about it. "Oh yeah, sure, tell her to come on back and say hi," so I went back to say hi and he was, I felt, just completely unreal. "Hi, hi, I hear you're running a school."

Up to now, I still wonder what Bobby thinks about me. You're bound to do that with somebody you loved once and who it seems, turned on you. But he would never. . . . Superficially, he'd say, "Turn on her? Wha? You know I talk to her, 'How you doing, you got a nice school.' " But inside you're wondering what does Bobby really think? I mean people want to be loved, want to be accepted, and when you feel as though somebody slapped you in the face you always want them to reassure you that they haven't. And so that also is what I was feeling. But I have the going backstage things mixed up. I can't remember which year is which and which night I stayed on and saw him afterward and had that discussion about Hanoi and which time I went home. When I wrote the "Dada King" was the time I went back home. And I did have this wonderful feeling afterwards, just tenderness, complete tenderness. I didn't feel demanding, like "Why doesn't Bobby spend time with me, and what's he doing with that stupid girl in the polka dot dress?" which is what I thought when I saw him at the party. I just thought, "I hope somebody takes care of that kid."

Reminisce a little about some of your memories of Bobby, personally and professionally.

JOAN. Oh, I think of the time at Woodstock. That was one of the nicest times we ever had. We were all staying out at that, ugh, Bearsville, the big house, the big haunted house.

Why do you say it's haunted? I don't know that story.

JOAN. Just gave me the fuckin' willies. People talking. . . . Well, I had nightmares. You know, when you're in a place and you wish you weren't there. . . . And it happened that night. The next morning, Dick Fariña, who was *always* into that kind of thing, he was staying there. Mimi, Dick, and Bobby and I, and I guess a bunch of other people around the house. And in the morning I looked like hell. I was just all green. I just passed through the house all night long in my dreams, and Dick, suspicious, said, "Did you have bad dreams?" And I said, "Yeah," and he said, "This house, isn't it?" And he went into this long great history of the house and how it used to have these pictures in the halls. I had dreamed about axes, I had dreams about people chopping up people all night, and Bobby—you couldn't get anything out of Bobby. When Bobby was out he was completely out, and I didn't want to wake him. I didn't want to scare him by telling him his house was haunted anyway. And the next day, Bobby and I went on a motorcycle ride. I can't remember who was driving. I think he was driving. I had dreamed about axes all night long. We talked about axes all morning long. We came to this fork in the road, and there was an axe lying there in the middle of the road. I was terrified. Gad, it was one of those dreams where it hangs over you the whole next day.

Another thing that I remember Bobby saying. We were sitting out, there was a lot somewhere in Woodstock near the antique stores. We were just sitting out on a little knoll. He used to go out a lot. He managed to go places in Woodstock. That was in the old days, though. I mean, it would be different for him now, anyway. But we used to go to that little coffee shop all the time. We had fun then. But he just said something about his memory. He said, "Hey, hey, tell ya one thing, hey. I got a fantastic memory, right? I don't never forget nothing." And I think it's probably true. I mean he forgets what he wants to forget, but if he wants to remember something, he'll remember. He'll go to his grave with it.

I used to drive his motorcyle around. I used to prefer to drive because he was a terrible driver, just terrible. I mean, I figured he was writing ten songs at once and trying to drive at the same time, and I always feared for us. So I'd always say, "Could I drive?" He drove so sloppy, he used to hang on that thing like a sack of flour. I always had the feeling it was driving him, and if we were lucky we'd lean the right way and the motorcycle would turn the corner. If not, it would be the end of both of us. So I'd say, "Bobby, you cheat, remember you've got somebody on here with you. Maybe that'll help you steer it, an' everything, better." Once when we got out of a store I said, "Let me drive," and he said, "Okay." So he got on the back and I drove and went over a bump and he said, "Hey, watch it, waddaya think I am, a fucking can of tomatoes?" What a nut. And I laughed. Sometimes when he'd say something like that I'd laugh for an hour. I laughed all the way home, and then he'd try to be serious and I'd look out the window and I'd think of that and I'd start laughing again.

Did he ever talk about when he learned to drive the motorcycle, in the early days driving the motorcycle as a kid?

JOAN. No. But every time we turned a corner if there was like a hill or something blocking the view, he'd slow down. I always had the feeling he'd been in an accident. So he was doing that once and I said, "Were you ever in an accident?" and he made some wisecrack about how I was "guessing shit." So I didn't push it, but I think he had been.

Yeah, he hit a kid once, when he was sixteen or seventeen. Didn't hurt him badly but it shook him up.

JOAN. Well, it didn't help his driving much. Oh, another time, he got drunk after a concert. He wanted to drive us. Victor was always

a good driver, and Neuwirth was a good driver. And Fariña was not.
I was never comfortable with Dick driving. He wanted to be the best
driver in the world, so he'd go fast and he could never quite handle
it. But Bobby insisted on driving one night and we got in the old
station wagon. He was driving us all from the city to Woodstock,
Mimi and Dick and Bobby and me and maybe somebody else. And
he was driving horrendously. We were just all terrified. Gee, he
terrifies you. You're afraid to say anything. And I was thinking "I
wonder if I took the keys out, like that (snaps fingers) if that would
do it," because we all said, "Oh Bobby, let me drive, hah hah," you
know, pussyfooting around, and he was having a wonderful time.
"Hey, I don't know what everybody's so fuckin' scared about. I can
drive, right? I can drive." I mean, if he'd taken his glasses off it
wouldn't have made any difference. He really nearly killed us. Finally Mimi and I said, "Oh, we have to go to the bathroom," so he
had to pull in, and we all got out of the car and he got out of the car,
and somebody else jumped in the driver's seat. And he laughed when
he came back from going to the bathroom, "Oh, man I can't believe
it. Everybody's so fuckin' scared. Everybody's so chicken. Wow, I
can't believe it." And I said, "Oh shut up," and he got in the back seat,
put his head in my lap and was asleep in about thirty seconds. Sweet
little baby.

*Was there ever discussion between you in the early days about
going down South?*

JOAN. Not that I remember, anyway. I was so inarticulate politically
in the early days. Bobby did do some political stuff, or stuff that he
thought was political. Like he accepted that Tom Paine award—that
big fiasco—and blew that scene.

It was a disaster for the people. I knew from their end because they
were friends of mine, the Foremans, and how terrible that was for
them. They loved Bobby, and here he stood up and just damned
them all to hell. I mean they saw the humor in it too, but it was very
hard, for they were responsible for that evening. Probably he was just
scared, I guess, got loaded and mouthed off. But I remember one
time, it was when we were giving concerts together. I think it was
after the discussion about Madison Square Garden, and I said,
"Bobby, we're alike up to a point, and then we're just split. We're
both agreed that the world is just terribly fucked and it's really a
mess, but I think there's something we can do about it. But you
don't." And he gave me a long rap, a very cynical rap, a good deal
of which was true, talking about the American white liberal mostly,
who goes campaigning into the South, and he said, "Hey, how many

people do you know who are willing to die for the cause? How many do you know?" And I named a couple of people.

White people?

JOAN. Yeah. I mean not necessarily just that cause, but willing to put their body really where their words were. And I considered myself one of them. . . ; I thought. I mean that may not be true because you never know until the very last minute. But I feel that way now and I felt that way then. I said, "Why do I think that there's something that can be done," and he said, "Maybe because you're a chick," and that's all he said.

What was his reaction to the Civil Liberties fuss? He ever talk about it?

JOAN. It was sort of like, "Oh, wow, fuck it all. Oh God." He knew he'd been awful. He was torn because Albert on the one hand was telling him, "You don't have to worry about that, you're a star. You don't owe them anything." And Bobby's inner conscience was saying, "You really screwed a bunch of people," and so he wrote them that apology.

Sort of an apology. He went to great lengths to put them down again.

JOAN. Yeah, right, but somehow in his mind he tried to get it straightened out. But I think the whole Albert thing was so destructive for him at every turn. And it's so sad, because Albert used to think he was doing right by people . . . money and fame. I mean, Grossman would say to me, "What do you want, who do you want to meet, hey you're a star, you can meet anybody you want to meet. What do you want, hey, we'll get it for you." I'd say, "Albert, don't talk to me that way. One, it makes me nauseated. Two, it's destructive."

You mean, "If you want to meet Marlon Brando, I'll get Marlon Brando for you?"

JOAN. Exactly. In fact, it was probably Marlon we were talking about. Then I could see how Dylan's mind was.

Was Albert screwing up his mind this way?

JOAN. Well, first of all, everybody was around Bobby 'cause he's so powerful. And unless you have something else to stand on, you know, you automatically feed on people. In England the biggest fantasy I had was of smacking Bobby in the face and saying "Stop it!" And sending everybody out of the room, and saying, "You want to completely destroy him, or you want to just half-way destroy him? Why don't you stop feeding that to him?" You have these dreams of making somebody see. I knew it was impossible. But I thought he was completely blind, and he was acting absolutely foul and everybody there was feeding it. Including Neuwirth. Which was sad.

You started to say earlier that you, at that point, weren't politically articulate.

JOAN. I had all the feelings and urges, but no clear direction.

Was Bobby saying to you at that point, "Hey, you don't know where it's at," as Farina quoted him as saying?

JOAN. Bobby had some faint respect for me. I think he recognized that I was real, even if I hadn't put it together yet, I think that he gave me credit for it.

Was he attempting to get you to put it together? Was he verbalizing any of it?

JOAN. No. The most he said, like for instance when we talked about Madison Square Garden, he didn't try to convince me that I shouldn't be responsible for the kids. He didn't put me down. Well, I'm sure he did, but I don't think he did much of it.

Not necessarily put you down, but attempting to guide you?

JOAN. I don't think so. Sometimes it came through Neuwirth. I had the feeling that Bobby and Neuwirth had talked about it, that I didn't really know what I was doing, or that non-violence meant absolutely nothing to them, and they figured that I didn't understand it well enough to be preaching about it.

Fariña quotes you at one point saying, "I don't like the word bomb *in a song, people don't listen to words like* bomb." *That was around the time that Dylan was moving away from explicit protest.*

JOAN. Well, at that point I wasn't talking about his music. I was talking about the people who wrote crummy protest songs.

I realize that. But it was in that period that he was moving away from the protest songs?

JOAN. Oh, you see I'm sort of puritanical and stiff. I could never enjoy the things that he did that wasn't protest until a year later. I'm still like that with a lot of his stuff because I felt so abandoned by his saying "I won't be responsible for those kids," in his music and in his words. I just felt sad, and so I was determined not to listen to the other stuff. Like I didn't like *Highway 61* until three years after it was written. I was mad at it, I was furious. I thought it was a bunch of crap. I didn't really listen to the words. But I felt as though he was inching around being committed. Well he was. Now it's hard to figure out exactly what I feel about that because Bobby did what he had to do, and he did leave a lot of us in the lurch. But he wasn't made to do the other things, so you can't push him. I feel sad about it, but why bother feeling sad, you know. Just go ahead and dig what he does. A lot of what he does is probably. ... The music to me is wrapped up in nostalgia. I mean I can never figure out whether it's a life force or a death force. Let's put it that way. Some of his songs, even like *Lay, Lady, Lay.* . . . I mean it's beautiful, it makes people reminisce, it makes people nostalgic.

Reminisce a little more about some of those concerts where he was your guest.

JOAN. You know when he wrote *When the Ship Comes In?* That was amazing, the history of that little song. We were driving around the East Coast, we were out in the boondocks somewhere, and I had a concert to give. I don't even know whether he was singing with me at that point, but he and I were driving together and we stopped. I said, "Run in and see if this is the right place," so he went in and came out and said, "Hey there's no reservations here." I said, "You sure?" and I went in and they said, "Hello, Miss Baez, we've been waiting for you." And I said, "Hold it a minute. I want an extra room, please." And then Bobby walked in, and he was all innocent and looking shitty as hell and I said, "Give this gentleman a room." And they said, "Oh certainly," but they wouldn't talk to him. He had said, "Does Joan Baez have a room here?" and they had said "No." And he went out. So then he went to his room and wrote *When the Ship Comes In:* "Your days are numbered." He wrote it that night, took him exactly one evening to write it, he was so pissed, "Hey, hey I'm writin' something. Hey, I'm writin' something." I couldn't believe it, to get back at those idiots so fast.

Did he do a lot of writing in your place at Carmel? Somebody was telling me he would sit in a corner with a Coke bottle and typewriter.

JOAN. Well, he was writing his book then. God, I still have a great hunk of it. If he wants it back he can have it. He wrote like a ticker tape machine. He'd just stand there with his knees going tung, tung, tung, back and forth. He was standing, and he'd smoke all day and drink wine. The only way I could get him to eat was to go over and eat right next to him, just peer over his shoulder and chew, and right away he'd start picking at whatever I had in my hand. So I made picking food. Otherwise I'd say, "You want something to eat?" and he'd say, "No, no." One time he was visiting, he wrote *Hattie Carroll,* and one time he wrote *Four Letter Word,* and a couple of other things. But mostly the second time he was there, he was writing his book *Tarantula.*

He ever talk about the name, talk about the book, what he was trying to do?

JOAN. No, he just said, "Hey, hey, writing about my childhood. Wait'll you meet the girl named Mona, right?" So fifteen pages he'd write about Mona. He wrote some beautiful things about running up to his own house and trying to get in. He had to pee, something about his mother behind the screen door and he was jumping up and down —he had to pee. I mean, they were beautiful. He never edited anything. He couldn't bear to take anything out of the sentence he'd written.

I was thinking of how at first I didn't want to talk about Bobby. But when I got started I realized that everybody who talks about him must really like it because in all of our lives there's so few little things that ring real. Most people are half dead and Bobby may be on a death trip, but he's got more life, more zonk or something to him. So you start talking about him.

What makes you think he may be on a death trip?

JOAN. I always pictured Bobby with a skull and crossbones on his forehead. I guess it's because I've seen him be destructive to himself and to other people. I've seen him not take care of himself. But see, I haven't seen him in years. . . . But back then I would say he was on something of a death trip, in a way. A withdrawal from life to me always seems like that, a withdrawal from commitment. But whenever somebody is mystical, I mean, you have to be a mystic to be a saint, and you don't have to be a saint to be a mystic. And Bobby's a mystic. He may be more devil than he is saint, I don't know. But he gave us a lot.

You don't have any idea where his head may be now, from having known him well, back then?

JOAN. No. I think he'd like to be somewhere comfortable and I don't know if that's possible for somebody with a mind like that. I think he's attempting that, from everything I've heard about him, he's attempting it with wife and children. I mean I hope he finds something there. Maybe he has. Some people say he's happier.

And others say he seems to be searching for something he lost back along the way. That is, he bought the house in the Village, and he's back down there because he's looking for something.

JOAN. Yeah, I can't imagine Bobby sitting back and saying, "Oh, hi," or "I've finally found peace." But then who the hell would say that except some moron? Especially because I think he's gonna try to be isolated and I don't think you find it that way. I think you'll always feel guilty enough in that isolation that you can't find peace. But I do think he's calmed down and I think that maybe some of the worst times of his life may be over. Like England. I mean England was hell. And I think it was as much hell for him as for anybody else. He was tied up in knots. That's what I thought anyway. He was treating everybody like shit and screamin' and hollerin', having fits.

Earlier we were talking, a couple of times you talked in terms of loving Bobby, can you expand on that?

JOAN. I think it's hard not to love somebody like Bobby. For me, maybe part of it is because of what I said, I'm really drawn to people who are exceptional, but also with him there's that maternal thing that we talked about. That feeling—you know—somebody's got to take care of him because he sure as hell is not going to take care of himself. And then just really loving his music. I mean you love it. You want to hear it over and over and over again, most of the stuff he does.

Were you able to separate loving his music and loving the man?

JOAN. Oh, I don't know, that's a hard question to answer. I mean, how could you imagine Bobby not ever having written that stuff? He wouldn't be Bobby if he didn't write that, and if he weren't a genius I. . . . It was everything, you know. It was the whole combination that makes up Bobby that made him irresistible. His humor, his warehouse eyes.

One time, it was his super grubby days, we were driving somewhere and I looked through his glasses when he turned his head or something. I said "Jesus, Bobby," and I took his glasses off and cleaned them, and he said "Oh hey, wow, hey, I can see." And I said, "How'd you like to be able to *hear?*" He was pretty low, and it made him laugh. He was really a grubby cat. He threw up out the window that night. He got drunk on wine, and in a tunnel somewhere he threw up, just had time to holler to whoever was in the back seat to shut their windows.

But some of it was just really beautiful. I remember days. . . . I guess we were with Victor and Dick and Mimi and Bobby. We'd stop on the highway and get out and dance and horse around—be crazy. Then Bobby and I would just fall asleep in the back of the station wagon. That was just really, really nice. Because I mean if you're with somebody for a long period of time, they're bound to have to calm down.

Once he bought me a beautiful coat, a blue-green corduroy thing. I wore it with a silk scarf. And I bought him a black jacket, and some weird lavender cuff links, and a white shirt. I remember it was winter then, and we were staying at the Earle in the Village. We were leaning out the window one morning and watching the kids. I felt as if I'd been with Bobby for a hundred years, and all those kids wondering around out there were our own children, you know? This couple looked up and I know they recognized us. They were beautiful . . .

1965: *Like A Rolling Stone*

AFTER THE ENGLISH tour, Dylan said, he decided to quit because it was too easy for him. It was down to a pattern, he complained.

He told one friend: "I play these concerts and I ask myself: 'Would *you* come to see me tonight?' and I'd have to truthfully say: 'No, I wouldn't come. I'd rather be doin' something else, really I would.' That something else is rock. I'd rather see me do rock. That's where it's at for me. My words are pictures and the rock's gonna help me flesh out the colors of the pictures."

The decision was made: Dylan had to get into rock, get a band behind him. Several rock musicians he began to work with at this time helped him flesh out the pictures, helped him take the step into electrified sound. Mike Bloomfield was one. Another was Robbie Robertson, of the group now called The Band. Some months after his return from England, Dylan met Robertson and the other members of the group—Rick Danko, Levon Helm, Garth Hudson and Richard Manuel. They then called themselves Levon and The Hawks. They had been together since 1959, and had been a backup band for Ronnie Hawkins who billed himself as "the king of rockabilly." But they had left Hawkins and were trying to make it on their own. John Hammond Jr., the blues guitarist and singer, son of the Columbia executive who had first signed Dylan, had met The Hawks at the Concord Tavern in Toronto in 1963, and they had played together as often as they could. Hammond brought them to New York in 1964, and with Mike Bloomfield sitting in on electric piano, they cut an album for Vanguard Records. The Hawks continued to work in the New York area, and Hammond got them together with Dylan. By the summer of 1965, Dylan had grown very close to Robertson and they frequently jammed together; Robertson, one of the more dynamic lead guitarists around, frequently sat in as Dylan was writing some of his songs, lending a counterpoint to Dylan's melody, following Dylan's lead and directions to make it possible for him to capture in sound what was in his head. (The long-accepted story, that Dylan called The Hawks while they were playing a gig in New Jersey and, without ever having heard them work, asked them to join him on a tour, is just another one of those pieces of misinformation that seem to swirl around Dylan.) Eventually, Robertson would be credited as tune writer on a couple of Dylan songs. "Robbie is an inspiration to be around," Hammond says. "He can only inspire you to play, and he inspired Bob."

Dylan had gone into the studio at the end of May and recorded a single, *Like A Rolling Stone.* "I wrote it soon as I got back from England," he told writer Jules Siegel. "It was ten pages long. It wasn't called anything, just a rhythm thing on paper—all about my steady hatred directed at some point that was honest. In the end it wasn't hatred. Revenge, that's a better word. It was telling someone they didn't know what it's all about, and they were lucky. I had never thought of it as a song, until one day I was at the piano, and on the paper it was singing. 'How does it feel?' in a slow motion pace, in the utmost of slow motion. It was like swimming in lava. Hanging by their arms from a birch tree. Skipping, kicking the tree, hitting a nail with your foot. Seeing someone in the pain they were bound to meet up with. I wrote it. I didn't fail. It was straight."

Revenge: Most of his songs from this point on would be songs of revenge. Dylan angrily sticking the hatchet into people who had hurt him, or whom he believed were destroying themselves and trying to destroy him because they didn't know truth. They were shadow-people, alienated from experience, divided from their true natures, so deluded by illusion that they were cut off from the inner reality. *Rolling Stone* could have been written for Neuwirth, as Joan Baez believes; it could have been written for her; more likely it was written for everyone Dylan believed had been trapped by the poison, including Dylan himself.

When you heard *Rolling Stone* back then it was like a cataclysm, like being taken to the edge of the abyss, drawn to some guillotine of experience. The rock band set up an enormous tension. Bloomfield on guitar, Al Kooper on organ, Bobby Gregg on drums, and four other musicians. *Wham!* It opened with a quick drum beat, and then organ and piano and guitar rolling over the listener, setting up an overwhelming sense of immediacy, drawing the nerves taut. And then Dylan: *"Once* upon a time ..." Biting off a word, spitting out venom, spreading a virulent emotion, infecting the listener. It is still probably the best song Dylan has ever done. Six years later it still moves, still bites. Back then, it destroyed the Dylan worshippers and brought him many new ones. Released in June, it quickly moved up the charts, hitting number one on some charts in August, the first popular hit by Bob Dylan.

The depth of the change in Dylan was fully revealed on Sunday night, July 25, 1965, at the Newport Folk Festival. Dylan was introduced by Peter Yarrow, but no one paid attention to his words this time, for Dylan needed no introduction. *Bringing It All Back Home* was selling several thousand copies a week. *Rolling Stone* was being played on Top 40 AM radio, music for teenyboppers. Unforgivable!

When he came running out on stage there was little doubt this was a new Dylan. Gone were the boots and the jeans and work shirts. When Dylan made himself over in a new identity, he did it inside and out, and the outside was now a reflection of the sights he had seen in England: kids expressing themselves and demonstrating their disdain of authority in wild and freaky clothes. Dylan had returned with a wardrobe of the latest London mod fashions, and he came out onto the Newport stage in a black leather jacket, black slacks, a dress shirt, and pointed black boots with Chelsea heels. Carrying a solid body electric guitar.

The audience sat transfixed as someone plugged his guitar into the amps and as a rock combo took its place behind him—the Paul Butterfield Blues Band. Dylan launched immediately into *Maggie's Farm*. He's not going to work on that farm—society—no more because he's trying his best to be what he is, inside, but everyone is trying to force him to be like them, and so he's quitting. The audience was bewildered, upset. This wasn't Bob Dylan. There were a few boos, mixed in with a smattering of applause. Most of the audience simply sat on its hands. Dylan plunged on and the boos grew more insistent. When he swung into *Like A Rolling Stone* no one clapped, and the boos and the heckler's shouts rang through the Festival site. "Go back to the Sullivan show!" someone shouted and laughter rolled up from the audience and across the stage. Dylan turned and stalked off, driven from the stage. Some who were there, behind the scenes, said there were tears in his eyes as he made his way backstage, and tears in the eyes of Pete Seeger, who was standing off to one side while rock was desecrating the hallowed Folk Festival ground.

"I did not have tears in my eyes," Dylan said in one of our talks. "I was just stunned and probably a little drunk."

Peter Yarrow returned to the microphone, obviously upset. "I don't know what to say," he mumbled. Then he raised his voice: "Want to hear more? Bob's gone to get his acoustic guitar if you want to hear more from him." Someone in the audience shouted: "Get his folk guitar!" To some folk "experts" the acoustic guitar was another instrument in the commercial plot to prostitute art.

Bob returned to the stage and quickly launched into *It's All Over Now, Baby Blue*, from the non-rock side of his latest album. The folk fans didn't understand that the song was Dylan again bidding the old allegiance goodbye. *(Baby Blue* can be interpreted on several levels. Friends say it was written for blue-eyed Paul Clayton, marking the end of a very close and warm relationship, although Dylan denies it. On a deeper level, Dylan again is saying that he must "start anew" because the old anthems don't work, the old society is useless; that he must face himself with honesty in order to continue.) But the fans cheered now because they believed they had won Dylan back to "pure" folk, had forced him to accede to their demands. They gave him a standing ovation, shouting "More!" and someone called out *"Tambourine Man."* Dylan said: "All right, people. I'll sing that for ya." The audience applauded again, once more not recognizing that the song was calling for the razing of all barriers that keep a man from getting to the truth within him (including the labels that artificially made some music "good" and some "bad"). The folk crowd knew only that he was using the *proper* guitar.

It has always been believed that Dylan was driven off the stage because a majority of the audience would not stand for his rock. But most of the audience was more open than that; many of his fans would have been willing to follow him wherever he took them. Ric von Schmidt has another explanation for what happened at Newport, one that makes a little more sense. Says von Schmidt:

"That historic '65 thing with the Butterfield Band has been totally misconstrued by everybody, including Dylan. The resulting thing, the attacks on him, would probably have happened anyway, but they happened at Newport in a bizarre fashion. The von Schmidt Theory of Newport goes like this:

"The Butterfield group had been invited to play there for the first time. They were gung ho to make a big statement. They played Sunday afternoon, but that was like the kiddy show, the matinee. You kind of had a feeling as a performer that if you really had it you should be on the Sunday night bill. Butterfield was great and it was obvious they should get some spot in the Sunday night performance.

"Dylan had heard Butterfield in the blues workshop a couple of days earlier and realized they were a great blues band, and he said, 'Wanna do *Maggie's Farm?*' And they played, and at least one night they also jammed, I think. As far as I know Dylan was planning to use the acoustic guitar for his set Sunday night, but then he realized these guys were just fantastic and they rehearsed for the show, practicing.

"Nobody knew Butterfield was going to back him up, that Sunday night. They just showed up there on stage. It was remarkable in that Bob, who always seemed to know when to make the moves, this one time he got taken advantage of—the Butterfield band was so anxious to be on stage and inadvertently they took advantage of him.

"What happened was, whoever was controlling the mikes messed it up. You couldn't hear Dylan. It looked like he was singing with the volume off. He got through the first song, with the Butterfield band pulling out all the stops, Sam Lay beating hell out of the drums, the whole thing sounding like a Butterfield boogie and no Dylan.

"We were sitting in the press section, maybe thirty yards back, and yelling, 'Can't hear ya!' and 'Cut the band down!' Only about four or five people were hollering. Then they went into the next song and no one had changed any dials. It was the same thing, no voice coming through at all, just the band doing a solo. After that more people began shouting, 'We can't hear Bobby!' and like that.

"This is the crux of the von Schmidt Theory. The people who first started shouting were not putting Bobby down for playing electric; it was just that we couldn't hear him. Nobody in the press section was yelling about bring back the old Bobby or get the acoustic guitar. That started with the people in the back, a misunderstanding about what we were shouting. They might not have started hollering back there if they hadn't heard hollering from the front. They thought we were putting Bobby down, so they started putting him down, and it just built from there.

"And Bobby didn't know what was happening. He was shocked by the band doing the Butterfield boogie, and he was so confused by where these voices were coming from and what they were saying. And then, once the people in the back started it, and changed it by putting Bobby down, just chanting at him, what was to have been his big moment turned out to be a massive confused thing between audience and performers.

"It seemed to be one of the few times that Dylan was not in control."

Bob was deeply hurt by the reaction at Newport. He hadn't expected it, and he was enormously upset. Upset at the reaction, and upset that he had apparently misjudged his audience, had lost control. But as events unfolded, Newport worked out to his advantage. Although he may have lost a few folk fans, the publicity helped him gain an even wider audience among the young disaffected. His album began to sell at a quickened pace, and *Rolling Stone* shot up the charts.

Dylan told Shelton, of *The Times:* "It's all music, no more, no less. I know in my own mind what I'm doing. If anyone has imagination, he'll know what I'm doing. If they can't understand my songs, they're missing something. If they can't understand green clocks, wet chairs, purple lamps or hostile statues, they're missing something, too. .... What I write is much more concise now than before. It's not deceiving."

A friend later asked what he meant by "deceiving" and he replied: "Deceiving means when I wrote a lot of those protest songs, they were written in a small circle of people. Then when they were brought to the outside, other people who heard them, heard them in their own way. They could think something was happening which wasn't happening. But what I'm doing now, my stuff now is *me,* what seems to be happening in the songs is really happening."

On Saturday night, August 27, more than 14,000 people filled the Forest Hills tennis stadium in Queens for Dylan's first concert since Newport, the previous month. Dylan went out to the stadium early in the afternoon, with Grossman and his musicians—Robbie Robertson and Levon Helm of The Hawks, Al Kooper and Harvey Brooks. There would be no Butterfield boogie this time out; hopefully, no problem with the sound system. They worked on the acoustic hazards of the large open air stadium, running over the music they would play, making certain the mikes, instruments and amplifiers were properly placed.

At nine o'clock the spotlight picked out Dylan, frail, young, dressed in a black suit and striped shirt with a collar clasp, and black high-heeled boots, the wind whipping his already tousled hair. Dylan carried only his acoustic guitar, and wore the harmonica on its holder around his neck. He did seven songs, forty-five minutes worth, "folk" style. Among them were *Tambourine Man* and *Love Minus Zero/No Limit,* from his last album, a song possibly to Sarah, about a woman who winks at life and doesn't care about anything happening in the outside world or about the people who are hungup and mentally fettered; a woman who has too much wisdom "to argue or judge." And he sang *Desolation Row,* his absurdist poem, a collage of dream-visions that seem to be describing the American landscape, a peculiar form of hell on earth.

Even though there wasn't a real folk song in the collection, the crowd gave him a tremendous ovation. No sign of hostility. But Dylan wasn't fooled. During intermission he talked to his musicians, almost like a football coach at half time. "Anything can happen with that crowd out there," he said. "If they start yellin' and booin' don't let it bother ya. Just keep playin' the best ya know how. Don't pay attention to anythin' the audience does."

He ran out, carrying his electric guitar, the four musicians taking

their places behind him. Some people in the stands began to boo at
the sight of the band, but the music started up fast, loud, intense,
crackling, overpowering the discontent of some of the fans. They sat
listening to his first number, most of them obviously wanting to hear
what he had to say. When Dylan and the band finished there were
scattered shouts of, "We want the old Dylan!" and scattered boos,
and some applause. Most seemed neutral. They listened at the start
of the next number and when it was concluded again there were
shouts: "We want Dylan! We want Dylan!" Bob plunged on, and by
the time he finished up his set, with *Rolling Stone*, the majority of
his audience was singing along with him. Not a clear victory, but
better than Newport.

As they drove back to Manhattan in the getaway car, Neuwirth
behind the wheel, Dylan kept asking: "Was it my sound? Was it all
right?" Later, at a party in Grossman's apartment, Dylan was almost
interrogating a young woman who had been at the concert, demanding to know her reactions. She finally admitted, somewhat ashamed,
that she hadn't particularly liked his new sound.

"Did you boo?" Bob asked.

"No, I didn't," the girl replied.

Bob stood up and began to lecture her. "Why not?" he demanded.
"Why didn't you let me know what you were feeling? You got feelings, then express them. Don't keep them inside. You should have
booed me. You should have reacted. That's what my music's all
about."

A month later Dylan gave a concert at Carnegie Hall, repeating
the Forest Hills format—acoustic guitar for the first half, and the rock
band behind him after intermission. This time the audience's response was enthusiastic, calling for more when the program ended,
and Dylan was up high with the excitement of it.

"I knew they'd understand me," he said. "Knew it wouldn't take
'em long to catch on."

His friends were not surprised that Dylan had moved into rock.
Phil Ochs, Dave Cohen, Eric Andersen, so many others, all believed
it was the most intelligent thing he could have done. Rock is where
everyone was headed, that was understood by all the young professionals in the field.

But others attacked him again, charging him with selling out, or
felt sympathy because Dylan had been forced up against the realities
of commercialization. Israel Young, writing in his column in *Sing
Out!*: "Bob Dylan has become a pawn in his own game. He has ceased

his Quest for a Universal Sound and has settled for a liason with the music trade's Top 40 Hit Parade." And, in the *Village Voice,* Arthur Kretchmer wrote that Dylan was being destroyed because he was forced to "act out his horrors in public instead of in the lonely privacy that other generations imposed upon their poets." Other critics were even more shrill, charging that Dylan had even been faking it back in his protest period. He had no real anger back then, but had been manufacturing passion in poetry, instead of writing about basic issues in folk song.

Dylan shrugged it all off. "That's their problem. It doesn't matter what they say about me. I mean, if they can just understand, as long as they're troubled about me, that I'm still gonna be around when everybody gets their heads straight. This thing about my not singing protest songs any more—I have no respect for what they're writing about. It's vulgar, the idea that somebody has to say what they want to say in a message type song. It's a stagnation kind of thing. Maybe people are afraid of words. That's who you're dealing with, people who are afraid of words. That's a shame, worse than being a pregnant dog.

"I know what folk music is, that's why I don't call myself a folk singer. Most of the people down on me because of folk music just don't know what they're talking about. They always say folk music should be simple so people can understand. *People!* That's insulting somebody, calling them people. But the truth is, there are weird folk songs that have come down through the ages, based on nothing, or based on legend, Bible, plague, religion, just based on mysticism. Those old songs weren't simple at all. What's happened is the labor movement people, *they're* talking about keeping it simple. All these labor people, rich suburban cats telling their kids not to buy Bob Dylan records. All they want is songs from the Thirties, union hall songs. 'Which side are you on?' That's such a waste. I mean, which side can you *be* on?"

None of those who were now most strongly moved by Dylan believed he had sold out. While Baez accused Dylan privately, and the critics said it in print, those whom Dylan now reached didn't care about the accusations. They had, most of them, grown up in a different kind of world. Alger Hiss had been sent to prison before most of them were born; he was a part of history, something barely real, like George Washington, cherry trees and silver dollars flung across the Potomac, not part of their reality or their fears. Dylan, who had created his own myth, was part of their reality. They did not care when they read that he was getting rich, when writers estimated that his song royalties alone would earn him $80,000 a month in the next year or two, as dozens of artists raced into the studios to record his songs. If anything, that only confirmed a feeling that Dylan was an important poet of the streets, the man who had taken poetry out of the hands of the dinosaurs and returned it to the citizens.

His fans knew what Dylan was feeling, from his music, from what they heard about his life style on the campus grapevine, and through the underground press where Dylan was getting as much play as Bardot was getting in *Time* and *Life*.

"Today counts, not tomorrow," he had said.

"If somebody told me right now that I was going to die in an hour I could accept it, because there's really nothing I have to clean up, no unfinished business. I gotta die, and that's it," he had said.

"I don't worry whether I'll be around in a year or five years. I just don't worry about it. I'm not counting on being around, and I'm not counting on *not* being around."

Dylan had now plunged into a complete search for the self that he had denied during his protest period. He was into life, in all its forms: into drugs more heavily, establishing friendships with Allen Ginsberg and other poets and artists. "Doing things for kicks, that's why I do things, without hangups, just an attitude of 'Why not?' I tell you, I'm willing to try anything once. Turn on to a realization of things." He was deliberately experiencing life in all its ugly-beautiful forms, living a life of total freedom, no matter where it led. He was attempting to come to a "realization of things" by completely throwing off all the learned attitudes imposed by society, attitudes that have repressed naturalness and sexuality, imposed a false consciousness over man's natural drives.

Dylan did not intellectualize it; he seldom discussed with anyone exactly what he believed, possibly because he did not know what he believed. But this time he did talk about it—into a friend's tape recorder— in his inarticulate manner, and out of his emotions rather than logic.

"I think maybe people can get less hungup. What it comes down to is the kid who's learned by the time he's twenty-one that it's all bullshit. Even some people have been turned on when they're forty-five—not turned on by pot but the realization of things, and they see what a waste their lives have been. They're happy now, after they see, they just quit their jobs and sit around the house and laugh. People can understand at forty-five that they been hungup all their lives, that it's not necessary to worry about your chick being with somebody else because the world's full of people, man. There's a thousand ways to get to the realization of what's inside your head, but the thing is to get there."

Later, they were talking about college and Dylan began thinking aloud, almost: "Going to college and learning why things happen is ridiculous in the face of the realization that things are going to happen whether you know why they're happening or not. And it's not a question of what they should be doing instead of college. They should be doing anything they want to do, hang around in Mexico four years, maybe. But learn a lot of things that people keep you away from until you reach a certain age, and by then you're trapped like them: learn about sex and drugs and your head. Do handstands even, the kind of habits that are looked at as if they're going to kill you. They're not going to kill you. Maybe they'll shake you up. We all need some shaking up. . . .

"What Joan Baez is doing, and all those people demonstrating, they're not gonna save the world. It's not true they can change men's hearts. I don't know how long these people want to live, don't know if they're looking for eternity, if they want to be immortalized, or what. I mean, a lot of people take it very seriously. None of it's real. Just slogans. I went through that. Everybody talks about names that strike familiar chords. Jesus Christ. They say, 'Look at all the good He did.' But I ask, where? How? When? For who? And look at what they *did* to him. Everybody's talking about how He really felt, but it's such a long time ago you can't really know. You really just have to believe. And that's a dangerous business, just believing. You have to sacrifice a lot.

"For me, it's live my own life the best way I can. Find out what *I'm* all about. Not what the slogans and the fakeness out there is all about. I want to know myself in my own mind. I don't have time to worry about those things outside.

"Nobody's gonna learn by somebody else showing them or teaching them. People have to learn for themselves, by going through it all until they come to the center of it through something which relates, and then coming out the other side. Like people who don't care about going to jail. They're still with themselves as much as when they were in the streets. They can make it if they go through some kind of scene with themselves and other people and dig that it's going to grind into them and be them and then come out something else. I can't put it into words better than that, except maybe that I don't think in terms of society because society just fights among itself. I'm part of me, the me that's *inside* me, not part of society in any way. Society's just trying to fuck up your head, and it don't make sense to walk around with a fucked up head."

And, finally: "You gotta read the *I Ching*. I don't wanna talk about it, except to say it's the only thing that's fantastically true. You read it, and you gotta know it's true. It's something to believe in." He added, giggling: "Of course, I don't believe in anything."

1965: *Positively 4th Street*

HIGHWAY 61 REVISITED was at that time—and may be still today —one of the most brilliant pop albums ever made. As rock, it cut through to the core of the music—a hard, driving beat without frills, without self-consciousness. *Like A Rolling Stone, Tombstone Blues,* among the finest rock ever recorded. As living poetry the album demonstrated that Dylan's talent had matured to the point that it seemed capable of expressing in word-rhythms the depth of his visions. Despite what the literary keepers of the esoteric flame may say, no matter how much they sneer, Dylan's works are poetry: *Desolation Row,* for just one example, amply demonstrates that. It is a descent into a modern Inferno, an eleven-minute freak show that portrays a world of alienation ruled by madmen, a world in which humanity has been estranged from its own possibilities, a world in which man's once free mind has been so totally suffocated by the one dimensional society that it accepts lies as truth and beauty, permits creativity and naturalness and Eros to be perverted by the social "reality." Not since Rimbaud has a poet used the language of the streets to expose all the horrors of the streets, to describe a state of the union that is ugly and absurd.

Phil Ochs: "From the moment I met him I thought he was great, a genius, Shakespearean. Every succeeding album up to *Highway 61,* I had an increasing lot of secret fear: 'Oh, my God, what can he do next? He can't possibly top that one.' And then I put on *Highway 61,* and I laughed and said it's so ridiculous. It's impossibly good, it just can't be that good. And I walked away and didn't listen to it again right away because I thought this was too much. How can a human mind do this? The writing was so rich I just couldn't believe it. What I felt at that time is what I said in a *Broadside* interview right after the album came out. I said I knew he'd produced the most important

222

and revolutionary album ever made, the best album, because he reached such heights of writing. . . . Listening to Dylan is like climbing a ladder; you look at it as you would a painting. You don't look at a painting and say, 'That's great,' and walk away from it. And you don't listen to Dylan once and say, 'That's good.' It's the kind of music that plants a seed in your mind and then you have to hear it several times—ten times. And as you go over it you start to hear more and more things. . . . He's done it. He's done something that's left the whole field ridiculously in back of him. He's in his own world now. . . ."

Bob Dylan: "I'm not gonna be able to make a record better than that one. *Highway 61* is just too good. There's a lot of stuff on there that *I* would listen to."

Bob Dylan—superstar. Three of his records were now on the charts and only the Beatles and Stones could generate more excitement. And the Beatles and Stones and Andy Warhol and all of the Big Names of pop culture were trying to get Dylan to decorate *their* parties because he was the most impressive catch around. Folk rock, a term coined by *Billboard* to describe what Dylan and the Byrds were doing ("It's nose-thumbing," Dylan said of the term, "sounds like you're looking down on what is fantastic, great music."), folk rock became a trend seized upon by the money-grubbers of a new Tin Pan Alley, who were advising singers, songwriters and performers: "Get with the Dylan sound, baby, that's where it's at." Dylan had fulfilled Baez's prophecy and accusation, he was the rock-and-roll king. Yet, in a little while even those mourning his lack of commitment would use electric instruments. Pete Seeger eventually turned out an album with three members of the Blues Project as a backup group.

Columbia quickly capitalized on the furor Dylan had created by releasing two singles: *Positively 4th Street* in September and *Please Crawl Out Your Window* in December. And Dylan was ecstatic at this new music he was creating, thrilled with the pure joy of performing it. "Now when I ask myself would I wanna come hear this tonight I gotta say I would. I dig it. You know? I really dig it. I don't think about quitting any more."

Bob Dylan had always wanted to reach a mass popularity, comparable to Presley's fame. He had said it repeatedly, starting back in Hibbing and even during his folk period, and many of his friends felt it in him. But he had not yet made it. In just a matter of months, he had become the most exciting pop music force in the English-speaking world, but he had not yet captured the mass audience that the Beatles had. That would take a little bit more stretching. The Beatles affected the minds of a vast audience of the young, from pre-teens who just adored them, to older teens who danced to them, to young men and women who listened to them as rebels and smoked dope to their music. Dylan had only a part of this audience.

The Presley-fame was in his grasp, but he would never pull it off.

Phil Ochs: "Just before *Positively 4th Street,* around the time of *Rolling Stone,* I started taking a very musical and commercial view of Dylan. I started to look at Dylan at a certain level: that what he was doing musically and lyrically was so exciting I thought there was no end to what he could do now. I thought then that he could become Elvis Presley on that level. Essentially he could physically represent rural America, all of America, and put out fifteen gold records in a row. Meaning fifteen grandly produced, musically exciting hit singles, with all the great lyrics, and thereby revolutionize the music business. My first reaction when *Positively 4th Street* came out was the thought, 'Oh, no, that's not a hit single at all. What are they trying to do? They're gonna blow it.' It was a hit anyway, but I thought it was a disastrous thing to do. Then they released *Please Crawl Out My Window* and stuff like that, and he threw it all away.

"I think he definitely could have pulled it off. I have no idea what short-circuited it. If he would ever talk about it he might say it wasn't important to him, he didn't want that, it didn't occur to him. My feeling at the time was that he *did* want that. There was that one flash, that one moment he could have done something on a whole higher level. In essence what happened then was the Beatles got in the way. Dylan wrote the lyrics, and the Beatles captured the mass music. There's no reason why Dylan with a straighter head could not have done an equivalent thing as the Beatles, musically. But it was just thrown away. It's too late now. That was the moment, that rare moment. It can never happen again on that level. He could have gone on to the whole thing, but he blew it."

The Beatles got in the way, certainly, but there were deeper reasons why Dylan blew it. Mostly, it seemed to be a recurrence of Dylan's fear that he would be swallowed by it all, destroyed by fame. He was becoming too visible once more in a world full of danger; that inner self was being threatened again.

"They want me to handle their lives," Dylan told a friend at this time. "That's a lot of responsibility. I got enough to do handling my own life. Trying to handle somebody else's life you gotta be a very powerful person. The more people's lives you got responsibility for, the bigger the weight is. I don't want that. Too much for my head."

The quality of the fame troubled him, and brought enormous pressures on him. To many who heard him and believed they understood

him, he was almost a Christ. Seriously. Those who knew him personally were struck by his magnetism, the power of his personality.
"He's got the heaviest vibes I've ever felt on anyone," Eric Andersen
says. "His power, his mystique, just affected people in crazy ways,"
says Dave Cohen. "Even just from hearing him on records you have
to say, 'This guy knows, this guy feels,' and want to be with him." And
a young Australian actress, who would meet him a few months later:
"He was Christ revisited. I felt that everything fitted, without being
Christian-religious or anything. I began to feel Dylan was sacrificing
himself in his whole philosophy, and that eventually he would
die. ..."

Those feelings were communicated to Dylan. He knew people
were making him an idol; that thousands of men and women, young
and old, felt their lives entwined with his because they saw him as
a mystic, a messiah who would lead them to salvation, or they saw
him as a titan pamphleteer bringing them the textbook of a new
radicalism. It disturbed him. "He was terribly frightened at this
Olympus people were putting him on, at this cross everybody expected him to bear for them," one close friend recalls. "He didn't
want to be a Christ, but that's what people were making him, and
it really shook him up."

Those who really listened to Dylan came away changed. Dylan
affected their lives. His incredible sensitivity to the moods of his
times and of his contemporaries led him to visions that forced his
audience to face themselves, to stop and ask: "Am I real?" Woody
Guthrie once said his aim in life was to be "the man who told you
something you always knew," and this is what Dylan had done.

When Allen Ginsberg was asked by some reporter whether Dylan
had sold out, he replied: "Only to God." To Ginsberg, and to less
learned students of Eastern religions, Dylan's voice was filled with
the philosophy of the prophets, the mystics, bringing vividly down
to modern terms what they had been reading in Zen and Hesse and,
later, in the writings of existentialist-psychiatrist R. D. Laing. Dylan,
rather than "sing sad and bitter songs of disillusion and defeat"
(Laing), was telling us that rejection is the first step to salvation.
Ginsberg even had the audacity to link Dylan and Buddha. In a letter
to Defense Secretary Robert McNamara advising him that if he could
be Zen-calm, then the illusion that is war and hatred and conflict
would go away, Ginsberg wrote: "Both sides are an illusion—you
must by now have read basic Buddhist or Bob Dylan heard, texts &
advices how to escape from that trap."

It was an irony. If Bob Dylan had sold out by leaving protest behind
and moving into rock and lyrical introspection, the sellout had a

reverse effect. In extending his audience, and in demonstrating to other musicians and writers that popular music did not have to be senseless pap, Dylan proved that "the times they are a-changin'." All of the folk songs and all the folk singers—including Guthrie and Seeger and Baez—were unable to create the sort of revolution that Dylan helped create. Folk artists, working within the framework of the established societal structure, were basically hoping to turn the citizenry from the right and center to the left; toward a gentle socialism for the most part, sometimes with the hope of eventual communism. Few of them were preaching deeper revolution. Dylan, however, by sparking his contemporaries to create tiny pop symphonies for the counter-culture, laid the groundwork for attacks on the system by college students, ecologists, activists. "He may be the greatest influence on the generation," Eric Anderson suggested, a feeling echoed by many. "I think the seeds of the future were laid down by him right there. I don't see any force quite like what Dylan did. Keats said the artist is the antenna of the race. Dylan is the antenna of the race."

Again and again, those within the Movement describe varying debts to Dylan. While he may not have created the youth revolution, may not have been the leader or chief spokesman, he summarized, focused, highlighted the discontent, delineated the problems. The social power of Bob Dylan lies as much in the pulpit from which he was able to disseminate his ideas as in the man and his talents. No prophet in the past had so many instant-followers; they could not reach the audiences that Bob was able to reach. He was the first mass media poet, the first poet of the jukeboxes, and he hit many hundreds of thousands in the mind and in the guts. One result is the explosive growth of the counter culture. To Dylan must go some of the responsibility for the many hundreds of thousands of freaks around the country, trying to make a life outside the established society, into drugs and mysticism and communes, determined not to be caught in the traps of what is called civilization. Dylan's influence can be felt in those who are attacking the system by refusing to cooperate with it, or are mounting direct assaults against it as they did during the 1968 Democrat convention. Dylan was only one factor in this revolution. Marcuse, Hesse, Fanon, Sartre, Camus, Proudhon and others, provided the ideology. But Dylan provided the emotional drive that brought it all home.

"Don't interpret me!" Dylan once snapped to a writer. "My songs don't have any meaning, they're just words." And, another time: "I'm not trying to teach anybody anything. That's obscene, that idea." But he has been interpreted and acclaimed as a teacher, revolutionary, firebrand, messiah, mystic, prophet.

And it all weighed heavily on him. To be famous was one thing; to have entered the minds and souls of so many was something else again. He had only wanted to be another Elvis Presley, not Jesus Christ.

"Who do you want to meet? Marlon Brando?" Harlow's had opened in New York in June, 1965, and became an important meeting place for the In Crowd, and other discos and private clubs were becoming gathering places for famous personalities. Dylan swung into it. "He enjoyed that scene," Dave Cohen recalls. "He really dug it."

More than ever now, he needed protection; more a bodyguard than the mindguard that had originally surrounded him. The Dylan Village group was a tight little circle: Victor Maimudes as bodyguard; Phil Ochs, Eric Andersen, Dave Van Ronk and Tom Paxton as sort of anvils off which he could flash his verbal pyrotechnics; Bob Neuwirth and Dave Cohen straddling both roles. Few others could break into their scene. Tom Clancy, for example, recalls that period when fame really hit: "I saw him a lot, but he was always surrounded by people. He would sort of say hello and go by, and I'd have the feeling I'd be barging in if I tried to get closer than that."

Of the singers and writers on the scene at this time, Dave Cohen appears to have been closest to Dylan. He became Dylan's bodyguard and companion around the 1965 Newport Folk Festival. "He needed a friend," Cohen says. "So he started including me in his scene and I got tight with him. He didn't like to be alone. He couldn't go out alone, but the *scene* had to be made because he was the number one star. My role was like protection. It wasn't stated, but I responded that way. A lot of people did.

"I didn't feel it was Dylan and me, two guys going places. It was him, and I'd go out and get a cab if he needed a cab. Not like a lackey, but just that *he* couldn't go out and get a cab. But it was an equal exchange. He'd do something for you. Like needs. I had a need for him. It was his scene, that's what he gave. I got a lot of notoriety. Not looking for it, but it was there."

When Cohen began singing professionally, at the urging of Dylan and others, he changed his name to Dave Blue (he's since taken his own name again). Blue was suggested by Eric Andersen because it fit Cohen's personality at the time: gruff, nasty, unsmiling, suspicious. He looked and acted a lot like Dylan. "I was unable to make contact with people," he says, "and when I hooked up with Dylan I became even more sarcastic. I fell into a pattern, a routine, of cutting people up." Cohen is not so mean today, but he still resembles Dylan somewhat, and doesn't smile much. He remembers those months in 1965 with a great deal of fondness.

"Dylan was very hostile, a mean cat, very cruel to people," Cohen says. "But I could see the reasons for it. It was very defensive, for one thing. Just from having to answer too many questions. The big thing was that his privacy had been invaded. It was just too heavy for him, being the center of attention, having people all around, asking things and demanding answers—'What is life all about?' and 'What did you mean by that song?' He was a street cat, man, and he lost it. He lost his freedom. In the early days he'd be able to go into a bar alone, and meet people. Then he couldn't do it any more and that kind of pressure is fantastic on a guy. The crowds, the feeling of being rushed by hundreds of people. It scares you. Crowds put your head in a funny place. Dylan hates it.

"Another thing about his hostility, we were the competition. All the singers, like Ochs, were in competition with Dylan. All writing songs, competing for an audience. Even I was writing at this time. But Phil especially was the competition. He always expected to be as big as Dylan, saying, 'I'm gonna go that far.' He thought he would be playing that big. Ochs wanted to take Dylan's place and it must have seemed absurd to Dylan, that Ochs would dethrone him. Dylan had it almost by accident, he never dreamed it was going to happen. At one point he figured he would just be as big as Van Ronk. Never beyond that. There was no beyond in the folk scene. It just didn't exist. Then everything went crazy. And everybody wanted what he had."

Van Ronk recalls: "I remember sessions at the Kettle of Fish where Dylan was especially obnoxious to Ochs, Andersen and Dave Cohen. And I realized something: Bobby came over like that because he knew something about those guys, he was into them—they wanted to get rich. They were hungry, scuffling cats looking to grab the brass ring. I felt it, I saw how hungry they were. They wanted to be honest, but they suddenly realized they could say what they wanted to say and make a million dollars. Dylan was a terrible influence, not through any fault of his own, but he tickled everybody's opportunism. None of us were poor, exactly. But then—wham! 250 billion dollars and an infinity of chicks to play with. And they reached out and grabbed for that brass ring.

"The big thing to keep in mind is that Bobby wanted to be a superstar. When he discovered the reality of being a superstar he freaked out."

Cohen: "And Dylan got cruel. Like, one night we're sitting in the Kettle and Dylan says to us all: 'Hey, maybe you think you're gonna make it like me. Nobody's gonna make it. Maybe you think you're gonna do what I did. Nobody's gonna do it.'

"But a lot of it was defensive, sort of offense as a defense, like building a fortress around ourselves. When you go somewhere with Dylan you have to be critical about the absurdities in the scene, especially at places like Harlow's, absurd scenes and people and ideas. And, like, you're very aware you're the scene, the center of attention, your little group. Instead of going over to somebody's table, they all come over to you because Dylan was the number one star around. So, it was like having fun, laughing at the absurdity of it all, of all these stupid scene-people. And attacking. Attacking first, before you were attacked.

"I don't know if he really meant to hurt anybody. He was really a nice guy. It was his life form at the time to make himself appear hostile. Actually he was a kind person, not really cruel to others. It was just a banter, a rap. If you could stand it, if you actually had not done anything to him or crossed him, if you could take it, then it was great. But if you couldn't be like him, then it was bad for you."

Andersen, the most sensitive of all Dylan's friends and victims, seems to have been hurt the most by it all. "That hostility thing was mental gymnastics, and it was really bitter at times," he recalls. "Neuwirth was just egging it on, and doing a lot of it himself. They were just like little kids. It was juvenile. It wasn't real, like how real people felt. Just assumed attitudes. But it promoted bitterness in people, bad feelings. I think later Dylan was sorry about it, but while he was doing it, it was rough. But I could understand it. He was under great pressure as the hip hero, and from the fame. And Dylan was feeling pretty negative about it all."

One night Bob trained his guns on Ochs: "You oughtta find a new line of work, Ochs. You're not doin' very much in this one." Andersen, uncharacteristically, leaned over and told Dylan: "Why don't you lay off him? Leave him alone." Bob looked hurt, and very angry. "What do ya want me to talk about?" he shouted. "I buy your wine, I try to be your friend. What do ya want me to talk about? The rats in the sewers? Or the sunrise over the Hudson?"

"He got real uptight," Andersen says. "Nobody dared to ever say anything to Dylan. Everybody had this awe of Dylan—not awe behind his back, but to his face. He knew it. Even Jack Elliott was smitten by the Dylan fame. Phil worshipped him. Dave worshipped him and sort of hung out. I could feel the presence of someone with the strongest vibes ever, but I wasn't awed by him and that's why he kept getting on my ass.

"But it wasn't like that all the time, understand that. He didn't come down to hassle anybody, he came down to have some drinks and rap. He would just get negative, though, and turn on somebody. But not too often."

The awe in which they held Dylan, the fear of saying anything to him that might annoy him, was a very real factor in their relationship, hanging over them, no secrets to conceal. Ochs, who was the most immediate competition—*Sing Out!* said he was the wave of the future because he continued to write protest songs after Dylan turned away from them—sometimes forgot, in his joy at being alive in such heady times, that Dylan would not permit direct criticism of his work. One night Dylan played his new single, *Can You Please Crawl Out Your Window,* for Ochs and Cohen. Before he put it on he told them: "This is the one I've been trying to do for years, this is the record that's really got it." He played it and asked: "What do ya think?" Cohen said he thought it was simply great, a good driving rock piece. Ochs said: "It's okay." Dylan reacted as if he'd been knifed. "Whattaya mean?" he shouted. "Listen to it again." He played it once more and again asked: "Well, what do ya think?" And Ochs replied: "It's okay, but it's not going to be a hit." Dylan's anger turned to cold fury. "What do ya mean, it's not going to be a hit? You're crazy, man. It's a great song. Ya only know protest, that's all." At that point a limousine arrived to take them to one of the uptown discos. They all climbed in and after the driver had moved up Sixth Avenue a few blocks, Dylan shouted at him: "Pull over." When the car stopped at the curb Dylan turned to Ochs and said: "Get out here, Ochs." Ochs was appalled, frozen. He wasn't certain whether Dylan was serious. "Get out, Ochs," Dylan repeated. "You're not a folksinger. You're just a journalist." Except for a momentary, traumatic incident a few months later, it was the last time he saw Dylan.

"He wasn't used to being criticized," Ochs says today, and is able to smile at it. "That was a sacrilegious thing to have said to him."

Ochs looks back on it, even on Dylan's viciousness, with an almost positive glow: "At first it was really a great time, thrilling, exciting, energetic, before the vicious aspect that it sort of became in the end. Just an endless series of great conversations at first, a huge speed trip. And singing all the time, writing all the time, everybody totally creative. Like one night Dylan came to my house in Bleeker Street and said: 'I want you to hear a new song.' And he sang *Tambourine Man.* What can you say? It's so outrageous to have something like that happen. But the other thing, the hostility, that didn't happen all the time. That came only in the last months we were all together. As he got bigger. You see, he had always talked about not placing any value in fame. But I also think he was afraid of fame. I think basically he was a very warm person and he wanted to keep human relationships from souring and he felt that slipping away because of the fame.

"Imagine someone that sensitive sitting at a bar and someone come in and say, 'Hey, you're Bob Dylan, tell me. . . .' It just drove him crazy. It spurred on that essentially huge defense system building up, plus the need for privacy. That's the kind of thing that really started him moving into hostility. And Bobby Neuwirth. He was Dylan's right hand man and *assassin.* They were a team sitting at the table doing it. It was also very clever, witty, barbed, and very stimulating, too. But you really had to be on your toes. You'd walk into a threshing machine if you were just a regular guy, naive and open, you'd be torn to pieces."

Dylan also used the threshing machine in song. *Positively 4th Street,* for one. It was released as a single in late September and quickly moved up the charts. It also moved a lot of temperatures up the scale. Dylan was either slicing up one specific individual on the Village scene or all of them, all of his friends and former friends. There is no line in all pop music filled with more hate than the last line of the song, which sums it up: *If you could stand in my shoes you'd see what a drag it is to be you.*

Everyone in the Village wondered who the song was about, and many took it personally and were hurt by it. Terri Van Ronk: "Everybody was especially upset by the song because they felt *they* were the people he was talking about. We didn't think the nastiness was called for, or the putting down." And Israel Young: "At least 500 people came into my place in a few months time and asked me if it was about me. I don't know if it was, but it was unfair. I'm in the Village twenty-five years now. I was one of the representatives of the Village, there is such a thing as the Village. Dave Van Ronk was still in the Village. Dylan comes in and takes from us, uses my resources, then he leaves and *he* gets bitter. *He* writes a bitter song. He was the one who left."

1965–1966: *I Pity the Poor Immigrant*

BOB MARRIED SARAH Lowndes on November 22, 1965, in a quiet civil ceremony performed by a State Supreme Court judge in suburban Nassau County and attended by Grossman, their lawyer, and a couple of close friends. There was no public announcement of the marriage. Bob kept Sarah a secret as he had kept so many things secret, until Nora Ephron broke the story in a New York newspaper the following February.

He even pulled a mask over the marriage with some friends. Jack Elliott recalls: "I saw him right after he was married and I said: 'Congratulations, I heard you got married.' And he said: 'I didn't get married. You'd be the first cat I'd tell, man, if I got married.'"

"Bob needed Sarah very desperately," a close friend from that period says. "His head was all screwed around from the pressures, the fame, that whole insane thing that was happening to him, and Sarah represented some solid ground. She was mystical, into Zen and all, and seemed to have found her own head and maybe seemed to have some answers from Zen, and Dylan needed that. Also, she was sort of Zen-egoless. She didn't try to get into Bob's head the way people always do, because that's not where it was at for her. And Bob needed that kind of unthreatening woman. She seemed to be able to give herself over to him and his special needs. Besides which, she is very beautiful and very tender."

The marriage was immediately followed by a grueling concert tour that Grossman had set up for him. It lasted through the end of 1965 and into the first months of 1966, a succession of one night stands broken by a week or two of rest before he was off again. Writer Jules Siegel accompanied Dylan and his entourage on a tour of Canadian cities a couple of months after the marriage, for a *Saturday Evening Post* article. Siegel was struck by an incident in Vancouver that demonstrated both Dylan's need for privacy and Sarah's sympathetic responsiveness. She visited Bob in Vancouver to attend the concert. They were in his dressing room before the show and Dylan was disturbed because two Canadian writers were coming up to interview him and he felt he had to hide Sarah from them. Dylan went to a large closet and opened the door. "Sarah," he said, "when they arrive I want you to get in here." Sarah looked at him quizzically, but didn't argue. Then Dylan began to laugh at the absurdity of his act, and closed the door.

That little scene is also an indication of Dylan's scorn for the press. He hated reporters even more than he hated the man in a bar who asked what a particular song or line meant. The press was a part of society's conspiracy for repression. Yet Dylan needed at least some press coverage.

With rare exceptions, his meetings with writers and reporters turned into little set pieces, stylized tennis games, almost, in which Dylan never lost control of the ball. If you saw the film made of the 1965 English tour, *Don't Look Back,* in which Dylan attacks and destroys a reporter from *Time* and a student interviewer, you see only one particularly vicious facet of Dylan's reaction to questions. But some interviews and press conferences were simply extensions of playful word games he ran on friends. At these press conferences, working with a larger canvas, Dylan's responses became more surrealistic, more absurdist, because the people he was dealing with didn't know how to react to him, and because they often were not even aware he was playing with them.

Nat Hentoff's *Playboy* interview (March, 1966) is an interesting example of how Dylan confounded those trying to understand him. Hentoff, one of the more knowledgeable writers in all forms of music, in politics, the youth culture and the inanities and insanities of society, has been scoffed at for having played straight man to Dylan's comedy routine. But, as usual with Dylan, the truth is not quite what it seems.

Hentoff will only talk about part of it. When he asked Dylan to do the interview Dylan at first refused, Hentoff says, because he felt that he no longer needed the sort of publicity *Playboy* would bring him. It wasn't worth the effort to Dylan, a friend adds. But Dylan finally agreed to the interview as a favor for Billie Wallington, a Columbia public relations woman, one of the warmest and gentlest press agents in the business. Hentoff says he and Dylan did a long interview at Columbia, an interview that came off well.

Hentoff won't say any more, but Dylan's friends pick it up from there. Hentoff, it seems, polished off the rough edges and, showed it to Dylan to get his approval. (That's standard procedure in such interviews, which would be comparable to an autobiographical piece written by Dylan himself. There is a difference between the question-and-answer interview which is designed to give the subject a chance to express his ideas to the public, and the regular magazine profile in which the writer is *expected* to be subjective, even if the result is unflattering, and which Grossman and Dylan usually tried to control.) Hentoff sent the approved script off to the magazine. Some heavy-handed editor practically rewrote it and when the copy was sent to Dylan for final approval he grew furious at the revisions. He called Hentoff and began to scream. When Hentoff got him calmed down, Dylan said: "I wanna do another interview. I'll ask the questions, and I'll answer them." Hentoff is said to have been delighted with the idea and they worked out a Dylan performance on the phone, in a conversation that lasted more than six hours. Except for some comments that actually reflected what Dylan was feeling at the time—on the futility of protest, his love of the rock music he was writing and singing at the time, and his insistence that he would not be responsible for the "destiny" of his fans—most of the interview as finally published is a Bob Dylan comedy script.

For example, Hentoff asked Dylan why he decided to "go the rock-and-roll route," and Dylan replied:

"Carelessness. I lost my one true love. I started drinking. The first thing I know, I'm in a card game. Then I'm in a crap game. I wake up in a pool hall. Then this big Mexican lady drags me off the table, takes me to Philadelphia. She leaves me alone in her house, and it burns down. I wind up in Phoenix. I get a job as a Chinaman. I start working in a dime store, and move in with a thirteen-year-old girl. Then this big Mexican lady from Philadelphia comes in. . . . The first guy that picked me up asked me if I wanted to be a star. What could I say?"

The tour schedule that Grossman set up for Dylan was a tortuously heavy one, a series of one and two night stands. Dylan was running from fans, running from interviewers, racing into a limousine, dashing to the private Lodestar jet he was using. Out of motels, into concert halls, off again before the kids grab you, try to unwind later with everyone pulling at your body and your head. "It's lonely where I am," Dylan remarked at one of the press conferences, and you know he meant it.

One stop on the tour was Minneapolis, a concert for the Dinkytowners and the students at the University. Some reporters wrote that he slipped into town and refused to have anything to do with his parents. Actually, he drove up to Hibbing and spent a little time there. And he called Echo, talking with her for about an hour. Echo recalls:

"I had gone home from work sick that day, for the first time the whole year, and as soon as I got home the phone rang and he said: 'Hi, it's Bob.' I told him: 'You put a hex on me. I haven't been sick all year.' And he said: 'Yeah, I did, but after a while you'll feel a lot better.' He asked me to come to his concert that night, and I said I couldn't because the guy I was going with was very jealous of him, going out of his mind knowing Bob was in town. So we just talked for a long time. He said he wanted to see me and I told him I just couldn't, and he said he was lonesome in the hotel room with just the company of the guys in the band. But I couldn't see him, so that was that. He didn't really talk much. As usual, I did most of the talking, as usual he was pretty secretive about what he was doing. I told him something like: 'The happiest people are those that are married and live an ordinary life and have the sense to appreciate what they do have,' and he said: 'Yeah, I've always felt that's true. But I never expected you to become a philosopher.' I think he was married at this time but he didn't say it and I knew better than to pry into his affairs."

At the end of that tour through Canada and to the West Coast, Dylan went into the studio again to cut several new songs, part of the album that would be called *Blonde on Blonde.* He was back on the West Coast by the end of March, 1966, performing at concerts from Los Angeles up to Vancouver and back again. He had put Levon and The Hawks on salary; they were his band by now, and his concerts were becoming wilder and more surrealistic, the sound of electricity like a squadron of jet planes, a pulsing, leaping, crushing sound that tore the air and seemed to make the seats rise. The audience listened, absorbing the experience, letting it all wash over them and finding understanding that way—viscerally.

"I'm not on drugs," Dylan had said at a California press conference around this time. "I just have a nervous disorder." But he was on drugs. Those who saw him say he was using speed and he has admitted (in the *Rolling Stone* interview) that he was using a good deal of dope to keep going. He was in bad shape by early April, physically and mentally. The pressures of the tour were driving him down; he was totally exhausted by the one night stands, and he seemed to almost hate Grossman for doing that to him. And the West Coast was not the end of it. He was scheduled to give a concert in Honolulu on April 9, spend more than a week touring Australia, and then on to Stockholm, Copenhagen, Paris, Rome, Ireland, England, Wales and Scotland. Still two months of hell in front of him.

Jack Elliott saw him at the house in the Hollywood Hills where he was living just before going to Hawaii: "He was going through a strange period. We had a conversation that lasted about one minute. I said: 'How ya doin', Bob?' He said: 'Fine, just played a gig at the Ash Grove, just playin' around a lot.' Somebody out in the kitchen was eating a baked ham and we could smell it out in the living room. Bob was eating ginger snaps. He said: 'You hungry?' I said: 'Sure am.' He said: 'Have a cookie.' I took one and he said: 'You *very* hungry?' And again I said: 'Sure am.' And Bob said: 'Have two cookies.' Then he just dove out of there."

That was where Jules Siegel, on assignment from the *Saturday Evening Post,* finally caught up with his subject. Siegel says: "I was out on the Coast and Ochs came to my place and I said: 'Let's go over to the house and see if Dylan is there.' When we got there the front door was open and we just walked in. Dylan was sitting there. He didn't pay any attention to Ochs. He started screaming at me: 'You got a hell of a nerve walkin' in on me, you got no respect for my privacy . . .' and I just screamed back: 'Don't yell at me like that. If you want to forget the interview, okay. I think you're a shit anyway. . . .' and so on and on. We finally left and Ochs had broken out in hives, and he said: 'I think I hate him. He's probably clinically insane.' The next day Dylan called me back and apologized and asked me to come around for the interview. He asked me: 'Who was that with you?' and I told him it was Ochs. He said: *'Really?* I was just blind. I didn't know.' He was always putting Ochs down, telling him things like: 'Ochs, you should be arrested for defamation of character, calling yourself a songwriter.'

"When I got there next day Dylan just tore into me, just tore me apart. It was about *Tarantula.* He couldn't bring himself to publish it. He was afraid. Afraid he'd be attacked by the critics. Ginsberg had told him the academic people were laying for him, and he said I was part of the academic community."

It was grinding on Dylan: the drugs, the endless tours, the threat-ening fans. At one concert a mob of girls broke through police lines and overwhelmed him. One tall blonde with a huge pair of shears snipped off some of his hair and ran away weeping, and Bob later sat in his dressing room, even paler and more wasted than usual, and cried: "Did ya see that? I mean, did ya *see* that? I don't care about the hair but she could have killed me. I mean, she could have taken my eyes out with those scissors." He looked like death during that tour, friends say. Baez had felt that Dylan was on some kind of death trip. Ochs was saying in an interview: "Dylan is LSD on stage. Dylan is LSD set to music. . . . I don't know if Dylan can get on stage a year from now. I don't think so. I mean that the phenomenon of Dylan will be so much that it will be dangerous. One year from now I think it will be very dangerous to Dylan's life to get on the stage. Dylan has become part of so many people's psyches and there are so many screwed up people in America, and death is such a part of the American scene now . . . I think he's going to have to quit."

Bob flew off to Australia, appearing in Brisbane on April 15, performing seven times in nine days, and ending up in Perth for a concert April 23. It was a vicious schedule and he hated it, but somehow he continued to be totally enthused about the rock music he and the band were making; it came together, it all made sense, and the crowds loved it.

An Australian actress, twenty years old and very beautiful, who wrote occasional newspaper pieces, spent several days with Dylan in Perth, before and after his concert at the Capitol Theater. She described her encounter with him under a promise of anonymity. She knew nothing about Dylan and his music, but friends were telling her that Dylan's poetry meant a great deal to them. Meanwhile, Dylan was telling the press that his words were meaningless. She decided to find out for herself. Dylan had a press conference scheduled on the afternoon of his concert and she attended. When it was over she saw Dylan alone and managed to break through his defenses. He invited her to see his show and to visit him backstage later.

She saw the second half of the concert and when it was over Dylan told her he had to go to a party. He asked her to meet him in his motel room in a couple of hours. She agreed.

"It was two in the morning and guards outside tried to stop me. Dylan leaned over the railing and told them to let me up. I went up and he was smoking and drinking Coke. He was sort of jumping around, excited, saying: 'What did you think of the music? Wasn't it good? Wasn't it terrific?' And I told him that it was marvelous, but that I didn't understand a lot of the words he had sung because they were colloquialisms, Americanisms, and he said: 'Yeah, right. Maybe I'll tell you about them.' What I felt was that he cared so much for that music that it was unbelievable.

"In the meantime, what had happened was Dylan sort of learned he could trust me. A friend of mine, Adrian Rawlings, a poet living in Melbourne, was the only person Dylan had gotten close to in Australia and Adrian rang Dylan up a couple of times in those hours between the first time I met Dylan and the next morning when I was in his motel room. Adrian had mentioned me and they talked about me, and that was another way Dylan found out I was okay.

"Dylan was on some kind of drugs. He said it was pot and I said to him I had never had marijuana—this dear little innocent girl—and I said I'd really like to try some. He said: 'You mean you never smoked anything?' I don't think he ever met anyone who was so not into anything. He was incredulous. 'No, I'm not gonna give you any, I'm not gonna start you off on anything.' And he wouldn't let me smoke.

"We reached a kind of impasse, we were just sitting there, and he said: 'You write what you want to write and I'll write what I want to write,' and he went to write more of his book. He said it was distinct from his poetry and songs, that he couldn't say what it meant, particularly. It didn't mean anything, but he was writing anyway. He wrote and did drawings, and I wrote some feeble kinds of observations about him. That went on for about an hour and then he suddenly jumped up and said: 'Look, this is all very stupid. You don't really want to write a story about me, do you?' And I said, after really wanting to do it: 'No, I don't, really.' And he said: 'Basically we're here with each other and there's not much point telling other people about it.' I said: 'Yes, that's right,' and he said: 'Well, you won't write anything so now you can stay.' "

They began to talk with mostly Dylan doing the talking:

"To start with, he was talking about being honest," she recalls. "This honesty is, basically, telling things and expressing things the way you really want to. That everybody should be honest, really honest, to start. I remember him saying: 'Honesty, that's just another *word.* These words, *truth, honesty,* they mean nothing.' But then he was saying that more important than just words is being completely honest, frustrating yourself as little as possible. Except for one thing which was forbidden, and that was to be unkind. That doesn't mean you can't be cruel, can't hurt. He was saying that small unkindnesses were not necessary, but when it came to things that involved your feelings, things you had to *tell* people, then it was okay to be cruel, if necessary. That is, be kind to people where you can, but be honest even if it is cruel, even if it hurts them.

"He was saying he could be cruel—we should all be cruel—to show someone what was wrong with her life.

"Basically what Dylan was telling me was that people should be ultimately what they are, as they see themselves. That this should be their religion, if any. That it's their duty to manifest this, openly, not keep it in but be that way with other people.

"The feeling of everything that came out of what he said was that he was interested in Self, and this is where the truth lay—he wasn't preaching to anyone, just telling them what he had discovered. And what he had discovered was the truth, was It. And that was that he had come to know that he must go back inside himself, that everything that happens comes out of reexamination and sort of drowning with your spirituality and your sensitivity. You go down into the deeper self and go through it all and come out the other side, and then you're going to *know* the way Dylan knew. Go back into your own self, get deeper than the surface world outside, and you won't need religion or philosophy because you will *know.*"

Dylan related a little story to illustrate a point he had been making, that part of society's trap that has destroyed the natural inner man was getting people hung up on wealth and material possessions. He told her:

"The last time I went to London I stayed at John Lennon's house. You should see all the stuff that Lennon bought: big cars and a stuffed gorilla and thousands of things in every room in his house, cost a fortune. When I got back home I wondered what it would be like to have all those material things. I figured I had the money and I could do it, and I wondered if it would feel like anything real. So I bought all this stuff and filled my house with it and sat around in the middle of it all. And I felt nothing. It didn't do anything for me. It wasn't real, part of life. Just a trap. I don't put down Lennon for it, that's his thing. But I know that material stuff is just a trap."

"He said we have to escape from the trap," she recalls. And part of the trap is our belief that wise men can teach us how to escape: possibly we can be taught knowledge by wise men and teachers, he told her, but not wisdom. Wisdom must come from within; from an understanding of our own inner being. She adds:

"But he would never use the word 'we' because he objected to being held up as a teacher or being apart from everyone else. My feeling was that he realized he was a teacher and apart, but he objected violently to it. Yet another side would be him saying 'I, I, I,' all the time, being a teacher, showing the truth of it all. There were these two conflicting points about him, and he changed radically from one to the other. Almost like dealing with two people. I'm not saying there was anything like schizophrenia, understand, but something was happening to him that was beyond his control. I think he was frightened by what people expected of him, what they had begun to think of him, what place they had put him into as to what he could tell them about truth, and I think he wanted to escape. It seemed, almost, that he courted a way of escape through doing anything that he could do to himself, such as drugs.

"I came to believe that Dylan was Christ revisited. I felt that everything fitted, without being Christian-religious or anything, I felt that what he had to say about living and communication with people was the truest, most honest and most Christ-like thing I've ever heard. I began to feel that Dylan was sacrificing himself in his whole philosophy, his thinking. That he would eventually die or that something horrible would happen to him. I felt it psychically, I felt it strongly. I must have been going slightly unhinged. But I know that other people felt Dylan was a Christ, sacrificing himself. Adrian Rawlings came to that conclusion the same time I did. Other people felt it.

"Dylan knew it, and he was so afraid of it. So very afraid. In that context, of being afraid of it, he said to me: 'I'm only a musician.' He said it with that kind of child-like thing when people say they are something they know they're not, when they know they're more. I know he didn't want to think himself as any sort of prophet, or that important, but he knew other people thought it of him and he was afraid of it. So was Christ, He was afraid of it, too."

Dylan was afraid, she said, and it is not difficult to understand why: If you are not Jesus Christ, but many people believe you could be and are asking you to cure their blindness and perform other miracles, then even crucifixion in the 20th century could seem a very real possibility. Especially if you are Bob Dylan, a highly sensitive man who periodically sniffed danger and made himself invisible to escape it.

One incident made it clear that Dylan was in a very fragile emotional state. The actress went home at about nine the next morning, after listening to Dylan talk for more than seven hours. That night she saw Dylan again briefly, but he was busy with some friends he and Robbie Robertson had made. He told her to return the next morning because he wanted to talk to her some more. She returned about five in the afternoon. Dylan, Robertson and other members of the group were going to catch a flight to Stockholm at 11 the following morning and they intended to stay awake until the plane left, "so we can get that wasted feeling and then sleep on the plane." The actress walked into Robertson's room, where everyone was sitting around jamming with Dylan. She slipped inside quietly and watched and made some sketches and listened, from around five in the afternoon until eight the next morning, some 15 hours. She recalls:

"It was amazing to see him work on a song. He would have the poetry of it worked out in his head and he would say to Robbie: 'Listen, Robbie, just imagine this cat who is very Elizabethan, with garters and a long shepherd's horn, and he's coming over the hill in the morning with the sun rising behind him. That's the sound I want.' And then they would begin to play and out of this would come some kind of rhythm, and then the music would take shape. They did this for hours and hours, Dylan setting a scene and everybody playing music to create the sound of that scene. And they were loving it so much. Somebody was sitting there, one of the other guys in the band, writing it down as music when it took shape. That's how Dylan was writing his songs at that time."

About eight the next morning Dylan suddenly turned on her and ordered her to leave, shouting at her, hurling his verbal hatchet at her. It was what somebody described as a "psychic storm," she says. "Something was really disturbing him. When I thought about it later I realized there was something almost crazed about him.

"I finally said to Dylan: 'Look . . .' and he started shouting: 'Go! Go! Go!' and I shouted back: 'I'm not going until you get me a taxi.' And he called a taxi. As I was going down the stairs to wait for it, he shouted from the balcony at me: 'Happy hunting.' After accepting me, after all the closeness that had been built up, he just went mad."

The reception he received in some European cities on his tour did nothing to brighten the oppressive cloud that seemed to hang over him more and more. It was Newport 1965, all over again, and Bob reacted venomously. At the Royal Albert Hall in London during the first half of the show in which he played on an acoustic guitar, he seemed to deliberately put down his audience. He would take about ten minutes between each number, casually tuning his guitar and commenting in a series of short expletives on everything from the vapidity of most rock being played to the stupidity of fans and pundits who tried to say Bob Dylan was writing "drug" songs. The second half, the electric part of the concert, drew scattered boos and several fans stalked out, Dylan shouting at their retreating backs. The boos grew louder after each song and Dylan fought back with angrier words. Finally, he shouted at the audience: "I'm never gonna play in England again. This is my last visit here." (He returned in 1968, to play a concert on the Isle of Wight.)

In Paris, at the Olympia, Bob ran into the same kind of audience resistance. Once more he took long breaks between each song, and at one point the audience became so restless that some began whistling to show their disapproval. Bob looked down at them and said: "I'm just as anxious to go home as you are. Don't you have any paper to read?" He was attacked the next day in the French press, one newspaper carrying a banner headline: "Bob Dylan Go Home!" and another prophesying that the concert marked "the fall of an idol."

1966–1967: *The Drifter's Escape*

BLONDE ON BLONDE was just being released when Dylan returned to New York at the beginning of June. With that album, the fourth in a series of song-poems that began with *Another Side of Bob Dylan*, we see what Dylan has discovered about *himself.* And that is an important point to keep in mind: Dylan was not only describing other mindless people in those bitter songs. In a discussion of his work during one of our conversations, he said that years after writing these songs he discovered that "I was really talking about no one but me."

Dylan signaled the onset of his interior struggle with *My Back Pages* and *Lay Down Your Weary Tune*. In both of these songs he writes that he is finished with protest and political activism. He was so much older then, he sings, and he's younger than that now—a hint of rebirth. He is going to leave his "weary tune," and he hopes to pause for a while to listen to "strings that no voice can hope to hum."

Another Side of Bob Dylan already contained the seed of salvation that Dylan would be stressing more and more. In *Spanish Harlem Incident*, for example, the woman represents a pure aboriginal state, sexuality without guilt, and personal freedom. This is something that Dylan covets, the ability to be totally free, to feel with the flesh, and not a detached intellect. Civilization as it has evolved is not geared to meet the needs of the human spirit, but the woman from Spanish Harlem *is* human spirit—and Dylan is seeking that spirit within himself.

In this album, Dylan mounts an attack on the tyranny of logic and morality that nails man to a cross: the dictatorship of the rational order of time and space, of science and reason, a civilization that is "binding with briars my joy and desires," as Blake expressed it. Dylan condemns all psychic straitjackets in *I Shall be Free #10* (a parody of Cassius Clay), in *To Ramona,* and in *Motorpsycho Nightmare* (really an old-style talking blues number).

Bringing It All Back Home, the second album in the series, continues the same motifs. The first cut, *Subterranean Homesick Blues* has become a radical hymn, offering such advice as *Don't follow leaders, watch parking meters; you don't need a weatherman to tell which way the wind blows* (from which the Weathermen took their name). Actually, Dylan was not writing about political revolution. Dylan, the author, is warning Dylan the "kid" that he must break loose from the debris that has cluttered all of our natural perception; the theme is repeated in another song in the album, *Maggie's Farm*.

At the same time that he is describing one aspect of the universal *angst*, Dylan celebrates the ability of some to break free from society's dungeon, women who have reached a stage of development he is striving for. *She Belongs To Me* and *Love Minus Zero/No Limit* describe two women who hold out the promise of the future's possibilities; women who have discarded all the falseness, who knew too much to *argue or to judge*. In so many songs where Dylan seems to be writing about women, he is really writing about Dylan. There is much that is androgynous in Dylan. One result of being an inner-directed man whose life is based on feeling and not intellect, is to break down the distinctions between the strong, unemotional rational male, and the emotional, sensual, unstable female. Friends have recognized a good deal of each in Dylan.

Dylan zeros in on the problem of self-realization with increasing bitterness in *Like A Rolling Stone*. In the song, which is in the *Highway 61 Revisited* album, Dylan once more judges himself. He thought he was invulnerable and he ignored the warnings of friends. But now that he has fallen—psychically—everything has been transformed. How does it feel to be without a home, to be lost inside while seeming to have so much on the outside? Denying the inner self—the "mystery tramp" with whom he tried to make a deal—was simply an attempt to escape the truth of his existence. Now he has "no secrets to conceal." When the pain becomes overwhelming, when it is so very clear that life is meaningless, then the soul opens, and he can see how he and all men and women blind themselves.

In *It's Alright Ma (I'm Only Bleeding)*, Dylan writes that he has been evading life, and he castigates those who tried to make him over in their image; those who fail to recognize that the "hollow horn" of the wordmongers and philosophers is empty of meaning. But there is a road to freedom, Dylan writes. When he stands alone and a "trembling distant voice unclear" calls to him, then questions are lit in his mind and he realizes he belongs to no one but himself. When he awakens to the fact that there *are* questions, he must break free of false gods, even if they kill him. It's alright, Ma, because "it's life, and life only." Dylan, affirming life. This is the road to salvation.

Dylan describes what he hopes to find at the end of that road in *Gates of Eden*. There are no truths outside the gates, only spiritual paupers who are coveting "what the other has got," and people who argue over "what's real and what is not." Inside Eden, it doesn't matter at all; there are no kings inside, no sins, no trials.

But it is not easy for him to stop wasting his life on the trivialities that most men believe define the real world. Dylan criticizes himself for being unable to cast off the ego blocking the Way to his inner being. In *Queen Jane Approximately,* he faces the truth that all his "creations" are part of life's artificialities. Don't come around, he sings, until you can rid yourself of all the clowns you have commissioned to entertain you, all the advisors who pile their plastic at your feet in obeisance to your fame, until all the useless repetitions of your life have made you sick.

Most of the remaining songs on the first three albums of the series are Dylan's explorations of his struggle to break free, to use the force of his will to reach a greater meaning in his life. *Desolation Row,* for example, Dylan's epic portrait of a crazed society, must be seen as more than simply an indictment of the souring of America, more than political ideology. Most of those inhabiting Desolation Row are imprisoned—Cain and Abel, the hunchback of Notre Dame, and even the Good Samaritan who is busy getting dressed for a carnival —all have been turned into symbols by intellectual system-makers to blind us to the men they had been. A typical woman on the Row wears an iron vest, perhaps to encase the heart and the soul; her "sin is her lifelessness." But among the zombies, there are several people filled with life, totally free: mermaids and calypso singers and fisher-men—men and women of the spirit who laugh at it all, and who "don't have to think too much" about the absurdity they see all about them.

In his work Dylan makes it clear he knows that it is cowardice to live by an abstraction that society calls order and morality. Chaos must be confronted. True salvation can come only after a descent into chaos, an inner wrenching that will alter his individual character and change the flow and direction of his life. Only then will Dylan be able to answer the questions: "Who am I?" and "What shall I do with my life?"

With *Blonde on Blonde,* the last album of the series, Dylan reflects on Zen. Man intrinsically lacks nothing; man is whole, a perfect circle which cannot be subtracted from or added to. But man is conned into believing that his body and his mind are separate from that of other beings, and he becomes obsessed by the idea of "I" or ego. This disorder leads to such ideas as "this is mine and that is yours." But man cannot know the meaning of life, by controlling the external conditions, by organizing institutions, writing laws, moral codes. Man must turn inward. He must accept the inner being—a transcendent godhead—as the meaning of life. Buddhists call it Enlightenment. If Dylan called it anything, he would have named it Truth—or *Visions of Johanna* which "conquer" his mind, and make it clear that the people around him, the people out on the streets, the friend who "whispers small talk at the wall," the museums where "infinity goes up on trial," are completely unreal. He speaks of them almost with compassion, a new voice for Dylan. Certainly Dylan's most beautiful song, *Visions of Johanna,* may have been written for Joan Baez—the name and the line about her farewell kiss supports that view. But more importantly Dylan is describing an awareness that has brought him to a stage where his "conscience explodes." He must be freed from the prison in which Dylan the star and the symbol has been locked. The visions hold out hope for beauty and truth in his life.

The other songs on *Blonde on Blonde* are mostly Dylan "coming down hard on all the people, not just specific people," as he expressed it in one of our conversations. This was during a discussion of whether such songs as *Leopard-skin Pill-box Hat* were written about actual individuals he had known. In most of them Dylan is saying that we must all break out of society's straitjacket.

The intense pressures of touring, the demands of recording, of being a star, of being worshipped as a public deity, were as much an obstacle to personal salvation as everything he had condemned in song. The prisoner could not leave the prison. The pressures did not let up with the end of the 1966 world tour. *Blonde on Blonde* was released. *Tarantula* was still being touted as almost ready for publication. Macmillan printed up ten thousand shopping bags with Bob's portrait on it and large type: *"Tarantula,* by Bob Dylan?" The question mark was not as cute as the ad writer probably believed, for Dylan by now was telling friends that he didn't think he wanted to see it published. By the time it got into the stores it would no longer represent what Dylan was all about. He also had two major concerts scheduled for August, at the Yale Bowl in New Haven and at Shea Stadium, the scene of the Beatles' insane love affair with fifty-five thousand screaming teenyboppers.

As soon as he returned from Europe, Bob was thrown into the midst of a rather ugly commercial scene, which he always genuinely abhorred. Grossman was finally ready to get Dylan away from Columbia. Dylan's contract expired in the spring of 1966, and Grossman had been busy sorting out offers from other companies. The best of them turned out to a million-dollar package from MGM, which would include handling Dylan's records, song publishing, and films. But a number of hitches developed. For one thing the MGM board of directors took a more critical look at the reports of Dylan's very negative European reception, rumors that he was into drugs, and assorted other tales growing out of the Dylan myth. Another problem was that Columbia owed a large sum of money to Bob, most of which could end up in the federal treasury if he left the label. John Hammond explains: "I had made a terrible goof in signing Dylan. Usually there is an automatic escalation clause, if a man starts at four per cent he moves right up to five per cent for the second record. I had requested it in the requisition form for the contract, but when the contract was drawn up the escalator was inadvertently left out and Bob signed it that way. I didn't know it, and Bob didn't know it. By the time the contract ran out five years later, that one per cent we owed Bob worked out to many hundreds of thousands of dollars. It was a wonderful bargaining point for Columbia because if it was released at one time Uncle Sam would get ninety per cent of it."

Before Grossman and Dylan could decide what to do with their very commercial problem, a macabre edge was honed onto the sword of Dylan's public mystique, creating a series of new rumors that put fresh masks over all the old ones. On the afternoon of Saturday, July 30, pop radio stations across the country interrupted their broadcasts with a bulletin: Bob Dylan had a motorcycle accident in Woodstock the day before, had been hospitalized, and appeared to be seriously hurt. Vague details came out in succeeding days: he had been riding his Triumph 500 bike near his home, heading for a repair shop and followed in a car by either Sarah or a friend, depending on the version. The back wheels of the bike suddenly locked, throwing it into a skid and dashing Bob to the pavement. He was lifted into the car and taken to Middletown Hospital, where his injuries were diagnosed as a broken neck (that is, several broken vertebrae), a concussion, and lacerations of the face and scalp.

Suddenly, the cataclysm that had always been expected to fall on him—the James Dean end—had happened. And the rumors began to spread: Dylan was dead; his brain had been crushed and he was no more than a vegetable; he was an incurable drug addict, hospitalized for treatment; he was in a psychiatric ward somewhere, totally insane; he was so badly scarred his public would never see him again. His wife was rumored to be turning away almost all visitors, permitting only the closest friends into the house. They could communicate with him only over an intercom because he refused to come out of the bedroom where he was hiding in the sprawling ranch house he had recently bought in Woodstock.

Attempts to turn back these stories added grist to the rumor mill. Grossman, Columbia, Macmillan, ABC-TV (which had given Bob a

$100,000 advance a few months earlier to do a TV special) and others with a commercial stake in Dylan insisted the accident had not been serious, but no one believed them. In some circles, a Johnson-Pentagon-CIA conspiracy was seriously given as the reason for Dylan's accident. As the months passed and Dylan remained hidden from sight, the rumors seemed to take substance.

The accident was indeed a cataclysm, but not in the sense his fans believed. Physically, Bob had been injured quite seriously. Those who were closest to him at the time and had refused to talk about it, now concede that the broken neck almost killed him. They say doctors told Sarah and Grossman that a fraction of an inch difference in the way his head had struck the pavement was the difference between injury and death. "He almost died," one friend says. "It really almost killed him. His neck is still stiff, still gives him trouble." Dylan was unconscious for a while, from the brain concussion, and had a short spell of amnesia. He was also paralyzed for a brief period, and internal injuries seemed particularly dangerous to his doctors. He remained in the hospital for more than a week, and when he was returned to his Woodstock home he remained in bed for more than a month. Recovery was slow because Dylan was in poor physical shape. He had never been a strong person, physically, and his condition at the time of the accident was as poor as it had ever been because of the exhaustion of the concert tour, the drugs, and the enormous conflict between his fame and his fear. "He was more scared by the accident than scarred," another friend says. The Australian actress's feeling, that he was a Christ offering himself up for sacrifice, had been communicated to Dylan over and over again in the previous year or two, and it terrified him. He had always dwelt on death, as far back as his first album which ends with *See That My Grave Is Kept Clean.* James Dean could not be dismissed from the memory, nor could his brush with death back in Hibbing when he was on his motorcycle and the train almost hit him, or when he knocked down a child with his bike. Death was personally close to him at this time. While Bob was in Australia the previous April Richard Fariña had been killed in a motorcycle accident. Paul Clayton committed suicide the April before Dylan's accident, jumping out of a window after a three-day LSD trip. Peter La Farge had committed suicide. Death lurked all around.

But Dylan also used the accident, not deliberately to create a new myth, although his withdrawal from public view did stimulate sales of his albums. The accident gave him a chance to sort things out in his head, to try and decide where he wanted to go from here. In discussing it with me years later, Dylan remarked:

"You were right on it when you described all those pressures. But you really only touched the surface. The pressures were unbelievable. They were just something you can't imagine unless you go through them yourself. Man, they hurt so much."

During his recuperation, Dylan let things slide. The MGM deal fell through, and he did nothing to rescue the deal. He also gave up on *Tarantula.* He told one friend it was the "wrong time to write a book," and he told another that the book was so meaningless and absurdist that he was "sure it won't be accepted, so I'm dropping it." (He told me in early 1971 that he planned to release the book "because I dig it now. It's a good book. I didn't dig it back then, but I dig it now." *Tarantula* was finally published in May, 1971.)

Robbie Robertson and the other members of the old Hawks went up to Woodstock to be with Dylan. "He just needed some friends, that's all," Robertson later said. Eventually their families joined them, and they rented an old house on a mountaintop in West Saugerties, a few miles away, that they called Big Pink. Dylan and the band, as it was informally called then, began to play together while Dylan was recuperating. They were important to his head, musically; not simply bringing him back to the relative simplicity of country music, but also in emphasizing his music which had always taken second place to his poetry. "We taught him what we knew about rock and roll," Robertson has said. And they knew a great deal. Some of it shows up on the so-called basement tape, recordings of about a dozen songs Dylan did with the group in the basement of his Woodstock home in the summer of 1967. The tape was bootlegged around the country a couple of years later. Some of the songs point the direction in which Dylan was heading, which would mark his *John Wesley Harding* album many months later.

Dylan remained holed up in his Woodstock home for more than nine months after the accident, refusing to see any but close friends and growing into an American legend at twenty-five. *Blonde On Blonde* was certified as a million-dollar best seller, and more than fifty other artists raced to record Dylan songs, some of which hit the pop charts. Columbia released an album, *Bob Dylan's Greatest Hits,* simply to have something on the market. That one quickly hit the million dollar mark, and two earlier Dylan albums broke through it.

But there was no public word from Dylan, and the mystery and rumors continued until early May, 1967, when Michael Iachetta, of the *New York Daily News,* got to see Dylan. Iachetta had interviewed Dylan in October, 1963, for an article on folk protest and had given him a good writeup and impressed him as someone who could be trusted. When he found Dylan standing there behind the screen he blurted out with genuine relief: "It's great to see you're up and around and the rumors aren't true." Dylan invited him inside for coffee. They talked for a while, Dylan telling him:

"What I've been doin' mostly is seein' only a few close friends, readin' little about the outside world, porin' over books by people you never heard of, thinkin' about where I'm goin', and why am I runnin', and am I mixed up too much, and what am I knowin', and what am I givin', and what am I takin'. And mainly what I've been doin' is workin' on gettin' better and makin' better music, which is what my life is all about."

Dylan added: "Songs are in my head like they always are. And they're not goin' to get written down until some things are evened up. Not until some people come forth and make up for some of the things that have happened." He would not elaborate. *"Somethin' has got to be evened up is all I'm goin' to say,"* speaking almost in italics, as he frequently did. *Evened up:* Revenge, again?

The answer, he was telling friends, would be forthcoming in the new album he was ready to cut—the answer to all the questions about what happened to him and where his head was at; all would be explained in the new album.

Dylan went down to Nashville with a batch of songs in October, 1967, almost fifteen months after the accident. He selected only three musicians—Charlie McCoy, bass; Kenny Buttrey, drums; and Pete Drake, steel guitar—and got down to work, putting in two days of intensive music making. When it was over he had most of the cuts for the new album, *John Wesley Harding.* He taped the rest of it a short time later, on another quick trip to Nashville.

The album, released in January, 1968, was a stunning reversal on what had been happening in pop music. The Beatles had released *Sergeant Pepper* a few months earlier. One report had it that when Dylan heard the first few cuts of that album he snapped: "Turn that off!" indicating to some that he was afraid rock was leaving him behind. And after *Pepper* the rock recording scene turned almost into a game of "Can You Top This?," culminating in a Christmas album by the Rolling Stones, *Their Satanic Majesties Request,* with a 3-D cover and musical content that was a parody of all the insanity. Rock had become almost a toy of studio engineers fiddling with control knobs and super-charged electricity. And Dylan's new album pulled out the plug.

The opening phrases of the title song were the strumming of an acoustic guitar. The electricity was muted, and his melodies had undergone structural changes. They are simple folk melodies, only lightly emphasized by the tranquil backbeat, a muted, low-volume rhythm section—drums, bass, an occasional piano. And his voice is for the most part flowing more naturally than at any time before.

Dylan explained the musical changes to me this way: "You see, that album was all I could come up with musically. It's the best I could have done at that time. I didn't intentionally come out with some kind of mellow sound. I would have liked a good sound, more musical, more steel guitar, more piano. More *music.* At that time so many people were into electronics, and I didn't know anything about that. I didn't even know anybody who knew it. I didn't sit down and plan that sound. It wasn't a question of this is what I'm doing and come over here."

Still it's difficult to believe that. Dylan's new sound moved away from rock because he hoped to shake up the industry and, most of all, because he wanted his poetry to carry the album, he wanted his words—and their meaning—fully understood.

1968: *I'll Be Your Baby Tonight*

JOHN WESLEY HARDING is infused with a belief in God, with self-discovery and compassion. It is Dylan's version of the Bible, songs written as parables describing the fall and rebirth of one man—Bob Dylan.

The album is Dylan's avowal of faith.

When we sat and talked about this album, Dylan told me: "Before I wrote *John Wesley Harding* I discovered something about all those earlier songs I had written. I discovered that when I used words like 'he' and 'it' and 'they' and talking about other people, I was really talking about nobody but me. I went into *John Wesley Harding* with that knowledge in my head. You see, I hadn't really known before, that I was writing about myself in all those songs."

In *Harding,* then, he is describing the fires that almost consumed him. He is saying: "This is what I was like, this is what I have gone through." And, in writing about himself Dylan drew on the Bible for

250

the form and content on which to build his poems, further emphasizing his search for redemption and salvation.

The biblical quality is first apparent in the notes on the album jacket, a parable of three "jolly" and disreputable-looking kings who are searching for the "key"—the key to the Kingdom and the key to Dylan. An ironical touch: You made me a Christ, a keeper of the keys. The kings decide that the key is Frank, who is Dylan, hiding as he has always done. They knock on his door and when Frank opens it they crawl in. They are no longer the wise men they had been at Christ's birth, but are now representatives of a structured society. "Please lead us inside to the true meaning of Dylan," they ask, "Just far enough so's we can say that we've been there." They prefer Dylan as symbol, not really wanting to know the truth of him. Frank bounces through a Chaplinesque pantomime, an absurdist-Zen routine that ends when he smashes his fist through a plate glass window. Glass hides the truth that is to be found beyond man's consciousness, by giving back man's own deluded reflection. The glass represents also the veil that covers the way from the Holy outer courtyard of the temple to the inner Holy of Holies where the Lord's ark was safeguarded; the veil which was rent at the moment Christ died.

The kings leave. As they walk along the road it is clear that the little glimpse Frank gave them of Dylan has transfigured them, but they are obviously still too blind to see the truth beyond that shattered glass. They continue to believe Dylan is the Messiah who works miracles.

This tale that draws on Brecht's *The Good Woman of Setzuan* in which three grubby kings come to earth to search for a "good person" and, on choosing a prostitute almost succeed in civilizing her into lifelessness. Dylan uses this story to introduce the songs within. You idolized me as a savior, he is saying, and in my cupidity I went along with you, but now I'm going to tell you all that I've discovered about me, Bob Dylan.

John Wesley Harding, the title song is, on the surface, a simple tale about the famous Western outlaw (with a final "G" added to the name) who was a friend of the poor, a man with a gun in each hand who robbed the rich but "never hurt an honest man." But for Dylan he is more than that: He is Christ, and he is also Dylan, who is saying that he was cast in the role of the Messiah and had come to believe that it was real, to believe he could save people's souls. He never realized that it was all ego, and that he had been caught in a false posture, trapped into believing he was more than a man.

Like Christ, Harding is an outlaw and outsider who tries to bring wisdom to the people of his land, who travels with his weapons, shooting down all men who will deny him. "Think not that I come to send peace on earth; I come not to send peace, but a sword," Christ told the apostles. Harding roamed the land, opening "many a door," and as he spread the Word he was hunted by the forces of repression. But there was no man around who could "chain him down," who could crucify him or civilize him into one of society's living dead. Harding escaped that fate because he "never made a foolish move" —a phrase of deepest self-irony for Dylan, as the next songs demonstrate.

As I Went Out One Morning extends this theme: they will do to you what they had done to Christ. Dylan sings that one morning— which in the Bible represents the beginning of true spiritual life— he went out to "breathe the air" around Tom Paine, a symbol of myth-exploding liberty. A statue of Paine was part of the ECLC award, a statue that Dylan said he thought was almost human because there was such tenderness in the eyes. The moment he began breathing that air he spied a "damsel" who was in chains; she is institutionalized religion and the establishment that has polluted God's and Christ's teachings. She has been chained by Western culture's evasions, hostilities and vanities, all of which separate us from Truth and make us blind. Dylan offered his hand, to free her from the chains, but she seized his arm and enticed him to give up his soul and become like her. As he struggled in vain to break free of her grip, Tom Paine rescued him and apologized for what society had tried to do to him.

He has continued to escape the traps, but he still believes in symbols like Tom Paine and has not become aware that he must go through chaos to find spirituality. Dylan describes some of that chaos in the next song, *I Dreamed I Saw St. Augustine,* which is in part a reworking of the idea expressed in *My Back Pages,* that the moment he preached society's sermon he joined the enemy. Augustine represents the duality of man's nature. Natural man has no place in most institutionalized religions. Good is at one pole, evil at the other; all is black and white. That view is a lie, Dylan maintains. There is actually no conflict in duality: good and evil are simply parts of the whole. As the Lord tells Isaiah: "I form the light, and create the darkness; I make peace and create evil. I, the Lord, do all these things." Lucifer, after all, is the light-bearer, and he is also an angel of darkness. But Augustine permitted himself to be torn by a duality that he should have recognized as unity. Eventually he resolved the conflict by insisting that the evil earthly life is just a temporary sojourn, and that only in the life hereafter will man find truth and beauty.

252

Augustine is Dylan in this song. Dylan-Augustine was caught up in the greatest "misery" because of the conflict over his duality; he had "a blanket under his arm" symbolizing the prophet who wanders the earth; at the same time he wore a "coat of solid gòld"—symbol of our corruptibility. Augustine continues to cry "Arise! Arise!," trying to rescue the very souls he has helped to destroy. And Dylan is saying he has been a false prophet, that he knows the only way to find salvation is by casting off all the artificiality, the rings and jewels and coats of gold, and ego. "Nobody is among you," Dylan-Augustine cries: I can't really be a savior, that is a false pose.

Dylan's dream continues. He saw Augustine alive "with fiery breath," shouting Jehovah's message of Jehovah's destruction that will purify the world. Dylan was one of those who put Augustine to death; he dreamed of killing one part of himself, destroying his God-given duality. When he awoke, Dylan writes, he put his fingers against the glass and cried. He did not break the glass, as Frank did in the liner notes, because he is still afraid to break through the doors of perception.

In *All Along the Watchtower,* the finest song on the album, Dylan is describing a turning point in his life when he became aware of the sham and began to speak to himself about it, trying to understand that his own life was false. In *Watchtower,* Dylan borrowed heavily from the book of Isaiah. Isaiah prophesies the Lord's wrathful destruction of a corrupt world: "And the Lord said ... watch in the watchtower. . . . go, set a watchman, let him declare what he seeth." Eventually the watchman saw riders approach and asked the news of one of them: "And he answered and said, Babylon is fallen, is fallen; and all the graven images of her gods he hath broken unto the ground." The watchman added: "The morning cometh, and also the night"—the Lord's cataclysmic destruction.

Dylan, the joker in *Watchtower,* complains that there must be a way out of the cage. Businessmen take his wine, plowmen dig his earth, and no one knows what it is worth. The wine is the blood of Christ now commercialized into organized religion. The plowmen have ignored the Lord's other commandments to Moses, among them the instruction that in the "seventh year shall be a sabbath of rest unto the land, a sabbath for the Lord." Instead of understanding the truths of Jesus and the Lord, we have corrupted all. In our perversion of truth we don't recognize the potential within us for joy and salvation. The thief answers the joker, speaking "kindly": although many feel life on earth is a joke, is evil and simply a time of waiting for the better life beyond, we've seen through those lies.

Let's not speak falsely, for time is running out. Life is too short to be wasted worrying about society's delusions.

And from the watchtower the believers see the Coming. Riders approach, the wind howls; chaos is on the way, as in Isaiah. And Dylan understands that in spreading the Word as a prophet, he has become as false as the idols of Babylon. He is facing a personal Armageddon, he writes. He must die now, in order to live.

He knew the thief spoke wisely but he did not listen, Dylan writes in *The Ballad of Frankie Lee and Judas Priest*. Dylan is Frankie Lee, a simple and natural man. And in naming him Judas Priest Dylan symbolized not only the betrayer of Christ but also the institutional religions and the ruling establishments. Frankie and Judas were best friends. When Frankie needed money, Judas reached down and pulled out a roll of tens and placed them on a footstool "above the crowded plains": The Lord had told Jesus to "sit on my right hand, until I make thy foes thy footstool," and Dylan is saying he was placing himself above all people, exalting himself.

Judas tells Frankie to take whatever he needs from the roll of bills. "My loss will be your gain." This is an ironic inversion, for if Frankie is seduced, then Judas's gain actually will be Frankie's loss—end of freedom, soul, the inner being. Frankie Lee resists the seduction at first, and Judas warns him quickly to choose the bills he wants, for there are many willing to accept Judas' blandishments. In giving Frankie a choice, Dylan reflects the Biblical teaching that a man can choose life, or he can choose death; choose to be a man who is natural and full of life, but mortal; or can choose to be the Priest, who is false, valueless, without a soul, and as immortal as Satan.

Judas leaves, pointing down the road saying he will be waiting in "eternity," but you may know it as paradise. Another ironic stab: Judas Priest is putting down the paradise of the Lord. Frankie Lee sits there, pondering his choices, when a stranger bursts in and tells him Priest is calling him. He is stranded in a house, the stranger says, and in panic Frankie drops everything and runs down the road until he finds Judas. He asks what kind of house this is and Judas says, "It's not a house, it's a home," a house of prostitution, society's house of harlotry.

Frankie Lee loses control of his senses and runs into the house, now completely owned by Judas and all his harlots, falls into Judas's arms and dies of thirst, recalling Christ nailed to the cross and complaining of thirst. This is Revelation: Dylan should never have entered society's whorehouse, should never have been seduced by their offerings; he had been made to believe he was above all men and the result of that huge ego trip was the death of his soul.

After he died they carried out his body and, he writes, "nothing is revealed." Christ's demand that the priests of the Temple should reveal all the wisdom of the Lord instead of holding it back to enhance the power of the inner circle, has not come to pass. Judas Priest poses as the angel of life to lure us to death.

The Drifter's Escape is the judgment of Bob Dylan, who had accepted the house because he believed it was a home. He is man who drifts through life. The drifter asks for help in his weakness; Dylan has reached the point at which he knows he is neither prophet nor idol, that he is only a weak man. The drifter is taken into a courtroom, where he has already been judged, but he does not know what he had done wrong. And now everything is revealed; the judge tells him he failed to understand and should not even try to understand. According to the Lord, or to the Zen masters, the search for knowledge is in itself a snare; knowledge becomes a system replacing wisdom, destroying intuition. As the judge spoke the crowd outside began stirring. The jury "cried for more"— all the actors in the divine comedy groaning in their wretchedness, still demanding from him the Word, a message from the cross. Then, suddenly, the courthouse is struck by a bolt of lightning, an illumination from the Lord. While everyone kneels to pray the drifter escapes, slipping out of the grasp of the idolizers.

Dear Landlord has been seen by many critics as a message from Dylan to Albert Grossman and other commercializers, telling them that he is finished with them. Some friends say Grossman saw it that way himself. But that interpretation misses the point, for the song is Bob Dylan describing his attempts to come to grips with the split between the inner being and the outer man. In it, Dylan's soul appears to be talking to his body, the landlord that has given a wordly shelter to his soul. Don't put a price on that soul, he asks. I am me, I have dreams and visions and a life force which I can't control. Don't *you* try to control it, body. Don't make a judgment on me. You are only a body; but I am a soul, in touch with something you will never be able to grasp. My soul is the master of my own fate, he says from the first line, the "steamboat whistle" that alludes to the ship's captain in "Invictus": master of his fate, captain of his soul. His soul says it is going to give the outer being all the support he can, and hopes it is received well. But landlord, he continues, heed me: I know you've suffered a great deal, but you are not unique in this world of suffering. I know that things have come to you "too fast and too much," that you have filled your life with trivialities you can see but can't touch, fame, ego, wealth, pride. But listen to me landlord, "don't dismiss my case." I'm not going to fight you and I certainly can't move out and find a more willing body. We each have something to give the other. If you don't deny my life force, I will not criticize your special needs.

I Am a Lonesome Hobo is intimately connected with everything that has gone before in this album detailing Dylan's road to self-discovery. Dylan is the lonesome hobo, friendless, without family. He is alone now, and glad of it because he has recognized that you must stand alone in order to find Self. My life ends, he sings, where another man's might begin: again, the words of Jesus—"Except a man be born again, he cannot see the kingdom of God."

I've been through it all, he sings, tried "bribery, blackmail and deceit." I've served time, meaning he was in death, was frozen in lifelessness. I did everything loathesome and false, except "begging on the streets." I never really humbled myself, which is where I lost my way, for man must be humble. I was proud. And what I got were the lies that are the world's truth: fame, becoming a wealthy superstar with 14-carat gold teeth and silks on my back. But I didn't trust my brothers; I never had faith; I never gave of myself. And that brought my "fatal doom," which is to wander around in shame, with guilt in my soul. I am going to leave soon, he writes. I will pass on. —*A man must die to be reborn.*

But, Dylan continues, before I leave you to find my own road to salvation I want to lay one more message on you: Don't get trapped in "petty jealousies," and don't accept any man's code. Don't fall for the rules laid down by the masters and merchants, but search within yourself for the faith to sustain you. And, most of all, don't make judgments on people or you will be tramping along the same terrible road I have traveled.

In the next song-parable, *I Pity The Poor Immigrant,* Dylan sees himself as an outsider, an immigrant, a man who did not really know his inner Self and had no place in the outer world. A man who is evil because he is playing society's vainglorious game. A man who believes life was created to cheat and lie and pretend. A man who hates life, but is afraid to die so that he can be reborn. The portrait he paints of himself is a cruel one. He writes that his heaven is like "ironsides," a battleground, not a place of peace and rest, not the source of beauty he wants in life. The tears he has spilled are like rain, the hard rain again, the lies. He was guilty of spreading the lies that society thrives on. Most of all, he says, he was a man who can hear "but does not see"—a visionary who does not use his vision, who has no faith. He pities the man who loves only wealth, who denies the existence of an inner being in his search for wealth; a man who performs horrendous acts and then "fills his mouth with laughing," which is a derision reserved for the gods. Dylan behaved as if he were indeed one of the gods.

But in the end, he writes, his visions will shatter like glass and he'll see the truth of existence beyond the illusion of this outer world. When that happens he is going to be a pitiable man because he will learn that he was living a deception. When it comes down to the end of the game, when the awakening comes, when you find that some simple thing you love is what existence is all about, and you finally learn to walk in peace, you're going to cry out in anger and pain for not having understood before.

And then, Bob Dylan's last self-flagellation, *The Wicked Messenger*. This is Dylan at his best, juxtaposing his Biblical metaphors against an incredible descending, unsettling, blues line that is wracked with tension. It tells of the death and rebirth of Bob Dylan. The wicked messenger is Satan, who is also Dylan. Satan, who has been sent to earth by Eli, the most intellectual of God's servants, wanders around as in Job, trying to cast doubt in the minds of God's children. Dylan writes that he took one of God's forms, the Devil, and wandered the earth attempting to deceive people into believing he was a prophet who had been given Truth. Then, suddenly, he disappeared one day and left behind a note that said the soles of his feet are burning, which is the hell fire: God's revenge on him for trying to intellectualize and philosophize, thereby destroying the intuitive sense that knows more truth than any philosopher. And when his feet were burned—Dylan's motorcycle accident, perhaps, as a form of punishment—the seas begin to part, as they did for God's chosen people during the Exodus, and he was told a few words that "opened up his heart." Bring good news or don't bring any at all is the message he was given; the Glad Tidings of the ancient Jewish texts and Luke's "glad tidings" of the Messiah's birth. If you must preach then preach the sermon of faith, preach the Word, Dylan was told.

And that is what he sings in the last two cuts of the album, good-time upbeat songs of love that are hymns to the joys of life.

Down Along The Cove is a new kind of Dylan, one that had never been heard publicly before. He sings what appears to be a playful ballad and bangs a boogie beat on the piano. The simplicity is deceptive. There is a depth of meaning in that little song. "Lord have mercy," he sings, for he and his true love are walking hand in hand and all the world knows they're in love. Most important, he says: "Yes, we understand"—only within love can man deal with a depth of reality that is akin to faith. Christ had said his main commandment is to love: "For now abideth faith, hope, charity, these three; but the greatest of these is charity." And charity, of course, is love of fellow man. The love that Dylan speaks of is not the social straightjacket that suppresses sensuality but a recognition of all that is implicit in a human relationship, an understanding that one is really loving if he is giving. Those who institutionalized religion considered sensuality a lure of the Devil, but poets and children know that to deny Eros is to deny life.

And in *I'll Be Your Baby Tonight* Dylan is a man who is able to give love without reservation. He tells his woman to close her eyes, that she need never be afraid because he'll be there and will take care of her. And, he assures her, the mockingbird is going to sail away and they'll bid it goodbye and good riddance—Bob Dylan, mockingbird, is going to get off that stool which the Lord had offered his Son. He and his woman are going to kick their shoes off, take a few swigs of the bottle, and dig into the pleasures of living.

And there will be no more sad songs from this singer; not for a long time to come.

1968–1970: *Country Pie*

DYLAN'S AMBIGUITY AND mystique continued to dominate his public image even after *John Wesley Harding* was released. He remained in Woodstock, leading the life of the simple country man, in near retirement with Sarah and her daughter, Maria, and their son, Jesse Byron, and Anna, born in 1967. He continued to make music with The Band, as the old Hawks were now officially calling themselves, and with any of dozens of friends who took up residence in the area or came up to visit occasionally. Those who saw him say that, generally, he seemed to be content. "He calmed down," Eric Andersen recalls, "got into his family, got into something more real, more tangible, and he was really grooving on it for a while. There's a happiness in the songs he was writing in that period." He appeared to be drawing considerable joy out of the life he was leading, particularly after *Harding* was well received. He had been worried about that album, friends say, afraid his audience wouldn't like it, worried about its effect on others. It was the first time anyone remembers him conceding that kind of worry; it was unusual for the only pop figure who had never set up a fan club or hired a public relations man. Part of Dylan's fear was stimulated by Grossman, friends say. Grossman didn't like the album, which is not too difficult to understand since many believed that Grossman was among the things Dylan said he was now rejecting. They had an argument over it, a rift that widened and resulted in Dylan refusing to sign a new contract in the spring of 1969. Dylan no longer has a manager.

Although he may have calmed down, Bob continued to play his wry public games. And as the *Harding* album was being snapped up by his fans, Dylan came into Carnegie Hall on a Saturday in January, 1968, for a concert in memory of Woody Guthrie, a folk concert with Jack Elliott, Judy Collins, Pete Seeger, Arlo Guthrie, Odetta, Tom Paxton, Richie Havens and others. And he came with The Band: electric and electrifying, Dylan howling *Grand Coulee Dam* and *Mrs. Roosevelt* and *Roll On Columbia,* thirteen minutes of a hip-grinding, Presley-style rockabilly that shook the theater and a lot of folk purists. This was the Bob Dylan of *Like A Rolling Stone:* Did it mean country sound was just a temporary diversion and Dylan was still into rock? Keep them guessing, Bobby.

Dylan's second son, and their fourth child, was born a few months later, named Seth Abraham Isaac Dylan. The Abraham was for Dylan's father, who had died in May, just before Sarah had given birth. Seth Abraham Dylan, it was going to be, but the initials would have spelled "sad," and Bob told friends he didn't want that, so he added Isaac. Dylan returned to Hibbing for his father's funeral and spent a few days there, but remaining completely aloof outside the immediate family. And then back to Woodstock.

Bob was now a mature family man who seems to have found at least a degree of peace. At the end of 1968 he flew down to Nashville again and taped the songs that would become *Nashville Skyline.* He had only four songs with him, he later told Jann Wenner, not enough for a full album. But then Johnny Cash dropped in for a visit one day and they sang together—*Girl From the North Country,* Echo's song —and it worked. He wrote a few songs in his motel room at night, and a couple of others during studio sessions. "Then pretty soon the whole album started fillin' in together, and we had an album. I mean, we didn't go down with that in mind ... It just manipulated out of nothing."

Dave Cohen was Dylan's guest in Woodstock for a few days, just before *Nashville Skyline* was released. "He was subdued, quiet, very humble," Cohen says. Bob told him: "*Nashville Skyline* is the best record I've ever done." Cohen continues: "He was proud of it. When I heard it I knew he was going to be torn apart, even though I thought it was marvelous. That's where he was at at that time, that's where it's all at, at this particular time. People getting away from the freaky psychedelic crap. Bob, and a lot of others, got to country at the same time, a reaction to the freakiness. And by using Cash on the album, he was going for a broader audience. For something that would last a long time.

"*Nashville Skyline* seemed to be a big change, but it wasn't a surprise, it wasn't like something out of the blue. It took him where he wanted to be: sitting with his wife and kids in the country, going in the studio and playing songs with good musicians, getting that incredible interchange of ideas going. And coming up with a great album."

Eric Andersen: "The way he talked around the time of *Nashville Skyline*, he said he had learned to sing for the first time in his life. Now he knew something about music, knew how to play and sing, and he was very proud of it."

Nashville Skyline is as clear as a country stream, without irony or ambiguity. Or anger. A healthy Dylan so in love with life that it has even changed his voice: gone is the sound of the prairie dog caught on a barbed wire fence, as one folkie used to call it. Now it's Bob Dylan, pop singer, lighthearted country twanger, sounding as if he's taken a few lessons from Professor Cash. It is a good album, possibly a great one, but it is not the old Bob Dylan. It's not even Bobby Zimmerman. Hank Williams, perhaps, or Hank Snow. Bob sings a duet with Cash on *Girl From the North Country,* the closest thing to parody on the album. His *Country Pie* sounds something like old Nashville man, Ray Stevens, might have done, an ode to the good old lazy country life. *Lay Lady Lay* is pure lyrical folk song. All of them are songs celebrating love, or love's slight twinges of pain, without the old Dylan bitterness that once cut so deep.

Nashville Skyline came just as country music swept the rock field, a boom for the old down-home stuff. To see Dylan jump into this brand of apple pie wholesomeness struck many as a sellout. For years he had transformed original country sources into music hard as city asphalt, and now it seemed like a complete turnabout. "With that record Bobby's neck went from a size 14 to a size 16, and got very red," one old friend says. For country is the music of the South, the very bigoted South, redneck music. The music of a South trying desperately to hold onto those customs and values that were characteristic of an older, simpler, more secure America, an America that was very sure of God, country, flag and white supremacy. The South of William Zantzinger and Hattie Carroll. You simply had to know that the men who murdered Emmett Till went back to their front porches, picked up their geee-tars and banjoes, and relaxed with some Carter Family licks.

On the face of it, Bob Dylan as a country gentleman seemed absurd, some sort of Kafkaesque brain-washing by a crew of mind doctors from desolation row. Or just good business, like Muzak. "I got a hit album," Dylan told Terri Van Ronk about *Nashville Skyline*, implying it was all a shuck for the masses.

That's how a lot of the critics saw it. While some recognized that the album demonstrated a high degree of artistry, that Dylan showed a large talent as singer-musician-songwriter; while some believed singing with Cash and doing simple, undemanding songs was the temporary aberration of a happy man going back to his roots; while many warned against trying to interpret Dylan or predicting what he might do in the future; most critics writing in both the mass and underground press appeared distraught at the loss of their leader and their dream.

"Dylan is a businessman first and a prophet some time later," one wrote in the *New York Times*. "To the people Dylan is writing for now, the action is down in God's country in places like Nashville, Tennessee. And there's old Bobby Dylan, fat and sassy, grinning out from the album cover. Just him and his guitar and the Columbia Records logo, saying 'Howdy folk. Want to buy some wacky-do songs for sitting and toe-tapping, come by the shop and I'll give you a free listen.' Dylan may have hung out in the Village for a time, but now he's up there in the big time with Johnny Cash and Kate Smith and the other greats."

At the same time that some critics believed Dylan's next stop was the Sullivan Show, singing *God Bless America*, others saw *Nashville Skyline* as Dylan's search for a new political constituency. Perhaps it was, as Joan Baez said, that the Movement "loved" Dylan and interpreted him in the light of that love, but for many the album also represented a voice that was still in step with the cause. Former SDS president Oglesby, for example:

"I could see *Nashville Skyline* as nothing other than Dylan becoming interested in the white working class at the same time the Movement did. As the Movement was getting turned on to the alienated, displaced white hillbillies in Northern cities and more and more convinced that if we didn't reach the white working kids there would be no future, he comes along with *Nashville Skyline*, which says in so many words that the problem from now on is to talk to America. It's a move to working class language. 'Love makes the world go 'round.' When Ralph Gleason points out that this kind of language is used by the guy who wrote 'the ghost of electricity howls in the bones of her face' then you have to ask: 'Why is he using this language?' You have to ask what objective has he in mind, what tactic is he using? You can't understand it unless you presuppose he had something on his mind. To me it leads to the decision that it is a conscious manipulation of a stereotype. It becomes intelligent, Dylan as strategist, Dylan making a decision to reach another constituency. And the Movement was making that decision, that it has to go to the working class."

Both views seem wide of the target. Dylan was neither becoming another Johnny Cash (or Kate Smith), nor was he trying to be a leader of anything or any group. Both views ignore Dylan the private man. Commenting specifically on *Nashville Skyline* during one of our conversations, Dylan said:

"There's no attempt there to reach anybody but me."

Rather than simply a series of pretty little songs written by a tunesmith who has returned to the country sound in search of a million-dollar album, *Nashville Skyline* is a natural extension of *John Wesley Harding*. Bob Dylan celebrating the joy of living, Bob Dylan, celebrating his own salvation.

In any case, it is the Dylan magic again: everyone has a strong opinion, everyone's talking about it, everyone's running out to buy the album. Only the money men at Columbia didn't worry about what he had in mind, as they rushed to the bank.

The change in Dylan's music was reflected in a change in his manner. He was going out of his way to be nice to people, many of those to whom he had not been nice in the past began to notice. On St. Patrick's Day, a month before *Skyline* was released, the Clancy Brothers were giving a concert at the Westchester County Community Center in White Plains, just north of New York City and about a hundred miles south of Woodstock. Bob unexpectedly showed up before the concert and sent a message backstage, and the Clancys urged the guards to bring him in. He walked in with Sarah and their two eldest children. Tom and Pat Clancy remember asking him where he'd come from, and Bob replied:

"I drove a hundred miles just to see you guys. I want to be with you guys for a while. It's great to see you again after all we've been through."

He had a beer with them and talked about himself and his family, about the Clancy Brothers and the old Village days, and about the possibility of buying a farm in Ireland. Seriously, the Clancys felt: Bob Dylan, Irish farmer. "I'm happy now," he told them. "I'm at ease with myself. And I just had to hear you guys sing." He sat out in the audience and after the show he went backstage again.

Pat Clancy recalls: "He was very serious that night. About coming to Ireland to visit us and have a look around. He seemed to be kind of anxious to renew old acquaintances, like looking up friends from back in the old days. He was being kind of genuine, after being through all the stuff he's been through." And Tom Clancy adds: "He seemed changed from when we last saw him during the big fame thing. He was communicating a lot more. He came across very much like a guy who had been through the mill and was coming back again, looking for where he began, back to where he really belonged. He was back again to being the Bobby Dylan I knew in the beginning, always bouncing, saying things like: 'Man, this is great. . . .'"

Johnny Cash asked Dylan to make an appearance on the first show in Cash's new TV series and Dylan agreed, reluctantly. He did the guest spot only because Cash was such an important influence in his life at this point, was at least partially responsible for getting Dylan into country music and into the simple verities, as they used to say. Cash had been through it all himself, through the drugs and the near-loss of his head, and his life. Bob sought him out, after recovering from the accident, and visited Cash and his wife, June Carter of the Carter Family, at their home in Nashville. Cash told one friend that there was an unusual bond between them, the kind of bond that permitted them to stand together fishing in a stream for four hours without needing to say a word.

Being nice again: Hibbing, August 2, 1969. The Moose rooms on Howard Street. Reunion of the Hibbing High School Class of 1960. Echo Helstrom, standing there, waiting:

"I got a phone call from a friend a couple of days before. 'You of all people have to know this,' she told me. 'Bob Dylan's coming. Don't tell anyone, but be there.' I went. I was a nervous wreck, waiting. I was so afraid he'd be mad at me for talking to Toby Thompson, the guy who wrote the *Village Voice* articles on Dylan as a kid, a few months before. When Bob finally showed up it was around eleven at night. He was a lot thinner than when I saw him last, he had his hair cut real short. His wife was there, a tiny little delicate princess, long brown hair, very cute and very quiet, just standing by his side.

"Everybody was standing around waiting for him and he just kind of showed up, walked down the stairs and in the doorway and everybody crowded around him. I headed for the bar and stayed there a while. Then I told my best girl friend to walk over with me, to his table.

"I thought, 'I can't go up to him like everybody else. I have to do something he would do himself.' So I put on these great big dark sunglasses and took the reunion booklet over there, where everybody was putting it down for him to sign. And I put mine down in front of him. I was going to say something like, 'You probably don't· remember me, but I'd like your autograph,' but he saw me and he said, 'Hey, I talk about you all the time,' and he turned to his wife and said, 'This is Echo.' He asked how I was and what I was doing, and we talked a little, but we couldn't really talk because there were all these people around. I don't know if he was being nice because he really wanted to be, or polite because of the crowd. He said, 'Hey, I saw that thing in the *Voice*,' and he laughed about it, he wasn't mad. I said, 'Hey, I wrote you a song.' He asked, 'What do you call it?' and I said, 'Boy From the North Country.' He started laughing a little bit, kind of embarrassed.

"He stayed about an hour. And then some dumb-dumb guy tried to start a fight with him and all of a sudden Bob was gone. That town, really impossible."

If Bob had indeed been content as a country squire, it didn't last very long. In fact, at the same time he was telling some friends how relaxed and happy he was, others were sensing the tension and hearing him hint that he was almost miserable. Bob had always been restless and deeply curious, the kind of man who returned to Gerde's on hoot nights after making it big just to see what was going on. And he began to feel he was missing something down in the city. A conflict was set up between city and country—with country becoming less enjoyable because of the split with Grossman, who had begun to build a restaurant in Woodstock and was becoming the local rajah. There was also the great influx of rock musicians and their camp followers, which made Woodstock less of the country retreat. His disaffection grew more severe with the passing months.

Eric Andersen was up in Woodstock for a couple of days around the time *Nashville Skyline* was being readied for release and Dylan was preparing for the Cash TV show. "He was very much into his kids but I didn't feel he was very relaxed," Andersen says. "I got the feeling he was very restless, thinking about making a move, getting out of there and getting more in touch with things. He seemed to be bored, and wanting to trace his roots again, get back to the vibes on the streets—*those* roots. The trees are pretty in the country but when you're not doing anything, not writing, they can get boring. That's why he wanted to get back to the streets. He told me he didn't have anything to write about, he felt sort of lost being in the woods all the time.

"He was trying to be nice, when I saw him, saying nice things about my records, being very positive and sweet, but you could tell that behind it a lot of things were going on. Just before I left he stood in front of his door with his guitar, blocking the door, and he sang that one about the old worker who worked and toiled all his life, with 'these old hands.' It was very touching. I got the feeling that Bob was sort of trying to be like a woodsman, out gathering sticks for the fire.

"I felt a kind of sorrow for him, for this great suffering that was going on inside of him, sort of grappling with himself as a person, his mind just flying all over the place. And trying to be nice. And at the same time all the dark feelings he's had, all the suffering. He's had a lot of suffering in his life."

Dylan moved back to the Village in the summer of 1969, occupying a duplex in a townhouse he bought on MacDougal Street just a shuffle away from the old scenes, near the Gaslight, Kettle of Fish, Bitter End, Gerde's. One friend says: "His biggest worry was where to send the kids to school, which were the best schools around. He didn't really want a private school, but he worried about the public schools." He settled on a public school just a few blocks from his home, sending Maria and Jesse there. The Dylans' fifth child, Samuel, was born at the end of 1969.

The return to the Village, the uncharacteristic trip to the Hibbing school reunion, the attempts to be warm and gentle with old friends, did not soothe Dylan's inner turmoil. That turmoil became clear during a visit to Terri Van Ronk at the end of 1969, the first time Dylan set foot in that apartment in years.

"He was looking for a piece of his past," she said a few months after that visit. "That's the feeling I got in like the four hours we talked. When he made it he disappeared, up to Woodstock, cut himself off, and now he seemed to be looking to find out what he'd been missing in the music world. The music, plus actually looking to catch up with his past. How far back, I don't know.

"When he came, he looked at his old corduroy cap which I still have. He said he wanted to see it. I held it and he looked at it and he said, 'Wow, what a great cap.' I asked him, 'Would you like to hold it, take it?' and he said, 'No, I don't want it.' He just wouldn't touch it. There's also this poster by Eric von Schmidt that Bobby gave to

265

me and he wanted to take it back, but I wouldn't let him. He asked, 'You got any other old stuff has anything to do with me?' I showed him this coloring book I have. We couldn't afford presents in the old days so I bought David a coloring book and we all colored in it, including Bobby, and he looked at it like he was looking into the old times."

Terri also felt stresses in Bob, and confusion. "He said he was uptight, has all this money and doesn't know what to do with it, not the foggiest notion what to do with all his money. He talked about his wife and kids, how beautiful they are. He said he couldn't perform any more, that he doesn't like performing in front of big audiences, but he's going to perform again because he doesn't have anything else to do."

Bob had tried making a couple of public appearances a few months earlier, to make contact with the audience out there. The Band was on tour in July, and during a concert in Edwardsville, Illinois, Dylan came out and did a song, a four minute surprise appearance, getting the feel of it again.

The next month Dylan gave his first paid performance ($75,000) in four years, at the Isle of Wight off England. Dylan was the headliner at the two-day festival, closing it off with the final performance on the last Sunday in August. All through Saturday and into Sunday evening everything was building up for Dylan's appearance; other performers did a large number of Dylan songs, and some sang their own songs that seemed to have been written for Dylan. Tom Paxton, for example, singing his *Rambling Boy,* hoping that all his ramblings have brought him joy, and sounding as if he were saluting Dylan although the song had been written in another time for another friend.

They had come to see Dylan, the 200,000 fans who filled the festival grounds, wandering over from England, the Continent, the United States and Canada, a month after Woodstock supposedly ushered in a new age. The nomads created a huge tent city on the landscape of that middle-class vacation isle. One shack, built by Americans and Canadians, was constructed of iron and plastic sheets and a grass roof, and was called "Desolation Row."

"We're here to see Dylan," the kids said. One of them told a writer: "I mean, well, he kinda says what we feel and don't know how to say, right?"

The Dylan magic worked once more. Although upset that he came on at eleven Sunday night, three hours later than announced, and that he performed only for an hour, the audience was swept up by Dylan's charm. While he was performing, at any rate. But after the concert ended, many came away with a dissatisfied feeling: this was not the old Dylan, whose rasping voice had been the conscience of an age, that made the young clutch him to keep the coffin lids from closing on them. This was Dylan singing in a new voice, closer to the earth and its promise of renewal, its sense of the joys of life.

Among those who had loved Dylan the prophet, the sense of disappointment began to grow at the end of 1969. "That lamentable *Rolling Stone* interview," as Carl Oglesby puts it, was the first indication that Dylan was no longer in touch with the distressing reality of our psychotic times, that he was out of step with the radical movement. The interview was published in November, a long talk between Dylan and Jann Wenner, publisher of the paper.

It was frustrating to read. It is Bob Dylan, but not the Bob Dylan everyone thought he knew. It is a Bob Dylan who talks in terms of his music, that's all. Dylan seemed unconcerned with his effect on his audience, and what comes across in the interview is Mr. Music Man: a shallow songwriter not interested in much else in the world except writing and singing pretty little songs that will keep his audience happy and his bank balance full.

The overwhelming feeling is of a Career man with a capital C; a man complaining that he was never paid a cent for *Don't Look Back*, that the film was almost an imposition on him while the producers got rich; a man who admits he no longer keeps in touch with what is blowin' in the wind; a dutiful son complaining that the writer for the *Village Voice* who went back to Hibbing to peer into Dylan's early life "talked about my father who has passed away."

It's not that Wenner didn't try. Some of the questions may sound like something for a teen fan magazine, but what do you ask a man who no longer seems to know (or pretends not to know) what is being done to the world in which he lives? Dylan said some of his most important song-poems were written simply because they were what his audience wanted to hear at the time, nothing more than large noisy song productions; he doesn't seem aware that his songs were, to so many, Doomsday poems. He discussed them as a Cole Porter or Irving Berlin might have talked about their songs. *John Wesley Harding,* he said, was just "a silly little song." *Sad Eyed Lady of the Lowlands* was a song he started to write in the studio one day because he needed something to flesh out an album and it turned out seventeen minutes long because "I just got carried away by the whole thing," and he couldn't even remember what he had started to say at the beginning of the song. Almost denying the force, the drama, of that pageant that had meant so much back then.

Wenner kept after Dylan on his role as youth leader, his feelings about being deified, and Dylan dodged, tried not to answer. And when Wenner wouldn't let go, Dylan finally commented about being a "leader":

"If I thought I was that person, wouldn't I be out there doing it? ... I can see that position filled by someone else. ... I play music, man. I write songs. I have a certain balance about things, and I believe there should be an order to everything. Underneath it all."

Some who read that interview came away with the feeling that it was another Dylan put-on. But to many it wasn't that easy to ignore. The interview seemed to present a new Bob Dylan: a very rich, white musician of enormous talent, but with a limited commitment to the world's problems; a human being, distressingly human, not a god. A false prophet, in fact.

As if to emphasize his apostasy, Dylan in the summer of 1970 drove down to Princeton, where he accepted an honorary Doctorate of Music from the university's president Robert F. Goheen; the parchment scroll said, in Latin, that Dylan was being honored because he is one of "those who have conferred the greatest benefits either upon their country or upon mankind as a whole. ..." The roars of dismay along the underground press system made it sound as if Dylan had written a song in support of war, or genocide. One pop newspaper described Princeton as the "home of Amerika's wealthy, alcoholic post-adolescents" and went on: "Up on the roster are a gaggle of seventy-five-year-old academic fascists, taking time off from their war contracts to be trustees. Up there with them is Robert Zimmerman, alias Bob Dylan, gown and all. ... Bob Dylan has ceased to grow and has slipped back into the slime with the rest of us. ..."

At the same time, Dylan had just completed another album. The reports coming out of Columbia were too incredible: Dylan had put together an album tentatively called *Blue Moon,* filled with his interpretations of other artists' works, songs by Rodgers and Hart, Paul Simon, Gordon Lightfoot, and a large number of the old traditional country and folk things he had been doing back in Minnesota. Bob had cut a couple of dozen songs in New York and had to discard many of them because they simply didn't turn out well at all. He then went to Nashville for some help from the country boys, but things were only slightly better down there.

When the album was finally released in June, 1970, the most insane rumors seemed to be true: Bob Dylan had put out a *product,* a two-record set mysteriously called *Self Portrait,* filled mostly with the works of others and some examples of Americana, produced in a style that appeared to be almost Mantovani music, dreary enough to pipe into elevators or corset *shoppes*. You laughed when you first heard it—Bob Dylan trying to turn his nasal twang into a bass baritone, in the style of Johnny Cash. It seemed to be a huge joke. Bob Dylan as commercial popular songwriter and singer, a one-man Simon and Garfunkel. Or, perhaps, the Dylan Brothers—his version of Simon's *The Boxer,* Dylan dubbing harmony with Dylan, sounded so lame at first hearing that it had to be a parody of Simon, except that Dylan was spending a lot of time with Simon in New York and out on Fire Island, and parody doesn't make sense.

None of the album made sense, at first. *Self Portrait* was the ultimate disillusionment for many Dylan freaks. *Rolling Stone* had nominated Bob for president in 1968—had come into being mostly because of what Dylan, the Stones and the Beatles had done to awaken the minds of a generation. Now it pulled out its large stable of thinkers and wordsmiths to tell Dylan he was through, and that the counter-culture was through with him. In a symposium led by Greil Marcus, one of the more perceptive rock critics around, a half-dozen writers, intellectuals and hangers-on simply pulled the album apart. From the first line—"What is this shit?"—to the last, the four-page "review" condemned Dylan to the same limbo in which Rimbaud had ended his life. Dylan had been the Rimbaud of his age, someone said, but now he has followed Rimbaud into Abyssinia, turning his back on the inner vision for the safety of a merchant's life. (Not realizing Rimbaud gave up poetry and Paris in order to reach deeper into his inner being.)

Critic-columnist Ralph Gleason expressed his sadness over what he felt was Dylan's role in the commercialization of rock that threatened to overwhelm the counter-culture. Gleason actually called for a boycott of Dylan:

"We cannot make an artist do anything. Nor can we tell him what to do. But we have, I think, a debt to him and a contract exists between us. And that is simply never to accept anything less than their best."

The new side of Bob Dylan created a trauma among those who continued to expect him to prescribe medicine for their souls. Even after a second wave of favorable reviews, many radicals could not forgive him for demonstrating that he really meant it when he said he refused to be a leader. It was Newport, 1965, all over again. A few underground critics even accused Dylan of being a "capitalistic pig," of "ripping off the youth culture," of becoming part of an oppressive society that rules and destroys us all.

In our conversation, seven months after *Self Portrait* Dylan appeared to be of two minds about the attacks on him. As a popular artist trying to reach a wide audience he emphasized that the disillusioned are in the minority. "You can talk to some radicals who are up on me, right?" he asked at one point. "I hope you just don't paint me on one side of the radical thing." He is, of course, correct. Dylan continues to be meaningful to many of those he reached back in 1964 and 1965, while at the same time affecting younger listeners with both his earlier albums and his latest work.

Dylan is somewhat defensive about the *Stone* interview, while sounding absolutely certain about the worth of *Self Portrait:* "It's a great album," he said to me. "There's a lot of damn good music there. People just didn't listen at first." As for the interview, Dylan said Wenner had been after him for almost a year and Dylan had resisted. "I decided finally to do it because I figured something should be out. But I didn't pay any attention to what was happening when we sat down to do the interview because I was doing a few things and had my head on them and wasn't paying much attention to what I was saying." Dylan said the interview did not represent what he was actually thinking and feeling at the time because he did not have the energy to concentrate on it. "That thing about my father," he said, "I was going to ask Wenner to cut that, and to cut a few other things, because it wasn't what I really felt, but by that time it was all too much trouble and I lost interest completely. I get that way."

Dylan appears to have no patience with those who insist that if he doesn't become a street fighter then he is a heretic. At first, he resisted talking about the radicals who want him to lead them, to give them the answers. Finally, he summed up his attitude: "It's all bullshit. It's petty." And, during several conversations, he elaborated:

"I told them not to follow leaders, to watch parking meters. I wasn't going to fall for that, for being any kind of a leader. The magazines fed that pap—that Dylan, the Stones, the Beatles, we were all leaders. And because I wanted out they all started to rap me. But who could live up to that kind of thing? I wasn't into politics. I didn't want any part of that.

"But the times are tough. Everybody wants a leader. They only want somebody to lead them out of their troubles."

Later, Dylan insisted that "people shouldn't look to me for answers." He added: "I don't know what's going down on the campuses, what's in their heads. I have no contact with them, and I'm sorry they think I can give them any answers. Because I can't. I got enough to keep me busy without looking for other people's problems." Reminded that he had said, during a 1965 radio talk show, that he didn't know why he should be "expected to carry the world on my shoulders," Dylan smiled and said:

"Yeah, I felt it then. And I still feel it."

Dylan also seems to feel that, like at Newport, he will eventually be understood, that his audience will follow him into his next stage. "I still have a lot of talent left," he said. "I can still do it. None of it has left me. All those people who are down on me, they'll catch up. They'll understand someday. They've got a surprise coming."

At the same time, Dylan was saying that he would accept whatever his fans thought of him, would accept it all on their terms. To refute it would mean he was being forced into a mold; any reaction on his part would limit his freedom of movement. And he wasn't about to do that. "I don't want to be out front," he said. "I have to keep something in reserve." A major part of the mystique of stardom is to be unobtainable; that fans must project their fantasies on a man like Dylan or John Lennon, but once a star reveals too much of himself —leaving nothing in reserve—then the mystique vanishes. Bob Dylan must be a public figure, at the same time that he remains a very private person.

And suddenly there was another Dylan album, only a few months after *Self Portrait*. Almost as if Dylan was so concerned with the dislocation of the Dylan myth that he had to show the world he could still affect it. Or, as one critic said, perhaps Dylan was hoping to distract us from *Self Portrait*.

"New Morning" was released in October and the critics and fans immediately hailed the album: Dylan had returned to the fold. Gleason, in *Rolling Stone,* headed his column: "We've Got Dylan Back Again."

"New Morning" works. It is effective both because it is marvelous entertainment—a series of tightly written songs—and because it overflows with Dylan's visions of his search for salvation, with his philosophy (although he would never call it that). The album is a letter from Dylan, something the mature Bob Dylan might have written to his father were he still alive, explaining himself a little bit, where he'd been and what he'd been feeling and thinking ... and suffering; and explaining that he has found a degree of peace. Much of the album is a love song to life. An autobiography, that's the feel of it, that's what makes it all come together. Dylan is once again writing about himself, giving us a few preview pages from the autobiography he said he is writing; a portrait of the artist as a young man. To cite a few examples:

If Not For You, the first cut, is a dedication: To Sarah. A love song for Sarah; "I'd be nowhere at all," he writes, "if not for you." Dylan *has* found some beauty in his life.

Day of the Locusts, inspired by the Princeton honorary award, but more likely Bob Zimmerman back in Hibbing High School. The locusts are singing while he is picking up his degree, emphasizing the reality of nature and freedom as against the illusions of society. Outside, the locusts are singing and inside is society's tomb, the dark chamber where the judges are ready to confer their approval on the student machines. A man's head is exploding, Dylan writes—which is what society's pellets of poison can do to you. And he escapes the pellets, driving to the hills of North Dakota with his sweetheart.

Time Passes Slowly: Dylan reminiscing, sitting by a stream, possibly up in Woodstock, lazy, warm, content, dreaming about the sweetheart he once had, a woman who was fine and good-looking. A dream about some of the more pleasurable Hibbing days, with Echo. But there's a touch of sadness: even the search for love is an illusion, Dylan seems to be saying, a social formality that brings the prison bars clanging down.

Winterlude: An ice skater's waltz, right off one of those old Victor records that were cut only on one side. But refreshingly sexual: Bob Zimmerman and his little apple, in love, cruisin' around the ice-locked Midwest, finding little nooks where they discover the beauties of their sexuality, blanking out the rest of that ugly world out there.

If Dogs Run Free: Bob Dylan, hearing things other people don't hear, seeing things other people don't see, knowing that the symphonies his mind weaves, the tapestries of rhyme, are something well beyond what his elders have to offer when they tell him "the best is yet to come." Dylan, in anguish, questioning his existence, questioning the reality of the prison in which everyone else is content to live. Trying to break free.

New Morning: The morning in the biblical sense, a rebirth. The song is a celebration of his escape from the prison, a celebration of nature, feeling, women, men, the pleasures of life: the dog has broken free.

The Man In Me: One of the more exuberant love songs in pop music, a song to Sarah telling her she's the only one who could have gotten "through to the man in me"—the only woman or man ever to understand that the man in Bob Dylan must hide sometimes so that he won't turn into some machine; one aspect of Bob Dylan summed up in four lines. But, most important, it is Dylan saying what a T. S. Eliot character says to *his* woman in the play, *The Family Reunion:* she opened a door that brought sunlight and singing, when he was so certain that life led only to a blank wall.

Three Angels: Dylan, back in the Village, near the church where the 10th Avenue bus goes West instead of its normal North-South route, and wondering why no one is able to hear the music of the angels—the voice of the inner, the cosmos—why the entire world doesn't hear, refuses to even try and hear. Dylan, standing there on a desolate big-city corner, commenting with sadness on mankind's blindness, inhumanity, stupidity: Can't they hear? Won't they ever listen?

Father of Night: Bob Dylan, in touch with the Father, with the unknown which doesn't have to remain unknown. A hymn of discovery, a hymn to the mysteries. "Not the God of philosophers, but the God of Abraham, Isaac and Jacob," Pascal wrote. And, Dylan seems to be saying, not the God of logic and reasoning, but the God that is within each of us, the God that is "I."

1971 : *Father of Night*

THE SETTING WAS Madison Square Garden, August 1, 1971: George Harrison, former Beatle, leading a group of fellow-superstars in a Sunday benefit performance to aid the citizens of Bangladesh. Twenty thousand fans were at each of two performances, and thousands of others in the street hoping to crash inside, for the concerts promised to be one of those *events* that later become part of a larger myth.

"Bob Dylan's gonna be here." Through the lobby, up in the galleries, down on the sports floor where music industry executives had paid $100 each for the privilege of settling their $400 suits into hard wooden folding chairs, spread the rumor, the hope: Bob Dylan, whose own myth surpasses the hyped-up mystique of the entire rock culture, might possibly make one of his rare public appearances.

For a while the concert almost made the audience forget Dylan. Ravi Shanker and Ali Akbar Khan, two giants of raga, played the classical music of their suffering land. And then Harrison and his gang of friends, including Ringo Starr, Eric Clapton, Leon Russell and Billy Preston, pranced through a dozen numbers, bringing the house roaring down after each song.

Near the end of the concert, Harrison, deliberately low key, announced : "Here's a friend of us all, Bob Dylan."

The words jolted, as if 20,000 people of all ages and life-styles were playing Ben Franklin, kites in the storm clouds, getting an electric charge. One young man, about 19, cried without embarrassment; a young woman, in a long purple velvet gown from the nineteen-twenties that barely covered her scruffy second-hand Army boots, leaped up and cried : "I can't believe it. I'm really seeing *Dylan*." Even a hardened rock writer turned to his lady and said : "Are we really seeing this?"

It was indeed Dylan, looking as young as on the cover of some of his earliest albums, carrying his acoustic guitar and singing those songs that had so much power in the days of protest and radicalism, among them, *Blowin' In the Wind*, *Mr. Tambourine Man*, and *A Hard Rain*. The concert was no longer simply an event. This was Dylan, singing songs many thought he would never do again, and his audience hung on every word and note.

"He's coming back to protest," said one older record company executive, who would probably rush into his office the next morning and tell his stable to "write it like the old Dylan, baby."

Two months later, before an overflow audience at Carnegie Hall, Joan Baez introduced a new song.

"This is a song I've written for Bobby Dylan," she said (and did one simply imagine that her voice grew husky?). "I haven't seen him in four years. I'd be ashamed to sing it to him, but I'll sing it for you." And she sang a song she had just written, "To Bobby", which is both a love song and a plea for Dylan to return to active social protest. "You left us marching on the road/And said how heavy was the load," she sang, and she told Dylan that although he had cast off his "cursed crown" the people who are still marching on the streets have reserved a special place for him in the struggle. Please come back, Bobby, sang from every line.

"To Bobby" received the longest ovation at the concert. For the audience knew that years before Dylan had provided her with the finger-pointing songs that enabled her to raise her voice in protest. They knew she and others have accused Dylan of turning his back on social commitment; many in the audience felt that of Dylan. They knew that some critics have charged Dylan with caring more about the steady growth of his investment portfolio than the problems of the world; of being a "capitalist pig" to use the shrill rhetoric of the radical movement.

Those accusations clearly have stung Dylan. He denied during several conversations that he was being affected by the anger directed against him by a small group of critics. "It's all petty," he said. Yet a week later, at the beginning of November, Dylan went into the recording studio to cut a new single called *George Jackson*—a "protest song" about the slaying of the Black Panther in San Quentin, a song that could have been written by the young Bob Dylan who wrote *Blowin' in the Wind* in 1962.

The reaction of the audiences at Madison Square Garden and Carnegie Hall reflect the conflict that enveloped Dylan's fans and former fans ten years after they first began to worship him as a "prophet" of the youth revolution. That deification has made him wealthy. Nine of his albums have been gold records, those selling more than $1 million at wholesale prices. His recording royalties alone have come to more than a million. He has undoubtedly received much more than that from royalties on sheet music, from radio air plays, and from recordings of his songs by other artists.

Dylan's songs are among the most recorded today, but record sales and income cannot measure his effect. It is difficult to write of Dylan and his decade as a force among the young without making it all sound an exaggeration. He touched the young deeply. He sang "in a voice that came from you and me", as folk singer Don McLean put it in his 1971 hit, *American Pie*, a song lamenting the rock era's lost promise. For millions of the young, Dylan has been a poet of the streets, crying out in pain against society's indifference and stupidity; his voice, his words, his visions, gave substance to their radicalization.

But in the years after *Nashville Skyline* some who deified him as a leader of the radical movement have expressed fears that he is no longer lashing out against a System into which he refused to fit. He has burned himself out, they charge with much passion, has grown old, physically soft and mentally mushy, with a wife and five children and a great deal of wealth to protect. Among his harshest critics are other singers, not only Baez, who have written of Dylan's apparent loss of commitment and who are, in effect, throwing down a challenge to him. McLean, in *American Pie*, writes of Dylan as "the jester ... in a coat he borrowed from James Dean", who stole the king's "thorny crown" and then became the "jester on the sidelines in a cast".

It seemed to many, by the time of the Bangladesh benefit, that

Dylan was deliberately telling them he has backed away from whatever power he once had to affect their lives, telling them he must be left alone, that all he wants from life is to write and sing pretty country tunes or Cole Porter-style lyrics. Even his voice had changed enormously. Back in the early years he sounded honest and full of pain, with a nasal quality that made him sound like a man from a chain gang whose nose had been broken by a guard's rifle butt.

Most recently, in his records and occasional appearances, Dylan has been singing in his richer, natural voice—the voice that only close friends were permitted to hear in the privacy of their living rooms, when he would sing *This Land Is Your Land* and other Woody Guthrie songs. It is a voice that some critics insist proves he wants to play the big prime-time TV shows, and the hell with his *real* audience.

Bob's reaction to the continuing attacks on him is, basically, that they are attempts to dictate to him, and he is not about to permit anyone to dictate his life, or his art. In one conversation I had with him in October, 1971, Bob paraphrased an earlier remark he had made about those attacks. He said:

"It's fantasy, created by cowardly men who turn wheels."

"What kind of wheels?" he was asked.

"Media wheels. I said not to follow leaders, to watch parking meters. It was that simple. I wasn't going to fall for that, for being any kind of leader. The media made up that crap, that Dylan, the Stones, the Beatles, were leaders. We didn't know anything about it, and what's more didn't want any part of it . . ."

"Nobody should look to anybody else for their answers. But the times are tough. Everybody wants a leader. In fact, everybody wants to *be* a leader . . ."

In all our conversations during the fall of 1971, Bob has stressed that he is simply trying to be as good a musician and songwriter as he can and that everything else is extraneous, and even destructive. More than six weeks after his Madison Square Garden appearance, still up high with excitement over the performance, full of that enthusiasm that has always been so infectious, he asked me:

"Did you see that concert, man? Wasn't it the most incredible show ever? The audience has changed. They're into the music now. They've grown up, and it's the music that's most important. They heard it and dug it. Just incredible."

What Dylan has been doing over the past couple of years is

simplify his life, so he can focus completely on the music he is writing and recording.

He had worked in a converted store near his Greenwich Village home almost every day he was in New York through 1970 and part of 1971, but even that studio hideout began to make too many demands on his time and his head. The phone number had a way of getting around, and friends who wouldn't dream of knocking at his door at home would knock on his studio door. "I don't have a studio anymore," he said.

He no longer has a manager, either. His contract with Grossman ran out in 1969. Dylan refused to renew it. "I haven't seen him in years," Dylan says, and other remarks he's made about Grossman indicate at least a small degree of distaste. Bob's only aides now are his secretary, Naomi Saltzman, and her assistant, who spend much of their time protecting him from hucksters who want him to endorse guitars, sweat shirts or soapsuds, as well as from writers and fans who want to pick his brain, and mendicants who want him to perform at benefit concerts.

"I'm just doing what I used to do in the old days," Bob says. "My music. Trying to keep my life simple. I'm making a new album and I'm trying to devote all my energies to that. I'm helping other people out, making records with people like Dave Bromberg, helping George (Harrison) edit the Bangladesh film."

In one phone conversation he joked: "I'm studying agriculture. Doing what you're doing, man, just standing in a phone booth. Hang out in the garment center a lot. Garment center's dirty and dank, but I like it.

"Just trying to keep things nice and simple."

Now that he is living in the Village again Bob is almost as anonymous as in the days when he was unknown and a street cat able to wander along Bleeker Street and into bars and folk clubs without being besieged by fans. He takes long walks along Village streets, sometimes drops in at some of the clubs to see musicians who interest him (like Dave Bromberg) and is seldom recognized. But when he is spotted, especially in a crowd situation, Dylan displays some of the old fears. One night he sat in the Gaslight to watch Bromberg work. He had entered after the lights went down and slipped into a seat against a wall. After a while the word spread through the house: "That's Dylan." As heads turned and fingers pointed, Bob said to one of the group accompanying him: "Too many people see me. Let's split." They left by a back door.

Generally, though, Dylan is almost invisible in the Village; a great number of young men affect a Bob Dylan look. Even when he is recognized, he is seldom accosted. Walking down Mcdougal Street late one afternoon with an interviewer, Bob seemed to tense slightly when a young man who passed him flashed a look of recognition and turned to pass again. It seemed likely he would ask for an autograph, or demand an explanation of the songs Bob was writing, as so many had done in the *Blowin' in the Wind* days. But he simply checked Bob out, satisfied himself that he had actually seen Bob Dylan, and walked away.

One minor indication of what has happened to Bob's head since those insane years of his first big fame, came while we were sitting in his studio on a January afternoon. By 4:30 it had begun to grow dark and Bob, ignoring the glasses in his denim jacket pocket, started to squint. I suggested we turn the lights on, and he did. When he sat down again he was practically smack against the bamboo blinds that offered no protection from a street filled with pedestrians and rush hour traffic. I asked him:

"Don't you have any problems with people gawking in at you?"

"No, man, not at all," Dylan replied. "If *you're* uptight about it we can move to the back."

Dylan fits every possible definition of the term "superstar", but he refuses, for the most part, to play the role. He has no personal press agent, no fan club. He refuses to make the TV talk show circuit. He has given only one official Dylan concert (the Isle of Wight) since his motorcycle accident, preferring to show up as a surprise guest, as at the Bangladesh concert, and a Carnegie Hall concert by The Band on New Year's Eve. Or as part of a larger crowd, as at the 1968 Guthrie Memorial Concert. While there was some talk that Joan Baez had asked Dylan to perform at a benefit concert with her, scheduled for the Spring of 1972, nothing much ever came of it. Dylan seldom grants interviews, and then usually only to those whom he can trust or whom he is trying to keep from writing something he may not like.

But Dylan is a complex man, and his words and actions are often a series of contradictions. He carefully gauges the span between interviews and periodically sits down for one of those inane question-and-answer periods he honestly loathes because, as he put it in discussing one such interview, "I felt it was time to have something out about Bob Dylan." And, although he has denied it during our conversations, Bob also seems concerned to a degree about his public image. Dylan's reaction to A. J. Weberman is a case in point. Weberman is the self-styled "Dylanologist"

278

who has made a career of interpreting Dylan's lyrics and going through his garbage to learn all he can of the man he both idolizes and hates (and mostly, to make himself as famous as Dylan). Weberman loves Dylan for what he had been, back in his radical period in the mid-sixties, and he hates him now because he believes Dylan has sold out to the commercializers, has grown rich and sleek and fat and is now ripping off the youth culture that puts so much faith in him. For months, at the end of 1970 and into the beginning of 1971, Weberman began widely hinting in the radical press—and then saying outright—that Dylan was a heroin addict. Weberman, who spends most of his waking hours interpreting Bob's lyrics through some kind of tortured mental filter and has actually used a computer to put together a "concordance" of almost every word Dylan has ever written or uttered or belched, claimed he found the evidence of Dylan's addiction in his lyrics and, almost incidentally, in his behavior.

Dylan is not an addict. I've known addicts, as a police and court reporter some years ago, and on a deeply personal level. I've known addicts who have enough money—as Dylan does—to feed their addiction and continue to function in highly skilled professions. During all the time I spent with Bob I watched for the signs of addiction I have known in others; for almost four hours Dylan and I sat together, in one stretch, and none of those signs ever revealed themselves. Dylan is no addict.

In any case, Dylan would have simply ignored Weberman years ago, as he ignored so many others who had attacked him. He would have been pained, and angry, but he would have kept it to himself. But Dylan is now concerned with public statements and rumors about him. As a result he cultivated Weberman for a while, spent many hours with him, trying to convince him that Bob Dylan is not addicted to anything. Dylan even went so far, on his first meeting with Weberman, to roll up his sleeves, baring his arms to show there were no needle tracks. When Weberman remained unconvinced, Bob offered him a job as a chauffeur. "You can hang around me and see I'm clean," Bob said. Weberman responded: "I won't let you bribe me"—blowing a chance to share a good piece of his hero's working hours.

Weberman has since admitted he was wrong about Dylan's addiction. But the daylight was a long time coming and before Weberman gave up his attacks on Dylan he became personal witness to Dylan's very strong desire to protect his wife and children, to extend his need for privacy to those closest to him.

In all our discussions about what I was going to reveal of his private life in this book, Bob's greatest concern ("Like any man's," he insists) was over his wife and children. "You can leave them out of it, right?" he asked. Told it was impossible to write of Dylan without writing of his family, he said, simply: "Bullshit." I asked him whether he would leave his wife and children out of his autobiography. Bob replied: "Sure, I'll write about them, of course. But in my style, not yours."

Years ago, anger would make Dylan appear to be a spoiled child, about to throw a tantrum. Now he has much greater control over his anger, the fury smoldering and ready to explode but held in check by a great discipline. Except when he feels Sarah and the children are threatened.

That anger exploded one evening in early October, 1971. Weberman was sifting through the Dylan trash can for the first time in months, after promising Bob he would never do it again. Sarah came out the front door. She became understandably enraged at the sight of the scavenger on her doorstep. "Get out of here," she shouted. "Get out of that garbage, you leech." Weberman muttered something about the garbage being "public property" and Sarah turned to chase a magazine photographer who was with him down the street. A TV cameraman shooting a feature on Weberman packed up his equipment and left, with Weberman sheepishly following.

Several hours later Bob came home, learned of the incident which had upset his wife a great deal, and went over to Weberman's tenement home at Bleeker Street and the Bowery. He found Weberman out front and jumped him, wrestling him to the sidewalk and bouncing his head against the pavement several times. Weberman says he fought Dylan to a draw (he has at least thirty pounds and a couple of inches on Dylan) but witnesses say Dylan was still pounding Weberman's skull against the sidewalk when a couple of men came along and broke it up. Dylan dusted himself off and strolled away.

Bob has put on a little weight in the last couple of years, but he is still very thin. He is several inches under six feet and weighs not much more than 135 pounds. His face is less drawn, is fleshing out somewhat, but the skin is still taut and almost translucent. When he speaks, the cowboy sound he had affected in the early years slips through only occasionally. Today, there are traces of his Midwest background in his voice, with phrasing from the city streets, Oklahoma, and upstate New York thrown in. For the last couple of years he wore a mustache and a wispy beard around his jawbone, but he shaved them off after the Bangladesh concert. Months later he grew the beard again. "All depends on how I feel," he explained. His brown hair once more rises from his head in a profusion of curls.

He now looks somewhat like the photos on his 1965 album, *Bringing It All Back Home*, his first album to use electric instruments, which contained some of his most effective "radical" songs. The change in Bob's appearance is one of those "clues" that Dylan freaks always search for. This one makes some Dylan watchers believe he will once more write songs of commitment, for Dylan's outer appearance has always changed with every change in his style and mood, from folk, to protest, to radical rock superstar, to country and western singer.

Ever since his motorcycle accident Dylan has gone through what some have called a metamorphosis. In working through the chaos that fame made of his life, he has returned to Judaism, a heritage he had always denied. He has studied Hebrew and has made several trips to Israel (he visited the Wailing Wall on his thirtieth birthday). He has reportedly donated some of his funds to help support at least one kibbutz there. Folk singer Theo Bikel says: "Dylan has told me that Israel appears to be one of the few places left in this world where life has any meaning." And Bob has celebrated his renewed belief in God in many songs written since the accident.

Dylan's interest in Israel and Judaism led him, late in 1970, into an unexpected relationship with Rabbi Meir Kahane and the Jewish Defense League. He attended several meetings of the J.D.L. and is rumored to have donated money to the organization; Rabbi Kahane will say only that Dylan has "come around a couple of times to see what we're all about." Dylan's enthusiasm for the militant Jewish organization has brought down the wrath of some in the radical movement. To many young radicals, including Jewish kids, Israel is simply another one of those fascist states propped up by a fascist American government, and Dylan's rumored support of Israel and his over-publicized contacts with the J.D.L. are to them a further indication he has sold out to the political right he once condemned.

Bob finds it difficult to express his feelings about J.D.L. and Israel. Not because he is unable to articulate them, but because, "If you print exactly what I feel it's going to hurt some people, and I don't want to hurt them," he said during one of our talks. "I don't know how you can say it, but just make it clear my enthusiasm has diminished." Asked why, Bob said: "If you want to see it, you only have to check what's going down. Just read the *Daily News*." (For months that paper had been filled with stories about the organization's militancy, which included attacks on Russian property and harassment of members of the Russian delegation to the U.N.) "I lost my enthusiasm rather quickly," Bob concluded. As for Israel, Dylan went into a long off-the-record discussion of what he had seen on his visits there; he did not like what he had seen. He also talked about organized religion: "I get twenty or thirty letters a day asking me to speak on Judaism at some temple or other. I don't have anything to say about it. Those people have nothing to do with me. I feel that far away from it."

None of these feelings, Dylan made it clear, detract from the reality of his return to his roots: the Judaism of the individual.

Among a certain element of the radical movement that is distressed by Dylan's "sellout", a story is making the rounds concerning a meeting between Dylan and Black Panthers Huey Newton and David Hilliard. Some time in the fall of 1970 attorney Gerald Lefcourt wrote a letter to Dylan at Hilliard's request, asking Bob to do a benefit or in some way help raise funds for the Panther trials. Many months later Dylan met with Newton and Hilliard. Dylan was still enthused about Israel and as soon as they sat down Dylan began to lecture them on the Panthers' anti-Zionist pronouncements. Within moments Hilliard leaped up, angry, and headed for the door shouting: "Let's get out of here! We can't talk to this Zionist pig!" Newton said to "cool it" and Hilliard returned to the discussion. It lasted for another hour or more, but was a standoff. "I can't help you as long as the Panthers are against Israel," Dylan is said to have told them.

Asked about the story, Bob said: "What meeting? Why don't you talk to Huey about it?" Newton was in China at the time, Hilliard in prison, and the story could not be confirmed. Dylan won't concede it took place. Those radicals who tell the story insist they heard it from Newton.

If his political commitment seems to have faded, as some critics charge, Dylan has not lost the enormous capacity for work which his friends remember from his early Village days. He's up and working by 10 a.m. or so, and often goes late into the night. Among his projects over the past year has been his autobiography. "I never thought of the past," he told me. "Now I sometimes do. I think back sometimes to all those people I once did know. It's an incredible story, putting together the pieces.

It's like a puzzle, as far as stories go. I meditate on it sometimes, all that craziness . . . I really like to work on it."

He spends much of his days, and many nights, in the recording studio, laying down tracks of new songs he has written, working with other artists (including George Harrison, Jerry Garcia of the Grateful Dead and Leon Russell). He had also begun to work on the format for a one-hour TV special which he had planned to tape just before Christmas, 1971. "A TV show with just songs," he said. "One hour of songs. There'll be a lot of new stuff, from my new album."

That new album will contain totally fresh material, and friends who have heard some of the songs believe it will be another reversal of field that will startle Dylan fans and other pop artists much as *Nashville Skyline* did in 1968, when Dylan went country.

Dylan insisted his friends are hearing things in his new songs that are not there. "Nobody's going to be startled," he maintained. He refused to discuss the album further, except to say he produced it himself. He is so secretive about his new work that few people at Columbia Records have heard the tapes. They are reportedly locked in a vault and only Columbia president Clive Davis has access to them. The album, and the TV show, had been scheduled for public release in June, 1972, but there was no sign of either by midsummer. "The album is all ready to go," a Columbia executive said at that time. "The TV show seems to be holding things up."

But in November, 1971, Bob released a two-record set called *More Greatest Hits*. That title is not quite accurate. While it contains primarily songs from previous Dylan albums and singles, there is some fresh material on it. One cut is *Tomorrow Is A Long Time*, recorded live at Carnegie Hall in 1963, a strangely moving love song written to Suze Rotolo while she was in Italy, and never before released by Dylan. Another is *When I Paint My Masterpiece*, a song Bob wrote about a year earlier that was recorded by The Band. Three other cuts are newly-recorded versions of old Dylan songs, *I Shall Be Released, You Ain't Goin' Nowhere* (with Happy Traum singing harmony on both) and *Down In the Flood*.

Bob had come over to my apartment one afternoon a couple of months before the album was released and he put his copy of the acetate on my turntable. He then wandered over to stand under the speakers suspended near the ceiling, listening intently, appearing quite serious. The song he seemed most excited about was *Masterpiece*. I remarked that his version, which he had greatly rewritten, had created a completely different song from The Band's, because The Band sort of ran through it nice and easy while Dylan had built a suspense and tension that approaches some of the more stunningly angry—and questioning—songs he was doing back in 1965. "Yeah, maybe so," he said. "Glad you like it."

Masterpiece begins with Leon Russell on the piano for a couple of bars, joined by an electric guitar riff, the whomp of a drum, and Dylan suddenly coming in: "Oh, the streets of Rome . . ." Immediately, the sensation is a flashback: This sounds almost like the Dylan from six years before, the days of *Like A Rolling Stone*, which is probably still the most moving song he has ever recorded. Bob's voice on *Masterpiece* reinforces the *deja vu* mood. The rich country sound is less noticeable than at any time in the last couple of years; his voice is harsh and grating once more, not quite filled with the youthful anger that had struck so deep, but approaching it. And the haunting images of the lyrics ("Oh, the hours I've spent inside the Colliseum/Dodgin' lions and wastin' time") bring to mind again Dylan's struggle to understand himself, his life, his relationship to his God.

Some critics saw the album as a piece of product put out by Columbia executives simply to coin another million dollars; the new Dylan cuts were added, they charged, so that fans who already had all the old recordings would be forced to buy those cuts again in order to get the new material.

Actually, that album is Dylan's concept from beginning to end, every single note of it, even including jacket photos. "I produced every bit of it," Dylan told me. "Been doin' my own producin' for a while now." The album is as carefully structured as any Dylan concert ever was—and Bob always devoted an enormous amount of energy to planning the sequence of his songs so that he could create precisely the right amount of tension and response from his audiences. Dylan conceives an album the way a writer conceives a book of poetry, or a novel.

As an aside, this is the basic reason Dylan gets so angry about the bootleg tapes and albums that are circulating. During one of his visits to my apartment I was playing one of the bootlegs, the double album with a plain white jacket (*Great White Wonder*) which contains mostly songs Dylan recorded with The Band in 1967, after he had completely recovered from his accident. When he walked in the door and heard the album, he said: "Oh, the basement tapes. You should hear the originals. They are just

fantastic. The crap they're putting out doesn't even sound like
me. And they're sure not in the order I'd put them on an album."

After playing *Masterpiece* for me, Dylan bounced back to the
turntable and placed the needle down at the end of *Baby Blue*.
And he said: "Listen to this. Running right into the next song,
from *Baby Blue*, I didn't think it worked. But now I do. They
go together." At that point, almost on cue, *Tomorrow Is A Long
Time*, the song to Suze, came on: "Only if she was lyin' by
me/Then I'd lie in my bed once again."

Baby Blue, Dylan waving goodbye to political and social traps
("Strike another match/Go start anew"), and *Tomorrow*, Dylan
saying he may be king in his own folkie world but he ain't nothing
at all without the real, human, one-to-one relationship his woman
had brought him. His woman, and love, as reality; the society
out there, and politics, as illusion. Those songs indeed "go together". They reflect like a mirror the pain Dylan was feeling
back then.

Dylan sees the album as a "reintroduction": The artist wanting to turn on all of us once more to the many faces and masks
of Bob Dylan, in twenty-two songs that delineate the painful and
sometimes joyous road Dylan has travelled. *Watching the River
Flow*, the first song, is so obviously the old Dylan; starting off
the album with the lines, "What's the matter with me?/I don't
have much to say ..." is a bit of irony and wry humor that takes
you back to those press conferences and interviews that he always
turned into absurdist word games. Leading off a fresh creation
—and that's what the album is—with that song, could only
have been a very deliberate act of introduction to Bob Dylan:
"I've got a hell of a lot to say, and here it is," he is in effect saying.

And then, with *Don't Think Twice*, we're catapulted back to
those devastating days in 1963–64, when so many fans first got
hooked on Dylan, that period of bittersweet love songs with a
gentle slap of the left hand and a sly knife in the right, hiding
behind what at first appeared to be ordinary love songs. Somehow, Dylan has us marching back in time, all the way: Dylan
juggling time, taking us back to the beginning. And once we're
comfortable there, all prepared for an early-sixties nostalgic
wave, he hits us with *Lay Lady Lay*, from the period when he
was deliberately seeking a respite from the superstar-insanity
that had almost overwhelmed him, and had begun to discover
who Bob Dylan really is, to discover his relationship with his
God. And he follows *Lady* with *Memphis Blues*, and we are
there, back with Dylan to the very brink of the abyss he had

approached and almost stepped over. "Oh, Mama, can this really be the end?"—and the tension of the electricity counterpointing his anguished voice and lyrics makes us realize it *could* have been the end for him. He sounds close to the edge of psychic destruction.

On listening to this album one begins to understand that Dylan meant it almost as an epic poem, the epic of a man who was nearly destroyed by the superstardom he had consciously sought but couldn't cope with once he got it, but who had the inner strength to pull himself out of the chaos his life had become and survive with his humaneness intact. It is the story, in song, of Dylan's search for salvation.

Dylan himself has made it clear that such was his concept. Peter Knobler, editor of *Crawdaddy*, had written that Dylan was attempting to draw a portrait of his life on the album, and when Dylan read it he told a close friend: "That guy's absolutely right."

After listening to the songs on *Greatest Hits* I asked Bob if it was possible, as some Dylan confidants suggest, that these songs and the material he is said to have written for the new album signal the return to commitment that has been demanded of him. I didn't get the answer from Dylan:

Q. Bob, one guy who apparently is pretty close to you tells me, "Dylan's still the same cat who wrote *Blowin' in the Wind*. When he's moved by something he jumps into it, and it's possible the Bangladesh benefit means he's taking a stand again on what's going down in the world. I think his next album will put him right in the center of the action again." Unquote. That statement, and some other clues that Dylan freaks say they're sniffing in the breeze, seem to make people feel you're coming back.

A. I don't understand your question.

Q. Okay. Are you returning to some form of political commitment?

A. I was talking to (Village radical) Louis Abolafia last night, the guy who ran for President. Told him he should run for President again. He was ahead of his time and should run again. (Pause.) Maybe I should run. (Grin.) Maybe you should run.

Q. That's no answer. You're being vague.

A. That's because I'm a vague kind of guy.

Q. You haven't answered the question.

A. Just use the quote. Let the quote stand.

Even as he was saying this, Dylan had written and was preparing to record *George Jackson*.

Dylan has been sincerely troubled by the attacks on him for refusing to speak out on public issues. He has made that clear in a number of conversations about the radicals who now accuse him of becoming part of the System he once abhorred. But, recently, even some of those critics have once more embraced him as a prophet. Since *"New Morning"* there has been an attempt to dress him in a greening of America politico-religious cloak, an attempt to deify him again as the Prophet leading us into Consciousness III: "Dylan has been, from the very beginning, a true prophet of the new consciousness," Charles A. Reich writes in his Utopian primer of the new world a-coming. Bob insists on denying that view. Those commentators, he says, are completely misguided.

"They're all just songs," he says. "Songs that are transparent so you can see every bit through them. They're just songs to me, that's all. Seriously, I'm writing songs. With a capital S." He added:

"You see, my thing has to do with *feeling*, not politics, organized religion, or social activity. My thing is a *feeling* thing. Those other things will blow away. They'll not stand the test of time."

For the last several years Dylan has been examining his relationship with his God. Commenting on Terri Van Ronk's feeling that he was searching for a piece of his past on his return to the Village in 1969, Bob says: "I actually was searching for myself."

Dylan's experience has always been that of an alien in a mechanistic culture. Throughout, he has been trying to answer the questions: Who am I? What is existence? Dylan has been and is today a man seeking *personal* salvation. That search has led Dylan to religion. Not institutional religion, but the religion of the inner being, the unknown inside us all. God is "I"—before He becomes socialized. In attempting to reconcile the conflict between the inner being and the outer world—a conflict Dylan has felt since his childhood—he has embraced Judaism, a religion that makes a great deal of sense, for Dylan. Not because it is the religion of his fathers, but because Judaism is an existential way of being in the world, a religion in which man may come face to face with his Creator and continue to maintain his own identity. "Though He slay me, yet will I trust in Him," Job says of God. And he adds: "But I will maintain my own ways before Him." This is, in its original form, a religion for the individual, not for the class known as man; a personal religion, not one of logic and rote. And it fits Dylan.

Attempting to freeze Dylan into a statue of Tom Paine or a wood carving of a latter-day Moses, blowing us the newest Ten Commandments on a mouth harp, as so many Dylan worshippers have tried to do, is absolute nonsense. The fact is that since rejecting the protest identity because it did not offer any solutions to his very personal pain, Bob Dylan hasn't cared in the least about political systems, philosophy, logical thought, or the theological questions of the age. He has cared only about Dylan, and how Dylan was going to get through the suffering and the seeking. His protest was a protest on behalf of his own confused and suffering being, his own will, against the abstract and impersonal world that seems to be trying to level us all after thirty centuries of civilization. If his songs seemed to be an attack on our social and political structures, a specific attack on Pentagon wars, industrial power, all the pellets of poison, they were that only tangentially. There are more critical things to worry about than society and civilization, Dylan has been saying. There is your personal salvation; *my* salvation. What Dylan represents is a religious way of being in the world—for him and him alone. His songs are a search for his solution, no one else's. They may touch a universal chord, but that was not his intention.

It is strange—or is it?—that all the rock critics and self-styled radicals who used Dylan to support their own crumbling lives, who fantasize on Dylan and believe they understand him, have missed the central point about him. Only a few writers, and especially Stephen Pickering (in two magazine-form books, *Dylan, A Commemoration* and *Praxis: One*) have recognized that point: that in all his songs since he waved farewell to protest almost ten years ago, Bob Dylan has been creating a body of work that is rooted in the Jewish mystical tradition. Not intellectually, but intuitively.

And yet, as has been their habit since his name began to be whispered around the Village, Dylan freaks are once more trying to force him to live up to their concept of what he should be. And so Dylan's battle to escape canonization (and the martyrdom that comes with it) continues.

"It's rough times," Bob commented during one of our talks. "Everybody needs a father."

1972: *Watching the River Flow*

SOME PERSONAL EXPERIENCES with Bob Dylan:
My first meeting with Bob was so heavily loaded with reality
that it didn't seem real at all. You expect Dylan to play games
with your head because he's always been a conjurer and jester,
he always seemed to be gleefully promoting the myth of Bob
Dylan, always playing an absurdist Chaplinesque role.

I suppose I expected the worst to happen, conditioned by
several viewings of *Don't Look Back*, by conversations with
friends who had spent much time with Dylan, by all those insane press conferences that Dylan always turned into a theater
of the absurd, and by all I had learned about him after hundreds
of hours of interviews with Bob's old friends, lovers, companions,
and enemies.

Primed for the Dylan word games, expecting him to behave
as he has always behaved with writers—fast, elusive, almost invisible, occasionally nasty—I was thrown completely off balance
that first time I met him. He had told me to come to his Village
studio at three o'clock on a January afternoon. I rang the bell at
that hour, waited at the door for a few moments, and was rather
shaken when another door opened several feet from the one at
which I was standing. Dylan was peering out from a second
door to his studio that I hadn't been aware of. The door opened
outward, toward me, and only Dylan's head showed around it.

And it suddenly flashed on me: this was the Bob Dylan almost
hiding behind those huge title cards in the opening frames of
Don't Look Back, a pixy who smiled slyly, as if saying: "Enter
the film and I'll twist your mind around." And the paranoia
descended on me: I could almost believe Dylan had rehearsed
the scene as a prelude to his running the usual numbers. On me,
this time.

But it didn't happen that way at all. "Got your copy of the
book?" Bob asked, pointing to a carbon of the manuscript I had
sent him two weeks earlier. And then we sat down at his desk,
getting right down to the business at hand, which turned out to
be a freewheeling interview-rap session about Bob Dylan—book
and man—in which Dylan talked about his life, his fears, some

of the forces that drove him, his pain at being a stranger in a strange land.

That first meeting turned out to be such a total inversion of what I had expected that I felt I was suffering delusions: Dylan, dressed in blue denims, with a wool pullover shirt under a denim jacket, boots, and a gray fur-lined hunter's hat he didn't remove in the three and a half hours we talked, was soft-spoken, gentle, warm and very open and talkative. He looked a little chubbier and a great deal less nervous and manic than he had ever appeared at concerts, press conferences or in films. He seemed to be a man who was now content after facing up to the chaos of his life. A man chatting amiably with a snoop and intruder, and being ... well, *charming* is the only word to describe him.

A flashback, to put it all into focus: when I first decided to write a biography of Bob Dylan I called his office and told Naomi Saltzman, his secretary, that I was doing the book and wanted an interview. She laughed, probably fell off her chair, then said somewhat somberly: "Bob doesn't give interviews." I asked her to pass the request along. About once a month, for more than a year, I repeated the request for an interview. The answer was always "No". In the meantime I had begun the interviews and research, pulling together the story of Bob Dylan. Finally, I called Mrs. Saltzman and asked her to tell Bob that I really had a *book*, that Joan Baez, Phil Ochs, Jack Elliott and so many others who had once been very close to Bob had talked to me at great length, telling stories about him and impressions of him they had never revealed publicly before, mostly because anyone who becomes part of Dylan's life feels an overwhelming need to protect him. Two days after that final request for an interview Mrs. Saltzman called me back and said: "I quote Mr. Dylan, 'Tell Scaduto as long as he's talked to everybody who knows everything about me, he doesn't need *me* to tell him about me.'"

I had a feeling I would have to finish the book without Dylan's cooperation. And then A. J. Weberman got to see Dylan and had a number of raucous arguments with him.—Weberman: "You're just a capitalist pig, Bob." Dylan: "You're the pig, Weberman, you're a fascist with a pig mentality."—and on and on, endless hours of name-calling. In his attempts to "liberate and re-radicalize" Dylan, Weberman said a number of outrageous things, among them: "I just wanna show the world you're ripping off the counter-culture. And if you think what I'm doing is hurting you, wait till you see what Tony Scaduto's gonna do to you. He's doing a book that will expose what you really are." It would be

290

a vicious exposé, Weberman said, filled with those dark secrets no man would want to see revealed.

Dylan reacted quickly: He called me the next morning and said he heard the book was finished. "Only about three-quarters finished," I told him. "I'd like to see it," Bob said, "because I heard a lot of rumors." What kind of rumors? "Well, Weberman told me your book is some kind of exposé about all sorts of things, dope-smoking, name it. I mean, I ain't never done nothin' to be exposed about."

After about twenty minutes of parrying and horse-trading I agreed to let Bob see the manuscript if he promised to sit and talk after he read it, and if he understood that I would not permit him to edit it in any way, that I would not make any changes unless those changes benefitted the book. He agreed. "Fine," he said, "just let me see the book." And, though he later pressured me to make changes—and though I did make some changes that strengthened the book—we stuck to those groundrules through all our conversations.

Ten days after I got the manuscript off to him we were sitting at his desk shoved against the front window of a heavily-travelled Village street, Dylan started off by telling me what he thought of my book about him:

"I thought it was great, it ran smooth and true until I got to the interview with Joan Baez, and right after that it began to change on me."

Flipping through the manuscript pages, finding what he was looking for about halfway through the book, a description of his relationship with his former manager, Albert Grossman, Dylan said:

"This is changin' drastically now. You get the impression there's some kind of gross *spirit* in the air. The book was changin' on me, starting around here. I liked the book, that's the *weird* thing about it. I start out as a lad from the Midwest, wanting to make it, and you described all that happened to me. And then it gets to *Albert...*"

What Bob objected to was the section that began: "Grossman appeared to be more than a manager at this point. He had become almost a substitute father..."

Said Dylan: "That's not *true*. You shouldn't put that in the book 'cause it's just not *true*." But it was true. At least, that's how most of Dylan's old friends saw it and my book was basically Bob Dylan as seen by his old friends—reality vs. myth—until Bob cooperated (to some extent) and added a new dimension.

In talking to me about the manuscript, Bob displayed some qualities I found disconcerting in a man who had been described as a manipulator, a self-centered man who used people and hurt them and later turned his back on them. He was deeply and honestly concerned about the way I had handled some of those he had once known well. I had characterized one old friend as a former Communist, and Bob was upset: "You shouldn't say that," he said. "I feel that strongly. He might get some problems if you call him a Communist. You're not doin' the right thing." At another point, on reading a section where I quoted Dylan from an old interview in which he discussed John Hammond, who had discovered Bob and was his first producer, he said: "I'd like you to insert 'Mr. Hammond' because I do respect that man. If I was talking about him I would have said 'Mr. Hammond.'" And, about another anecdote that was critical of Joan Baez—and which I later learned was untrue—Dylan asked: "Could this be dropped? It's cruel."

In our conversations, Bob seemed to be as heavily into reality as his old friends had been when they discussed him with me. He went much further than simply complaining about some of the things I had written, did more than attempt to get me to edit an anecdote here and there: Bob gave me information and insights from deep within, something I never expected from such a private man.

For example, at one point we had been talking about the enormous pressures Bob had been under during the year or two before his motorcycle accident, and his deliberate use of the accident to cut himself free of a destructive ego-scene. And, leaning back in his chair, staring at a point where the wall meets the ceiling, Bob began to talk about *John Wesley Harding*, the first album after the accident.

"Before I wrote *John Wesley Harding* I discovered something," he said. "I discovered that when I used words like 'he' and 'it' and 'they' and putting down all sorts of people, I was really talking about no one but me. I went into *Harding* with that knowledge about all the stuff I was writing before then. You see, I didn't know that when I was writing those earlier songs."

And he also talked about some of those song-poems he had writen from 1964 on, speaking elliptically, thinking aloud about some self-discoveries, about where the interpreters—myself included—had gone wrong.

"You're interpreting yourself for me," I said at one point, incredulous, just not believing that it was all happening. Bob smiled, shyly, and replied:

"I guess so. What I'm telling you is where Weberman and the others don't get the point. You see, your interpretation is as good as anybody else's. That's what bothers me about it. Because you've learned enough about me to get closer to the truth than that. Go back and listen to all those songs again"—and he named songs and even quoted lines I should listen to—"you'll hear what I was saying."

I went back, guided by what he had told me in that talk and in several phone conversations later on, and the interpretations in this book are the result of those broad hints, that outline of his thoughts and emotions, that he laid out for me during our talks.

What made that session with Bob so unreal is that he seemed to open himself up, again and again, telling me who and what he is, describing what he was thinking and feeling during various crises in his life. "Let me ask you something?" I said at one point. "Why are you telling me things I don't know about you? Why are you doing this for me?" Bob replied: "Because you wrote a good book and I want to help you make it better." And then he talked about his Gemini character, how he blows hot and cold about things and was hot at that point and anxious to contribute to the book.

But, although he had decided to cooperate, Bob made his suspicions about my motives in doing the book rather clear. During that first long interview in his studio, Bob revealed that he had checked out my background before agreeing to see me. "I hear you did a book on the Mafia." When I told him that wasn't so, that I had writen a number of magazine articles on organized crime and had been the "Mafia expert" for the *New York Post* for over a dozen years, Bob said: "Oh, I was wondering why anybody would want to do a book like that. It's like doing a book on Dylan—you can't ever get to the truth of the subject." I mentioned other books I had written and Bob said: "Yeah, I know all about them."

Over the next few weeks we had several phone conversations, Bob revealing a little more about himself in each one, removing a bit more of the mask he always wears in public.

It was not always smooth going. When he read the manuscript he asked me to delete all references to his wife and children. I refused. Later, when I finished the last chapters and sent them off to him, hoping to provoke another interview from him, Bob called, furious. "You gotta stop writing about my family," he said. I told him I thought he had understood that I could not ignore his wife and children and Bob said: "What about your wife and kids? I talked to your daughter the first time I called, and I talked to your son. Would you want somebody to write about them? What if somebody was doing a book about you? Would you want to see your kids in it?"

I was rather surprised at his anger, and I made some lame remark along the lines of: "If that time ever came I'd do my best to control what was written about them, sure, but ..." Dylan broke in: "I'm past playing games. I'm serious about it. I'm not gonna stand for it ... I'm not gonna take it, that's the way it stands, you should know that in front."

I told him once more that I would not delete the references to his family and Bob replied: "I'm known to retaliate you know; you should know I'm known to *retaliate*." And that, basically, was the end of the conversation. I was completely puzzled by his attitude.

Bob called again the next evening. "Listen," he said, "I just want to apologize for being a little hasty last night. I was misinformed." I asked him, misinformed about what? and he replied: "I just sort of got in a general bad mood because some people in the garden"—a common created of the backyards of all the homes on Bob's block—"they said you were asking questions at a party there. Somebody said you caught her in a corner, started asking questions about my family."

"It wasn't me," I told him. "I've never been in the garden." And Bob said: "Yeah, I know. I checked it out and we had you mistaken for somebody else. Anyway, I just want to apologize."

And then Bob became extraordinarily friendly again. I had told him I was leaving in a few days for Jamaica, a vacation with my family, and he went into a discussion about his experiences there: "The people are very strange. They're just so beautiful. They haven't lost that magic quality, I don't mean voodoo or that tourist crap, but the beautiful thing inside them. They're still real people, their heads haven't been fucked over ... But there's a lot of tension. I was there in, I guess it was 1965, and I could feel the tension. They're being held down by the whites, and they hate it, and you can feel it. Especially inland, away from the tourist areas. They look at you in strange ways. It's going to explode some day..."

And then I locked myself away to finish the book. I didn't hear from Bob for about nine months, when he began coming around to my apartment at the other end of Greenwich Village from his home, to talk about the profile of him I was writing for the *New York Times Magazine*.

Once more he was open and quite captivating. During one of Bob's visits a friend of mine stopped by, not aware that he was there. Bob appeared very shy when I introduced her to him, but after we sat together for a while the shyness seemed to leave him and he became very amusing, the old Dylan wit flashing. After Bob left my friend remarked: "He's acting like you've been best friends for years." And I told her something I think I've learned about Dylan: He is a manipulator, of media, events, people. The only reason he gets involved with people like Weberman, or with me, is that he wants to get so completely into our heads that we won't write or say anything that might hurt Dylan.

To a large extent, I had felt, there was an ulterior motive behind Dylan's friendliness, his almost bewitching approach, the enormously helpful way he filled in so many holes in my first draft of this book, and talked about himself for the magazine article. That motive was a manipulative self-protection, I felt. We would swap, he would give me enough material to flesh out the portrait I had done of him in exchange for permitting him to edit material to which he objected.

Bob continually denies he is as manipulative as he is pictured, and asked several times: "Why don't you show how much I've been used by other people?" And that's true. Among all the pressures that turned Bob Dylan into a recluse after his accident was that he knew so many people saw him as the road to easy riches and fame, and tried to get to him, to use him, to bask in the reflected glory of being close to Bob Dylan. Yet, the attempts to manipulate Dylan in no way lessens the impact of Dylan's manipulation of others.

What Bob was doing, in trying to get into my head, flashed in strange ways. For example, while we were reading a rough draft of my *Times* article together, Dylan commenting on it, expanding some thoughts and, of course, asking me to make changes, he stopped at one point and smiled. Bob pointed to the section (used in the previous chapter of this revised edition of the biography) in which I had written out in full the long question I had asked him about reports his latest songs marked his return to social commitment, with Dylan's answer: "I don't understand the question, man."

At that point in the manuscript Bob turned to me and said: "Why don't you write, 'I don't understand the question, *Tony.*' "?

I crossed out the word "man" and was about to substitute "Tony" when the thought flashed: Dylan was trying to turn me into one of his writer-groupies by making me his *friend*, in print—"Wow, Dylan calls you Tony"—and I told him: "Come on, I'm not into. that. Bob giggled a little (that adorable giggle that friends found so enchanting back in the old Village days), smiled broadly, and said: Okay, leave it alone."

And yet, as I think back upon it now, I wonder if perhaps I was being a bit paranoid about Dylan's ability to mind-rape. Was he being friendly and cooperative because he actually felt that way? I think, from the vantage point of a half year later, that perhaps he was. Bob certainly did seem to be very natural. During one visit I had the stereo on and while we were discussing his *More Greatest Hits* album, John Lee Hooker's voice came on. Dylan stopped talking, almost immediately, and stared into the fireplace across from the couch on which we were sitting. I remained silent, not quite understanding why he had broken off in the middle of a sentence and why he seemed almost to have left the room. Finally, he said:

"I'm listening to Hooker. Can't help it. The guy's incredible. You know I used to hang around with him at the Broadway Central Hotel? They were great times."

At another time, during an interview for the *Times* profile, I asked Bob for permission to quote lyrics from several of his songs. "Oh, yeah," Bob said, smiling slyly. "There's *that* problem for ya." Playfully; almost saying, Ah ha, I got ya now." But he promptly agreed to let me use his lyrics, which surprised me because months earlier he had turned down a similar request for use of the lyrics in this biography.

I said: "That's great. Now what I need is a note from you saying it's okay, 'cause I'm sure the *Times* editors and lawyers would want it in writing." Bob said: "Don't worry about it. I'll call my publishers and tell them it's okay." I continued to press for a note from him and he repeated several times that a phone call from him would be sufficient. I finally said: "Hey, I'm not going to sell your autograph," and Bob shot back: "Sure you will. I know you, You'll probably Xerox and sell it all over the Village." Another giggle.

Several days after my last conversation with Dylan I sent my completed article off to the *Times*. That evening I was sitting at home when a familiar voice singing an unfamiliar song roared out of my receiver: "Lord, Lord, they shot George Jackson down. . ." and I almost fell off my chair. After so many hours trying to get Dylan to talk about the rumors he may again write "protest" songs, so many hours of his dodging around my questions, here was the answer—on the radio. My first reaction was anger. Dylan had recorded his first "protest" song in nine or ten years while my article saying he wouldn't talk about his possible return to such blatant social comment was going into type.

My second reaction was to get something about *George Jackson* into the *Times* article. I called a number of friends—writers, radicals, musicians, Dylan watchers—asked them to listen to the song, and tell me what they felt about it. Dylan lost this particular jukebox derby—eight of eleven felt strongly that Dylan was not being honest in the song, that he had written it to get all the Webermans of this world off his back. I wrote it that way, for the *Times,* quoting one singer who said she could believe it when Dylan wrote about Hattie Carroll and the Masters of War, but couldn't believe Dylan actually felt strongly about the murder of Jackson.

That article, particularly the comments on *George Jackson,* eventually resulted in one of those absurdist-theater games that Bob enjoys so much. It began rolling into gear the week after my article was published, when a rock critic for the *Village Voice* criticized me for trying to force Dylan to return to protest. The writer added that it didn't matter whether Dylan actually meant what he wrote in *George Jackson,* the fact that the song was written at all should be good enough for us.

The *Voice* published my response a couple of weeks later: I wrote that the rock critic had been unable to understand that I had done a job of *reporting,* had written an objective article about Dylan and what Dylan freaks felt about the rather contented musical phase he had been going through. And I added that it made a large difference whether Dylan truly felt what he wrote in the song, because if he didn't feel strongly then he was simply turning out another piece of schlock-rock, like all the other hucksters mining rock's mountain of gold.

That letter angered Dylan. He began to write a larger than life script that he got onto videotape and says he will release some day. The first stage was a letter written to the *Voice* by one of Bob's friends and confidants, familiarly known around the Village as One Legged Terry—he has an artificial leg as the result of an accident. Terry's letter roundly condemned me, as a person and a journalist. The *Voice,* which will print almost anything in its letters column, refused to print Terry's letter because, as one editor put it: "The letter was malicious, insane, paranoid, vicious and probably libellous. And it wasn't even literate."

Terry called the *Voice* and demanded his letter be printed. After a long argument with an editor's secretary he was told to bug off, or words to that effect. A couple of days later One Legged Terry showed up at the *Voice* offices, accompanied by four or five other men and a large dog, loudly barking. "It was like a freak Mafia," one *Voice* staffer said about the scene that went down.

The scene: Terry standing in front of an editor, reading his letter aloud, stopping every couple of lines to demand: "Why can't you print that?" Some of his troops backing him up: "Sure you can print that!" The dog barking, loudly. And the official recorder of Terry's assault brigade, a skinny man standing outside the action, with a videotape camera in front of his face, getting the entire fantasy down on tape. When an editor realized he was being taped he pointed to the man with the camera and asked what the hell he thought he was doing. The camera came slowly down to reveal a familiar-looking face that was filled with a broad grin—Mr. Tambourine Man himself, Bob Dylan recording Terry's attempt to "liberate" the *Village Voice*.

It all ended when a *Voice* staffer, who did not recognize Dylan, shouted at the crowd: "Listen, you mothers, you better split because I just called the cops." Dylan, Terry, and the others left quickly. As he was going down the elevator Bob was overheard saying to his friends: "They don't give me a very nice reception here."

The word got around pretty quickly that Dylan was angry at me, and the story made a couple of the gossip columns. Some time after that scene Ernest Leogrande, who writes a column for the *Daily News*, decided to check out the story. He called Dylan's office and a short time later Bob returned the call. He told Leogrande:

"I got a friend who's got a videocamera and he wrote a letter to the *Village Voice* in reply to one of Tony's letters. The *Voice* didn't care to print it, so this friend of mine asked why and they didn't give him a satisfactory answer. He went down to find out why and I went with him to try out his camera." Leogrande asked what kind of reception Dylan got there and Dylan, misunderstanding the question, continued: "The reception isn't so good but the sound track is okay. They were pretty upset by the camera. There was an article about screaming people and a dog. Maybe it was a dog that was in the *Voice*. It's on the videotape.

There's some screaming but I think it might be a couple of *Village Voice* people.

"Tony's book is okay with me. It was the letter they wouldn't print. . . I'll put out the film of the *Voice* thing eventually. I was there mostly to practice using the camera. . ."

The last I heard, Dylan is still angry at me for what I've written about *George Jackson* and for my letter to the *Voice*. He'll probably be annoyed at some things I've written here.

With the benefits of hindsight, I think I was wrong about *George Jackson*, as were the people I talked to and interviewed for my *Times* article. *George Jackson* works, as music, and as an effective verbalization of the anguish so many felt over the killing. It works, despite the fact that so many critics are disappointed by the simplicity of the song's lyrics, for the song is filled with the compassion of Dylan's faith, almost a dialogue between Bob Dylan and his Lord.

But I was wrong, also, for a more vital reason: months after the song was released I learned from several of Dylan's friends that the impetus for the song came from a reading of Jackson's *Soledad Brother*. "Bob finished reading the book one night, and the next day he was moved to write the song," one friend said. "That's what he told us after coming out of the recording studio." The song was written November 3, 1971. That night Bob called a Columbia executive. "I just wrote a song. I wanna record it tomorrow. See if you can get a studio tomorrow." The studio was secured, and Dylan recorded it the next day. The recording was released within a week.

It's always unsafe to go out on a limb and predict where Dylan is headed. But I think it is possible, from my talks with Bob and from the word that gets out from his friends, that his voice may be raised once more to condemn the absurdities of our society. His new album will reportedly bring him back somewhere between *Blowin' in the Wind* and the *Highway 61* masterpiece. Further, Dylan and Allen Ginsberg have been writing and recording together, laying down songs with lyrics by Ginsberg and music by Dylan. At least some of the songs are "protest"— among them a song for Gay Liberation and one that was called *See You in San Diega* before the Republicans moved their 1972 Presidential convention to Miami.

But such a move back to an activist role could be enormously destructive for Dylan. He is a complex man, facing a complex dilemma: He said it all, in the Sixties, and "they never listened"— Bob Dylan's remark to a friend when he read of the Kent State

Massacre—and now we are in the Seventies and where do we go from here? The dream is over, after all—Dylan believed the dream was over, that activism and protest would not work, back around the time John F. Kennedy was murdered. But the Dylan freaks continue to demand that he orchestrate their dream, for Dylan continues to provide the stuff of fantasy for fans who seek to entwine their lives with his, to satisfy their own needs.

Dylan is also acutely aware of something that other pop star-artists—John Lennon, as a specific example—seem not to understand: Polemics overwhelm art; an artist who reaches for power and leadership, even if he does not understand he is reaching, cannot survive as an artist. Sartre comes immediately to mind; Stalinist Russia can be cited as an exaggerated example. Dylan fled such a role, that his fans tried to impose on him, by going into seclusion after his accident and remaining in hiding in a sense by refusing to use his talents as part of a "movement." Writing *Nashville Skyline* and *Self Portrait* and getting roundly condemned for it.

Watch the parking meters, he had said, and that summed up what he had written in so many of his most effective songs: Don't follow leaders, don't try to make Bob Dylan a leader.

If Dylan returns to the streets, if he assumes an activist role, the conflicts that almost destroyed him years ago could be awakened. Dylan is very much aware of this.

During one of our long talks about the accusation that he refused to speak out when so many felt that just a word from him, just a song or two, could help change society, that political activism by pop stars will have an effect on the history of our times, Bob said:

"That's an illusion. There's a deeper reality than that. But the media feeds the illusion, and will eventually destroy it all." I asked: "You mean you're a puppet?" Bob replied: "Yeah, I'm a part of it." Unspoken, but so very clear, Dylan was saying: "If I'm really a part of it I will be destroyed with all the rest."

But Dylan is six years older than when he last wore the "crown" of the pop culture, when he last was enveloped in an ego bubble. He has moved, in his songs, from self-concern to a larger understanding and consciousness—reflected most clearly in the relationship between his songs since his accident and the Judaic mystical ethic. From a dialogue with his Maker, Dylan seems to have moved to a dialogue between men. It is possible he will be able to undertake that dialogue without becoming a puppet of that illusion he perceives.

During one discussion of politics and activism, I remarked that a large number of radicals were angry because he had given up his "crown" of leadership. Bob said something that appeared to come from deep within him :

"A lot of kings throw their crowns around. What's so sacred about a crown?"

A Dylan Discography

NASHVILLE SKYLINE (April 1969): *Girl From The North Country* (with Johnny Cash); *Nashville Skyline Rag; To Be Alone With You; I Threw It All Away; Peggy Day; Lay Lady Lay; One More Night; Tell Me That It Isn't True; Country Pie; Tonight I'll Be Staying Here With You.*

SELF PORTRAIT (June 1970): *All the Tired Horses; Alberta # 1; I Forgot More Than You'll Ever Know; Days of 49; Early Mornin' Rain; In Search of Little Sadie; Let It Be Me; Little Sadie; Woogie Boogie; Belle Isle; Living the Blues; Like A Rolling Stone; Copper Kettle; Gotta Travel On; Blue Moon; The Boxer; The Mighty Quinn (Quinn The Eskimo); Take Me As I Am; Take a Message To Mary; It Hurts Me Too; Minstrel Boy; She Belongs To Me; Wig Wam; Alberta # 2.*

NEW MORNING (October 1970): *If Not For You; Day Of the Locusts; Time Passes Slowly; Went To See the Gypsy; Winterlude; If Dogs Run Free; New Morning; Sign On the Window; One More Weekend; The Man In Me; Three Angels; Father Of Night.*

CONCERT FOR BANGLADESH (1971): *Hard Rain; It Takes A Lot To Laugh; Blowin' In The Wind; Tambourine Man; Just Like A Woman* (all with Leon Russell, George Harrison, Ringo Starr).

WOODY GUTHERIE MEMORIAL CONCERT VOL. 1 (1972): *Mrs. Roosevelt; Ain't Got No Home; Grand Coulee Dam.*

MORE GREATEST HITS (November 1971): *Watching the River Flow; Don't Think Twice; Lay Lady Lay; Memphis Blues Again; I'll Be Your Baby Tonight; All I Really Want To Do; Back Pages; Maggie's Farm; Tonight I'll Be Staying Here With You; She Belongs To Me; Watchtower; Mighty Quinn; Tom Thumb's Blues; Hard Rain; If Not For You; Baby Blue; Tomorrow Is A Long Time; When I Paint My Masterpiece; I Shall Be Released; You Ain't Goin' Nowhere; Down In The Flood.*

Singles

Mixed Up Confusion/Corrina, Corrina (1962); *On the Road Again/Bob Dylan's 115th Dream; Gates of Eden/She Belongs to Me* (1965); *Like a Rolling Stone/Gates Of Eden* (1965); *From a Buick Six/Positively 4th Street* (1965); *Can You Please Crawl Out Your Window/Highway 61 Revisited* (1965); *One Of Us Must Know/Queen Jane Approximately* (1966); *Rainy Day Women/Pledging My Time* (1966); *I Want You/Just Like Tom Thumb's Blues* (1966); *Just Like a Woman/Obviously Five Believers* (1966); *Leopardskin Pillbox Hat/Most Likely You'll Go Your Way And I'll Go Mine* (1966); *Rainy Day Women/Like A Rolling Stone* (1966); *Just Like A Woman/I Wait You* (1967); *I Threw It All Away/Drifter's Escape* (1968); *Lay Lady Lay/Peggy Day* (1969); *Tonight I'll Be Staying Here With You/Country Pie* (1969); *Copper Kettle/Wigwam* (1970); *Watching The River Flow/Spanish Is the Loving Tongue* (1971); *George Jackson/George Jackson* (1971).

A Discography of Unreleased Recordings

The following list of tapes of Dylan recording sessions never officially released by any record company, and bootleg albums mastered from the tapes, includes everything known to be in the hands of Dylan collectors in England and America up to November, 1972. My special thanks to Sandy Gant for providing most of the information, and to Jeff Thomas for additional material.

Tapes

East Orange, N.J. (Feb.-Mar. 1961), home of Bob and Sid Gleason: *San Francisco Bay Blues; Jesus Met the Woman at the Well; Gypsy Davey; Pastures of Plenty; Trail of the Buffalo; Jesse James; Sweetheart Remember Me.*

Minneapolis, Minn. (May 1961): *Railroad Bill, Will the Circle be Unbroken; Man of Constant Sorrow; Pretty Polly; Railroad Boy (Little Willie); Times Ain't What They Used to Be; Why'd You Cut My Hair; This Land Is Your Land; Two Trains; Wild Mountain Thyme; Howja Do; Car Car; Don't Push Me Down; Come See; I Want My Milk; San Francisco Bay Blues; A Long Time A-Growin'; Devilish Mary; Death Don't Have No Mercy; It's Hard to be Blind; This Train; Harp Blues; Talkin' Fisherman; Pastures of Plenty.*

Riverside Church, N.Y., WRVR-FM (July 1961): *Handsome Molly; Naomi Wise; Poor Lazarus; Mean Old Southern Railroad* (plays harp for Danny Kalb); *Acne* (with Jack Elliott).

Carnegie Recital Hall, N.Y. (Nov. 1961): *Where Did You Sleep Last Night (In the Pines); Pretty Peggy-O; Gospel Plow; Song to Woody; Fixin' to Die.*

McKenzie's home, N.Y. (1961-1963): *Hard Times in New York Town; Lonesome Whistle Blues; Worried Blues; Baby Let Me Follow You Down; San Francisco Bay Blues; You're No Good; House of the Rising Sun* (standard arrangement); *Highway 51; Donald White; Hard Rain; Times Ain't What They Used to Be; Long Time Gone; Only a Hobo; Rising Sun* (Van Ronk arrangement).

Whittaker's home, Minneapolis (Dec. 1961): *Candy Man; Baby Please Don't Go; Hard Times in New York Town; Stealin'; Poor Lazarus; I Ain't Got No Home; Hard to be Blind; Drink's Song; Constant Sorrow; East Orange monologue; Naomi Wise; Wade in the Water; Young When I Left Home; In the Evening; Let Me Follow You Down; Sally Gal; Gospel Plow; Long John; Cocaine; See That My Grave is Kept Clean; Rambling Round; VD Blues; VD Waltz; VD City; VD Gunner's Blues; Hezekiah Jones* (Black Cross).

Leeds Music demos, N.Y. (early 1962): *He Was a Friend of Mine; Man on the Street* (2 versions); *Hard Times in New York Town; Talkin' Bear Mountain; Standing on the Highway; Poor Boy Blues; Ballad for a Friend; Ramblin' Gamblin' Willie.*

The Gaslight, N.Y. (1962): *Man on the Street; Friend of Mine; Talkin' Bear Mountain; Song to Woody; Pretty Polly; Car Car* (with Dave Van Ronk); *Motherless Children; Go Down Old Hannah.*

WBAI, New York (May 1962): *Donald White, Emmett Till; Blowin' in the Wind.*

Gaslight, N.Y. (1962): *Barbara Allen; Hard Rain; Don't Think Twice; Hezekiah Jones; No More Auction Block; Moonshine Blues; Hiram Hubbard; Blowin' in the Wind; Rocks and Gravel; Quit Your Low Down Ways; Friend of Mine; Let Me Die in My Footsteps; Two Trains; Ramblin' On My Mind; Muleskinner's Blues; Rocks and Gravel; Emmett Till; Stealin'.*

Oscar Brand Show, WQXR, N.Y. (Oct. 1962): *Girl of the North Country; Only a Hobo.*

BBC, London (Jan. 1963): *Blowin' in the Wind; Swan on the River.*

Broadside Magazine, N.Y. (1963): *I'd Hate to be You on That Dreadful Day; Oxford Town; Paths of Victory; Walkin' Down the Line; I Shall be Free; Train A-Travelin'; Cuban Missile Crisis; Farewell* (with Gil Turner); *Masters of War; Playboys and Playgirls.*

"Banjo Session" with Happy Traum, N.Y. (Jan 1963): *Lonesome River Edge; I'd Rather See My Coffin Coming; Bob Dylan's Dream; Farewell; All Over You; Masters of War; Keep Your Hands Off Her; Honey Babe, Back to Romance; Stealin'.*

Witmark demos, New York (1963): *Only a Hobo; Emmett Till; Ain't Gonna Grieve; Babe, I'm in the Mood For You; Quit Your Low Down Ways; Bound to Lose, Bound to Win; John Brown; Long Ago, Far Away; Long Time Gone, Hollis Brown; Hard Rain; Let Me Die in my Footsteps; All Over You; Baby Let Me Follow You Down; Bob Dylan's Blues; Talking John Birch; Hero Blues; Farewell; Walkin' Down the Line; Gypsy Lou; Whatcha Gonna Do; Paths of Victory; I'd Hate to be You; I Shall be Free; Seven Curses; Tomorrow is a Long Time; Don't Think Twice; Oxford Town; Masters of War; Girl of the North Country; Boots of Spanish Leather; Bob Dylan's Dream; Blowin' in the Wind; Guess I'm Doin' Fine; When the Ship Comes In; Times They Are A-Changin'; I'll Keep It With Mine.*

Freewheelin' sessions out-takes (1963): *Let Me Die in my Footsteps; Rocks and Gravel (Solid Road); Ramblin' Gamblin' Willie; Talkin' John Birch; Baby Please Don't Go; Milk Cow Blues; Talkin' Bear Mountain; Corrina, Corrina; Emmett Till; Talkin' Hava Negeilah; Babe, I'm in the Mood for You; Low Down Ways; Worried Blues; Going to New Orleans; Lonesome Whistle Blues; Wichita Blues.*

Town Hall, New York (Apr. 1963): *Rambling 'Round; Bob Dylan's Dream; Tomorrow is a Long Time; Bob Dylan's New Orleans Rag; Masters of War; Halls of Red Wing; Hero Blues; Davey Moore; God on Our Side.*

Studs Terkel Show, WFMT, Chicago (May 1963): *Farewell; Hard Rain; Bob Dylan's Dream; Boots of Spanish Leather; John Brown; Davey Moore; Blowin' in the Wind.*

Greenwood Miss. civil rights rally (July 1963): *Only A Pawn in Their Games.*

Songs of Freedom, WNEW-TV New York (Aug. 1963): *Blowin' in the Wind; Only A Pawn in Their Game.*

Washington Civil Rights March (Aug. 1963): *Pawn in Their Game* (complete version).

Times They Are A-Changin' sessions out-takes (Aug.-Oct. 1963): *Eternal Circle; Paths of Victory; Cough Song; I'll Keep It With Mine; California; Percy's Song; Red Wing; Only a Hobo; Moonshine Blues; Lay Down Your Weary Tune; Eternal Circle (alternate version); Seven Curses; Percy's Song (alternate version); Mama, You've Been On My Mind.*

Carnegie Hall (Oct. 1963): *When The Ship Comes In; John Brown; Davey Moore; Poem To Woody/Last Thoughts On Woody Guthrie; Lay Down Your Weary Tune; Dusty Old Fairgrounds; Percy's Song; Bob Dylan's New Orleans Rag; Seven Curses.*

Steve Allen TV Show (Feb. 1964): *Hattie Carroll.*

Another Side sessions out-takes (June 1964): *Bob Dylan's New Orleans Rag (two versions); Denise, Denise; That's All Right, Mama; East Laredo Blues (piano solo); Farewell.*

Forest Hills, New York, Joan Baez concert (Aug. 1964): *Mama/Papa You Been On My Mind; It Ain't Me Babe; God on Our Side* (duets with Baez).

Philharmonic Hall, New York (Oct. 1964): *Times They Are A-Changin'; Spanish Harlem Incident; Talkin' John Birch; To Ramona; Gates of Eden; If You Gotta Go, Go Now; It's All Right, Ma; I Don't Believe You; Davey Moore; Talkin' World War III Blues; Don't Think Twice; Hattie Carroll; Mama/Pappa You Been on My Mind* (with Baez); *God on Our Side* (with Baez); *It Ain't Me, Babe* (with Baez); *All I Really Want to Do.*

San Jose Auditorium, Calif. (Nov. 1964): *Times They Are A-Changin'; John Birch; To Ramona; Gates of Eden; If You Gotta Go; It's All Right, Ma; Tambourine Man; Hard Rain; World War III Blues; Don't Think Twice.*

Berkeley University, Calif. (Nov. 1964): *Gates of Eden; If You Gotta Go; It's All Right, Ma; World War III Blues; Don't Think Twice; Mama/Papa You Been On My Mind* (with Baez).

Bringing It All Back Home sessions out-takes (Dec. 1964): *Baby Blue; She Belongs To Me; Love Minus Zero/No Limit.*

WABC-TV New York, Les Crane Show (Feb. 1965): *Baby Blue; It's All Right, Ma* (both with Bruce Langhorne).

Los Angeles Calif. Civic Auditorium (Apr. 1965): *To Ramona; Gates of Eden; If You Gotta Go; It's All Right, Ma; Love Minus Zero; Tambourine Man; Don't Think Twice; God on Our Side; She Belongs to Me; It Ain't Me Babe; Hattie Carroll; All I Really Want To Do; Baby Blue.*

London, Albert Hall (May 1965): *Times They Are A-Changin'; To Ramona; Gates of Eden; If You Gotta Go; Tambourine Man; World War III Blues; Don't Think Twice; God on Our Side; She Belongs to Me; It Ain't Me Babe; Hattie Carroll; All I Really Want To Do; Baby Blue; It's All Right, Ma; Love Minus Zero.*

BBC, London (June 1965): *Hollis Brown; Tambourine Man; Gates of Eden; If You Gotta Go; Hattie Carroll; It Ain't Me Babe; Love Minus Zero; One Too Many Mornings; Spanish Leather; It's All Right, Ma; She Belongs to Me; Baby Blue.*

Studio sessions (1965): *Crawl Out Your Window; Killing Me Alive; It Takes A Lot To Laugh, It Takes A Train To Cry; I Wanna Be Your Man; She's Your Lover Now.*

Newport Folk Festival (July 1965): *Maggie's Farm; Tambourine Man* (in F); *Tombstone Blues; Like A Rolling Stone; Baby Blue.*

Forest Hills, New York (Aug. 1965): *She Belongs To Me; To Ramona; Gates of Eden; Love Minus Zero; Desolation Row; Baby Blue; Tambourine Man; Tombstone Blues; I Don't Believe You; From A Buick 6; Tom Thumb's Blues; Maggie's Farm; It Ain't Me Babe; Ballad of A Thin Man; Like A Rolling Stone.*

Please Crawl Out Your Window; I Wanna Be Your Lover; Number One Band Session (Dec. 1965): *Medicine Show (Temporarily Like Achilles);* (instrumental); *Seems Like A Freeze Out (Visions of Johanna); She's Your Lover Now.*

Westchester County Center, New York (Feb. 1966): *She Belongs To Me; To Ramona; Visions of Johanna; Baby Blue; Desolation Row; Love Minus Zero; Tambourine Man; Tell Me Mama; I Don't Believe You.*

Hempstead, New York (Feb. 1966): *She Belongs To Me; 4th Time Around; Visions of Johanna; Baby Blue; Desolation Row; Love Minus Zero; Tambourine Man; Tell Me Mama; I Don't Believe You; Let Me Follow You Down; Tom Thumb's Blues; Pill Box Hat; One Too Many Mornings.*

Unidentified concert (1966): *Like a Rolling Stone; One Too Many Mornings.*

Dublin, Adelphi (May 1966): *Johanna; 4th Time Around; Baby Blue; Desolation Row; Just Like a Woman; Tambourine Man.*

Bristol, Colston Hall (May 1966): *She Belongs to Me; 4th Time Around; Johanna; Baby Blue; Desolation Row; Just Like a Woman; Tambourine Man; Tell Me Mama; I Don't Believe You; Let Me Follow You Down; Tom Thumb's Blues; Pill Box Hat; One Too Many Mornings; Ballad of a Thin Man; Rolling Stone.*

306

London, Albert Hall (May 1966): *Tell Me Mama; I Don't Believe You; Let Me Follow You Down; Tom Thumb's Blues; Pill Box Hat; One Too Many Mornings; Ballad of a Thin Man; Rolling Stone.*

"Basement Tapes" demo series with The Band, W. Saugerties, N.Y. (Spring 1967): *Million Dollar Bash; Yea Heavy and a Bottle of Bread; Please Mrs. Henry; Down in the Flood; Lo and Behold; Tiny Montgomery; This Wheel's on Fire; Ride Me High; I Shall Be Released; Too Much of Nothing; Tears of Rage* (3 takes); *Mighty Quinn* (2 takes); *Nothing Was Delivered* (2 takes); *Open the Door Homer/Richard* (3 takes); *Apple Suckling Tree* (2 takes); *Talkin' Clothesline Blues; I'm Not There; Odds and Ends; Get Your Rocks Off.*

Another Band session, perhaps from the Basement Tapes (1967): *Sign on the Cross; Don't Tell Henry.*

Nashville, Johnny Cash TV documentary (Jan. 1969): duets with Cash on *Girl of the North Country* (included in 'Nashville Skyline' album); *One Too Many Mornings.*

Nashville, Johnny Cash Show, ABC-TV (taped May 1969): *I Threw It All Away; Living the Blues; Girl of the North Country* (duets).

Nashville, Columbia studios, duets with Cash (1969): *I Walk the Line; Wanted Man; Big River; Understand Your Man; Careless Love.*

Nashville sessions (June 1969): *Folsom Prison Blues; Ring of Fire.*

Isle of Wight concert (Aug. 1969): *She Belongs To Me; Mighty Quinn; Minstrel Boy; Rolling Stone; I Threw It All Away; Maggie's Farm; Wild Mountain Thyme; It Ain't Me Babe; To Ramona; Tambourine Man; I Dreamed I Saw St. Augustine; Lay Lady Lay; Highway 61; One Too Many Mornings; Pity the Poor Immigrant; I'll Be Your Baby Tonight; Rainy Day Woman.*

Nashville and N.Y., Self Portrait sessions (1970): Roughly a dozen outtakes from the sessions are believed circulating, including Eric Andersen's song, *Thirsty Boots.*

Nashville and N.Y., "New Morning" sessions (1970): Another dozen outtakes, including *Jamaica Farewell.*

Earl Scruggs TV documentary (1970): *East Virginia Blues; Nashville Skyline Rag.*

Concert for Bangladesh, N.Y., takes from afternoon concert not released on Apple Records concert album, (Aug. 1971): *Hard Rain; Takes a Lot to Laugh; Blowin' in the Wind; Just Like a Woman.*

Carnegie Hall, The Band's New Year's Eve Concert (Dec. 1971): *Rolling Stone; Please Mrs. Henry.*

New York, sessions with Alan Ginsberg (1971–1972): *Song for Women's Liberation; See You in San Diego;* several William Blake poems read by Ginsberg, Dylan guitar accompaniment.

New York, sessions with the Grateful Dead (summer, 1972): tracks not known.

New York, sessions with Dave Bromberg, Dr. John (Mack Rebennack), Fathead Newman, Doug Sahm and other musicians, (Sept.-Oct. 1972): *Faded Love; Wildflower; Tom Thumb's Blues;* plus songs by Hank Williams, Doug Sahm; Atwood Allen; Johnny Bush and Ray Price.

Bootleg Albums

All the cuts on bootlegs have been mastered from tapes in circulation, with one exception: The last disc listed contains a barely audible version of Help!, reputedly sung by Dylan with the Beatles backing him and cut sometime in 1964–65 in either London or N.Y. Authenticity could not be determined at press time.

THE ACETATE: 14 songs from the Basement Tapes on some discs, an additional six cuts from the same source on other discs.

MOTOR CYCLE: Fourteen Basement Tapes songs.

GREAT WHITE WONDER VOL. 1: Nine songs from the Dec. 1961 Minneapolis session, plus two songs and part of an interview with Pete Seeger from an unreleased N.Y. radio show, 1961 or 1962, plus seven cuts from the Basement Tapes, and six other songs from various sources.

GREAT WHITE WONDER VOL. 2: Twenty-eight cuts on a double album, mostly out-takes from recording sessions, tracks from single releases, and six tracks from the Basement Tapes. Dreadful quality, most material available on other bootlegs.

GREAT WHITE WONDER VOL. 2: Another version of above, quality even more dreadful, several tracks missing.

STEALIN': Unusually good quality, containing out-takes from Highway 61 and 1965 studio sessions, plus tracks from a variety of sources recorded between 1961 and 1965. Fifteen cuts.

BOB DYLAN, THE VILLAGER: Double album, mostly cuts from the Gaslight tapes, and the East Orange N.J. tapes. Fourteen cuts.

THE KINDEST KUT: Seventeen tracks, mostly from the Dec. 1969 Minneapolis session and the Broadside Magazine session.

BLIND BOY GRUNT: Same tracks as The Kindest Kut.

JOHN BIRCH SOCIETY BLUES: Mostly versions of the Great White Wonder cuts. Thirteen tracks.

TALKIN' BEAR MOUNTAIN PICNIC MASSACRE BLUES: Colour-printed album, good quality, containing different recordings of tracks on the previously-listed bootlegs, primarily from material taped from 1961 to 1963. Contains fourteen cuts.

24: Despite title, contains fourteen cuts, probably studio tracks from 1963 and 1964.

VD WALTZ: The VD songs from Dec. 1961 Minneapolis session, several studio cuts from 1963 and 1964, and several from the Basement Tapes. Contains fifteen cuts.

40 RED WHITE AND BLUE SHOESTRINGS: Out-takes from 1965–66 studio sessions, a duet with Johnny Cash, and several others. Nine cuts.

BLACK NITE CRASH: Eleven tracks, all-live from the May 1966 Dublin concert (four tracks) and from the April 1963 Town Hall tape.

DYLAN WITH THE BAND LIVE 1966: The eight tracks from the 1966 Albert Hall concert.

LIVE: Double album, terrible quality, five tracks from the Albert Hall concert, seven from the 1969 Isle of Wight concert, two from the Dublin concert.

DYLAN AT THE ISLE OF WIGHT: Fifteen tracks from that concert.

BOB DYLAN, LONG TIME GONE: Two 7-in. discs containing nine tracks available elsewhere, plus Help! reputedly cut with the Beatles but possibly a fake—if it is imitation Dylan, the imitator has done a marvellous job.

Index

310

312

Mail Order

All Helter Skelter, Firefly and SAF titles are available by mail order from the world famous Helter Skelter bookshop.

You can either phone or fax your order to Helter Skelter on the following numbers:

Telephone: +44 (0)20 7836 1151 or Fax: +44 (0)20 7240 9880
Office hours: Mon-Fri 10:00am – 7:00pm,
Sat: 10:00am – 6:00pm, Sun: closed.

Postage prices per book worldwide are as follows:

UK & Channel Islands	£1.50
Europe & Eire (air)	£2.95
USA, Canada (air)	£7.50
Australasia, Far East (air)	£9.00
Overseas (surface)	£2.50

You can also write enclosing a cheque, International Money Order, or registered cash. Please include postage. DO NOT send cash. DO NOT send foreign currency, or cheques drawn on an overseas bank. Send to:

Helter Skelter Bookshop,
4 Denmark Street, London, WC2H 8LL, United Kingdom.
If you are in London come and visit us, and browse the titles in person!!

Email: helter@skelter.demon.co.uk
Website: http://www.skelter.demon.co.uk